PHP & MySQL® Everyday Apps

FOR

DUMMIES®

PHP & MySQL® Everyday Apps FOR DUMMIES®

by Janet Valade

WILEY

Wiley Publishing, Inc.

PHP & MySQL® Everyday Apps For Dummies®

Published by
Wiley Publishing, Inc.
111 River Street
Hoboken, NJ 07030-5774

www.wiley.com

WILEY

About the Author

Janet Valade has 20 years of experience in the computing field. Her background includes work as a technical writer for several companies, as a Web designer/programmer for an engineering firm, and as a systems analyst in a university environment where, for over ten years, she supervised the installation and operation of computing resources, designed and developed a statewide data archive, provided technical support to faculty and staff, wrote numerous technical papers and documentation, and designed and presented seminars and workshops on a variety of technology topics.

Janet currently has two published books: *PHP & MySQL For Dummies,* 2nd Edition, and *PHP 5 For Dummies.* In addition, she has authored chapters for several Linux and Web development books.

Dedication

This book is dedicated to anyone who finds it useful.

Author's Acknowledgments

I wish to express my appreciation to the entire Open Source community. Without those people who give their time and talent, there would be no cool PHP for me to write about. Furthermore, I never would have learned this software without the PHP lists where people generously spend their time answering foolish questions from beginners. Many ideas have come from reading questions and answers on the lists.

I want to thank my mother for passing on a writing gene and a good work ethic. Anything I accomplish has its roots in my beginnings. And, of course, thank you to my children who manage to remain close, though far away, and nourish my spirit.

And, of course, I want to thank the professionals who made it all possible. Without my agent, my editors, and all the other people at Wiley, this book would not exist. Because they all do their jobs so well, I can contribute my part to this joint project.

Publisher's Acknowledgments

We're proud of this book; please send us your comments through our online registration form located at www.dummies.com/register/.

Some of the people who helped bring this book to market include the following:

Acquisitions, Editorial, and Media Development

Project Editor: Nicole Sholly

Acquisitions Editor: Terri Varveris

Copy Editor: Virginia Sanders

Technical Editor: Craig Lukasik

Editorial Manager: Kevin Kirschner

Permissions Editor: Laura Moss

Media Development Specialist: Travis Silvers

Media Development Manager: Laura VanWinkle

Media Development Supervisor: Richard Graves

Editorial Assistant: Amanda Foxworth

Cartoons: Rich Tennant, www.the5thwave.com

Composition Services

Project Coordinator: Nancee Reeves

Layout and Graphics: Andrea Dahl, Joyce Haughey, Clint Lahnen, Barry Offringa, Lynsey Osborn, Melanee Prendergast, Heather Ryan

Proofreaders: Leeann Harney, Jessica Kramer, Carl William Pierce, TECHBOOKS Production Services

Indexer: TECHBOOKS Production Services

Special Help: Kim Darosett, Andy Hollandbeck

Publishing and Editorial for Technology Dummies

Richard Swadley, Vice President and Executive Group Publisher

Andy Cummings, Vice President and Publisher

Mary Bednarek, Executive Acquisitions Director

Mary C. Corder, Editorial Director

Publishing for Consumer Dummies

Diane Graves Steele, Vice President and Publisher

Joyce Pepple, Acquisitions Director

Composition Services

Gerry Fahey, Vice President of Production Services

Debbie Stailey, Director of Composition Services

Contents at a Glance

Table of Contents

Introduction

●●●

*B*ecause you're looking at a book called *PHP & MySQL Everyday Apps For Dummies,* I assume you want to build a Web application with the PHP scripting language and a MySQL backend database. If you need to build a dynamic Web application for a specific purpose, you're in the right place. You will find six popular applications in this book and one additional application chapter on the CD. If the exact application you need isn't here, you can probably adapt one of the applications to suit your needs.

About This Book

This book is a practical introduction to dynamic Web applications. It provides the code and information needed to build several of the most popular applications on the Web. The applications in this book allow you to

- Restrict your Web site or part of your Web site to authorized users
- Sell products on your Web site
- Provide a place where users can communicate with each other online
- Allow users to publish and edit their documents on a Web site
- Manage mailing lists

You can use these applications as is, modify them for use on your Web site, or build your own application by using techniques that I show you in these applications.

Conventions Used in This Book

This book includes many listings of PHP code. Line numbers appear at the end of some of the lines in the listings. I explain the code after the code listing. The line numbers in the explanation refer to the specific line in the code.

In MySQL queries in the code listings, the SQL commands and key words appear in uppercase letters. The parameters specific to your application, such as the database name and field names, use their specific names, usually lowercase letters or, sometimes, lowercase letters with a beginning uppercase letter. For example, look at the following SQL query:

```
SELECT name FROM Customer WHERE account_number="$acc_no"
```

The all-uppercase words are SQL commands and keywords, which must be spelled exactly as shown. The words with lowercase letters are the names of items in your database, such as the table name and field names.

A continuation symbol (↪) appears at the end of some lines of code to indicate when a line is too long to fit in its allotted space on the printed page.

Foolish Assumptions

I assume that:

- ✔ **You're building your Web application in an environment that includes access to PHP and MySQL.** This might be your own computer or a Web hosting company. This book doesn't include instructions for installing PHP or MySQL. I assume that your environment is already installed and working.

- ✔ **You have some experience with PHP.** You don't need to be an expert PHP coder. You don't need advanced PHP skills. You only need a basic understanding of how PHP works and its basic features, such as if statements and `foreach` loops.

  When I explain the code in the listings, I don't explain each line in detail. I provide a general description of the tasks performed by the script and tasks performed by specific loops. I provide a detailed explanation only for parts of the script that are specialized or potentially confusing.

  Even if you don't have experience with PHP, if you have programming experience in another language, such as Perl or C, you might be able to understand and use the applications in this book. PHP is close to C syntax and is designed to be easy to use. Its features are quite familiar to anyone with programming experience.

- ✔ **You have a basic understanding of MySQL.** I don't explain how to create MySQL databases. I don't provide any description of SQL. I *do* provide SQL queries that you can use to create each database, but assume that you know how to use the SQL query.

✔ **You know HTML and a little CSS.** If you have experience with PHP, you necessarily have experience with HTML. I also assume a slight acquaintance with CSS. The applications in this book display some Web pages, such as the catalog or the login screen, so HTML and CSS are included in the code listings. I keep the HTML as simple as possible so that it doesn't interfere with your understanding of the PHP. However, some HTML is necessary. In general, I use in-line CSS code to format the HTML. I don't explain the HTML or CSS.

How This Book Is Organized

This book is divided into six parts, with two chapters in each part. Chapters 3 through 8 present applications. An additional bonus application chapter is included on the CD. Each application chapter includes the following information:

✔ Discussion of issues

✔ Structure of the database

✔ Code listings

✔ Explanation of the code

Each application chapter presents both procedural code and object-oriented code for the application.

The additional chapters provide information that's useful when building applications (for example, I demystify security considerations).

Part 1: Introducing Application Development

Chapter 1 in this part provides the information needed to use the applications in this book. It discusses PHP and MySQL versions, installing and modifying applications, and procedural versus object-oriented programming. In Chapter 2, you find out how to write secure code.

Part II: Building a User Authentication Application

This part provides information and code to build a user login application. I present two types of applications: user authentication using HTTP authentication (Chapter 3) and a user login application that allows users to register their own accounts, as well as log in to a secure Web site (Chapter 4).

Part III: Building Online Sales Applications

This part provides information and code for online sales applications. In Chapter 5, you find out how to write code for an application that provides an online catalog. Chapter 6 covers writing an application that allows customers to buy products from the catalog.

Part IV: Building Other Useful Applications

In Part IV, I present two other applications that you may find useful. In Chapter 7, I describe how to build a content management system (CMS). I describe how to build a Web forum in Chapter 8.

Part V: The Part of Tens

This part provides a useful list of important things to keep in mind when building an application (Chapter 9). I also provide a list of Web sites offering useful resources, such as code libraries, tutorials, articles, and so on (Chapter 10).

Part VI: Appendixes

This part provides instructions for object-oriented programming. Appendix A provides an introduction to the object-oriented programming features of PHP for people who know PHP, but are unfamiliar with the concepts and terminology of object-oriented programming. Appendix B describes the syntax of PHP object-oriented features for those who are familiar with object-oriented programming in another language. Appendix C provides information on PHP functions used to interact with MySQL. It provides tables for converting from mysql functions to mysqli functions and/or mysqli objects. Appendix D describes in detail what you can find on the CD accompanying this book.

About the CD

The CD at the back of this book contains all the source code you need to run the applications that I describe throughout. You also find a list of links to Web sites that offer PHP-related code libraries, tutorials, and articles. Lastly, I include a bonus chapter on the CD that simply wouldn't fit in the book. The bonus chapter covers building and managing a mailing list.

Icons Used in This Book

Tips provide extra information for a specific purpose. Tips can save you time and effort, so they're worth checking out.

Always read the warnings. Warnings emphasize actions that you must take or must avoid to prevent dire consequences.

This icon is a sticky note of sorts, highlighting information that's worth committing to memory.

Where to Go from Here

This book is organized around the applications. My suggested approach is to install an application from the CD and get it working. Then when it's working as is, modify it by making one small change at a time. Get each change working before starting on another change. The first chapter provides the information that you need to install, run, and customize the applications in this book.

If you're interested in object-oriented programming in PHP, using the new object-oriented features added in PHP 5, you might want to check out the appropriate appendixes first. Appendixes A and B describe the syntax and features of PHP available for object-oriented programming.

If you modify an application for use on your own Web site or build your own application by using the book applications as a pattern, you need to consider security issues. Security is a major issue for Web applications. Chapter 2 explains the security issues and describes how to write secure programs in PHP.

Part I

Introducing Application Development

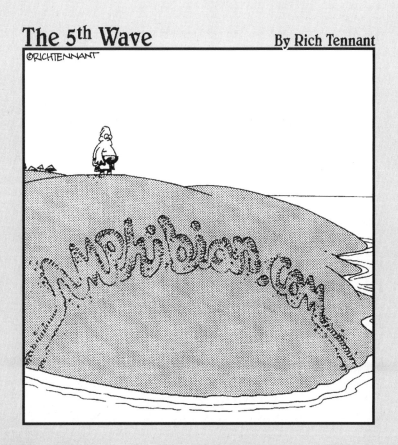

The 5th Wave   By Rich Tennant

In this part . . .

This part contains the information that you need for implementing the applications in this book. Here you find details about the applications, how to find them, where to put them, how to understand them, and how to modify them.

When building Web applications, you also need to keep security in mind. These chapters explain security issues and show how to write secure code.

Chapter 1

Building Your Application

*Y*ou know PHP. Or at least you've been introduced and have spent some quality time together. You know PHP syntax, control structures, and some built-in functions. You can display a form and retrieve the information from it. You can interact with a database. You have the basics down.

Or, perhaps you're an expert programmer in another language. You've been using C for years. You know the basics of programming. You don't know exactly how the familiar programming features are implemented in PHP, but you believe you can understand quickly from seeing examples. After all, a `for` loop is a `for` loop and an `if` statement is an `if` statement. Other programmers have told you how easy PHP is and how similar it is to C.

Now, you want to write a practical application. You need an application quickly. Perhaps you need to provide a login application to protect a Web site or part of a Web site. Perhaps you need to provide an online catalog for a store. Perhaps you need to implement a forum on your Web site where your customers can interact.

This book provides complete applications. Chapters 3 through 8 provide all the code for six popular applications. An additional bonus chapter on the CD provides a seventh application. You can copy the code from the CD to your Web site and have a working application. Of course, nothing is ever quite that simple. You probably need to modify the application; you might need to make a small modification, such as adding your company logo, or a larger modification, such as removing or adding features to an application. Thus, I provide explanations with the code so that you can more easily modify it. The applications are

- ✔ **User authentication:** The user authentication application uses HTTP (Hypertext Transfer Protocol) authentication. This feature is built in and useful for simple user/password authentication. It is quick and easy, but also limited and not very flexible. (See Chapter 3.)

- ✔ **User login:** In the user login application, the user/password authentication is written from scratch in PHP. This application allows users to register and set up their own user IDs and passwords, as well as log in to the Web site. (See Chapter 4.)

- ✔ **Online catalog:** Displays product information stored in a MySQL database on a Web site where customers can view it. (See Chapter 5.)

- ✔ **Shopping cart:** This application allows customers to purchase the products that they find in an online catalog. (See Chapter 6.)

- ✔ **Content management system:** This application allows users to post, delete, and edit information on a Web site. (See Chapter 7.)

- ✔ **Web forum:** This application functions as a public bulletin board. Users can read the posted messages and post messages of their own or responses to current messages. (See Chapter 8.)

- ✔ **Mailing list management:** This application allows users to subscribe to one or more mailing lists. An authorized administrator can use the application to create new mailing lists. (See the Bonus Chapter on the CD.)

You can copy an application from the CD to your Web site and have a working application instantly — well, assuming you have the correct versions of PHP and MySQL. In the first section ("Understanding PHP and MySQL Versions"), you find out more information about the versions that I use in this book. You also have to put the application files in the correct place, and I tell you how to do that in the "Using the Application Source Code" section.

Understanding PHP and MySQL Versions

Because PHP and MySQL are open-source software, new versions are released often and sometimes without much warning. Sometimes new releases include changes in the way the software works or the installation procedure that require changes to your application — not often, but occasionally. The software developers try to maintain *backward compatibility* (meaning old programs can run on the new versions), but sometimes it's just not possible. Consequently, you need to be aware of versions and keep informed about PHP and MySQL versions, changes, and problems.

MySQL

Currently, MySQL offers three versions: MySQL 4.0, MySQL 4.1, and MySQL 5.0. At this time, MySQL 5.0 is a developmental version, not recommended for production uses. It's fine for testing or experimenting, but if you have a Web site that users are accessing, I recommend not using a developmental version.

MySQL 4.0 and 4.1 are stable versions, recommended for use on active Web sites. MySQL is maintaining and improving both versions. The current versions are MySQL 4.0.24 and 4.1.11.

Version 4.1 added many new features and is the currently recommended version. If you don't have an existing MySQL server, install MySQL 4.1.

If you upgrade from version 4.0 to version 4.1, one change, starting with version 4.1.1, is longer passwords for MySQL accounts. That is, when you set a password for a new account using SET PASSWORD, PASSWORD(), or GRANT, the password is longer (and more secure) in 4.1 than in 4.0. Therefore, after you upgrade, you need to run the mysql_fix_privilege_tables script that is provided with the MySQL installation. This script changes the tables in MySQL that hold the account and password information, making the password column wider to hold the new, longer passwords. In addition, you need to access the database with a client that understands MySQL 4.1 passwords, such as the mysql client provided with MySQL version 4.1. (See http://dev.mysql.com/doc/mysql/en/password-hashing.html for more information on passwords in version 4.1.)

This book avoids the use of complex SQL queries, making the applications as easy to read and understand as possible. All SQL queries used in the applications in this book can run with either version 4.0 or 4.1. However, the functions used in PHP might or might not run correctly. See the following section for information on PHP versions.

PHP

Currently, PHP is maintaining two versions: PHP 4 and PHP 5. The current versions are PHP 4.3.11 and PHP 5.0.4.

PHP 5 is a major change from PHP 4. Enhancing object-oriented programming features was an important goal in the development of PHP 5. The creation and use of objects runs much faster, many object-oriented features have been added, and exceptions are introduced. Programmers who prefer object-oriented programming will be much happier with PHP 5. Most object-oriented programs that run with PHP 4 can run under PHP 5.

With PHP 5, the directory structure was changed. The executable programs have different names. The extension files are located in a different directory. Functions were added or enhanced. (For a complete list of new functions, see www.php.net/manual/en/migration5.functions.php.)

Each application provides procedural scripts and object-oriented programs. The procedural scripts in this book run with either PHP 4 or PHP 5, with the exception of the MySQL function calls. See the following section, "PHP and MySQL together," for further information on the MySQL function calls. The object-oriented programs in this book run only with PHP 5.

PHP and MySQL together

PHP interacts with MySQL by using built-in functions. Currently, PHP provides two sets of functions for use when accessing MySQL databases: the MySQL extension and the MySQL Improved extension. The MySQL Improved extension was made available with PHP 5 for use with MySQL 4.1.

When you install PHP, you activate either the MySQL or the MySQL Improved extension. PHP 4 activates MySQL automatically during installation. You don't need to activate it yourself. PHP 4 activates the MySQL extension. The MySQL Improved extension isn't available with PHP 4. You can use the MySQL extension with MySQL 4.1; you just can't use some of the new version 4.1 features.

PHP 5 doesn't activate MySQL automatically. You need to enable MySQL support yourself either by using the installation option — with-mysql or with-mysqli — on Linux/Mac or by uncommenting one of the following lines in php.ini:

```
;extension=php_mysql.dll
;extension=php_mysqli.dll
```

In general, it's best to use mysql with MySQL version 4.0 and mysqli with MySQL version 4.1.

To access MySQL from a PHP script, you use the appropriate functions, depending on which extension you enabled. The functions are similar to the following:

```
$cxn = mysql_connect($host,$userid,$password);
$cxn = mysqli_connect($host,$userid,$password);
```

The applications in this book use the mysqli functions. Consequently, you must use PHP 5 to run these scripts in their current format. However, if you need to run the applications with PHP 4, you just need to use the mysql function calls instead of the mysqli calls. If you revise the script and change the mysqli functions to mysql, you need to change the format of some of the functions.

In the preceding `mysql_connect` functions, the syntax of the two function calls is the same. However, many of the function calls differ slightly, such as the following:

```
$db = mysql_select_db("dbname");
$db = mysqli_select_db($cxn, "dbname");
```

The mysqli function requires a database connection parameter before the database name. Other functions require similar minor changes. Appendix C shows the differences between mysql and mysqli syntax for the functions used in this book.

Using the Application Source Code

All the code for the applications in this book is provided on the CD. Each application is in its own directory. If you copy all the files from a specific directory to your Web space, you can run the application in your browser.

Choosing a location

Copy all the files from the CD directory to your Web space. You might want to put all the files into a subdirectory in your Web space, such as `c:\program files\apache group\apache\http\catalog`. The files include three types of files:

- ✔ **PHP scripts:** The files contain the scripts with the PHP code that provides the application functionality. PHP script files end with a `.php` extension.

- ✔ **Include files:** The files are called by using `include` statements in the PHP scripts. Include files end with a `.inc` extension.

- ✔ **Classes:** The files contain class definitions for object-oriented programs. The files are called at the beginning of the PHP scripts using include statements. Class files end with a `.class` extension.

If all the files are together in a single directory, the application runs. However, you might want to organize the files by putting them in subdirectories. If you put the files in subdirectories, you need to modify the script to use the correct path when including or calling the files.

One of the include files, named Vars.inc, contains the sensitive information needed to access the MySQL database. You should secure this file by putting it into your *include directory* — a directory where PHP looks for the files specified in an include statement. The include directory can be located outside your Web space, where visitors to your Web page cannot access it. You set up your include directory in the php.ini file. Look for the include_path setting. If the line starts with a semicolon (;), remove the semicolon. Add the path to the directory you want to use as your include directory. For example, you could use one of the following statements:

```
include_path=".;c:\include";          #Windows
include_path=".:/include";            #Linux
```

Both of these statements specify two directories where PHP looks for include files. The first directory is dot (meaning the current directory), followed by the second directory path. You can specify as many include directories as you want, and PHP searches through them for the include file in the order in which they are listed. The directory paths are separated by a semicolon for Windows and a colon for Linux.

If you don't have access to php.ini, you can set the path in each individual script by using the following statement:

```
ini_set("include_path","c:\hidden");
```

This statement sets the include_path to the specified directory only while the program is running. It doesn't set the directory for your entire Web site.

The catalog application in the book includes images, but the images aren't included on the CD. Any catalog you implement will need specific product pictures. The application expects to find image files in a subdirectory named images.

Understanding the PHP code

The PHP code in the applications consists of only basic PHP statements. It doesn't use advanced PHP concepts or statements. Anyone who has a basic understanding of PHP can understand the code in the applications. You don't need to be an expert.

In the application, most of the code is included in the main PHP script(s). When building PHP scripts for an application, good programming practice dictates that you look for opportunities to use functions. Any time you find yourself using the same code more than once, you can place the code in a function and call the function at the appropriate locations in the script.

In the applications in this book, I don't use functions nearly as often as I could (or should). I believe that you can understand the code and follow its flow more easily when the code is in a single file, rather than when you must jump from page to page and back again, looking for the listing of functions. So, I present the code in the listings in a less disjointed manner — in fewer files showing the code in a top-down listing. In the explanation of the code, I point out locations where functions would be better coding style.

After each listing, I explain the code. Numbers in the explanation refer to line numbers shown in the code listing. I assume you know how control structures work in PHP and can follow the program flow. I provide some general description and some detailed description for more difficult or complex coding blocks.

Procedural versus object-oriented programs

Each application in this book is built with both procedural code and object-oriented code. That means that the CD contains two sets of independent programs for each application in the book. The mailing list application, described in the bonus chapter on the CD, however, is provided only with procedural code.

I am providing both types of code with the intention of producing a useful book for the following readers:

- ✔ **Inexperienced PHP programmers who have written only procedural code and who need to build an application for a real-world Web site:** You can install and use the procedural version of the application.

- ✔ **Programmers experienced with procedural programs in PHP who want to find out how to write object-oriented code in PHP:** You can compare the two versions to understand how to build object-oriented code. Appendixes A and B provide the concepts and syntax of object-oriented programming.

- ✔ **Programmers experienced in writing object-oriented code in another language who want to build an object-oriented application in PHP:** You can install and use the object-oriented version of the application. Appendix B describes the syntax of object-oriented programming in PHP.

Procedural and object-oriented methods are more than simply different syntax. As I describe in Appendix A, object-oriented programming is a different way of approaching programming projects. In the object-oriented approach, the programming problem is modeled with objects that represent the components of the programming problem. The objects store information and can perform needed tasks. The code that defines the object is stored in a class, which can then be used anywhere in the application that it's useful. The programmer using the class doesn't need to know anything about what's happening inside the class or how the class performs its tasks. The programmer can just use it. Thus, one programmer can develop a class that works in programs for many other programmers.

Developing really large, complex applications, involving several programmers or teams of programmers, is pretty difficult without using object-oriented programming. With object-oriented programming, programmers can develop their parts of the application independently. In addition, if something needs to be changed later, only the class with the change is affected. The other components of the application need not change. For the same reasons, maintenance of the application is much easier.

Modifying the Source Code

In most cases, you need to modify the application code. For one thing, the Web page design is very plain. Nothing in the page design will excite visitors or win you that Designer of the Year award. So, you undoubtedly want to customize the look and feel of the page. If you're adding one of these applications to an existing Web site, you can modify these pages to look like the existing page. Or, you might want to design something creative to impress your customers. If nothing else, you surely want to add your logo.

Because the source code provided with this book is a simple text file, you can use your favorite text-editing tool to modify the PHP source code files. You wouldn't be the first person to create scripts with vi, Notepad, or WordPad. However, you can find tools that make script editing much easier.

Check out programming editors and Integrated Development Environments before creating your PHP scripts. These tools offer features that can save you enormous amounts of time when building your application. So download some demos, try out the software, and select the one that suits you best. You can take a vacation on the time you save later.

Programming editors

Programming editors offer many features specifically for writing programs. The following features are offered by most programming editors:

- **Color highlighting:** Highlight parts of the script — such as HTML tags, text strings, keywords, and comments — in different colors so they're easy to identify.

- **Indentation:** Automatically indent inside parentheses and curly braces to make scripts easier to read.

- **Line numbers:** Add temporary line numbers. This is important because PHP error messages specify the line where the error was encountered. It would be cumbersome to have to count 872 lines from the top of the file to the line that PHP says is a problem.

- **Multiple files:** You can have more than one file open at once.

- **Easy code inserting:** Buttons for inserting code, such as HTML tags or PHP statements or functions are available.

- **Code library:** Save snippets of your own code that can be inserted by clicking a button.

Many programming editors are available on the Internet for free or for a low price. Some of the more popular editors include the following:

- **Arachnophilia:** This multiplatform editor is written in Java. It's CareWare, which means it doesn't cost any money.

  `www.arachnoid.com/arachnophilia`

- **BBEdit:** This editor is designed for use on a Mac. BBEdit sells for $199.00. Development and support have been discontinued for BBEdit Lite, which is free, but you can still find it and legally use it.

  `www.barebones.com/products/bbedit/index.shtml`

- **EditPlus:** This editor is designed for use on a Windows machine. EditPlus is shareware, and the license is $30.

  `www.editplus.com`

- **Emacs:** Emacs works with Windows, Linux, and UNIX, and it's free.

  `www.gnu.org/software/emacs/emacs.html`

✔ **HomeSite:** HomeSite is designed for use with Windows and will run you $99.00.

www.macromedia.com/software/homesite

✔ **HTML-Kit:** This is another Windows editor that you can pick up for free.

www.chami.com/html-kit

✔ **TextWrangler:** This editor is designed for use on a Mac. It's developed and published by the same company that sells BBEdit. TextWrangler has fewer features than BBEdit, but has most of the major features useful for programmers, such as syntax highlighting and automatic indenting. And it's much cheaper than BBEdit — as in *free*.

www.barebones.com/products/textwrangler/index.shtml

✔ **Vim:** These free, enhanced versions of vi can be used with Windows, Linux, UNIX, and Mac OS.

www.vim.org

Integrated Development Environment (IDE)

An *Integrated Development Environment (IDE)* is an entire workspace for developing applications. It includes a programming editor as well as other features. Some features included by most IDEs are the following:

✔ **Debugging:** Has built-in debugging features.

✔ **Previewing:** Displays the Web page output by the script.

✔ **Testing:** Has built-in testing features for your scripts.

✔ **FTP:** Has built-in ability to connect, upload, and download via FTP. It also keeps track of which files belong in which Web site and keeps the Web site up to date.

✔ **Project management:** Organizes scripts into projects, manages the files in the project, and includes file checkout and check-in features.

✔ **Backups:** Makes automatic backups of your Web site at periodic intervals.

IDEs are more difficult to get familiar with than programming editors. Some are fairly expensive, but their wealth of features can be worth it. IDEs are particularly useful when several people will be writing scripts for the same application. An IDE can make project coordination much simpler and make the code more compatible.

The following are popular IDEs:

- **Dreamweaver MX:** This IDE is available for the Windows and Mac platforms. It provides visual layout tools so you can create a Web page by dragging elements around and clicking buttons to insert elements. Dreamweaver can write the HTML code for you. It includes the HomeSite editor so you can write code. It also supports PHP. Dreamweaver will set you back $399.00.

  `www.macromedia.com/dreamweaver`

- **Komodo:** Komodo is offered for the Linux and Windows platforms. It's an IDE for open-source languages, including Perl and Python, as well as PHP. It's offered for $29.95 for personal or educational use, and $295.00 for commercial use.

  `www.activestate.com/Products/Komodo`

- **Maguma:** Maguma is available for Windows only. It's an IDE for Apache, PHP, and MySQL on Windows and comes in two versions at different costs: Maguma Studio Desktop and Maguma Studio Enterprise, which offers features for huge sites with multiple servers. Maguma Studio for PHP is a free version with support for PHP only.

  `www.maguma.com`

- **PHPEdit:** This free IDE is available only for Windows.

  `www.phpedit.net/products/PHPEdit`

- **Zend Studio:** Zend Studio is offered for the Linux and Windows platforms. This IDE was developed by the people who developed the Zend engine, which is the engine under the hood of PHP. These people know PHP extremely well. Zend Studio will cost you $195.00.

  `www.zend.com/store/products/zend-studio.php`

Planning Your Application

Planning is an essential part of building your application. The application design is the blueprint for building your application. Your plan should be complete enough to keep your project on track toward its goal and to ensure that all the needed elements and features are included in the plan.

Even if you're using one of the applications in this book, you need to develop your own plan first. With your plan as a guide, you can see whether the application meets all your needs as is or whether you need to modify the application, adding or removing features so the application fits your needs perfectly.

The larger and more complex your application is, the more planning is required. An application that displays Hello World on the screen, with five lines in the script, built by one person, requires little planning. The Amazon Web site requires mammoth planning.

Planning the software

Planning the application software includes the following steps:

1. **Identify the goal or goals of the application.**

   Is the application intended to collect information from users? Sell products to users? Entertain users? Create a community of users?

2. **Develop a list of tasks that the application needs to perform in order to meet the goal.**

   For instance, if the goal is to sell products, the application needs to, at the least, display the products information, provide a means for the customer to select a product, collect the information needed to fill the order, and charge the customer for the product.

3. **Plan the database.**

   Decide what information needs to be stored. Decide how to store it for quick and easy access.

4. **Develop a detailed plan for the methods to use in carrying out the general behavior tasks that you develop in Step 2.**

   For instance, "collect the information needed to fill the order" can expand to:

   a. Display a form.

   b. Verify the information submitted in the form.

   c. Store the information in a database.

5. **Plan the Web pages.**

   How many Web pages need to be displayed? For instance, do you need a form and a feedback page? A product information page? A page that looks like a chess board? Design the look and feel of the Web pages.

Additional planning

The application plan is a basis for other project planning. You need to develop a schedule for your project. You also need to develop a resource plan.

Developing a schedule

The most important date for your project is the date the application goes live. That is, the date when outside users can begin using the application. In some cases, you are given the date, and you need to determine the resources you need to meet the date. In other cases, you have finite resources and you must estimate the date when the application will be ready to go live.

You can use the application plan to estimate the number of man hours needed to build the application. The calendar time required depends on how many programmers are working on the application. A project that takes 100 hours will take one programmer 2½ weeks to finish, assuming the programmer makes optimum use of every hour of a 40-hour week. Two programmers can finish the application (theoretically) in 1¼ weeks.

When scheduling, be sure to allow some time for those tasks required by Murphy's Law — rewriting vanished code, time lost due to bubonic plague, electric outages caused by lightening, and so forth. Also, be sure to allow time for testing and writing documentation.

When planning your timeline, remember that some tasks can proceed simultaneously, but other tasks must proceed sequentially. For instance, if one of your tasks is to buy a computer, the programming can't start until after the computer arrives.

Project management software can be useful when developing a schedule. It keeps track of the tasks, the resources, and the critical events along the way. It charts the tasks into a timeline, showing the *critical path* — the series of tasks that must be completed on time in order for the project to be completed on time.

Planning the resources

Resources include both human and material resources. Your software plan and the project delivery date determine the human resources required. Your plan needs to schedule the availability of the human resources. If you need to hire more people, include that time in your schedule. If you plan to use existing staff, plan the project time into their schedules.

Make sure that material resources are available when they're needed. For instance, if you need to buy a new computer for the project, you need to start the purchasing process so that the computer will arrive before it's needed. For the applications in this book, you need PHP and MySQL, so you need to plan their availability. Is the software currently installed? Does it need upgrading? If it's not installed, who will install and administer it? When can the administrator have it available?

Include a list of resources needed, both human and material, as part of your project plan. For projects such as the applications in this book, personnel and computers are required resources. However, for your specific project, many other resources might be needed. For instance, artwork or photos of products may be required. Written copy for an online catalog might be needed. You might want a reference book or two. A list of resources can help prevent dead time spent waiting for needed resources.

Chapter 2

Building in Application Security

Security is an important issue for computing in general and Web sites in particular. Security is *not* an on/off condition; it's a continuum ranging from no security to total security. *No security* is a computer set up in the middle of a mall where anyone can use it. *Total security* is a computer locked in a safe where no one can use it.

Your Web site security is somewhere between the two extremes. Your Web site must be available for access from the Internet; otherwise, no one can see your Web pages. Your goal is to limit what visitors to your Web site can do while allowing them to download your Web pages and, for the applications in this book, to enter information into a form. However, you certainly don't want visitors to be able to reformat your hard disk or delete all the files on your Web site.

Web site security is a tradeoff between security measures and ease of use. For instance, if you require visitors to log in, the Web site is more difficult for them to use. They must enter user IDs and passwords, which means that they must remember their user IDs and passwords (or at least remember where they put the papers where they wrote that information down). Some Web sites require a login for security, however, even though the site becomes more difficult to use. Just be sure that the login is really necessary. Some visitors might not use the site because of the login requirement.

The more security you add, the more difficult the site is to use, so you don't want to use more security than necessary. One consideration in deciding how tight your security needs to be is the importance of the information you are protecting. If you're storing top-secret government information or a treasure trove of credit card numbers, you must implement a high level of security. If you're saving family recipes, however, you probably need very little security.

PHP and MySQL each has its own security features and issues. I discuss these issues in detail in this chapter. In addition, there are security issues concerning the computer that houses your Web site and the Internet connection to your Web site. Computer and Internet security issues are the domain of the system administrator, not the programmer. This is a book about building applications, so I don't discuss system security.

Understanding Security Risks

Security is another word for protection. Just as you protect your home from invasion, you protect your computer from invasion. Although the majority of visitors to your Web site are customers with no intention beyond using the services you offer, not all people are honest and well-intentioned. Some are bad guys with nefarious purposes, such as:

- **Stealing stuff:** The intruder hopes to find a file sitting around full of valid credit card numbers or the secret formula for eternal youth.

- **Trashing your Web site:** The miscreant wants to destroy your Web site. Or add graffiti to it. Some people think this is funny. Some people do it to prove that they can. Or, you may have really annoyed someone.

- **Harming your visitors:** A malicious person can add things to your Web site that harm or steal from the people who visit your site.

When you design your Web site, you must consider security issues. You must design security as well as functionality. You need to consider the possible misuses of your Web site and design prevention for identified misuses into your site.

Building Security into Your PHP Scripts

PHP is used to build dynamic Web sites. Web sites are by definition accessible from the Internet, making them open to possible infiltration and theft. In addition, the dynamic aspect of PHP allows users to add information — possibly malicious information — to your Web site. However, alert and informed programming can minimize the security risks on your Web site.

Don't trust any information from an outside source

Don't store or use any information from an outside source without checking whether it contains the expected information. This is your number one commandment. If you remember this commandment, the applications you write won't be vulnerable to the common security problems present in many applications.

Identifying outside sources

Information in your PHP scripts is stored and used in variables. Your script assigns values to variables with statements of the following format:

```
$varname = value;
```

The value can be one of the following types:

- **A literal value:** A number or a string, as shown in a statement as follows:

```
$num = 1;
$str1 = "Hello";
```

The information originates in the script, not outside the script. This type of value is safe and can be used as is, without checking.

- **A variable:** Information from one variable is stored in another variable, as shown in the following statement:

```
$varname2 = $varname1;
```

This statement might be safe if $varname1 originates in the script. However, if $varname1 contains information from an outside source, it must be treated as suspicious information. Check it before storing or using it.

Some outside information sources are the following:

- **URLs:** PHP reads information from the end of the URL when a file is downloaded. The information consists of variable name/value pairs.
- **POST data:** PHP reads data that is submitted via the POST method.
- **Cookies:** PHP reads data from cookies. *Cookies* are information that's stored on the user's computer and sent to the server when the user accesses your site.

Information received from outside sources can contain anything, including information that can damage or compromise your Web site. All information from outside sources needs to be checked and filtered. The remainder of this section discusses some ways of checking and filtering the information.

Specifying the source of the information

When you use information from a source outside the script, be sure it's coming from the expected source. For instance, if you pass information in a hidden variable in a form, be sure you get the information from the $_POST array. For instance, suppose your application logs in a customer and then passes the authorization variable, such as login=yes, in a hidden variable in the form. When you check whether a user is authorized to view a Web page, you need to use code such as the following:

```
if(!$_POST['login'] == "yes")
{
    echo "You are not logged in";
}
```

Then, if a user tried to access your Web site with the following URL:

http://www.yoursite.com?login=yes

the user would not be able to see the page because the authorization variable is in $_GET['login'], not in $_POST['login'].

Getting form variables from the $_POST array is the most secure method. If you check the authorization variable in $_REQUEST['login'], the user would appear to be logged in because the elements of both the $_POST and the $_GET arrays are included in $_REQUEST.

Another method is to turn the register_globals setting on in php.ini. Then, a variable called $login would be available. You could use the following check:

```
if($login != "yes")
{
    echo "You are not logged in";
}
```

However, this code also doesn't check where the information came from. If the user accessed your site with the login variable in the URL, the user would appear to be logged in.

The most secure programming checks the source of the information. You should leave register_globals turned off, which is the default, and get the information from the appropriate superglobal array. This alone isn't enough for secure programming. However, it can help make your application more secure.

Checking the data type of outside information

Your PHP script should check all information received from an outside source to be sure it contains the expected information.

You can check the type of information contained in a variable. PHP provides functions that check information. For instance, if you expect the information to be an integer, you can check it as follows:

```
if(!is_int($_POST['age']))
{
  echo "Data is not an integer";
}
```

PHP provides several functions that check data type, such as `is_array`, `is_bool`, `is_double`, `is_float`, `is_numeric`, `is_scalar`, `is_string`, and others. Use these functions to check information from outside sources.

Cleaning outside information

A lot of the outside information is in strings. Strings can contain any characters, including characters that can cause problems for your application, your database, or visitors to your Web site. For instance, HTML tags can potentially cause problems. A user might enter script tags, such as `<script>`. The script can execute and perform actions, such as deleting all files or dropping a database.

PHP provides two functions that can clean the data, thus rendering it harmless:

✔ `strip_tags`: This function removes all text enclosed by < and > from the data. It looks for an opening < and removes it and everything else, until it finds a closing > or reaches the end of the string. You can include specific tags that you want to allow. For instance, the following statement removes all tags from a character string except `<b>` and `<i>`:

```
$last_name = strip_tags($last_name, "<b><i>");
```

✔ `htmlspecialchars`: This function changes some special characters with meaning to HTML into an HTML format that allows them to be displayed without any special meaning. The changes are

- < becomes `&lt;`
- > becomes `&gt;`
- & becomes `&amp;`

In this way, the characters < and > can be displayed on a Web page without being interpreted by HTML as tags. The following statement changes these special characters:

```
$last_name = htmlspecialchars($last_name);
```

If you're positive that you don't want to allow your users to type any < or > characters into a form field, use `strip_tags`. However, if you want to allow < or > characters, you can safely store them after they have been processed by `htmlspecialchars`.

Checking outside information with regular expressions

You can use regular expressions to check whether data is in a reasonable format. If the information doesn't make sense, it's probably not something that you want to store in your database. For instance, if the user types a name into a form, you can check whether it seems like a real name by matching patterns. You know that a name consists mainly of letters and spaces. Other valid characters might be a hyphen (–), as in the name *Smith-Jones,* and a single quote ('), as in *O'Hara.* You can check the name by setting up a pattern that's a string containing only letters, spaces, hyphens, and single quotes and then matching the name to the pattern. If the name doesn't match — that is, if it contains characters not in the pattern, such as numerals or a question mark (?) — it's not a real name.

Regular expressions consist of literal characters and special characters. *Literal characters* are normal characters, with no other special meaning. A *c* is a *c* with no meaning other than it's one of the 26 letters in the English alphabet. *Special characters* have special meaning in the pattern, such as the asterisk (*) when used as a wild card. Table 2-1 shows the special characters used in regular expressions.

Table 2-1	Special Characters Used in Patterns			
Character	*Meaning*	*Example*	*Match*	*Not a Match*
^	Beginning of line.	^c	cat	my cat
$	End of line.	c$	tic	stick
.	Any single character.	. .	Any string that contains at least two characters	a, I
?	Preceding character is optional.	mea?n	mean, men	moan
( )	Groups literal characters into a string that must be matched exactly.	m(ea)n	mean	men, mn
[ ]	Encloses a set of optional literal characters.	m[ea]n	men, man	mean, mn

Character	Meaning	Example	Match	Not a Match
–	Represents all the characters between two characters.	`m[a-c]n`	man, mbn, mcn	mdn, mun, maan
+	One or more of the preceding items.	`door[1-3]+`	door111, door131	door, door55
*	Zero or more of the preceding items.	`door[1-3]*`	door, door311	door4, door445
{ , }	The starting and ending number of a range of repetitions.	`a{2,5}`	aa, aaaaa	a, xx3
\	The following character is literal.	`m\*n`	m*n	men, mean
(|)	A set of alternate strings.	`(Tom|Tommy)`	Tom, Tommy	Thomas, To

Literal and special characters are combined to make patterns, which are sometimes long, complicated patterns. A string is compared to the pattern, and if it matches, the comparison is true.

PHP provides functions that compare strings to regular expressions. You can use the function `ereg()`, as follows:

`ereg("regexp",$varname);`

The following code fragment tests whether the information is a valid zip code:

```
$regexp = "^[0-9]{5}(\-[0-9]{4})?$"
if(!ereg($regexp,$_POST['zip']))
{
    echo "Not a valid zip code<br>";
}
```

The regular expression breaks down as follows:

   `^[0-9]{5}` — Any string that begins with five numbers

   `\-` — A literal hyphen

   `[0-9]{4}` — Any string of numbers that is four digits long

   `( )?` — Groups the last two parts of the pattern and makes them optional

Another useful code fragment might be:

```
$regexp = "^.+@.+\.com$"
if(!ereg($regexp,$_POST['email']))
{
    echo "Not a valid email address<br>";
}
```

This code accepts only e-mail addresses that end with .com. (E-mail addresses can end with other characters.) Another regular expression is used in this code:

```
$regexp = "^[A-Za-z' -]{1-50}$"
if!(ereg($regexp,$_POST['last_name']))
{
    echo "Not a valid name<br>";
}
```

This regular expression accepts only letters, single quotes, blank spaces, and hyphens. If any other character shows up in the string, the last name is rejected as invalid.

PHP also provides Perl-compatible regular expressions for people who are familiar with Perl. You can use the function preg_match with Perl-compatible regular expressions.

Storing information

In your scripts, you frequently need to store and retrieve information. For instance, in an online ordering application (such as the one in Chapter 6), you need to store the customer information, such as name and address, for shipping the order, and you also need to store the items that the customer orders. You can store information by using any of the following mechanisms:

✔ **Text file:** You can store information in a text file on the Web server. This solution is fast and easy. However, anyone who has access to the Web server can access the text file.

✔ **Cookies:** Small amounts of information can be stored in a cookie. However, the information is stored on the user's computer, not on the Web server, which means that it can be changed. In addition, bad guys have techniques for stealing cookies, obtaining the information stored in them.

✔ **Session variables:** PHP session information is stored in a file on the Web server. The file is stored outside the Web space, so no one can access the session file from the Web.

✔ **Database:** You can store the information in a database. This is the most secure method because the database has security features of its own in addition to the security features provided by PHP. However, this method requires the most work and the most overhead.

You must protect the information you store. The protection measures needed depend on the importance of the information stored. If you're storing a credit card number or social security number, you need much greater protection for the data than if you're storing the customer's favorite color.

Using system calls

Some scripts require you to access the operating system. None of the applications in this book need to use operating system commands, but some applications do, such as applications that manage files or disk space. You can perform tasks that access your disk space in either of the following ways:

- ✔ **PHP functions:** PHP provides many functions for use with files and directories, such as `copy`, `rename`, `delete`, `mkdir`, `readfile`, and many others.

- ✔ **Executing system commands:** PHP allows you to execute system commands. That is, you can enter a system command, just as if you were working in the operating system. You can put the command in backticks (' ') or use one of three PHP functions: `system()`, `exec()`, or `passthru()`.

As long as you execute commands by using only information from within the script, the commands are safe. However, if you use information from any outside source, the potential for damage is high. You certainly don't want your users to be able to execute a command such as `rm *`, which deletes all files in the current directory.

Executing system commands is more dangerous. For instance, suppose you want to allow your user to rename a file. You might allow the user to enter the filename to change in a form and then build the following statement in your script:

```
system("mv $_POST['oldname'] $_POST['newname'] ");
```

Then, suppose your user typed the following into the form fields:

```
file1.txt
file2.txt;rm *
```

The statement you build and execute is the following:

```
system("mv file1.txt file2.txt;rm *");
```

When the command executes, all the files in the directory are deleted.

Clearly, if you're going to execute system commands containing information from an outside source, you must check the information carefully. You find techniques for checking and cleaning data in the section "Don't trust any information from an outside source" earlier in this chapter.

Using PHP file system functions is much safer than executing system commands with the system functions. For instance, the previous operation could be done using a statement like the following:

```
rename($_POST['oldname'],$_POST['newname']);
```

The function accepts only valid filenames, and so it is much more secure. Use a PHP function whenever you can find one that does what you need to do. Use the general function that lets you execute any system command only when absolutely necessary. And check any outside information very carefully.

Handling errors

Error messages display information when errors are encountered. Some of this information can be very useful to bad guys. The more a bad buy knows about your system, the more likely he is to figure out a way to break into it. For instance, an error message can tell the bad guy which database you're using or how the Web page is programmed or designed.

When you're developing your application, you want PHP to give you as much information as possible to help you identify problems in your script. However, when your Web site is available to the public, you no longer want this information displayed.

One way to handle errors is to shut off the error functions in php.ini. Using PHP settings, you can stop error messages from being displayed in your Web pages. If you want, you can log errors into a file that you can review. Then, you can turn the error display functions on for specific files only. That is, when you're developing a script, you can turn errors on for that script only.

The following settings in php.ini are related to error message display:

```
display_errors = On  (displays error messages in a Web page)
log_errors = Off   (sends error messages to a log file)
error_log = filename (specifies the log file name)
```

Bad guys can deliberately send errors to your Web site, causing error messages to display useful information. The following settings are more secure than the preceding settings:

```
display_errors = Off
log_errors = On
error_log = /var/log/php_error_log
```

Setting `display_errors` to off prevents error messages from being displayed in your Web page. When you turn `log_errors` on, it sends the error messages to the log file. The `error_log` setting defines the log file.

When you're developing a script, you can put the following line in the top of the script:

```
ini_set("display_errors","On");
```

This statement in a script displays errors for this script only. Thus, you can see errors while developing, but you can remove the statement when your script becomes available to the public.

MySQL Security

Data in databases is more secure than in flat files, cookies, or sessions because DBMS (Database Management System) software provides its own security features. MySQL provides a security system for protecting your data that restricts access based on account names and passwords. In addition, each account has permission settings that specify what the user can do when using the account to access MySQL. MySQL security might seem complicated, but its security features provide valuable protection for your data.

Setting up accounts and passwords

Accessing a MySQL database is a two-step process:

1. **Connect to the MySQL server.**

   This step requires a valid user account and password.

   The MySQL server might be located on the same computer you are using to access it or on another computer that you access over a network. It's more secure to locate MySQL on a separate computer. Ideally, the MySQL computer is behind a firewall. If the MySQL computer accepts only internal traffic, such as traffic from your Web server, and not traffic from outside your organization, it's much more secure.

2. **Access the data in the database.**

   An SQL query is used for this step. MySQL provides a system of permissions that specify what an account can do to the data. For instance, an account might be set up so that users can select data but cannot insert nor update data.

When MySQL is installed, some accounts are set up by default. The information used to control access to your data is stored in a MySQL database named mysql.

Understanding the MySQL security database

When MySQL is installed, it automatically creates a database called mysql. All the information used to protect your data is stored in this database, including account names, hostnames, passwords, and permissions.

Permissions are stored in columns. The format of each column name is *permission*_priv, where *permission* is one of the query permissions you can set for MySQL. For instance, the column containing ALTER permissions is named alter_priv. The value in each permission column is Y or N, meaning *yes* or *no*. So, for instance, in the user table (which I describe in the following list), you would find a row for an account and a column for alter_priv. If the account field for alter_priv contains Y, the account can be used to execute an ALTER query. If alter_priv contains N, the account doesn't have permission to execute an ALTER query.

The mysql database has the following tables:

- ✔ **user table:** This table stores permissions that apply to all the databases and tables. It contains a row for each valid account with user name, hostname, and password. The MySQL server will reject a connection for an account that doesn't exist in this table.

- ✔ **db table:** This table stores permissions that apply to a particular database. It contains a row for the database, which gives permissions to an account name and hostname. The account must exist in the user table for the permissions to be granted. Permissions that are given in the user table overrule permissions in this table.

- ✔ **host table:** This table controls access to a database depending on the host. The host table works with the db table. If a row in the db table has an empty field for the host, MySQL checks the host table to see whether the db has a row there. In this way, you can allow access to a db from some hosts but not from others. For instance, say you have two databases: db1 and db2. The db1 database has information that is very sensitive, so you want only certain people to see it. The db2 database has information that you want everyone to see. If you have a row in the db table for db1 with a blank host field, you can have two rows for db1 in the host table. One row can give all permissions to users connecting from a specific host, whereas another row can deny privileges to users connecting from any other host.

✔ `tables_priv` **table:** This table stores permissions that apply to specific tables.

✔ `columns_priv` **table:** This table stores permissions that apply to specific columns.

You can see and change the tables in `mysql` directly if you're using an account that has the necessary permissions. You can use SQL queries such as `SELECT`, `INSERT`, `UPDATE`, and others.

Setting up accounts

MySQL is installed with default accounts, one of which is the root account. In some cases, the root account is installed without a password. In other cases, the installation procedure requests you to enter a password for the root account. The root account needs a password. If it is installed without a password, you should give it one immediately. The root account is well known, and a bad guy might try the root account on your system just to see whether it's there and unprotected.

REMEMBER

The root account is set up with all possible permissions, including the ability to shut down your server. You should restrict access to this powerful account. Never allow users to access your database with this account.

You should set up specific accounts for the purpose of accessing your databases from PHP. Give the accounts only the permissions they really need. If your script will only retrieve data from the database, only `SELECT` permission is needed by the account that accesses the database. You can provide even more security by using different accounts for different purposes. You can set up one account with `SELECT` permission only and a different account for use with `INSERT` queries that doesn't have `SELECT` permission. Thus, if one account is compromised, the damage it can do is limited.

When you set up an account, you specify the password, the name of the computer allowed to access the database using this account, and the permissions. However, you can change these at any time.

You can add or modify an account by changing the `mysql` database directly with `INSERT` and `UPDATE` queries. Or you can use the `GRANT` query, an SQL query for adding or modifying accounts.

Adding accounts with the GRANT query

Here is the general format for a `GRANT` query:

```
GRANT permission (columns) ON tablename
     TO accountname@hostname IDENTIFIED BY 'password'
```

You must fill in the following information:

- *permission (columns)*: You must list at least one permission. You can limit each permission to one or more columns by listing the column name in parentheses following the permission. If no column name is listed, the permission is granted on all columns in the table(s). You can list as many permission and columns as needed, separated by commas. See the MySQL manual for a list of all permissions (dev.mysql.com/doc/mysql/en/privileges-provided.html). For instance, a GRANT query might start with this:

```
GRANT select (firstName,lastName), update,
      insert (birthdate) ...
```

- *tablename*: This indicates which tables the permission is granted on. At least one table is required. You can list several tables, separated by commas. The possible values for *tablename* are

  - *tablename*: The entire table named *tablename* in the current database. You can use an asterisk (*) to mean all tables in the current database. If you use an asterisk and no current database is selected, the privilege will be granted to all tables on all databases.

  - *databasename.tablename*: The entire table named *tablename* in *databasename*. You can use an asterisk (*) for either the database name or the table name to mean *all*. Using *.* grants the permission on all tables in all databases.

- *accountname@hostname*: If the account already exists, it is given the indicated permissions. If the account doesn't exist, it's added. The account is identified by the *accountname* and *hostname* as a pair. If an account exists with the specified account name but a different hostname, the existing account isn't changed; a new one is created.

- *password*: This is the password that you're adding or changing. A password isn't required. If you don't want to add or change a password for this account, leave out the entire phrase IDENTIFIED BY '*password*'.

The GRANT query to add a new account for use in the PHP programs for a database named Catalog might be

```
GRANT select ON Catalog.* TO phpuser@localhost
             IDENTIFIED BY 'mysecretpassword'
```

If an account already exists, you can add or change passwords with the following GRANT query:

```
GRANT select ON * TO phpuser@hostname
             IDENTIFIED BY ''
```

The existing password is replaced with a blank, leaving the account with no password — and that isn't usually a good idea.

Accessing MySQL from PHP scripts

To access MySQL from PHP scripts, you need to use the account name and password that you have set up for use in your PHP scripts. Consequently, the account information must be available to your scripts. You need to protect this information as well as possible.

Don't put the account information in the script. Store the information in a separate file. For instance, you might use a file similar to the following:

```php
<?php
$host = "localhost";
$user = "phpuser";
$password = "asdf321";
$database = "Catalog";
?>
```

You can then include the file in your script, so that your MySQL connect statement would look as follows:

```
$connect = mysqli_connect($host,$user,$password,$database);
```

You can store the file in a secure location outside your Web space so that no one can access it from the Web. PHP allows you to specify a directory for include files. When you use the `include` statement in your script, PHP looks for the file in the include directory.

You specify the include directory in the `php.ini` file, as follows:

```
include_path = ".:/php/includes"     (Linux, Unix)
include_path = ".;c:\php\includes"    (Windows)
```

You can specify as many paths as you want. The preceding statements both specify two paths: dot (.), which means the current directory, and /php/ includes. The paths are separated by a colon (:) for Linux and a semicolon (;) for Windows.

You can store your file containing the account information in the include directory and access it in the script with the following statement:

```
include("Vars.inc");
```

PHP searches for `Vars.inc` in the paths specified in the `include_path` statement, searching the directories in the order they are listed.

Understanding SQL injection attacks

When you use information from an outside source to build an SQL query, you might be vulnerable to an SQL injection attack. In an *SQL injection attack*, a bad guy inserts characters into an SQL query, changing it into a query that affects your application.

Using quotes to change your query

When you use unchecked data from a form to build an SQL query, you provide the bad guy with a golden opportunity to create an SQL statement that serves his purposes. For instance, suppose you used the following code to allow a user to log in:

```
$user = $_POST['user_id'];
$password = $_POST['password'];
$sql = "SELECT COUNT(*) FROM Customer
        WHERE user_id='$user' and password='$password'";
```

If the SQL query returns any count higher than 0, the user_id and password exist in the database and the user is logged in. In this case, the data entered into the form by the user is used without any checking. Suppose a user entered the following user name into the form:

```
' or 1=1 --
```

Your SQL query would then be:

```
SELECT COUNT(*) FROM Customer WHERE user_id='' or 1=1 --
        and password='$password'
```

This query will always return a count higher than 1 because 1=1 is always true. In addition, the -- makes the rest of the query into a comment, which is ignored by SQL. Consequently, this user is now logged in.

Unauthorized access is bad enough. Depending on the structure of your database, however, a bad guy might be able to construct queries that seriously damage your database. For instance, a query might be changed into two or more queries, adding a damaging query. The use of multiple queries is discussed in the next section.

Building multiple queries

Many databases allow more than one query to be executed at a time, usually separated by a semicolon (;). A bad guy might be able to enter data into a field that creates a malicious SQL query. Suppose you're building a query from information the user enters into a form. The query you're building is:

```
SELECT email FROM Member WHERE last_name='$_POST['name'] '
```

Suppose the user enters the following into the name field in the form:

```
Smith';DROP TABLE Member --
```

Your query would then be:

```
SELECT email FROM Member
    WHERE last_name='Smith';DROP TABLE Member --
```

After you execute this query, you are left wondering where your database table went.

Adding a query that harms your application is less of a danger in MySQL than in other databases. Until MySQL 4.1, MySQL didn't accept multiple queries in a single request. Beginning with MySQL 4.1, multiple queries can be executed, but you must use a specific function, `mysqli_multi_query`, to send multiple queries. If you don't use this function, users can't use the type of attack shown in the preceding query.

Escaping quotes

One measure to protect your database is to escape the quotes in any information that is going to be sent to your database. With a \ in front of a quote, it is treated as a literal character by the database, not as a special character with special meaning. The quote is stored in the database as a character, rather than triggering the database to take an action. For example, if the example in the preceding section were escaped, it would look as follows:

```
SELECT COUNT(*) FROM Customer WHERE user_id='\' or 1=1 --
       and password='$password'
```

SQL would see the \' as any other character, not as the quote that closes the `user_id` field. It would interpret the entire string until the quote in front of `$password` as the `user_id`. The query is not valid SQL in this form. The query would cause an error.

PHP provides two features useful for escaping quotes, as follows:

✔ **Magic quotes:** A setting in your `php.ini` file that is turned on by default. When magic quotes is turned on, information received by the PHP script is automatically escaped. In other words, when you retrieve information from the `$_POST` array, any quotes are already escaped.

✔ **The `addslashes` function:** A PHP function that escapes quotes. A matching `stripslashes` function removes the slashes when needed, such as when you want to display the information on the Web page, without displaying a bunch of ugly slashes.

Magic quotes are turned on by default. However, not all data is meant to be sent to the database. When you display data, without storing it in the database, the slashes must be removed. In general, tuning magic quotes off is preferable. While magic quotes are handy to prevent beginners from making dangerous mistakes, adding/removing slashes with the functions allows you more control over your script. Just remember to add slashes to any data you send to your database.

Checking and filtering information

Escaping the quotes in data sent to the database is not enough to prevent all SQL injection attacks. The bad guys can be very creative. You need to check all data received from outside sources. (Heard that somewhere before?)

At the very least, you need to check for semicolons. Semicolons are seldom required in legitimate data. I know no one named Jo;ann. In most cases, you can check that the information is in a reasonable format. For more information about checking your data, see the section "Don't trust any information from an outside source" earlier in this chapter.

Backing up your databases

You must back up your databases. If an attack destroys your databases, you must be able to replace them quickly. MySQL provides a utility that creates backups for you.

To back up your database, use the `mysqldump` utility located in the `bin` subdirectory of the directory where MySQL is installed. You start `mysqldump` by typing a command. If you're using Windows, you need to open a command prompt window.

Use one of the following commands to back up a database:

```
mysqldump --user=accountname --password=password databasename
     >path/backupfilename
```

You can change into the `bin` directory to type the command. Or, you can type the path to `mysqldump` when entering the command, such as:

```
c:\mysql\bin\mysqldump ...
```

For example, to back up a database named `Catalog`, you might use the following command:

```
mysqldump --user=phpuser --password=bigsecret Catalog
      >../backups/Catalog.bak
```

After running `mysqldump`, the file `/backups/Catalog.bak` contains all the SQL queries needed to re-create Catalog.

Backups should be made at certain times — at least once per day. If your database changes frequently, you might want to back up more often. For example, you might want to back up to the backup directory hourly, but back up to another computer once a day. In fact, for monumentally important data, you should have more than one backup and store one backup off-site, in case the building burns down.

Using a Secure Web Server

Your Web server and the browsers of its visitors communicate by sending messages. The browser requests a file that contains the HTML for a Web page. The server sends the information in the file. The communication between server and browser is not secure. Someone on the Internet between you and the person requesting your Web pages can read the messages that are being sent. If your site collects or sends credit card numbers or other secret information, you must use a secure Web server to protect this data.

Secure Web servers use Security Sockets Layer (SSL) to protect communication sent to and received from browsers. This is similar to the scrambled telephone calls that you hear about in spy movies. The information is *encrypted* (translated into coded strings) before it is sent across the Web. The receiving software decrypts it into its original content. In addition, your Web site uses a certificate that verifies your identity. Using a secure Web server is extra work, but it's necessary for some applications.

You can tell when you're communicating using SSL. The URL begins with *HTTPS,* rather than *HTTP.*

Information about secure Web servers is specific to the Web server that you're using. To find out more about using SSL, look at the Web site for the Web server that you're using. For instance, if you're using Apache, check out two open-source projects that implement SSL for Apache at `www.modssl.org` and `www.apache-ssl.org`. Commercial software is also available that provides a secure server based on the Apache Web server. If you're using Microsoft Internet Information Server (IIS), search for *SSL* on the Microsoft Web site at `www.microsoft.com`.

Part II

Building a User Authentication Application

The 5th Wave · By Rich Tennant

"What I'm looking for are dynamic Web applications and content, not Web innuendoes and intent."

In this part . . .

In this part, I provide two applications that restrict Web sites (or sections of Web sites) to authorized users only. The two applications use two different methods — procedural and object oriented — to authorize users.

Chapter 3

User Authentication with HTTP

In This Chapter

▶ Understanding how HTTP headers work

▶ Using HTTP authentication with Apache

▶ Designing a PHP script that uses HTTP authentication for user login

▶ Building a PHP script that uses HTTP authentication for user login

*M*any applications require the user to log in. For example, most applications for online shopping require the user to log in before purchasing merchandise or services. Sometimes users can't view any pages in the Web site without entering a password, and sometimes only part of the Web site is password-protected.

Because requiring users to enter a user ID and a password before viewing Web pages is needed so often, user authentication is built into HTTP (Hypertext Transfer Protocol), the language that Web servers and browsers use to communicate when transferring Web page content. I provide a short refresher on the WWW (World Wide Web) and HTTP in the following section, "Understanding HTTP Authentication."

You can use HTTP's built-in user authentication features or build your own login application from scratch. HTTP authentication is quicker and easier because it's ready and able to collect and verify user IDs and passwords; you don't have to write code for this task. However, HTTP authentication has some disadvantages, as I describe in the following list:

✔ **Look and feel:** The screen that requests password info is presented by your browser. It's a simple gray screen where the user enters a user ID and a password. You can't control its appearance.

✔ **Behavior:** The response to valid and invalid user IDs and passwords is set and controlled by the browser. For example, Internet Explorer allows only three invalid entries and then stops, whereas Netscape allows the user to reenter the information forever. You can't change the set behavior.

✔ **Passwords:** Valid user IDs and passwords must be provided in advance. The HTTP authentication function checks the user information against stored valid information to verify the user ID and password. HTTP authentication provides no facility for users to register online.

HTTP authentication is most useful for simple applications. For example, you might want to protect sections of your intranet, making them viewable only by staff members from a specific department, such as accounting or sales. Simple password protection in which a user enters a password provided by the department head might work well for such an application. Because the Web page is internal, its appearance might be less important than the appearance of Web pages presented to potential customers. In this chapter, I show you how to develop an application by using HTTP authentication.

If you want a more complicated application, such as one in which users can register online, or if the look and feel of the application are important, you probably want to build the application by writing your own code for all the functions. In Chapter 4, you find out how to build a user authentication application from scratch.

Understanding HTTP Authentication

HTTP authentication is built into HTTP (Hypertext Transfer Protocol). HTTP is the language that browsers and Web servers use to communicate. HTTP is the foundation that makes the WWW work.

Understanding how the WWW works

When a user types a URL into a browser, the browser sends an HTTP message out onto the WWW, requesting to view the file specified by the URL. The HTTP request might look like the following:

```
GET /Index.php HTTP/1.1
```

In addition to the initial request for the file, other HTTP messages, called *HTTP headers,* can be sent. For instance, a header is sent specifying where the file is to be found, as follows:

```
GET /index.php HTTP/1.1
Host: www.myowncompany.com
```

When the Web server at `www.myowncompany.com` receives the request, it searches the root directory of its Web space for a file named `index.php`. If it finds the file, the Web server sends some HTTP headers to the requesting browser containing information about what is being sent, followed by the contents of `index.php`. For instance, the Web server sends a status line such as the following:

HTTP/1.1 200 OK

This status line informs the browser that the file was found. If the file isn't found, the following status line is sent:

HTTP/1.1 404 Not found

In addition, other headers can be sent following the status line, as shown in this example:

HTTP/1.1 200 OK
Date: Mon, 31 May 2004 10:05:44 GMT
Content-Type: text/html
Content-length: 210

The headers provide the current date and time and tell the browser what type of information to expect and the length of the file contents. After the HTTP headers are sent, the content of the requested file is sent.

Requesting a password-protected file

In some cases, when the Web server receives a request for a file, it finds the file but determines that the file is password-protected. For example, when you use the Apache Web server, you can specify to Apache that all the files in a directory require the user to enter a password before Apache can send the file contents to the browser. The details of designating files as password-protected are discussed later in this chapter.

When the Web server receives a request for a protected file, it responds with the following status line:

HTTP/1.1 401 Unauthorized
WWW-Authenticate: Basic realm="Realm"

When the browser receives the authenticate header line, it displays a dialog box requesting the user to enter a user name and password. The display differs somewhat by browser, but all are similar. Figure 3-1 shows the dialog box displayed by Internet Explorer.

Figure 3-1:
The Enter
Network
Password
dialog box
requests
a user
name and
password.

When the user enters a user name and password, the browser sends a second request for the file, followed by a header that contains the user name and password entered by the user, as follows:

```
GET /SecretFile.php HTTP/1.1
Host: www.myowncompany.com
Authorization: Basic stringofcharacters
```

stringofcharacters is the user ID and password, encoded and separated by a colon. The user ID and password are encoded for transmission, not encrypted for security. If you're building a high security application, you need to use SSL (Secure Sockets Layer) to protect the information during transmission, which I discuss in Chapter 2.

Authorizing access

When the Web server receives the file request with the authorization header, the included user name and password must be tested to determine whether they're valid. Apache automatically checks the password based on Apache directives that tell Apache what user name/password combinations are valid. If the information is valid, the contents of the requested file are displayed. If the user name/password combination is not valid, the user is given the opportunity to reenter the information one or more times, depending on which browser is being used. Setting up your Web site for Apache HTTP authorization is described in the section "Using HTTP Authentication with Apache."

Alternatively, you can write code in your PHP script that checks the user name/password information in the authorization header. The information is available in your PHP script in $_SERVER['PHP_USER_AUTH'] and $_SERVER ['PHP_USER_PW']. I show you how to build a login application with this method in the sections that describe designing and building the application with PHP, later in this chapter.

Using HTTP Authentication with Apache

You can set up HTTP authentication by using Apache alone, without PHP or MySQL. After you use this approach to set up authentication, Apache automatically prompts for a user name and password and checks the information that the user enters against a list of valid user names and passwords. Although this approach is quick and easy to set up, it's also simplistic, inflexible, restricted in scope and function, and slow if you have a large number of valid user names and passwords. However, it's perfect for some types of user login, allowing quick and easy authentication for situations with a restricted number of users and that don't require anything more complicated. For instance, you might want to set up a password-protected directory on your intranet for each department, providing the department staff members with a user name and password for their specific areas.

You use instructions to Apache, called *directives,* to set up your authentication application. Directives allow you to specify the files that are password-protected and the valid user names and IDs. The simplest way to use Apache directives for authentication is to create a file called .htaccess (notice the period at the beginning of the filename).

Configuring Apache

When Apache starts, it executes the directives in its configuration file, usually called httpd.conf, located in a subdirectory called conf in the directory where Apache is installed. This configuration file generally allows access to all the Web pages stored in files in your Web space — htdocs by default, unless the location was changed in the Apache configuration file. To restrict access to certain files, you put a file called .htaccess, which contains Apache directives that specify authentication, into the directory that you want to password-protect. The Apache directives in the .htaccess file override the directives in the configuration file that were executed when Apache started. However, an Apache directive in the configuration file can tell Apache to ignore the commands in the .htaccess file. Before you can password-protect directories with an .htaccess file, you must be sure that Apache can execute the directives in the .htaccess file.

To make sure that Apache can execute directives in the .htaccess file, open the file httpd.conf. In Windows, choose Start⇨Programs⇨Apache HTTPD Server⇨Configure Apache Server. Look through the file for a line similar to the following line that identifies the top directory in your Web space:

```
<Directory "C:/Program Files/Apache Group/Apache/htdocs">
```

This line means that the following Apache directives apply to this directory only. Shortly after this line, you might find a line similar to the following:

```
AllowOverride None
```

This line tells Apache to ignore all the directives in any `.htaccess` file. You can change this line to the following line:

```
AllowOverride Authconfig
```

This line tells Apache to allow the directives in the `.htaccess` file that are related to HTTP authentication to override the authentication directives executed when Apache was started.

Creating the .htaccess file

The `.htaccess` file contains the Apache directives needed for HTTP authentication. Create a file called `.htaccess` (notice the filename begins with a period) in the directory that you want to password-protect. The `.htaccess` file specifies directives that apply to the directory where it's located and all subdirectories under its directory. The contents of the file should be as follows:

```
AuthUserFile "c:\secret\.htpass
AuthGroupFile /dev/null
AuthName "Accounting Department"
AuthType Basic
Require valid-user
```

Here's a closer look at the file contents:

- ✔ The first line specifies a file containing the list of valid users for this directory. The procedures for creating the password file are discussed in the next section, "Creating the password file."

  Store the password file in a directory outside of your Web space. It's much more secure there than in a directory that visitors from the Web can access. In this case, the directory is in `c:\secret`, not anywhere under `htdocs`.

- ✔ The second line specifies a group file; in this case, no group file exists (designated by `/dev/null`). A group file contains a list of groups that are allowed to access the files in this directory.

- ✔ `AuthName` is the name of the section that is protected. This name can be anything you want and is displayed in the window where the user enters a user name and password.

- ✔ `AuthType` is specified as Basic. Digest is the other type of authentication, which is more secure but also more complicated. I don't discuss Digest authentication in this book.

- ✔ The last line states that only a valid user — a user found in the file specified on the first line — can access files in this directory.

The .htaccess file applies to the directory where it resides and all subdirectories of this directory. However, another .htaccess file in a subdirectory of this directory would override the directives in this .htaccess file.

Creating the password file

The password file contains all the valid user name/password pairs. Apache provides a program to use to create the password file. The program, called htpasswd, is automatically installed in the bin subdirectory in the directory where Apache is installed, such as c:\Apache\bin\htpasswd.exe.

To create a password file, type a command similar to the following at the command line (the command prompt in Windows):

c:\Apache\bin\htpasswd -c c:\secret\.htpass janet

This command creates a file called .htpass in the directory c:\secret. It adds one line to the file for the user name janet and prompts you to enter a password for the user name janet. The -c in the command line stands for create and should be used only when you're creating the file. You can add user name/password lines to the file as follows:

c:\Apache\bin\htpasswd c:\secret\.htpass boss

If you use -c with the command to add a line to an existing password file, the file is overwritten by a new file with the same name; any lines in the existing file are gone. Don't use -c unless you want to create a new file.

You can name the file that contains the valid user names anything you want. The name .htpass is commonly used but isn't required. The information is stored in the file and looks like this:

janet:$apr1$Hr......$DS8EPQBQbqxRXt9hUFoq3/

Notice that the password isn't stored in a form that humans can read.

Although you can store the password file anywhere on your computer, it's best to store it outside your Web space so that it's more secure. You tell Apache where the file is located with a line similar to the following line in your .htaccess file, as discussed in the preceding section:

AuthUserFile /usr/local/apache/secret/.htpass

This command tells Apache to look for valid user names in the file /usr/local/apache/secret/.htpass.

Apache HTTP authentication in action

After you create the `.htaccess` and password files, Apache implements user authentication without any further intervention by you. When Apache receives a request to view a file in a directory containing your `.htaccess` file, the dialog box requesting a user name and password is automatically displayed. When the user clicks the button to submit a user name and password, Apache compares the information entered to the list of valid user name/password pairs in your password file. If it finds a match, it sends the Web page contents to the user's browser.

The behavior when the user name and password are not found in the password file depends on the browser. For instance, Internet Explorer allows the user to try three times and then stops, displaying the message `Authorization Required`. Netscape, on the other hand, displays a message that says `Authorization Failed. Try Again?` and provides an OK button and a Cancel button. Netscape allows the user to keep clicking OK and reentering user name and password combinations forever or until the user clicks the Cancel button.

Most browsers offer the user the option to cancel by clicking a button. When the user clicks Cancel, the message `Authorization Required` is displayed.

After the user has entered a valid user name/password combination, the user is authorized to view all the password-protected Web pages during the session. The user does not have to reenter the password every time a new file is requested. The authorization is valid until the browser is closed, ending the browser session.

Designing an HTTP Authentication Application in PHP

In the rest of this chapter, I discuss using HTTP authentication in a PHP script. The basic function of the HTTP authentication application is to protect files. Only users who have entered valid user names and passwords are allowed to view the protected pages. The HTTP authentication application requires an existing set of stored user names and passwords. The application compares the provided user name and password to the stored list of valid information, and if the provided user name and password match a stored pair, the user is granted access to the protected files.

Using HTTP authentication with PHP on Windows

A PHP authentication script that uses HTTP headers to prompt for login information from the user won't work unless PHP is installed as an Apache module, not as CGI. If you currently have a working installation of PHP, you can determine which mode your PHP is starting with by checking your Apache configuration file `httpd.conf`. This file is usually installed in the subdirectory `conf` in the directory where Apache is installed, such as `c:\Program Files\Apache Group\ Apache\conf\httpd.conf`.

Open `httpd.conf`. You can usually open it by selecting a menu item on your Start⇨Programs menu. For example, on Windows 2000, choose Start⇨Programs⇨Apache HTTPD Server⇨ Configure Apache Server⇨Edit the httpd.conf Configuration File. The configuration file is opened in a default editor, such as Notepad or WordPad. Look for one or both of the following lines:

```
LoadModule php5_module
    "c:/php/php5apache.dll"
Action application/x-httpd-php
    /php/php-cgi.exe
```

If you're using Apache 2, the `LoadModule` line might look like:

```
LoadModule php5_module
    "c:/php/php5apache2.dll"
```

The `LoadModule` Apache configuration directive starts PHP as an Apache module. The `Action` directive starts PHP in CGI mode. In many cases, both directives are in the `httpd.conf` file, but one starts with a #, which means it's a comment and not an active directive.

If the `Action` directive is currently active (that is, the `LoadModule` directive is either missing or has a # as its first character), your PHP is installed as a CGI. You must change PHP to an Apache

module before HTTP authentication will work in your PHP scripts. To change PHP to an Apache module, follow these steps:

1. Find the `LoadModule` line mentioned previously in your `httpd.conf` file. If you find it with a # at the beginning of the line, remove the #. If you don't find the line, add it.

2. Find the `Action` line mentioned previously and insert a # at the beginning of the line.

3. Find the following line in your `httpd.conf` file and remove the # from the beginning of the line. If you don't find this line in your `httpd.conf` file, add it — without the #.

   ```
   #AddModule mod_php5.c
   ```

4. Be sure your `php.ini` file is in your system directory (Win98/XP: `Windows`; Win2000: `Winnt`).

5. Be sure your `php_mysql.dll` or `php_mysqli.dll` file is in your system directory (Win98: `Windows\system`; Win2000: `Winnt\system32`; WinXP: `Windows\ system32`). If your MySQL `dll` file isn't currently in your system directory, check your `php.ini` file to see which one is active in your current installation and copy the correct file to the system directory.

6. Restart Apache.

   You should be able to find a menu item on your start menu, such as Start⇨Programs⇨ Apache HTTP Server⇨Control Apache Server⇨Restart.

If you're using a PHP 4 installation, the steps are slightly different. For instance, the module `dll` is named `php4_apache.dll`. See the PHP Web site, `www.php.net`, for instructions for PHP 4.

To design the application, you specify in detail the functionality of the application, as follows:

1. Check to see whether a user ID and password have been sent by the browser with the request for the protected Web page.

2. If a user name and password are not included in the request for the Web page, prompt the user to enter a user name and password.

3. When the user enters a user name and password, resend the Web page request, adding a header containing the user name and password entered by the user.

4. When a user name and password are included with the Web page request, check whether the user name and password are in the list of valid user information. If not, display an error message and give the user the opportunity to enter another user name and password.

5. If the user has entered a valid user name and password, display the contents of the Web page in the user's browser.

To use HTTP authentication with PHP on Windows, you must have PHP installed as an Apache module, not as CGI. For more information, see the nearby sidebar, "Using HTTP authentication with PHP on Windows."

Creating a User Database

In the HTTP authentication application, a list of valid user names and passwords is stored, and the user name and password provided by the user are compared to the stored information to check whether they're valid. The list of valid information can be stored in flat files or in your favorite database. In this example, the valid user information is stored in a MySQL database. In the next few sections, I explain how to create the database.

Designing the user database

The database design is simple: It needs to contain only a user name and a password for each user account. The date on which the account was created is also useful information.

For this design, the database is named UserAccount. It contains one table called Valid_User, and the table design is shown in Table 3-1. The table contains three fields: user_name, password, and create_date. All the fields are required; none is allowed to be blank. The primary key is user_name.

Table 3-1	Database Table: Valid_User	
Variable Name	*Type*	*Description*
user_name	CHAR(10)	User name for the user account (primary key)
password	CHAR(255)	Password for the account
create_date	DATE	Date when the account was added to the table

Creating the user database

The following SQL statement creates the user database:

```
CREATE DATABASE UserAccount;
```

The following SQL statement creates the table:

```
CREATE TABLE Valid_User (
  user_name     CHAR(10)   NOT NULL,
  password      CHAR(255)  NOT NULL,
  create_date   DATE       NOT NULL,
PRIMARY KEY(user_name) );
```

Accessing the user database

You can access the database from your PHP script with the MySQL functions that are built into PHP. You can use either the mysql functions or the mysqli functions, depending on which version of PHP and MySQL you are using and which function module is activated in your php.ini file. In this book, the applications use the mysqli functions. I explain the version differences for PHP and MySQL in Chapter 1.

You need to provide the information that the MySQL functions need, such as a MySQL account name and password. This is not related to any other account name or password that you have, such as a password to log on to the system.

If you're using PHP 4, the mysqli functions aren't available. You need to use the mysql functions. The syntax is slightly different. You find out about the difference between the mysql and mysqli functions in Appendix C.

In this application, I have stored the information needed by the PHP mysqli functions in a separate file called Vars.inc. This file is stored in a directory outside my Web space, for security reasons. The file contains information similar to the following:

```php
<?php
        $host = "localhost";
        $user = "admin";
        $passwd = "";
        $database = "UserAccount";
?>
```

Notice the PHP tags at the beginning (<?php) and the end (?>) of the file. If these tags aren't included, the information might display on the Web page for the whole world to see, which is not what you want.

Building the Authentication Application in PHP: The Procedural Approach

One script can provide all the functionality needed for this application. When the script Auth.php is first accessed, it prompts the user for a user name and password. After the user types a user name and password and clicks the button to submit them, the program tests whether the user name/password combination is valid.

The flow of the application script is controlled by an if statement that tests whether a user name and password have been entered. The following is the general design of the application script:

```
if   (user name and password have not been submitted)
        Prompt the user to enter a user name and password

else (user name and password have been submitted)
              1 Test whether user name and password match a user
                name and password in the valid user database.
              2 If user name and password are valid, display the
                content of the protected Web page.
              3 If user name and/or password are not valid,
                prompt the user again for login information.
```

The HTTP authentication application script (Auth.php) is shown in Listing 3-1.

LISTING 3-1: THE SCRIPT THAT COLLECTS AND TESTS THE USER NAME AND PASSWORD

```php
<?php
/* Program: Auth.php
 * Desc:     Program that prompts for a user name and
 *           password from the user using HTTP authentication.
 *           The program then tests whether the user
 *           name and password match a user name and password
 *           pair stored in a MySQL database.
 */

//Testing whether the user has been prompted for a user name
if(!isset($_SERVER['PHP_AUTH_USER']))                          #10
{
    header('WWW-Authenticate: Basic realm="secret section"');
    header('HTTP/1.0 401 Unauthorized');                      #13
    exit("This page requires authentication!");               #14
}                                                             #15

// Testing the user name and password entered by the user
else                                                          #18
{
    include("Vars.inc");                                      #20
    $user_name = trim($_SERVER['PHP_AUTH_USER']);             #21
    $user_password = trim($_SERVER['PHP_AUTH_PW']);
    $connection = mysql_connect($host,$user,$password)
            or die ("Couldn't connect to server.");           #24
    $db = mysql_select_db($database,$connection)
            or die ("Couldn't select database.");
    $sql = "SELECT user_name FROM Valid_User
            WHERE user_name = '$user_name'
            AND password = md5('$user_password')";
    $result = mysql_query($sql)
            or die("Couldn't execute query.");                #31
    $num = mysql_num_rows($result);                           #32
    if ($num < 1)  // user name/password not found            #33
    {
        exit("The User Name or password you entered
                is not valid.<br>");
    }                                                         #37
}                                                             #38
// Web page content.                                          #39
include("Welcome.inc");                                       #40
?>
```

Some of the lines in Listing 3-1 end with line numbers. The following discussion refers to the line numbers in the listing to discuss the script and how it works:

#10 Begins an `if` block that executes when the script first starts, before the user has entered a user name and password. The `if` statement tests whether a user name has been entered by testing whether the element `PHP_AUTH_USER` exists in the `$_SERVER` superglobal array. If it does not exist, the user has not entered a user name, and the `if` block executes. The `if` block sends two HTTP headers (lines 12 and 13) that tell the Web server that this file is password-protected. The Web server then sends the headers that tell the browser to prompt for a user name and password.

#14 Is executed only if the user clicks the Cancel button.

#15 Ends the `if` block.

#18 Begins an `else` block that executes when the user has been prompted for a user name and password. The `else` block executes if the element `PHP_AUTH_USER` exists in the `$_SERVER` superglobal array. When the user clicks the button to submit a user name and password, the element is created. Even if the user didn't type anything in the user name field, the element is created containing a blank string, causing the `else` block to execute.

#20 Lines 20 to 31 create and execute the SQL query that tests whether the user name and password exist in the MySQL database of valid user name/password combinations.

> **#20** Includes the file `Vars.inc` that contains the information necessary to access the database.
>
> **#21** Gets the user name from the `$_SERVER` superglobal array. Trims the value to remove any blank spaces typed by the user. Line 22 does the same for the password submitted by the user.
>
> **#27** Lines 27 to 29 create the SQL query that tests the user name and password. Notice that the password supplied by the user is put into a `md5()` function. This is a MySQL function that encrypts the password for security reasons. The password stored in the database is encrypted with the MySQL md5 function. Therefore, when you test the password entered by the user, you need to use `md5()` on it before you compare it to the password in the database.

#32 Creates `$num`, which contains the number of records found containing the user name and password combination entered by the user.

#33 Begins an `if` block that executes if the user name and password entered are not found in the database. This `if` block prints a message and then stops the script.

#37 Ends the invalid user name `if` block.

#38 Ends the `else` block.

#39 The script from this line executes if the user name and password are valid. The contents of the Web page go here. This script just displays a welcome message. You can put anything you want on your Web page, such as a list of links to the Web pages in your password-protected area.

#40 Includes the file that contains the contents of the Web page. In this case, the file is named `Welcome.inc`. Listing 3-2 shows the contents of `Welcome.inc`.

When the script in Listing 3-1 first executes, it displays a window that prompts for your password (Lines 10 to 15). The exact appearance and function of the window depend on the browser. Figure 3-2 shows the dialog box displayed by Firefox with the user name and password already typed by the user.

Figure 3-2: The Firefox dialog box that requests a user name and password.

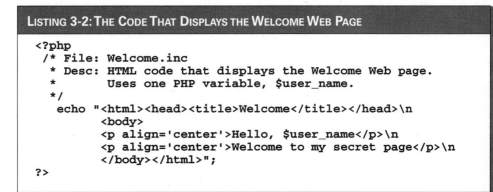

After the user types a correct user name and password, the Web page is displayed. In this application, a simple welcome page is displayed, using a PHP variable containing the user name. Listing 3-2 shows the code that displays the welcome page.

LISTING 3-2: THE CODE THAT DISPLAYS THE WELCOME WEB PAGE

```php
<?php
 /* File: Welcome.inc
  * Desc: HTML code that displays the Welcome Web page.
  *       Uses one PHP variable, $user_name.
  */
   echo "<html><head><title>Welcome</title></head>\n
         <body>
         <p align='center'>Hello, $user_name</p>\n
         <p align='center'>Welcome to my secret page</p>\n
         </body></html>";
 ?>
```

When the user enters a valid user name and password, the Web page shown in Figure 3-3 is displayed.

Figure 3-3:
The Web
page that
displays
when a user
enters a
valid user
name and
password.

Figure 3-3:
The Web
page that
displays
when a user
enters a
valid user
name and
password.

Building the Authentication Application in PHP: The Object-Oriented Approach

Object-oriented programming requires that you create and use objects to provide the application's functionality. You first identify the objects needed for the application, and then you write the classes that define the objects, including the methods that the application needs. When the objects are ready, you write the application script that creates and uses the objects.

Developing the objects

This HTTP authentication application must prompt for the user's login name and password. After the user submits the login information, the application must compare the information submitted against the user account information stored in a database. If the user name and password are valid, the application displays the contents of the Web page. The following objects are needed for the application:

- `PasswordPrompter`: Prompts for and collects the user's login information.
- `Database`: Container that stores the data for the application.
- `Account`: User account with its associated user information.
- `WebPage`: Web page to be displayed by a browser.

The details for each object are discussed in the next sections.

Writing the PasswordPrompter class

The PasswordPrompter object, which displays the prompt window where the user enters a user name and password, is central to the application. The PasswordPrompter object uses the built-in HTTP authentication features to display the window. When the user submits the information, it's available in the PHP script in the $_SERVER superglobal array.

The properties

The PasswordPrompter class requires only one property.

```
private $realm;
```

$realm is a string of your choosing that is displayed when the application prompts for the user name and password.

The code

Listing 3-3 contains the complete code for the PasswordPrompter class. The constructor and the single method are discussed in detail after the code listing. Notice the line numbers at the ends of some of the lines of code. The discussion following the listing refers to the line numbers.

LISTING 3-3: THE CODE FOR THE PASSWORDPROMPTER CLASS

```php
<?php
 /*  Class:   PasswordPrompter
  *  Desc:    Class that displays a window that requests
  *           a user password. The user name and password
  *           typed into the window are returned to the
  *           script in the superglobal array $_SERVER.
  */
class PasswordPrompter
{
   private $realm;    // String passed to constructor

   function __construct($realm)                              #12
   {
      if(is_string($realm))
      {
         $this->realm = $realm;
      }
      else
      {
         throw new Exception("Argument must be a string.");
      }
   }
```

Continued

```
function displayPrompt()
{
    header
    ("WWW-Authenticate: Basic realm=\"$this->realm\"");
    header('HTTP/1.1 401 Unauthorized');                #28
    // The following code executes when the user cancels.
    exit("This Web page requires authentication.");     #30
  }
}
?>
```

The constructor

The constructor expects a string to be passed into it. The string is stored as the *realm* (see line 12), the name of the section of the Web site that is password-protected. The name can be any string. It's displayed in the dialog box that prompts users for their login information. If the information passed is not a string, an exception is thrown with a message.

displayPrompt

Lines 26 to 28 send HTTP headers to the Web server. The Web server responds with headers that cause the browser to display a window that prompts for a user name and password.

The code on line 30 executes only if the user clicks the Cancel button.

Using the PasswordPrompter class

You can create a `PasswordPrompter` object as follows:

```
$prompt = new PasswordPrompter("secret place");
```

If the parameter passed isn't a string, an exception is thrown, with a message.

Writing the Database class

In order to authenticate the login information entered by the user, a list of valid user name/password combinations must be available. The `Database` class defines an object where the data is stored. In this application, it's a MySQL database. Listing 3-4 shows the code for the `Database` class.

The properties

The Database properties information needed to connect to the database.

```
private $connection;
private $database_name;
private $host;
private $user;
private $password;
```

$connection contains an object that represents the connection to the database. $database_name contains the name of the currently selected database. If no database has been selected, $database_name is NULL. The host, user, and password aren't required by the class as defined here; these properties aren't used. However, for a different application, additional methods might require these properties.

The code

Listing 3-4 contains the complete code for the Database class. The constructor and both of the methods are discussed in detail after the code listing. Notice the line numbers at the ends of some of the lines of code. The discussion following the listing refers to the line numbers.

LISTING 3-4: THE CODE FOR THE DATABASE CLASS

```php
<?php
 /*  Class:   Database
  *  Desc:    Class that connects to a MySQL database.
  */
 class Database
 {
   private $cxn;                    // database connection object
   private $database_name;
   private $host;
   private $user;
   private $password;

   function __construct($filename)
   {
     include("$filename");
     if(!$this->cxn = new mysqli($host,$user,$passwd))       #16
     {
         throw new Exception("Database is not available.
                              Try again later.");
         email("dbadmin@ourplace.com","DB Problem",
            "MySQL server is not responding. ".
             $this->cxn->error());
         exit();
     }
```

Continued

LISTING 3-4: *(Continued)*

```
      $this->host = $host;                                    #25
      $this->user = $user;
      $this->password = $passwd;
   }

   function useDatabase($dbname)
   {
      if(!$result = $this->cxn->query("SHOW DATABASES"))      #32
      {
         throw new Exception("Database is not available.
                             Try again later");
         email("dbadmin@ourplace.com","DB Problem",
            "MySQL server is not responding. "
               .$this->cxn->error());
         exit();
      }
      else                                                     #41
      {
         while($row = $result->fetch_row())
         {
            $databases[] = $row[0];
         }
      }
      if(in_array($dbname,$databases) ||
         in_array(strtolower($dbname),$databases))             #49
      {
         $this->database_name = $dbname;
         $this->cxn->select_db($dbname);
         return TRUE;
      }
      else                                                     #55
      {
         throw new Exception("Database $dbname not found.");
         return FALSE;
      }
   }

   function getConnection()
   {
      return $this->cxn;
   }
?>
```

The constructor

The constructor creates the connection and stores the properties. The host, user, and password must be passed when the new Database object is created so that the connection can be made. The following numbers refer to line numbers in the code in Listing 3-4:

#16   Begins an `if` block that executes if the database connection fails. The block throws a new exception with a message, e-mails the database administrator that the database is down, and exits.

#25   Lines 25 to 27 execute if the database connection is successful. The lines store the properties in the object.

The connection (`$cxn`) is stored in a property so that it can be used whenever the database connection is needed.

useDatabase

The `useDatabase` method selects a database. The name of the database is passed when the method is executed. The method checks to make sure that the specified database exists before selecting it.

The following discussion refers to line numbers in Listing 3-4:

#32   Begins an `if` block that executes if the database query fails. The block throws a new exception with a message, e-mails the database administrator that the database is down, and exits.

#41   Begins an `else` block that executes when the query runs successfully. The query returns a list of available databases in the result set. This block stores the database names in an array named `$databases`.

#48   Begins an `if` block that executes if the database the user wants to select exists. The database name is stored in a property. The database is selected. The method returns `TRUE`.

#55   Beings an `else` block that executes if the database passed in the method isn't found. An exception is thrown, with a message stating that the database isn't found. The method returns `FALSE`.

getConnection

The `getConnection` method returns the value stored in the `$connection` property — the connection for the database. This can be used wherever the connection to the database is needed.

Using the Database class

You can create a `Database` object as follows:

```
$filename = "Vars.inc";
$db = new Database($filename);
$select = $db->useDatabase("UserAccount");
```

If the `new` statement can't create a new `Database` object, it throws an exception with the following message:

```
Database is not available. Try again later.
```

After the statements, $select contains FALSE if the database doesn't exist. If the database is successfully selected, $select contains TRUE.

The database selected remains in effect until you select a different database or the script ends. You can change the database selected at any time by using the useDatabase method again.

Writing the Account class

The Account class stores and retrieves the information about a user. In this application, the user account contains only three bits of information: the user name, password, and date the account was created. For other applications, the user account might store more information, such as the user's address, phone, and credit card number. In the database for this application (described earlier in this chapter in "Creating a User Database"), the user's information is uniquely identified by the user_name.

The properties

The Account properties store the information needed to access the account row in the database.

```
private $userID = NULL;
private $cxn;
private $table_name;
private $message;
```

$userID is the field that identifies the account information in the table. $userID stores the information from the user_name field in the database. $table_name stores the name of the table in the database where the account information is located.

$cxn stores an object that represents the connection to the database where the account information is stored.

$message is a string that is stored by some methods when they execute.

The code

Listing 3-5 contains the complete code for the Account class. I discuss the constructor and each of the three methods in detail after the code listing. Notice the line numbers at the ends of some of the lines of code. The discussion following the listing refers to the line numbers.

LISTING 3-5: THE CODE FOR THE ACCOUNT CLASS

```php
<?php
 /*  Class:   Account
  *  Desc:    A user account stored in a database. Represents
  *           the account information stored in one record
  *           in a table.
  */
class Account
{
  private $userID = NULL;
  private $cxn;               // database connection object
  private $table_name;
  private $message;

  function __construct( mysqli $cxn,$table)
  {
    $this->cxn = $cxn;
    if(is_string($table))                                        #17
    {
      $sql = "SHOW TABLES LIKE '$table'";                        #19
      $result = $this->cxn->query($sql);
      if($result->num_rows > 0)                                  #21
      {
        $this->table_name = $table;
      }
      else                                                       #25
      {
        throw new Exception("$table is not a table
                                in the database");
        return FALSE;
      }
    }
    else                                                         #32
    {
      throw new Exception("Second parameter is not a
                              valid table name");
      return FALSE;
    }
  }

  function selectAccount($userID)
  {
    $userID = trim($userID);                                     #42
    $sql = "SELECT user_name FROM $this->table_name
            WHERE user_name ='$userID'";                         #44
    if(!$result = $this->cxn->query($sql))
    {
      throw new Exception("Couldn't execute query: "
                            .$this->cxn->error());
      return FALSE;
    }
```

Continued

LISTING 3-5: *(Continued)*

```
   if($result->num_rows < 1 )                          #51
   {
     $this->message = "Account $userID
                        does not exist!";
     return FALSE;
   }
   else                                                #57
   {
     $this->userID = $userID;
     return TRUE;
   }
 }

 function comparePassword($form_password)
 {
   if(!isset($this->userID))                           #66
   {
     throw new Exception("No account currently selected");
     exit();
   }                                                   #70
   $sql = "SELECT user_name FROM $this->table_name
           WHERE user_name ='$this->userID' AND
                 password = md5('$form_password')";
   if(!$result = $this->cxn->query($sql))              #74
   {
     throw new Exception("Couldn't execute query: "
                          .mysql_error());
     exit();
   }
   if($result->num_rows < 1 )                          #80
   {
     $this->message  = "Incorrect password for
                         account $this->userID!";
     return FALSE;
   }
   else                                                #86
     return TRUE;
 }

 function getMessage()
 {
    return $this->message;
 }
 }
 ?>
```

The constructor

The constructor tests the connection and the table name that are passed to it
to ensure that the parameters are in the proper format and stores them in
properties. There is no default for these values; the values must be passed
when the Account object is created.

#16 Stores the database connection in the property.

#17 Begins an `if` block that executes if the table name passed is a string. The table name is checked to see whether it exists.

> **#19** Lines 19 to 20 create and execute an SQL query that tests whether a table exists with the name that was passed to the constructor.
>
> **#21** Begins an `if` block that executes if the table exists. The table name is stored in the `$table` property.
>
> **#25** Begins an `else` block that executes when the table does not exist. The script throws an exception with a message and returns `FALSE`.

#32 Begins an `else` block that executes if the table name is not a string. The script throws an exception with a message and returns `FALSE`.

selectAccount

This method stores the `user_name` of the currently active account. The user name is passed when `selectAccount` is called. The method checks whether the user name exists in the database. If it's found, the user name is stored in `$userID`.

#42 The `userID` passed to `selectAccount` is trimmed to remove any blank spaces accidentally typed by the user before or after the user name.

#43 Lines 43 and 44 create an SQL query to select an account that has a `user_name` that matches the user name passed in `userID`. The table name property is used in the SQL query.

#45 Begins an `if` block that executes when the query fails. An exception is thrown, with a message, and the method returns `FALSE`.

#51 Begins an `if` block that executes when the number of rows returned by the query is less than 1, meaning that the user name passed to the method was not found in the database table. A message is stored in `$message`, and `FALSE` is returned.

#57 Begins an `else` block that executes when the number of rows returned by the query is not less than 1, meaning that the user name was found in the database table. The method stores the user name in the `$userID` property and returns `TRUE`.

comparePassword

This method compares the password passed to the method with the password stored in the database for the current account. This method fails if no account has been selected.

#66   Begins an `if` block that executes when no account has been selected. If no user name is stored in the `$userID` property, the script throws an exception with a message and exits.

#71   Lines 71 to 73 construct an SQL query that selects a record with the user name for the current account and the password passed to the method.

#74   Begins an `if` block that executes if the query does not execute successfully. The script throws an exception with a message and exits.

#80   Begins an `if` block that executes if the password provided by the user doesn't match the password stored in the database. That is, if the query returned less than 1 row. The method stores a message and returns FALSE.

#86   Begins the `else` block that executes if the password supplied by the user matches the password stored in the database table. The `else` block returns TRUE.

getMessage

This method returns the content of the `$message` property.

Using the Account class

To use the `Account` class, you must pass it a database connection. In addition, the correct database must be selected. Therefore, to create an account object, you can use statements similar to the following:

```
$db = new Database("Vars.inc");
$db->useDatabase("UserAccount");
$acct = new Account($db->getConnection(),"Valid_User");
```

When the new `Account` object is created, a previously created database connection object is passed to it, along with the name of the table where the account information is stored.

In most cases, you want to select a specific account from the database with a statement similar to the following:

```
$acct->selectAccount("janet");
```

If the user name `janet` doesn't exist in the database table, FALSE is returned. An account must be selected before you can use `comparePassword`, as follows:

```
$acct->comparePassword("secret");
```

If you use `comparePassword` before selecting an account, the script throws an exception and exits.

Writing the WebPage class

The WebPage class is used frequently throughout this book whenever a Web page needs to be displayed. The WebPage class has a single function: to display a Web page. The class expects the name of a file that contains the code that defines the Web page to be passed. If the Web page displays any information stored in PHP variables, an array of the data to be displayed in the Web page must also be passed.

The properties

The WebPage properties store the information needed to display the Web page.

```
private $filename;
private $data;
```

$filename is the name of the file that contains the code that defines the Web page — HTML code and perhaps some PHP code for parts of the Web page that use PHP variables. The file that defines the Web page for the authentication application presented in this chapter is named Welcome.inc. The same file is used for the procedural code and is shown in Listing 3-2.

$data is an array that contains the PHP variables for the Web page. If information contained in PHP variables is displayed on the page, the PHP variables must be passed in an array. If no PHP variables are displayed, $data can be NULL.

The code

Listing 3-6 contains the complete code for the WebPage class. The constructor and the single displayPage method are discussed in detail after the code listing. Notice the line numbers at the ends of some of the lines of code. The discussion following the listing refers to the line numbers.

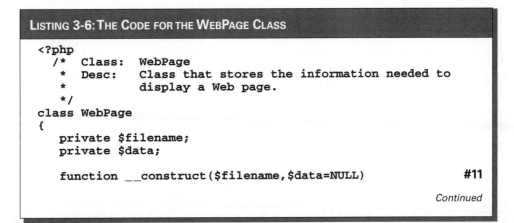

LISTING 3-6: THE CODE FOR THE WEBPAGE CLASS

```php
<?php
  /* Class:    WebPage
   * Desc:     Class that stores the information needed to
   *           display a Web page.
   */
class WebPage
{
    private $filename;
    private $data;

    function __construct($filename,$data=NULL)          #11
```

Continued

LISTING 3-6: *(Continued)*

```
    {
        if(is_string($filename))                          #13
        {
            $this->filename = $filename;
        }
        else
        {
            throw new Exception("Filename must be a string");
        }
        if($data == NULL or is_array($data))              #21
        {
            $this->data = $data;
        }
        else                                              #25
        {
            throw new Exception("Data must be passed
                              in an array");
        }
    }

    function displayPage()
    {
        @extract($this->data);                            #34
        include($this->filename);                         #35
    }
}
?>
```

The constructor

When a WebPage object is instantiated, the filename and the data that are passed to the constructor are stored in the properties.

#11 The constructor definition includes a default value for $data: NULL. If no value is passed for data, NULL is stored in the $data property. This gives the object the flexibility to store and display Web pages that are only HTML as well as Web pages that contain PHP variables.

#13 Begins an if/else statement that tests whether the filename passed is a string. If it's a string, it's stored in a property. If it's not a string, the else block executes, which throws an exception and exits.

#21 Begins an if/else statement that tests whether the data passed is in an array. The if statement executes if the data is NULL or is an array and stores the data passed to the constructor in the $data property. The else block that begins on line 26 executes when the data is not passed in an array. A new exception is thrown with a message, and the program exits.

displayPage

This method displays the Web page based on the information stored in the properties.

#34 Extracts the PHP variables for the `$data` array. If no PHP variables are used in the Web page, no data was passed, and `$data` is NULL. To prevent a notice from being displayed when `$data` is NULL, an @ is used before the extract function.

#35 Includes a file that defines the Web page based on the filename stored in the `$filename` property.

Using the WebPage class

A `WebPage` object is created with a statement similar to one of the following:

```
$page1 = new WebPage("Welcome.inc");
$page2 = new WebPage("Welcome.inc",$data);
```

You can use the first statement to create a `WebPage` object when the Web page contains only HTML code and no PHP variables. The second statement creates an object that contains PHP variables to display in the Web page.

When the second parameter is passed, it must be an array. If a second parameter is included that is not an array (for instance, just a string or an integer), an exception is thrown with the following message:

```
Data must be passed in an array
```

Writing the Auth-OO script

The application script creates and uses the objects to provide the application's functionality. For the HTTP authentication application, the script must prompt the user to enter a user name and password and then check whether the user name and password are valid. Listing 3-7 shows the application script `Auth-OO.php`.

The flow of the application script is controlled by an `if` statement that tests whether a user name and password have been entered, by testing whether the `$_SERVER` array contains the user name. The following is the general design of the application script:

```
if    (user name and password have not been submitted)
          Prompt the user to enter a user name and password

else (user name and password have been submitted)
          1 Test whether user name and password match a user
            name and password in the valid user database.
          2 If user name and password are valid, display the
```

content of the protected Web page.

3 If user name and/or password are not valid, prompt the user again for login information.

LISTING 3-7: THE APPLICATION SCRIPT THAT CREATES AND USES OBJECTS

```php
<?php
/* Program: Auth-OO.php
 * Desc:    Program that prompts for a user name and password
 *          from the user using HTTP authentication. The
 *          program then tests whether the user name and
 *          password match a user name and password pair
 *          stored in a MySQL database.
 */

require_once("PasswordPrompter.class");               #10
require_once("Database.class");
require_once("Account.class");
require_once("WebPage.class");

//Testing whether the user has been prompted for a user name
if(!isset($_SERVER['PHP_AUTH_USER']))                 #16
{
   try
   {
      $prompter = new PasswordPrompter("secret section");
      $prompter->displayPrompt();
   }
   catch(Exception $e)
   {
      echo $e->getMessage();
      exit();
   }
}

// Testing the user name and password entered by the user
else                                                  #31
{
   try                                                #33
   {
      $db = new Database("Vars.inc");                 #35
      $db->useDatabase("UserAccount");                #36
   }
   catch(Exception $e)
   {
      echo $e->getMessage();
      exit();
   }                                                  #42
   try                                                #43
   {
      $acct = new
            Account($db->getConnection(),"Valid_User");  #46
```

```
        if(!$acct->selectAccount($_SERVER['PHP_AUTH_USER']))
        {
            $mess = $acct->getMessage();
            echo $mess."<br>";
            exit();
        }                                                          #52
        if(!$acct->comparePassword($_SERVER['PHP_AUTH_PW']) )
        {
            $mess = $acct->getMessage();
            echo $mess."<br>";
            exit();
        }                                                          #58
    }
    catch(Exception $e)
    {
        echo $e->getMessage();
        exit();
    }
}                                                                  #65

$data['user_name'] = $_SERVER['PHP_AUTH_USER'];                    #66
try                                                                #67
{
    $welcome_page = new WebPage("Welcome.inc",$data);             #69
    $welcome_page->displayPage();                                 #70
}
catch(Exception $e)
{
    echo $e->getMessage();
    exit();
}
?>
```

The application program has a single `if/else` statement to prompt for and test a user name/password pair. If the user has not submitted login information, the script prompts for a user name and password. When the user submits the login information, the user name and password are compared to the valid user accounts stored in the MySQL database. If the information is valid, the contents of the Web page are sent to the user. (The following discussion refers to line numbers in Listing 3-7.)

#10   Lines 10 to 13 include the files that contain the classes needed for the application. `require_once` is used so that the class is not accidentally included more than once.

#16   Begins an `if` block that executes if the user has not submitted a user name. If `$_SERVER['PHP_AUTH_USER']` isn't set, the user hasn't submitted a password, so a `PasswordPrompter` object is created and displayed, resulting in a window that prompts for a user name and password.

#31 Begins an `else` block that executes when the user enters login information in the HTTP password window. The user name and password submitted by the user are available to the script in the `$_SERVER` superglobal array in the elements `PHP_AUTH_USER` and `PHP_AUTH_PW`.

#35 Creates a `Database` object.

#36 Selects the database that contains the user account information. If `useDatabase` fails (returns `FALSE`) because `"UserAccount"` doesn't exist, a message is displayed, and the scripts stops.

#45 Lines 45 and 46 create an `Account` object.

#47 Begins an `if` block that selects the account based on the user name submitted by the user. If `selectAccount` fails (returns `FALSE`) because the user name isn't found in the database, a message is displayed, and the scripts stops.

#52 Ends the `if` block that selects the account.

#53 Begins an `if` block that compares the password submitted by the user with the password stored in the database. If the passwords don't match (the method returns `FALSE`), a message is displayed, and the script exits.

#58 End of the `if` block the compares the passwords.

#65 End of the `else` block that tests the user login information against the valid login information in the database. The script goes past this line only if the login information submitted by the user is valid.

#66 Creates an array of data to be displayed on the Web page. The array contains only one element: `user_name`.

#69 Creates a new `WebPage` object containing the welcome Web page. The filename passed to the `WebPage` object is `Welcome.inc`. This is the same file that is used for the procedural script shown previously in Listing 3-2.

#70 Displays the welcome `WebPage`. The Web page that is displayed is the same welcome page displayed by the procedural script (refer to Figure 3-3).

Notice that many of the lines in the script are in `try` blocks. Methods that can throw an exception should be in `try` blocks. If an object method throws an exception that you don't catch, you get a fatal error similar to the following:

```
Fatal error: Uncaught exception 'Exception' with message
'Database is not available.' in c:\Database.class:18
```

Chapter 4

User Login Application

*M*any Web sites are secret or have secret sections. Such Web sites require users to log in before they can see the secret information. Here are a two examples of when Web sites might restrict access:

✔ Many online merchants require customers to log in so that their information can be stored for future transactions. These companies must protect the customers' information, particularly financial information, from public view.

✔ Many Web sites grant access only to certain people. For example, company information might be restricted to company staff or members of a certain department. Another example is when information is available for sale, so the information must be restricted to people who have paid for it.

If you have a Web site that needs protection, be sure to implement a *user login application.* User login applications can be quite simple, such as an application in which the administrator sets up a list of valid users. Anyone who tries to access a protected file is prompted to enter a user name and password that is checked against the list of valid users. A login application can also be much more complicated. It can allow Web site visitors to register for access, setting up their own accounts. The application might collect information from customers as they register. The application might provide the ability for users to manage their own accounts. The features that a login application can provide are wide and varied.

A user login application is one of the most common applications on the Web, so I'm sure you've had the experience of logging in to one. In this chapter, I show you how to build your own user login application.

If you need only a simple login screen, the application that I provide in Chapter 3 might be sufficient for your needs; it uses the built-in HTTP authentication features of browsers. The login application in this chapter is more complex. It allows users to register or to log in if they're already registered and collects and stores information from users when they register. It provides a fairly complex login Web page with two forms: one for login and one for registration. If you need to provide this additional functionality and control the look and feel of your login application, this chapter is for you.

Designing the Login Application

The basic function of the login application is to allow registered users to enter the Web site and to block access to users who have not registered. The application also allows users to register, storing their information in a database. To meet this functionality, the user login application should do the following:

- ✔ Give customers the option to register for Web site access or to log into the Web site if they're already registered.

- ✔ Display a registration form that allows new customers to type their registration information.

  I discuss the information you need to collect in the form in the following section, "Creating the User Database."

- ✔ Validate the information submitted in the form.

  Make sure the required fields are not blank and the submitted information is in the correct format.

- ✔ Store the validated information in the database.

- ✔ Display a login form that asks for the registered customer's user name and password.

- ✔ Compare the user name and password that a user enters with the user names and passwords in the database. If a match is found, send a Web page from the site to the customer. If no match is found, give the customer the opportunity to try to log in again.

Creating the User Database

The application design calls for a database that stores user information. The database is the core of this application. A login application must store user names and passwords, at the very least, but often you'll want to store additional information as well.

Designing the database

Your first design task is to decide what information you want to store. At a minimum, you need to store a user name and password that the user can use to log in. It's also useful to know when the user account was created. In deciding what information to collect during user registration, you need to balance your urge to collect all the potentially useful information that you can think of against your users' urge to avoid time-consuming forms and reluctance to give out personal information. One compromise is to ask for some optional information; users who don't mind will enter it, and those who object can just leave it blank.

Some information is required for your Web site to perform its function. For instance, users can readily see that a site that will be sending them something needs to collect their names and addresses. However, they might not see why it's necessary for you to have their phone numbers. Even if you require a phone number, users sometimes enter fake ones. So unless you have a captive audience, such as your employees, who must give you everything you ask for, think carefully about what information to collect. It's easy for irritated users to leave your Web site. It's not like they drove miles to your store and looked hours for a parking space. They can leave with just a click.

For the sample application in this chapter, the Web site is an online store that sells products. Thus, you need to collect the customers' contact information, and you need their phone numbers in case you need to contact them about their orders. Most customers are willing to provide phone numbers to reputable online retailers, recognizing that problems with an order might necessitate the merchant contacting them. The remainder of this section discusses the details of the information and its storage in a MySQL database.

The database contains only one table. The customer information is stored in the table, one *record* (row) for each customer. The fields needed for the table are shown in Table 4-1. The table contains 12 fields. The first three fields, `user_name`, `password`, and `create_date`, are required and cannot be blank. The remaining fields contain the customer's name, address, phone number, and fax number and are allowed to be blank. The first field, `user_name`, is the primary key.

Table 4-1	Database Table: Customer	
Variable Name	*Type*	*Description*
user_name	VARCHAR(20)	User name for the user account (primary key)
create_date	DATE	Date when the account was added to the table

(continued)

Table 4-1 *(continued)*

Variable Name	Type	Description
password	VARCHAR(255)	Password for the account
email	VARCHAR(50)	Customer's e-mail address
last_name	VARCHAR(50)	Customer's last name
first_name	VARCHAR(40)	Customer's first name
street	VARCHAR(50)	Customer's street address
city	VARCHAR(50)	City where customer lives
state	CHAR(2)	Two-letter state code
zip	CHAR(10)	Zip code, five numbers or zip + 4
phone	CHAR(15)	Phone number where customer can be reached
fax	CHAR(15)	Customer's fax number

Building the database

You can create the MySQL database with the following SQL statement:

```
CREATE DATABASE CustomerDirectory;
```

The following SQL statement creates the table:

```
CREATE TABLE Customer (
    user_name       VARCHAR(20)     NOT NULL,
    create_date     DATE            NOT NULL,
    password        VARCHAR(255)    NOT NULL,
    last_name       VARCHAR(50),
    first_name      VARCHAR(40),
    street          VARCHAR(50),
    city            VARCHAR(50),
    state           CHAR(2),
    zip             CHAR(10),
    email           VARCHAR(50),
    phone           CHAR(15),
    fax             CHAR(15),
PRIMARY KEY(user_name) );
```

Accessing the database

PHP provides MySQL functions for accessing your database from your PHP script. The MySQL functions are passed the information that's needed to access the database, such as a MySQL account name and password. This is not related to any other account name or password that you have, such as a password to log in to the system.

Several new features became available with MySQL 4.1. To access the new features, you must use the mysqli functions, rather than the mysql functions. To use the mysqli functions, you must use PHP 5. The mysqli functions are not available with PHP 4. You can still use the mysql functions and PHP 4 to interact with MySQL 4.1, but you can't use some of the new features. The mysqli functions are very similar to the mysql functions, but some differences exist. Read about MySQL and PHP versions in Chapter 1. Read about mysql/mysqli functions in Appendix C. Read about the mysqli (MySQL Improved) module at www.php.net/manual/en/ref.mysqli.php.

In this application, I have stored the information needed by the PHP mysql functions in a separate file called Vars.inc. This file is stored in a directory outside my Web space, for security reasons. The file contains information similar to the following:

```php
<?php
        $host = "localhost";
        $user = "admin";
        $passwd = "";
        $database = "CustomerDirectory";
?>
```

Notice the PHP tags at the beginning (<?php) and the end (?>) of the file. If these tags are not included, the information might display on the Web page for the whole world to see, which is not at all what you want.

Adding data to the database

This database is intended to hold data entered by customers — not by you. When the application is first made available to customers, it's empty until customers add data. When you test your application programs, the scripts add a row to the database. You might want to add a row with a user name and password for your own use when testing the scripts.

Building the Login Web Page

Customers log in to your protected Web site via an HTML form on a Web page. The login application design, developed earlier in this chapter, calls for two forms: one form to allow new customers to register and another form to allow registered customers to log in. You need to develop the login Web page, making decisions on its functionality and its look and feel.

Designing the login Web page

In your Web travels, you've probably seen many different designs for login pages. You might already have ideas for your login page. The design presented here is not the only possible one, just one I like. Feel free to change any part of it.

In this design, both forms are presented on a single Web page. The forms are displayed in two sections, side by side. Each form has its own section heading, form fields, and submit button. The login form allows people to enter their user names and passwords; the registration form requests much more information from customers. Figure 4-1 shows what the login Web page looks like when it's displayed in a browser.

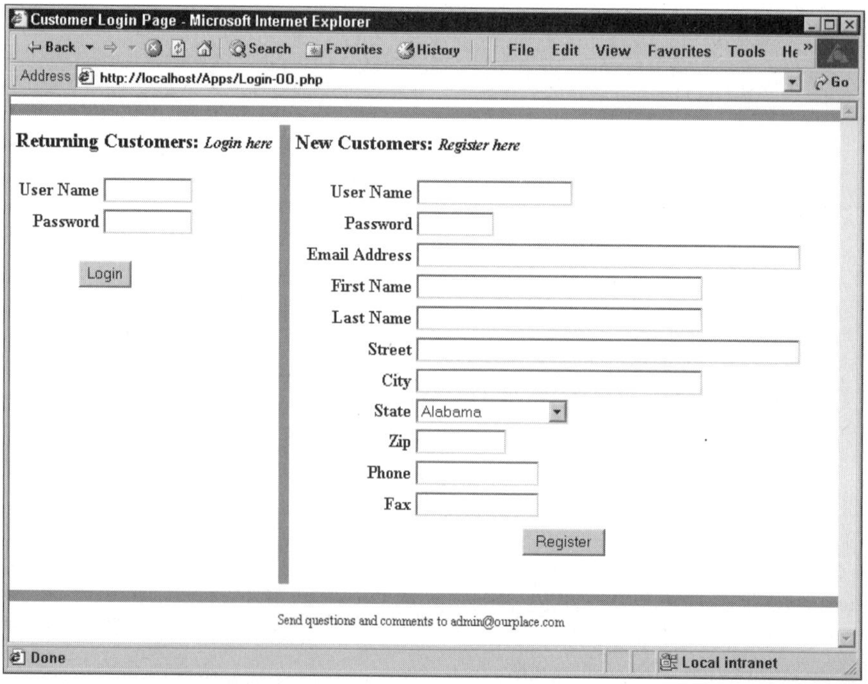

Figure 4-1:
The login
Web page
displayed
by the
user login
application.

The code for the login Web page is the same whether you're using the procedural approach or the object-oriented approach to build your application. The code for the login Web page is stored in separate files that are included when the application needs to display the login page. Thus, the code that defines the Web page is separate from the PHP code that provides the logic of the application.

The code for the login page consists of two files: the code that defines the look and feel of the page and the code that provides the specific information for the page.

Writing the code for the login page

The login Web page provides two forms: a login form and a registration form, side by side. The code that creates the page is in two separate files, as follows:

- double_form.inc: Contains the code that defines the look and feel of the Web page. It produces a Web page with two side-by-side forms and can be used to create any Web page that needs two side-by-side forms. This file does not include specific information, such as the names and values of the text fields displayed in the forms. You must use another file in conjunction with this file to create the Web page. The other file contains the specific information, such as field names, for the Web page.

- fields_login.inc: Contains the specific information for the login Web page. When used with double_form.inc, it displays a customer login Web page. A different file with different fields can be used with double_form.inc to create a Web page that displays forms with fields unrelated to customer logins.

The remainder of this section shows the details of these files. The second file is short and easier to understand, so I discuss it first in Listing 4-1. Then when explaining the first file (double_form.inc) in Listing 4-2, I refer to the information contained in fields_login.inc.

Writing fields_login.inc

The file shown in Listing 4-1 provides seven arrays that contain the specific information displayed in the login Web page. The arrays are as follows:

- $page: Elements that are displayed at the top and bottom of the page. These elements span the entire page, not just one of the forms.

- $elements_1: Elements that are displayed at the top and bottom of the first form (the form on the left). This array contains text to display at the top and bottom of the form and the text to display on the submit button.

- ✔ $elements_2: Similar elements for the second form (the form on the right).

- ✔ $fields_1: The names and labels for the fields to be displayed in the first form. The array keys are the field names in the form and the array values are the labels that are displayed in the form next to the fields.

- ✔ $length_1: The lengths of the fields in the first form. It's not necessary to define lengths for the fields, but you can if you want. For example, you can make all the fields the same length. I prefer to define lengths for fields as a security measure; it restricts the number of characters that a user can type into a field, limiting some of the opportunities for a bad guy to enter evil things into your forms.

- ✔ $fields_2: The names and labels for the fields in the second form. The array keys are the field names. Because these fields are stored in the database, the array keys are the same names used in the database table. The array values are the labels that are displayed in the form next to the fields. For instance, the field name used in the database is first_name, but the label in the form is much clearer and more attractive as *First Name*.

- ✔ $length_2: The lengths of the fields in the second form. The length of the fields is the same as the length of the fields defined in the database.

Setting up your elements and fields in this separate file, rather than including them in the file with the HTML code for the form, greatly simplifies the design and maintenance of the form. You can easily see the fields and elements in this separate file, as well as easily edit and modify them.

LISTING 4-1: THE FILE THAT CONTAINS THE ARRAYS NEEDED FOR THE LOGIN PAGE

```php
<?php
/* File: fields_login.inc
 * Desc: Contains arrays with the field names and form
 *       elements for the login Web page. The arrays named
 *       with 1 are displayed in form 1 and those named
 *       with 2 are displayed in form 2. The forms are
 *       defined in the file double_form.inc.
 */
$page = array( "title"  => "Customer Login Page",
               "top"    => " ",
               "bottom" => "Send questions and comments
                            to admin@ourplace.com",
             );

$elements_1 = array( "top" => "Returning Customers:
                              <span style=\"font-size: 80%;
                              font-weight: 100%\">
                              <i>Login here</i></span>",
                     "bottom" => "",
                     "submit" => "Login"
```

```
                          );
   $elements_2 = array("top" => "New Customers:
                                 <span style=\"font-size: 80%;
                                 font-weight: 100%\">
                                 <i>Register here</i></span>",
                       "bottom" => "",
                       "submit" => "Register"
                       );

   $fields_1 =    array("fusername" => "User Name",
                        "fpassword" => "Password"
                        );
   $length_1 =    array("fusername" => "10",
                        "fpassword" => "10"
                        );
   $fields_2 =    array("user_name"      => "User Name",
                        "password"       => "Password",
                        "email"          => "Email Address",
                        "first_name"     => "First Name",
                        "last_name"      => "Last Name",
                        "street"         => "Street",
                        "city"           => "City",
                        "state"          => "State",
                        "zip"            => "Zip",
                        "phone"          => "Phone",
                        "fax"            => "Fax"
                        );
   $length_2 =    array("user_name"      => "20",
                        "password"       => "8",
                        "email"          => "55",
                        "first_name"     => "40",
                        "last_name"      => "40",
                        "street"         => "55",
                        "city"           => "40",
                        "zip"            => "10",
                        "phone"          => "15",
                        "fax"            => "15"
                        );
   ?>
```

Notice that the arrays are defined in a structured format. You could use much less space to define the arrays, but this format makes the values clear and easy to change if necessary.

Notice that some of the values are blank, such as `$element_1["bottom"]=""`. In this particular Web page, I didn't want to include any text at the top of the page or at the bottom of the forms. However, for another form using `double_form.inc`, you might want to include values for these elements.

Writing double_form.inc

The script `double_form.inc`, shown in Listing 4-2, contains the code that defines how the Web page looks. It includes HTML code for the forms and for tables to organize the page. The code includes variables where specific information is needed. The variable values are provided in the previous file, `fields_login.inc`. For example, the script includes the following line that defines the Web page title:

```
<head><title><?php echo $page['title']?></title></head>
```

The variable `$page['title']` is found in the file `fields_login.inc`, where it is set to `"Customer Login Page"`.

LISTING 4-2: THE SCRIPT THAT DEFINES TWO SIDE-BY-SIDE HTML FORMS

```php
<?php
 /* File: double_form.inc
  * Desc: Contains the code for a Web page that displays
  *       two HTML forms, side by side in a table.
  */
include("functions.inc");                                      #6
?>
<head><title><?php echo $page['title']?></title></head>
<body style="margin: 0">
<h1 align="center"><?php echo $page['top'] ?></h1>
<hr size="10" noshade>
<table border="0" cellpadding="5" cellspacing="0">
<?php
    ############
    #  Form 1  #
    ############                                               #16
?>
  <tr>
    <td width="33%" valign="top">
      <p style="font-size: 110%; font-weight: bold">
          <?php echo $elements_1['top']?></p>
      <!-- Beginning of form 1 (left) -->
      <form action=<?php echo $_SERVER['PHP_SELF']?>
              method="POST">
      <table border="0">
<?php                                                         #26
  if (isset($GLOBALS['message_1']))                            #27
  {
      echo "<tr>
              <td colspan='2'
                style=\"font-weight: bold;
                  font-style: italic;
                  font-size: 90%; color: red\">
                  {$GLOBALS['message_1']}<p></td></tr>\n";
  }
  foreach($fields_1 as $field => $value)                       #36
```

```
      {
        if(ereg("pass",$field))                                      #38
          $type = "password";
        else
          $type = "text";
        echo "<tr><td style=\"text-align: right;
                    font-weight: bold\">$value</td>
                <td><input type='$type' name='$field'
                        value='".@$$field."'
                        size='{$length_1[$field]}'
                        maxsize='{$length_1[$field]}'>
                </td></tr>\n";
      }                                                              #49
?>
            <tr>
              <td colspan="2" style="text-align: center" >
                <br />
                <input type="submit" name="Button"
                    value="<?php echo $elements_1['submit']?>">
              </td></tr>
        </table>
        </form>
      </td>

      <!-- Column that separates the two forms -->
      <td style="background-color: gray"></td>
<?php                                                                #63
    ###########
    #  Form 2  #
    ###########                                                      #66
?>
      <td width="67%">
        <p style="font-size: 110%; font-weight: bold">
            <?php echo $elements_2['top']?>
        <!-- Beginning of Form 1 (right side) -->
        <form action=<?php echo $_SERVER['PHP_SELF']?>
            method="POST">
        <p>
        <table border="0" width="100%">
<?php                                                                #76
  if (isset($GLOBALS['message_2']))                                  #77
  {
    echo "<tr>
            <td colspan='2'
                style=\"font-weight: bold; font-style: italic;
                font-size: 90%; color: red\">
                {$GLOBALS['message_2']}<p></td></tr>";
  }                                                                  #84
  foreach($fields_2 as $field => $value)                            #85
  {
    if($field == "state")                                           #87
    {
```

Continued

LISTING 4-2: *(Continued)*

```
        echo "<tr><td style=\"text-align: right;
                    font-weight: bold\">State</td>
                <td><select name='state'>";
    $stateName=getStateName();                              #92
    $stateCode=getStateCode();
    for ($n=1;$n<=50;$n++)                                  #94
    {
        $state=$stateName[$n];                             #96
        $scode=$stateCode[$n];
        echo "<option value='$scode'";
        if ($scode== @$_POST['state'])
            echo " selected";
        echo ">$state\n";
    }
    echo "</select>";
    }                                                       #104
    else
    {
        if(ereg("pass",$field))
            $type = "password";
        else
            $type = "text";                                #110
        echo "<tr><td style=\"text-align: right;
                    font-weight: bold\">$value</td>
                <td><input type='$type' name='$field'
                        value=\"".@$$field."\"
                        size='{$length_2[$field]}'
                        maxsize='{$length_2[$field]}'>
                </td></tr>";                               #117
    }                                                       #118
    }                                                       #119
?>
        <tr><td colspan="2" style="text-align: center">
            <p style="margin-top: .05in">
            <input type="submit" name="Button"
                value="<?php echo $elements_2['submit']?>">
        </td></tr>
    </table>
    </form>
    </td>
  </tr>
</table>
<hr size="10" noshade>
<div style="text-align: center; font-size: 75%">
<?php echo $page['bottom']?>
</body></html>
```

The following numbers refer to the line numbers in Listing 4-2:

| **#6** | Includes a file containing functions used in this script. The file functions.inc is shown in Listing 4-3. |

#8   Lines 8 to 12 are an HTML section. The HTML code defines the top of the Web page. Lines 8 and 10 have a small PHP section that echoes a variable. The variable values are found in the `fields_login.inc` file. Line 12 begins the table that organizes the Web page.

#18   Lines 18 to 25 contain HTML code that opens the first table cell, displays the text at the top of the cell, and produces the form tag. A second table, inside this first cell, is started to hold the form fields.

#26   Opens the PHP section that produces the form fields.

#27   Begins an `if` block that displays a message. If the item `"message_1"` exists in the GLOBALS array, `message_1` is displayed. The message is set into the global array in the application script when errors are found in the information entered by the user. If the form is displayed for the first time, before the user enters anything, or if no errors occur, the GLOBALS element `message_1` doesn't exist.

#36   Lines 36 to 49 contain a `foreach` block that displays all the fields in the form. The `foreach` statement walks through the `$fields_1` array that is set in the file `fields_login.inc`.

     #38   Starts an `if` statement that sets a value for `$type` — a variable used in the input field code. The input field is type `text` for all fields except the password field, which is type `password`.

     #42   Lines 42 to 48 contain the `echo` statement that outputs the HTML code for the field. The `echo` statement is executed once for each element in the `$fields_1` array. PHP variables are used for the specific information, such as field names, in the statement.

#51   Starts an HTML section (lines 51 to 59) that displays the submit button for form 1 and closes the tags for form 1.

#62   HTML code that displays a column that separates the two forms.

#67   An HTML section (lines 67 to 75) that opens the second table cell, displays the text at the top of the cell, and produces the form tag. A second table, inside this second cell, is started to hold the form fields.

#76   Opens the PHP section that produces the form fields.

#77   Begins an `if` block that displays a message. If the item `"message_2"` exists in the GLOBALS array, `message_2` is displayed. The message is set into the global array in the application script when errors are found in the information entered by the user. If the form is displayed for the first time, before the user enters anything, or if no errors occur, the GLOBALS element `message_2` doesn't exist.

#85   Lines 85 to 119 contain a `foreach` block that displays all the fields in the form. The `foreach` statement walks through the `$fields_2` array that is set in the file `fields_login.inc`.

#87 Starts an `if` block that executes only for the `state` field. A drop-down list of states is displayed rather than the simple text field that is displayed for all the other fields. Lines 96 to 97 use the functions included on line 6.

#105 Starts an `else` block that executes for all fields except the `state` field.

#107 Starts an `if` statement that sets a value for `$type` — a variable used in the input field code. The input field is type `text` for all fields except the password field, which is type `password`.

#111 Lines 111 to 117 contain the `echo` statement that outputs the HTML code for the field. The `echo` statement is executed once for each element in the `$fields_2` array. PHP variables are used for the specific information, such as field names, in the statement.

#121 Starts an HTML section that displays the submit button for form 2, closes the tags for form 2, and displays the page text at the bottom of the Web page.

In `double_form.inc`, the `state` field in form 2 is a drop-down list. The code that creates the list uses two functions stored in the `functions.inc` file that's included on line 6. Listing 4-3 shows the code for the two functions.

LISTING 4-3: FUNCTIONS THAT CREATE ARRAYS OF STATE NAMES AND CODES

```php
<?php
function getStateCode()
{
    $stateCode = array(1=> "AL" ,
        "AK" ,
        "AZ" ,
        ...
        "WY" );
    return $stateCode;
}

function getStateName()
{
    $stateName = array(1=> "Alabama",
        "Alaska",
        "Arizona",
        ...
        "Wyoming" );
    return $stateName;
}
?>
```

The functions are called on lines 92 and 93 of Listing 4-2. The arrays created by these functions are used to create the drop-down list of states in the `for` statement that starts on line 94 of Listing 4-2.

Displaying the login Web page

The file `double_form.inc` is used in conjunction with `fields_login.inc` to display the login Web page. Although the approach to displaying the form might be different in the procedural script versus the object-oriented script, the code that displays the form is the same, as follows:

```
include("fields_login.inc");
include("double_form.inc");
```

The file containing the arrays of information used when the form is displayed must be included first so that the arrays are available when needed.

If you want to display any information in the form fields, the information must also be available. For instance, if the user submits a form with an error and you redisplay the form, you want the redisplayed form to contain the information the user typed. To do this, you use a variable in the value parameter of the input tag, such as `value="$first_name"`. The variables you use in the input tags must be available.

When the customer submits the form, the information the user typed is passed to the script in the `$_POST` superglobal array. If you redisplay the form, you can get the information from this array to display in the form by using the PHP `extract` function, as follows:

```
extract($_POST);
```

In this case, the following code displays the form:

```
extract($_POST);
include("fields_login.inc");
include("double_form.inc");
```

Building the Login Application: The Procedural Approach

The login application has one main script that's organized into three basic sections:

✔ A section that executes the first time the login page is displayed, before the user clicks a button

✔ A second section that executes when the user clicks the Login button

✔ A third section that executes when the user clicks the Register button

A `switch` statement controls the program flow based on which button is clicked. The following is an overview of the script's structure:

```
switch (Button)

   case "Login":
      1 Test whether the user name is in the database. If
        not, redisplay the form with an error message.
      2 Test whether the password is correct. If not,
        redisplay the form with an error message.
      3 When login succeeds, display the protected Web
        page.

   case "Register":
      1 Test whether all the fields are filled in. If not,
        redisplay the form with an error message.
      2 Test whether the information is in the correct
        format. If not, redisplay form with an error
        message.
      3 When information is correct, store it in database.
      4 When registration succeeds, display the protected
        Web page.

   case "default":
      Display the Login Web Page with blank form fields.
```

The default case executes if neither the Login button nor the Register button is clicked.

Writing the application script

Listing 4-4 shows the code for the login application script.

LISTING 4-4: LOGIN APPLICATION CODE

```php
<?php
/* Program: Login.php
 * Desc:    Main application script for the User Login
 *          application. It provides two options: (1) login
 *          using an existing User Name and (2) register
 *          a new user name. User Names and passwords are
 *          stored in a MySQL database.
 */
  session_start();                                        #9
```

```
    include("functions_main.inc");                               #10
    $table_name = "Customer";                                    #11
    $next_program = "SecretPage.php";

    switch (@$_POST['Button'])                                   #14
    {
      case "Login":                                              #16
        $cxn = Connect_to_db("Vars.inc");
        $sql = "SELECT user_name FROM $table_name
                WHERE user_name='$_POST[fusername]'";            #19
        $result = mysqli_query($cxn,$sql)
                    or die("Couldn't execute query 1");          #21
        $num = mysqli_num_rows($result);                         #22
        if($num == 1)                                            #23
        {
            $sql = "SELECT user_name FROM $table_name
                    WHERE user_name='$_POST[fusername]'
                    AND password=md5('$_POST[fpassword]')";
            $result2 = mysqli_query($cxn,$sql)
                    or die("Couldn't execute query 2.");
            $row = mysqli_fetch_assoc($result2);                 #30
            if($row)                                             #31
            {
              $_SESSION['auth']="yes";                           #33
              $_SESSION['logname'] = $_POST['fusername'];        #34
              header("Location: $next_program");                 #35
            }
            else                                                 #37
            {
              $message_1="The Login Name, '$_POST[fusername]'
                      exists, but you have not entered the
                      correct password! Please try again.<br>";
              extract($_POST);
              include("fields_login.inc");
              include("double_form.inc");
            }                                                    #45
        }                                                        #46
        elseif ($num == 0)   // login name not found             #47
        {
            $message_1 = "The User Name you entered does not
                        exist! Please try again.<br>";
            include("fields_login.inc");
            include("double_form.inc");
        }
      break;                                                     #54
      case "Register":                                           #55
        /* Check for blanks */
        foreach($_POST as $field => $value)                      #57
        {
          if ($field != "fax")
          {
            if ($value == "")
            {
```

Continued

LISTING 4-4: *(Continued)*

```
                    $blanks[] = $field;
                }
            }
        }                                                   #66
        if(isset($blanks))                                  #67
        {
            $message_2 = "The following fields are blank.
                Please enter the required information:  ";
            foreach($blanks as $value)
            {
              $message_2 .="$value, ";
            }
            extract($_POST);
            include("fields_login.inc");
            include("double_form.inc");
            exit();
        }                                                   #79
        /* validate data */
        foreach($_POST as $field => $value)                 #81
        {
          if(!empty($value))                                #83
            {
            if(eregi("name",$field) and
                !eregi("user",$field) and !eregi("log",$field))
                {
                if (!ereg("^[A-Za-z' -]{1,50}$",$value))
                    {
                        $errors[] = "$value is not a valid name.";
                    }
                }
            if(eregi("street",$field)or eregi("addr",$field) or
                eregi("city",$field))
                {
                if(!ereg("^[A-Za-z0-9.,' -]{1,50}$",$value))
                    {
                        $errors[] = "$value is not a valid address
                                    or city.";
                    }
                }
            if(eregi("state",$field))
                {
                if(!ereg("[A-Za-z]",$value))
                    {
                        $errors[] = "$value is not a valid state.";
                    }
                }
            if(eregi("email",$field))
                {
                if(!ereg("^.+@.+\\..+$",$value))
                    {
                        $errors[] = "$value is not a valid email
```

```
                                       address.";
            }
        }
        if(eregi("zip",$field))
        {
            if(!ereg("^[0-9]{5,5}(\-[0-9]{4,4})?$",$value))
            {
                $errors[] = "$value is not a valid zipcode.";
            }
        }
        if(eregi("phone",$field) or eregi("fax",$field))
        {
            if(!ereg("^[0-9](xX -]{7,20}$",$value))
            {
                $errors[] = "$value is not a valid phone
                            number. ";
            }
        }
    }
}                                                              #132
}
foreach($_POST as $field => $value)                            #134
{
  if($field != "Button")
  {
    if($field == "password")
    {
        $password = strip_tags(trim($value));
    }
    else
    {
        $fields[]=$field;
        $value = strip_tags(trim($value));
        $values[]=addslashes($value);
        $$field = $value;
    }
  }
}
if(@is_array($errors))                                         #151
{
  $message_2 = "";
  foreach($errors as $value)
  {
      $message_2 .= $value." Please try again<br />";
  }
  include("fields_login.inc");
  include("double_form.inc");
  exit();
}
$user_name = $_POST['user_name'];                              #162

/* check to see if user name already exists */
$cxn = Connect_to_db("Vars.inc");
$sql = "SELECT user_name FROM $table_name
```

Continued

LISTING 4-4: *(Continued)*

```
                WHERE user_name='$user_name'; #158
    $result = mysqli_query($cxn,$sql)
            or die("Couldn't execute query.");
    $num = mysqli_num_rows($result);                     #170
    if ($num > 0)                                        #171
    {
      $message_2 = "$user_name already used. Select another
                         User Name.";
      include("fields_login.inc");
      include("double_form.inc");
      exit();
    }
    else                                                 #179
    {
      $today = date("Y-m-d");                            #181
      $fields_str = implode(",",$fields);
      $values_str = implode('","',$values);
      $fields_str .=",create_date";
      $values_str .='"'.",".'"'.$today;
      $fields_str .=",password";
      $values_str .= '"'.",".".md5".("'".$password."')";
      $sql = "INSERT INTO $table_name ";
      $sql .= "(".$fields_str.")";
      $sql .= " VALUES ";
      $sql .= "(".'"'.$values_str.")";
      mysqli_query($cxn,$sql) or die(mysqli_error($cxn));
      $_SESSION['auth']="yes";                           #193
      $_SESSION['logname'] = $user_name;                 #194
      /* send email to new Customer */
      $emess = "You have successfully registered. ";
      $emess .= "Your new user name and password are: ";
      $emess .= "\n\n\t$user_name\n\t";
      $emess .= "password\n\n";
      $emess .= "We appreciate your interest. \n\n";
      $emess .= "If you have any questions or problems,";
      $emess .= " email service@ourstore.com";           #202
      $subj = "Your new customer registration";          #203
      $mailsend=mail("$email","$subj","$emess");         #204
      header("Location: $next_program");                 #205
    }
  break;                                                 #207

  default:                                               #209
      include("fields_login.inc");
      include("double_form.inc");
  }
?>
```

The numbers in the following explanation refer to the line numbers in Listing 4-4:

#9   Starts a PHP session.

#10   Includes the file containing the function `Connect_to_db`, which is used later in the script.

#11   Declares a variable that contains the name of the database table where your customer information is stored.

#12   Declares a variable that contains the name of the script that is the opening Web page of your protected Web site. The script executes when your customer successfully logs in.

#14   Starts the `switch` statement that comprises the rest of the script. The `switch` statement tests the value of the `Button` element in the `$_POST` superglobal array. The `Button` element exists only if a user has clicked one of the Submit buttons in the forms.

#16   Begins the `case` that executes when the `Button` element has the value of `Login` — that is, when the user clicked the submit button labeled Login. The statements from line 14 to line 52 are part of the `Login` case. This `case` block checks the user name and password submitted against the user names and passwords stored in the database.

#17   Connects to the database by using the function included on line 10.

#18   Lines 18 to 21 build and execute an SQL query to select a record from the database with the user name submitted by the user.

#22   Checks how many records were found that matched the user name submitted by the user. Possible values are 0 or 1.

#23   Begins an `if` block that executes if 1 record was found. This block checks whether the user entered the correct password.

       #25   Lines 25 to 30 build and execute an SQL query to select a record with the user name and password submitted by the user and, after the query is executed, check how many records were found.

       #31   Begins an `if` block that executes if a record was found, meaning that the password is correct. Two session variables are set, and the protected Web page content is displayed.

       #37   Begins an `else` block that executes if no record was found, meaning that the password was incorrect. An error message is created, and the login Web page is redisplayed with the error message.

#47   Begins an `elseif` block that executes if no record was found with the user name submitted by the user. An error message is created, and the login Web page is redisplayed with the error message.

#55 Begins the case block that executes when Button has the value of Register, meaning that the customer clicked the Register submit button. The statements from line 53 to line 180 compose the Register block.

#57 Starts a foreach loop that checks whether each field of the form is blank. If the field name is not fax (which is not a required field), the field name of any field with a blank value is added to an array named $blanks.

#67 Begins an if block that executes if $blanks is an array — that is, if any fields had blank values. An error message is created that includes the names of the blank fields, and the form is redisplayed with the error message.

#81 Starts a foreach loop that checks the format of the information in each field.

#83 Begins an if block that executes if the value is not blank. Lines 57 to 79 of the script processed the information for blank fields. Therefore, any fields that are blank when they reach this line are fields that are allowed to be blank because they're not required. The format testing is not needed on blank fields.

The if block (83 to 133) checks each of the fields with information to ensure that the information is in an acceptable format. An if block is executed when specific field names are found and compares the value in each field with a regular expression specific to the field. If the information in the field doesn't match the regular expression, an appropriate error message is stored in the array called errors.

#134 Starts a foreach loop that processes each field, removing any beginning or trailing blank spaces and any HTML tags. The password is stored in a variable named password. All other fields are stored in two arrays. $fields contains the field names, which need no extra processing. $values contains the values to be inserted into the database, with any quotes escaped. In addition, each value is stored in a variable named with the field name.

If you have magic quotes turned on in the php.ini file, you don't need to escape the quotes here. The quotes are escaped automatically for the POST data. However, you have more control if you turn magic quotes off and escape the quotes in the script. Whichever way you do it, it's important that the quotes be escaped before data is stored in the database. See Chapter 2 for a discussion of escaping quotes to protect against SQL Injection attacks.

#151 Begins an if block that executes when the $errors array exists, meaning that at least one error was found. An error message is created, and the form is redisplayed with the error message.

#165 Lines 165 to 170 create and execute a query to select a record with the user name entered by the user. Duplicate user names are not allowed in the database.

#171 Begins an `if` block that executes if a record is found, meaning that the user name is already in use. An error message is created, and the login page is redisplayed along with the error message.

#179 Begins an `else` block that executes if no record is found, meaning that the user name is not in use — it's available.

> **#181** Stores today's date.
>
> **#182** Lines 182 to 192 build and execute the SQL query that inserts the new record into the database. The `$fields` and `$values` arrays are converted to strings with the implode function. The strings are then used to create an `INSERT` query to add the record for the newly registered user.
>
> **#193** Stores a session variable indicating the user successfully logged in.
>
> **#194** Stores a session variable with the user's new user name.
>
> **#196** Lines 196 to 204 create and send an e-mail message to the new user.
>
> **#206** Displays the protected Web page content.

#209 Begins the default `case` block. This block executes if neither of the two preceding cases is true. That is, this block executes if the user didn't click either the Login or Registration submit button. This block displays the login Web page with blank form fields.

The login application script calls a function to connect to the database. The file containing the function code is included on line 9. Listing 4-5 shows the function code.

LISTING 4-5: THE CONNECT_TO_DB FUNCTION

```php
<?php
/*  Function:   Connect_to_db
 *  Desc:       Connects to a MySQL database. The name of
 *              a file containing the database variables
 *              is passed to the function.
 */
function Connect_to_db($filename)
{
    include($filename);
    $cxn = mysqli_connect($host, $user,$passwd)
            or die ("Couldn't connect to server.");
    $db = mysqli_select_db($cxn,$database)
            or die ("Couldn't select database.");
}
?>
```

This function gets the information it needs from a separate file. The filename is passed when the function is called. The file contents are something like the following, with your own information, of course:

```php
<?php
$host = "localhost";
$user = "admin";
$passwd = "";
$database = "CustomerDirectory";
?>
```

You should store this file outside your Web space for security reasons. If you set your include_path in your php.ini file to a location outside your Web space, you can store files there and include them without using a complete pathname.

Protecting your Web pages

The Web pages in your protected Web site or section of your Web site are no different than any other Web pages. You just want to restrict them to members who are logged in. To do this, you start a session and check whether the user is logged in at the top of every page.

If the user logs in through the Login.php application script described in the previous section, a session is started, and the value "yes" is stored in a session variable, as follows:

```php
$_SESSION['auth'] = "yes";
```

You probably want to use your own variable name and value as well as your own filename. Vars.inc is fairly obvious, as is $auth = "yes". It's better if the name and value are less guessable. For instance, you might want to use something totally irrelevant and misleading, such as Flower.inc, $Brad="Pitt". Of course, now that these suggestions are published in a book, they aren't good choices either.

Thus, at the top of every script, you check to see whether the auth session variable is set for the user. You must add the following statements to the top of every script that you want available only to logged in users:

```php
session_start();
if (@$_SESSION['auth'] != "yes")
{
    header("Location: Login.php");
    exit();
}
```

When session_start executes, PHP checks for an existing session. If one exists, it sets up the session variables.

The `if` statement checks to see if the `auth` session variable is set to yes. If it isn't set to yes or if it doesn't exist, it means the user is not logged in, in which case the script displays the login Web page and exits. Otherwise, if `auth` is set to yes, it means the user is logged in, and the script continues to display the Web page.

Building the Login Application: The Object-Oriented Approach

Object-oriented programming requires that you create and use objects to provide the functionality. You first identify the objects needed for the application, and then you write the classes that define the objects, including the methods that the application needs. When the objects are ready, you write the application script that creates and uses the objects.

Developing the objects

The login application needs to perform the following tasks:

- ✔ Collect and process information in a form
- ✔ Store information in a database when a customer registers
- ✔ Check a user's password
- ✔ Allow the authenticated user to visit pages on the Web site during the user session
- ✔ Send the user an e-mail

The following list of objects reflects the tasks this application must perform:

- ✔ `WebForm`: A form is central to this application. The form allows customers to register or to enter their user names and passwords if they're already registered. The `WebForm` class provides the form for the application. It collects and processes the information typed by a user.

- ✔ `Database`: The application stores the customer information in a database. The `Database` class provides the container that stores the data.

- ✔ `Account`: The information entered by the customer needs to be associated with a customer account. The `Account` class stores and retrieves the customer information.

- ✔ `Session`: Typically, you want customers to be able to view more than one page during a visit without having to log in to each page. The time period that a customer spends at your Web site, from when he logs in to your Web site until he leaves it, is called a *session*. The `Session` class allows a visitor to stay logged in for an entire session.

✔ `Email`: The application sends an e-mail to customers when they register, to let them know that the registration was successful. The `Email` class contains and manages the e-mail message.

The details for each object are discussed in the following sections.

Writing the WebForm class

One of the most important objects is the form. The definition for the form object is coded in the `WebForm` class. This class is a general class that can be used to display any form and collect and process the data from any form, not just from the login form used in this application.

The `WebForm` class displays a form on a Web page, collects the information, reformats the information, and validates the information format, redisplaying the form when incorrect information is detected. WebForm contains four properties, a constructor, and 13 methods.

The properties

The `WebForm` properties store information needed to define and manage the form and its data. The properties are as follows:

```
private $form;
private $fields;
private $data;
private $not_required;
```

The first two properties are the names of the files that are needed to display the form. These files are described in the section "Writing the code for the login page," earlier in this chapter.

The last two properties are arrays. `$data` contains the information submitted by the customer in the form. The key of each element is a field name — the field name used in both the form and the database table. `$not_required` is an array containing the field names of fields that are allowed to be blank. The `checkForBlanks` method uses this array to identify the fields that are not errors when left blank.

The code

Listing 4-6 contains the complete code for the `WebForm` class. Each method is discussed in detail after the code listing. Notice the line numbers at the ends of some code lines. The discussion following the listing refers to the line numbers.

LISTING 4-6: THE WEBFORM CLASS

```php
<?php
 /*  Class:    WebForm
  *  Desc:     Class that collects, stores, and processes
  *            information in an HTML form.
  */
class WebForm
{
   private $form;            //filename
   private $fields;          //filename
   private $data;            //array
   private $not_required;    //array

   function __construct($form,$fields,$data=NULL)
   {
      if(is_string($form) and is_string($fields))          #16
      {
         $this->form = $form;
         $this->fields = $fields;
      }
      else                                                 #21
      {
         throw new Exception("First 2 parameters
                             must be filenames");
      }
      if($data == NULL OR is_array($data))                 #26
      {
         $this->data = $data;
      }
      else                                                 #30
      {
         throw new Exception("Form data must be passed
                             in an array");
      }
   }

   function setFieldsNotRequired($not_required)            #37
   {
      if(!is_array($not_required))
      {
         throw new Exception("Fields must be passed
                             in an array");
      }
      else
      {
         $this->not_required = $not_required;
      }
   }
```

Continued

LISTING 4-6: *(Continued)*

```php
function displayForm()
{
    @extract($this->data);
    include($this->fields);
    include($this->form);
}

function getAllFields()
{
    return $this->data;
}

function checkForBlanks()
{
    if(sizeof($this->data) < 1 )                              #64
        throw new Exception("No form data available");

    foreach($this->data as $key => $value)                    #67
    {
        if($value == "")                                      #69
        {
            $match = false;
            if(is_array($this->not_required))                 #72
            {
                foreach($this->not_required as $field)        #74
                {
                    if($field == $key)
                    {
                        $match = true;
                    }
                }
            }
            if($match == false)                               #82
            {
                $blanks[] = $key;
            }
        }
    }
    if(isset($blanks))                                        #88
        return $blanks;
    else
        return TRUE;
}

function verifyData()
{
    if(sizeof($this->data) < 1 )                              #96
        throw new Exception("No form data available.");
    foreach($this->data as $key => $value)                    #98
    {
        if(!empty($value))                                    #100
        {
            if(eregi("name",$key) and !eregi("log",$key)
```

```
                    and !eregi("user",$key))                          #103
            {
              $result = $this->checkName($value);                     #105
              if(is_string($result))
                  $errors[$key] = $result;                            #107
            }                                                         #108
            if(eregi("addr",$key)or eregi("street",$key)
                or eregi("city",$key))                                #110
            {
              $result = $this->checkAddress($value);
              if(is_string($result))
                  $errors[$key] = $result;
            }
            if(eregi("email",$key))                                   #116
            {
              $result = $this->checkEmail($value);
              if(is_string($result))
                  $errors[$key] = $result;
            }
            if(eregi("phone",$key)or ereg("fax",$key))                #122
            {
              $result = $this->checkPhone($value);
              if(is_string($result))
                  $errors[$key] = $result;
            }
            if(eregi("zip",$key))                                     #128
            {
              $result = $this->checkZip($value);
              if(is_string($result))
                  $errors[$key] = $result;
            }
            if(eregi("state",$key))                                   #134
            {
              $result = $this->checkState($value);
              if(is_string($result))
                  $errors[$key] = $result;
            }
        }
    }
    if(isset($errors))                                                #142
        return $errors;
    else
        return TRUE;
}

function trimData()
{
    foreach($this->data as $key => $value)
    {
        $data[$key] = trim($value);
    }
    $this->data = $data;
}
```

Continued

LISTING 4-6: *(Continued)*

```php
function stripTagsFromData()
{
   foreach($this->data as $key => $value)
   {
      $data[$key] = strip_tags($value);
   }
   $this->data = $data;
}

function checkName($field)
{
   if(!ereg("^[A-Za-z' -]{1,50}$",$field))
   {
      return "$field is not a valid name.
              Please try again.";
   }
   else
      return TRUE;
}

function checkAddress($field)
{
   if(!ereg("^[A-Za-z0-9.,' -]{1,50}$",$field))
   {
      return "$field is not a valid address.
              Please try again.";
   }
   else
      return TRUE;
}

function checkZip($field)
{
   if(!ereg("^[0-9]{5}(\-[0-9]{4})?",$field))
      return "$field is not a valid zip code.
              Please try again.";
   else
      return TRUE;
}

function checkPhone($field)
{
   if(!ereg("^[0-9](Xx -]{7,20}$",$field))
      return "$field is not a valid phone number.
              Please try again.";
   else
      return TRUE;
}

function checkEmail($field)
{
```

```
        if(!ereg("^.+@.+\\..+$",$field))
            return "$field is not a valid email address.
                    Please try again.";
        else
            return TRUE;
    }

    function checkState($field)
    {
        if(!ereg("^[A-Za-z]",$field))
            return "$field is not a valid state.
                    Please try again.";
        else
            return TRUE;
    }
}
?>
```

The constructor

The *constructor* checks to see whether the information passed to the class is the correct type of data. If it is, it stores the data. If it isn't, it throws an exception with the appropriate message. On line 16, the constructor checks whether the first two parameters, which need to be filenames, are strings. On line 26, it checks whether the data that is passed in the third parameter is in an array. The data is also allowed to be NULL, which allows the form to be displayed the first time, before the customer has entered information and submitted it. Thus, you can create a WebForm object with either of the following statements:

```
$form = new WebForm("file1.inc","file2.inc",$_POST);
$form = new WebForm("file1.inc","file2.inc");
```

If you use the second form, the $data property is NULL. This won't cause an error.

setFieldsNotRequired

The setFieldsNotRequired method checks to see whether the parameter passed is an array. If it is, it stores it in a property. If not, it throws an exception with the appropriate message.

displayForm

This displayForm method displays the form. It extracts the data from the $data property where it's stored. An @ is used to suppress the error messages so that the form can be displayed without any data. The two files that define the form are then included. These two files can define any type of form with fields and elements you want to use. For this application, I use the files described earlier in this chapter that define a login Web page with two forms.

getAllFields

The `getAllFields` method returns the `$data` property array that contains the data in the form.

checkForBlanks

The `checkForBlanks` method checks each field in the form to see whether it contains information. If invalid blank fields are found, it returns an array containing the field names of the blank fields. The following explanation refers to line numbers in Listing 4-6:

#64   Checks whether `$data` contains an array of data. If not, it throws an exception stating that no data is currently in the form.

#67   Starts a `foreach` loop that walks through the `$data` array. The `foreach` loop checks for blank fields. An array is built that contains the field names of all blank fields.

#69   Begins an `if` block that executes if the field is blank. The block ends on line 86.

>   **#71**   Sets the variable `$match` equal to `false`.

>   **#72**   Starts an `if` block that executes if any field names are stored in `$not_required`. If so, the current field is compared to each value in `$not_required`, and if a match is found, `$match` is set to `true`. After the current field is checked against the field names in `$not_required`, line 82 checks whether a match was found. If `$match = false`, the current field name is not in the array of fields that can be blank, which means that the field is not allowed to be blank, and the field name is added to an array called `$blanks`.

#88   After all the blank fields are processed, an `if` statement checks whether any field names were added to the array `$blanks`. If so, the array is returned. Otherwise, if the `$blanks` array is empty, the method returns `TRUE`, meaning that all the fields are okay.

verifyData

The `verifyData` method checks each field to ensure that the information submitted in the field is in a reasonable format. For instance, you know that "hi you" is not a reasonable format for a zip code. A zip code must be in one of two formats: either 12345 or 12345-6789. If you check the information submitted by your customer for reasonable formats, you can catch many typos. You can also prevent the bad guys from entering malicious code into your form fields.

Checking data is a balancing act. You want to catch as much bad information as possible. However, you don't want to stop legitimate information from getting through. For instance, if you limit a phone number to numbers only, any phone numbers with a hyphen or parentheses — as in (123) 555-6789 — or other legitimate characters would be stopped as errors. Think carefully about what information you want to allow or screen out for any field.

This method checks the information from specific fields against regular expressions that match the information allowed in those fields. The following explanation refers to line numbers in Listing 4-6:

#96 Checks whether $data contains any information. If not, the method throws an exception with an appropriate message.

#98 Starts a foreach loop that walks through the array in the $data property. The foreach loop checks the format of all the data fields. Any format errors found are added to an array called $errors.

#100 Begins an if block that executes if the field is not blank. Blank fields are not checked because they would always be incorrect, but some fields are allowed to be blank. The method checkForBlanks is usually used before this method to catch any blank fields that are not allowed to be blank. In this if block, the information in each field is checked against an appropriate regular expression.

> **#102** Begins an if block that executes if the field name contains "name", such as first_name, and does *not* include "log" or "user". The requirements for names are more restrictive than for user names, so this statement excludes field names that might be user names. On line 105, the information in the field is passed to the checkName method, which compares the value to the regular expression for names. If checkName approves the value, it returns TRUE. If the value doesn't match the regular expression, checkName returns an informative message. The checkName method is discussed later in this section.
>
> Line 106 checks the value returned by checkName. If it's a string, which means that the value didn't pass muster, the string is added to an array named $errors.

#109 Begins an if block that executes if the field name contains "addr" or "street" or "city". It processes the field information as described for line 102. The method checkAddress is called.

#116 Begins an if block that executes if the field name contains "email". The method checkEmail is called.

#122 Begins an if block that executes if the field name contains "phone" or "fax". The method checkPhone is called.

#128 Begins an if block that executes if the field name contains "zip". The method checkZip is called.

#134 Begins an if block that executes if the field name contains "state". The method checkState is called. Even though the state field is a drop down list, you need to check its format. Bad guys can change the field to a text field and send it with some malicious code in the field.

> **#142** After all the field values have been processed, the method checks whether any strings were added to the array $errors. If so, the array is returned. If not, meaning that all the field information is okay, the method returns TRUE.

This WebForm class verifies fields that are commonly collected in forms, such as addresses and phone numbers. To use this class to verify data in a form with less common fields, such as age or birthday or favorite hobbies, you can add methods to the class that check your specific information.

Or, if you expect to use the different forms frequently, you can create classes to represent the different forms you use. For instance, you can have a class WebForm that contains all the methods in this WebForm class except the methods that verify data. Then you can have two (or more) classes, such as WebFormAddress and WebFormPersonal, that have WebForm as a parent and contain only the methods that verify data. For instance, you can define WebFormAddress extends WebForm and WebFormPersonal extends WebForm. In this case, the two child classes inherit all the methods of WebForm, so they don't need to contain those methods themselves. They need to contain only the methods for verifying data because those are the methods that are different in WebFormAddress than in WebFormPersonal.

trimData, stripTagsFromData

A PHP function is applied to each value in the $data property. The resulting values are stored in $data. The trim function removes leading and trailing blanks from a string. The strip_tags function removes any HTML tags from the string, which is important for security.

checkName, checkAddress, checkZip, checkPhone, checkEmail, checkState

These methods compare the values sent to them with regular expressions for the type of data expected. For instance, checkZip checks the string passed to it to see whether it consists of five numbers or five numbers followed by a dash and four numbers.

If the comparison against the regular expression fails, a message is returned stating that the field is invalid. If the string is okay, the method returns TRUE.

Writing the Database class

The Database class provides the connection to the database where the customer information is stored. The Database class is developed is Chapter 3; see Listing 3-4 for the Database class code.

The methods provided by the Database class are as follows:

- ✔ **The constructor:** Creates a connection to a MySQL database. Expects to be passed a file name, which contains the hostname, account name, and password necessary to access MySQL. A Database object is created with the following statement:

  $db = new Database("Vars.inc");

- ✔ useDatabase: Selects a database and stores the database name. Expects to be passed a database name. Checks whether the database exists and returns a message if the database doesn't exist. The method is used as follows:

  $db->useDatabase("Customer");

- ✔ getConnection: Returns the connection that is established and stored in the constructor. The method is used as follows:

  $db->getConnection();

Writing the Account class

The Account class specifies the record in the database table that contains the customer account information. The Account class that is developed in Chapter 3 is used in this application, but I've added a method in this chapter. See Listing 3-5 for the Account class used in Chapter 3. In this chapter, the method createNewAccount is added to the Account class. The code for this new method is shown in Listing 4-7.

Summary of account methods

The methods provided by the Account class are as follows:

- ✔ **The constructor:** Creates a connection to a MySQL table where account information is stored. Expects to be passed a database connection and a table name. The method checks whether the parameters passed are in the correct format. It also checks whether the database table exists.

  An Account object is created with the following statement:

  $acct = new Account($connection, "tablename");

  An Account object is often created for use with a Database object. You can create it with the following statements:

  $db = new Database("Vars.inc");
  $acct = new Account($db->getConnection, "tablename");

- ✔ selectAccount: This method stores the user_name of the currently active account. The user name is passed when selectAccount is called. The method checks whether the user name exists in the database. The method is used with the following statement:

  $acct->getConnection();

✔ getMessage: This method returns the content of the $message property. The method is used with the following statement:

$acct->getMessage();

✔ comparePassword: This method compares the password passed to the method with the password stored in the database for the current account. This method fails if no account has been selected. Use selectAccount to select an active account before using this method. The method is used with the following statement:

$acct->comparePassword("secret");

✔ createNewAccount: This method stores customer information into a new record in the database table, creating a new account. The information is passed to this method in an array. This method assumes that the data has already been cleaned and verified and is ready to be stored in the database. The method is used with the following statement:

$acct->createNewAccount($data_array);

createNewAccount

This method stores customer information into the database table in a new record. This method accepts the data from an array and stores it without checking it. The data should be cleaned and validated before it's passed to this method.

Each element in the array passed to this method stores the customer information with the field name as the key. This method first creates two arrays: one containing the keys and one containing the customer information. It then reformats each array into a string. Finally, it builds the SQL query to insert the new record, putting the strings in the appropriate location in the query, and executes the query to create the new record.

The code for createNewAccount is shown in Listing 4-7.

LISTING 4-7: THE CODE FOR THE createNewAccount METHOD

```
function createNewAccount($data)
{
    if(!is_array($data))                                        #97
    {
        throw new Exception("Data must be in an array.");
        return FALSE;
    }
    foreach($data as $field => $value)                          #102
    {
        if($field != "password" and $field != "Button")
        {
```

```
                $fields[] = $field;
                $values[] = addslashes($value);       #107
        }
    }
    $str_fields = implode($fields,",");                #110
    $str_values = '"'.implode($values,'","');          #111
    $today = date("Y-m-d");                            #112
    $str_fields .=",create_date";
    $str_fields .=",password";
    $str_values .="\",\"$today";
    $str_values .="\",md5(\"{$data['password']}\")";   #116
    $sql = "INSERT INTO $this->table_name ($str_fields)
        VALUES ($str_values)";
    if(!$this->cxn->query($sql))                       #119
    {
        throw new Exception("Can't execute query: "
                                .$this->cxn->error());
        return FALSE;
    }
    else                                               #125
    {
        return TRUE;
    }
}
```

The numbers in the following discussion refer to the line numbers in
Listing 4-7:

#97 Starts an `if` block that executes if the data passed is not an array, in
which case an exception is thrown.

#102 Begins a `foreach` loop that walks through the array of data that was
passed. The loop creates two arrays: `$fields`, which contains the
field names, and `$values`, which contains the field data.

#104 Screens out the fields password, which gets special processing later,
and Button, which should not be added to the arrays because it's not
really a field name.

#106 Builds the `$fields` array with the field names from the data **array** keys.

#107 Builds the `$values` array. Because the values in this array are going
to be inserted into the database, quotes are escaped before the
values are added to the array.

If you have magic quotes turned on in the `php.ini` file, you don't
need to escape the quotes here. The quotes are escaped automatically for the POST data. However, you have more control if you turn
magic quotes off and escape the quotes in the script. Whichever way
you do it, it's important that the quotes be escaped before data is
stored in the database. See Chapter 2 for a discussion of escaping
quotes to protect against SQL Injection attacks.

#110 Calls the PHP `implode` function, which turns the `$fields` array into a string, with a comma between each field name.

#111 Calls the PHP `implode` function, which turns the `$values` array into a string, with a quote, a comma, and a second quote (`","`) between each value. Notice that a double quote is added to the beginning of the string. This string forms the VALUES section of the query, and the values need to be enclosed in quotes.

#112 Stores the current date in `$today`.

#113 Lines 113 to 116 add the field names and values for the fields `create_date` and `password` to the appropriate strings.

#117 Lines 117 and 118 create the SQL query that inserts the data into the database table.

#119 Begins an `if` block that executes if the query fails. The `if` block throws a new exception with the MySQL error message.

#125 Begins an `else` block that executes if the query succeeds in storing the new account information. The block returns `TRUE`.

Writing the Session class

The `Session` class is used so that the customer doesn't have to log into every page on the protected Web site. The `Session` class starts a PHP session and stores session variables.

The properties

The `Session` class needs only one property, which contains a message stored by a method.

```
private $message;
```

The code

Listing 4-8 contains the complete code for the `Session` class. The constructor and each of the four methods is discussed in detail after the code listing. Notice the line numbers at the ends of some of the lines of code. The discussion following the listing refers to the line numbers.

LISTING 4-8: THE CODE FOR THE SESSION CLASS

```php
<?php
 /*  Class: Session
  *  Desc:  Opens and maintains a PHP session.
```

```
*/

class Session
{
    private $message;

    function __construct()
    {
        session_start();
    }

    function getVariable($varname)
    {
        if(isset($_SESSION['$varname']))                      #17
            return $_SESSION['$varname'];
        else                                                  #19
        {
            $this->message = "No such variable in
                                    this session";
            return FALSE;
        }
    }

    function storeVariable($varname,$value)
    {
        if(!is_string($varname))                              #29
        {
            throw new Exception("Parameter 1 is not a
                                    valid variable name.");
            return FALSE;
        }
        else                                                  #35
            $_SESSION['$varname'] = $value;
    }

    function getMessage()
    {
        return $this->message;
    }

    function login(Account $acct,$password)                   #44
    {
        if(!$acct->comparePassword($password))               #46
        {
            return FALSE;
        }
        $this->storeVariable("auth","yes");                   #47
        return TRUE;
    }
}
?>
```

The constructor

The constructor starts the PHP session. The PHP `session_start` function checks to see whether a session already exists. If not, it starts a new session. If so, it continues the existing session. The constructor doesn't expect any information to be passed. Thus, the statement to create a `Session` object is

```
$sess = new Session();
```

getVariable

This method returns the value of a stored PHP session variable. It checks whether the variable exists in the session. If it does, the method returns the variable value. If the variable doesn't exist, the method returns `FALSE` and stores an informative message.

storeVariable

This method stores a PHP session variable. The method expects two values: a string that is the variable name and a value for the variable. The following numbers refer to line numbers in Listing 4-8:

#29 Begins an `if` block that executes when the first parameter *is not* a string. The block throws an exception with a message stating that the parameter is not a valid variable name.

#35 Begins an `else` block that executes if the parameter *is* a string. The block stores the information in the `$_SESSION` superglobal array and uses the variable name as the key.

getMessage

This method returns the contents of the `$message` property.

login

This method logs an `Account` into the session.

#44 Notice that the method expects two arguments: an `Account` object and a string that is a password. The name of the object that is expected is included in the method signature. If `$acct` is not an `Account` object, a fatal error occurs, as follows:

```
Fatal error: Argument 1 must be an object of class
Account in c:\Session.class on line 39
```

#46 Calls the `comparePassword` method of the `Account` object that was passed to the `login` method. If the `comparePassword` method fails, the `login` method returns `FALSE`.

#47 If the `comparePassword` method does not fail, the `login` method stores a PHP session variable called `auth` with a value of `"yes"`. This variable can be checked on other pages in the session to see if the user is logged in. You can change this method to store a different variable name and value if you prefer. In fact, you can make the method more general by having the name and value of the authorization variable passed rather than coded right in the method.

#48 After storing the authorization variable, the login method returns TRUE.

Writing the Email class

After a new customer successfully registers, the application sends a verification e-mail message to the e-mail address provided by the customer.

The properties

The `Email` class stores the information needed to send an email message.

```
private $message;
private $addr;
private $subj;
```

`$message` contains the contents of the message. `$addr` contains the email address to which the message will be sent. `$subj` contains the text line that will be the subject line of the e-mail message.

The code

Listing 4-9 contains the complete code for the `Email` class. The four methods are discussed in detail after the code listing. Notice the line numbers at the ends of some of the lines of code. The discussion following the listing refers to the line numbers.

LISTING 4-9: THE CODE FOR THE EMAIL CLASS

```php
<?php
 /*  Class:   Email
  *  Desc:    Stores an email message.
  */
 class Email
 {
    private $message;
    private $addr;
```

Continued

LISTING 4-9: *(Continued)*

```php
    private $subj;

    function setMessage($message)
    {
       if(!is_string($message))
           throw new Exception("Message must be a string");
       else
       {
           $this->message = $message;
           return TRUE;
       }
    }

    function setAddr($addr)
    {
       if(!is_string($addr))
       {
           throw new Exception("Address must be a string.");
           return FALSE;
       }
       else
       {
           $this->addr = $addr;
           return TRUE;
       }
    }

    function setSubj($subj)
    {
       if(!is_string($subj))
           throw new Exception("Subject must be a string");
       else
       {
           $this->subj = $subj;
           return TRUE;
       }
    }

    function sendEmail()
    {
      if(!empty($this->subj) and                              #49
         !empty($this->addr) and
         !empty($this->message))
      {
          if(!mail($this->addr,$this->subj,$this->message))
            throw new Exception("Email could not be sent.");
          else
            return TRUE;
      }
      else                                                    #58
      {
```

```
                        throw new Exception("Subject, Address, and message
                                    are required. One or more is missing");
                    return FALSE;            }
            }
        }
    ?>
```

The constructor

The `Email` class doesn't need a constructor because no actions need to be performed when the `Email` object is created.

setSubj, setAddr, setMessage

These methods store the information needed to send the e-mail message. Each method checks to see if the information passed is a string. If not, it throws an exception with an informative message. If so, it stores the information in the appropriate property and returns TRUE.

sendEmail

This method sends the e-mail message.

#49 Begins an `if` block that executes if all the required information is available. If none of the required properties are empty, the e-mail is sent. If the e-mail send is successful, the method returns TRUE. If the send fails, an exception is thrown with a message.

#58 Begins an `else` block that executes if any of the properties are empty. An exception is thrown with a message.

This `Email` class is very simple. You can easily see where additional methods could be useful. For instance, a method that allows more than one e-mail address to be saved might be useful. Another useful method could set e-mail headers, such as a from header. However, for this application, the methods are sufficient.

Writing the login application script

After writing all the class code needed for the login application, you write the application script that creates and uses the objects to provide the application's functionality. The application script has the following general structure:

```
if (form has not been previously displayed and submitted)
        Display the Login Web Page with blank form fields

else  (if the form has been submitted by the user)

    if(the user submitted the login form)
```

1 Test whether all the fields are filled in. If not, redisplay the form with an error message.
2 Test whether the user name is in the database. If not, redisplay the form with an error message.
3 Test whether the password is correct. If not, redisplay the form with an error message.
4 When login succeeds, display the protected Web page.

elseif(the user submitted the registration form)
1 Test whether all the fields are filled in. If not, redisplay the form with an error message.
2 Test whether the information is in the correct format. If not, redisplay form with error message.
3 When information is correct, store it in database.
4 Display the protected Web page.

The application program creates objects and uses their methods to perform these tasks. The application program script is shown in Listing 4-10.

LISTING 4-10: THE LOGIN APPLICATION SCRIPT

```php
<?php
 /* Program:   Login-OO.php
  * Desc:      User Login Application script. The program
  *            displays the Login Web page. New customer
  *            registration information is validated and
  *            stored in a database. Existing customers'
  *            passwords are compared to valid passwords.
  */
require_once("WebForm.class");                              #9
require_once("Account.class");
require_once("Database.class");
require_once("Session.class");
require_once("Email.class");

try                                                        #15
{
  $form =
    new WebForm("double_form.inc","fields_login.inc",$_POST);
}
catch(Exception $e)
{
  echo $e->getMessage();
  exit();
}
//First time form is displayed. Form is blank. //
if (!isset($_POST['Button']))                              #26
{
   $form->displayForm();
   exit();
}
// Process form that has been submitted with user info  //
else                                                      #32
```

```
{
    $sess = new Session();                                          #34
    try
    {
        $db = new Database("Vars.inc");                             #37
        $db->useDatabase("CustomerDirectory");                      #38
        $acct = new Account($db->getConnection(),"Customer");
    }
    catch(Exception $e)
    {
        echo $e->getMessage()."\n<br>";
        exit();
    }

    // Login form was submitted  //
    if (@$_POST['Button'] == "Login")                               #48
    {
        try
        {
            $blanks = $form->checkForBlanks();                      #52
        }
        catch(Exception $e)
        {
            echo $e->getMessage();
            exit();
        }
        if(is_array($blanks))                                       #59
        {
            $GLOBALS['message_1'] =
                "User name or Password was blank.
                           Please enter both.";
            $form->displayForm();
            exit();
        }
        try
        {
            if(!$acct->selectAccount($_POST['fusername']))          #69
            {
                $GLOBALS['message_1'] = $acct->getMessage().
                            " Please try again.";
                $form->displayForm();
                exit();
            }
            if(!$sess->login($acct,$_POST['fpassword']))            #76
            {
                $GLOBALS['message_1'] = $acct->getMessage().
                        " Please try again.";
                $form->displayForm();
                exit();
            }
            header("Location: SecretPage.php");                     #83
            exit();
```

Continued

LISTING 4-10: *(Continued)*

```
        }
    catch(Exception $e)
    {
        echo $e->getMessage();
    }
}

// Registration form was submitted  //
elseif($_POST['Button'] = "Register")                           #93
{
    $not_required[] = "fax";                                    #95
    try
    {
        $form->setFieldsNotRequired($not_required);             #98
        $blanks = $form->checkForBlanks();                      #99
    }
    catch(Exception $e)
    {
        echo $e->getMessage();
    }
    if(is_array($blanks))                                       #105
    {
        $GLOBALS['message_2'] =
            "The following required fields were blank.
                Please enter the required information:  ";
        foreach($blanks as $value)
        {
            $GLOBALS['message_2'] .="$value, ";
        }
        $form->displayform();
        exit();
    }
    $form->trimData();                                          #117
    $form->stripTagsFromData();                                 #118
    try
    {
        $errors = $form->verifyData();                          #121
    }
    catch(Exception $e)
    {
        echo $e->getMessage();
    }
    if(is_array($errors))                                       #127
    {
        $GLOBALS['message_2'] = "";
        foreach($errors as $value)
        {
            $GLOBALS['message_2'] .="$value<br> ";
        }
        $form->displayform();
        exit();
    }
    $newdata = $form->getAllFields();                           #137
```

```
        try
        {
          if($acct->selectAccount($newdata['user_name']))      #140
          {
            $GLOBALS['message_2'] =
                "Member ID already used.
                      Select a new Member ID.";
            $form->displayForm();
            exit();
          }
          if(!$acct->createNewAccount($newdata))               #148
          {
            echo "Couldn't create new account.
                          Try again later.";
            exit();
          }
          $sess->storeVariable("auth","yes");                  #154
          $sess->storeVariable("logname",$newdata['user_name']);

           $em = new Email();                                  #156
           $em->setAddr($newdata['email']);
           $em->setSubj("Your new customer registration");
           $emess = "Your new customer account has been setup.";
           $emess .= " Your new user name and password are: ";
           $emess .= "\n\n\t{$newdata['user_name']}\n\t";
           $emess .= "{$newdata['password']}\n\n";
           $emess .= "We appreciate your interest. \n\n";
           $emess .= "If you have any questions or problems,";
           $emess .= " email service@ourstore.com";
           $em->setMessage($emess);
           $em->sendEmail();                                   #167
        }
        catch(Exception $e)
        {
            echo $e->getMessage();
            exit();
        }
        header("Location: SecretPage.php");
      }
    }
    ?>
```

Notice that many of the statements in this script are enclosed in `try/catch` blocks. If a method throws an exception and the exception is not caught, a fatal error occurs as follows:

`Fatal error:` **Uncaught exception 'Exception' with message 'Database is not available.' in c:\Database.class:56**

Therefore, you need to catch any exception thrown by a method either in the method itself or in the script that uses the method.

The following explanation of the script refers to the line numbers in Listing 4-10:

#9   Lines 9 to 16 include all the needed files.

#15   Begins a `try/catch` block that creates the `WebForm` object.

#26   Begins an `if` block that executes if no button was clicked, meaning the form has not yet been submitted. The block displays the login Web page with blank form fields.

#32   Begins an `else` block that executes if a button *was* clicked, meaning the user submitted the form. This block does all the form processing and password authentication.

#34   Creates a `Session` object.

#37   Lines 37 and 38 create a `Database` object and select the correct database.

#39   Creates an `Account` object.

#48   Begins an `if` block that executes when the user submits the login form. This block tests whether the user name and password submitted are valid.

> **#52**   Checks the login form fields for blanks. None can be blank.
>
> **#59**   Begins an `if` block that executes if any fields are blank. An error message is created, and the form is redisplayed. Notice that the error message is stored in the `$GLOBALS` array so that the `WebForm` method has access to the message.
>
> **#69**   Begins an `if` block that executes when the user name is *not* found in the database. An error message is created, the form is redisplayed, and the script exits.
>
> **#76**   Begins an `if` block that executes when the password from the form does not match the password stored in the database for this user. An error message is created, and the form is redisplayed.
>
> **#83**   Displays a protected Web page. The name `SecretPage.php` is just a sample name. You want to use the name of a script on your Web site that you want the customers to see when they log in — in other words, the main, or home, page of your protected Web site.

#93   Begins an `elseif` block that executes when the user submits the registration form. This block processes and stores the information from the form fields.

> **#95**   Creates an array containing the name of the field that is allowed to be blank. In this case, `fax` is the only field that can be left blank.

#98   Sets the name of the field that is allowed to be blank.

#99   Checks the form for blank fields. An array of the names of fields that are blank is returned. If `fax` is blank, it is ignored.

#105   Begins an `if` block that executes if the `$blank` array contains any elements — that is, if any fields are blank. An error message is created, and the form is redisplayed. Notice that the error message is stored in the `$GLOBALS` array so that the `WebForm` method has access to the message.

#117   Trims the data in all the fields.

#118   Removes any HTML tags from the data in the fields.

#121   Checks that the data is in the correct format. The methods return an array of error messages if any data is incorrectly formatted.

#127   Begins an `if` block that executes if the `$errors` array contains any elements — that is, if any fields contain bad data. An error message is created, and the form is redisplayed with the error message.

#137   Gets the data from the `WebForm` object. You need to store the data from the object. You don't store the data from the `$_POST` array that the user entered into the form because the data might have been changed on lines 120 and 121.

#140   Begins an `if` block that executes if the user name was found in the database. Duplicate user names are not allowed. An error message is created, and the form is redisplayed.

#148   Begins an `if` block that executes if the `createNewAccount` method fails. An error message is displayed, and the script exits.

#154   Stores the session variable that indicates that the user successfully logged in. The script reaches this line only when no error conditions were found.

#155   Stores the user name in a session variable for use later in the session.

#156   Lines 156 to 167 create and send an e-mail message to the customer that his or her new account has been successfully installed.

#174   Displays a protected Web page. The name `SecretPage.php` is just a sample name. You want to use the name of a script on your Web site that you want the customers to see when they log in — in other words, the main page (or *home* page) of your protected Web site.

Protecting your Web pages

The Web pages in your protected Web site or protected section of your Web site are no different than any other Web pages. You just want to restrict them to users who are logged in. To do this, you check whether the user is logged in at the top of every page.

If the user logs in via the `Login-OO.php` application script described in the preceding section, a session is started, and the value `"yes"` is stored in a session variable, as follows:

```
$sess->setVariable("auth","yes");
```

You can check this `$auth` session variable at the top of every protected Web page to see if it's set to `"yes"`. If so, the user is logged in. You can add the following statements to the top of every script to check the `$auth` session variable:

```
require_once("Session.class");
$sess = new Session();
if($sess->getVariable("auth") != "yes")
{
    header("Location: Login-OO.php");
    exit();
}
```

When you create the session object, PHP checks to see whether a current session exists for the user. If so, the current session variables are made available to the script.

The `if` statement tests whether the session variable `$auth` equals `"yes"`. If `$auth` is not set to `"yes"` or if `$auth` doesn't exist, the user isn't logged in, and the `if` block is executed, taking the user to the login Web page and exiting the current script. If `$auth` *is* set to `"yes"`, the script continues to display the Web page contents.

Adding Features to the Application

The login application in this chapter provides basic login functionality. Additional features can be added. Some common features of login applications that are not provided in this chapter are:

✓ **Forgotten password button:** It's almost guaranteed that users will forget their passwords. Many applications provide a button that users can click when they can't remember their passwords. Some applications e-mail the password to the user, and some provide a page where the user can change the password.

If you want to e-mail the user her password from the database, you need to use a different password encryption function, because md5(), used in this application, is a one-way encryption function. You can't retrieve the password in its original form. The password is protected from everyone, even you. Many users feel more secure knowing that no one can find out their password. If you want two-way encryption so that you can decrypt the password and e-mail it to the user, check the AES and DES functions in MySQL or the mcrypt function in PHP.

Rather than retrieve the password and e-mail it to the user, which is basically an unsecure procedure, you can provide the users with a Web page where they can change their passwords. However, you need to be sure that only the actual account owner can change the password. Many applications request and store the answer to a security question, such as your mother's maiden name, and require the correct answer before making any changes to the account.

✔ **Account management:** Users move and change their phone numbers. Their e-mail addresses can change. A feature that allows users to change the information stored for their accounts is handy. Many login applications provide a "manage your account" button that provides Web pages where a user can change his address, phone number, password, and so forth.

You can add these common features or features that are very specific to your Web site. But first, I suggest that you get the application working as it is. Then, when it's working, you can add features, one at a time. Don't change too many things at once. Troubleshooting one feature at a time is easiest.

In general, adding features to the object-oriented application is easier than adding to the procedural application. One of the strengths of object-oriented programming is that you can add code without needed to change the existing code. If you believe your application is likely to grow in the future, you might be wise to build the object-oriented application.

Part III
Building Online
Sales Applications

The 5th Wave   By Rich Tennant

"Ms. Lamont, how long have you been sending out
bills listing charges for 'Freight', 'Handling',
and 'Sales Tax', as 'This', 'That', and
'The Other Thing'?"

In this part . . .

In this part, I provide two applications related to online
sales. The first application displays a catalog of products (Chapter 5). The second application allows customers
to purchase products online (Chapter 6). For each application, I show two different methods — procedural and
object oriented.

Chapter 5

Online Catalog Application

*T*he online catalog application is one of the most common applications on the Web. Whether the Web site is offered by an individual with a handful of products or a huge company with gazillions of products, the principle is the same. The customer needs to see the products and information about them before buying anything.

On many Web sites with catalogs, customers can purchase the catalog items online. In this chapter, I provide a catalog application that doesn't include online purchasing functionality. The application in this chapter only displays the catalog. The application in Chapter 6 is an online purchasing application, which provides the ability to purchase catalog items online.

Designing the Online Catalog Application

The basic function of the online catalog application is to display a store's products to the customers. If a store offers only a dozen products, you can just display them all on one page. However, a store generally offers many products, more than you can reasonably display on a single Web page. Usually, the products are categorized. A small number of products can be successfully categorized by one category level. If the store offers a large number of products, however, you might need to use two, three, or more category levels to successfully categorize the products into categories small enough to be displayed. For instance, the example in this chapter is a store that sells food products. I use two category levels for this example. Foods are categorized first at the high category level, such as fruit, vegetables, herbs, and so on. Second levels within the high level of fruit might be apple, orange, and cherry. The product might be Delicious or Granny Smith, which would be in the category fruit: apple.

If your products are categorized, the online catalog typically first displays a page showing the categories available. The customer can select a category to see all the products in that category. If you have several levels of categories, the customer might need to select successive categories before reaching the product Web page.

Even with categories, some stores might have many products in a single category. For instance, Sears probably has many products in the category "Dresses" or even "Evening Dresses." A common practice when displaying a large number of products is to display only a certain number of products (often ten) on a page. The customer clicks a button to see the next set of products or the previous set of products.

To meet its basic functionality, the online catalog application should

- ✔ **Display the product categories from which the user can select.**

- ✔ **Display the products in the category the user selects.** It should display all the product information (price, description, and so on) needed by the customer. It should display the products one page at a time if the product list is quite long.

Creating the Catalog Database

The application design calls for a database that stores product information. The database *is* the catalog, the core of this application. The database stores the product names, ordering numbers, description, price, and any other relevant information, such as size, color, and so on.

Designing the Catalog database

Your first design task is to select the information you want to store. What you store depends on the type of product. You need to store any information that a customer might use when deciding which product to purchase. The store owner, who knows the products and what customers need to know, can provide this information along with graphics of the products. Some possible information to store might include

- ✔ **Product name:** Obviously, customers will need this information.

- ✔ **Product ID:** In most cases, the product name is not unique, so you usually need to store a *product number,* a unique number that identifies the product to the purchaser.

- ✔ **Product description:** A text description of the product.

✔ **Size:** A product might come in sizes. Even when only one size is available, customers need information about the size for some purposes. For instance, you might have only one size coffee table for sale, but the customers still need to know the size to know whether it will fit in their living rooms.

✔ **Color:** A product might come in several colors.

✔ **Price:** Customers will surely want to know how much the products cost!

✔ **Product availability:** Customers might also like to know when the product was added to the catalog, whether it's in stock, or when it's due to arrive.

You can add information for your use only to your product entry in the database. For instance, you might add information about the company that supplies you with the product. This information is stored in the database, but never displayed to customers.

The store in this example is called The Food Shop. It sells food items. At the present time, it sells fruit and vegetables, but the store owners hope to expand to other items soon.

The database contains only one table. The product information is stored one row per product. The fields needed for the table are shown in Table 5-1.

Table 5-1	Database Table: Customer	
Variable Name	*Type*	*Description*
catalog_number	INT(6)	Product identification number, assigned sequentially by MySQL (primary key).
name	VARCHAR(40)	Name of the individual product.
added_date	DATE	Date the product was added to the catalog.
category	VARCHAR(20)	First-level category name.
type	VARCHAR(20)	Second-level category name.
description	VARCHAR(255)	Description of the product.
price	DECIMAL(7,2)	Price of the product. All prices are entered at price per pound.
pix	VARCHAR(20)	Filename of the graphic file that contains an image of the product.

The table has eight fields. All fields except description are required and may not be blank. The description field is allowed to be blank when the product is entered. The description can be added later.

The catalog_number field is the product number that uniquely identifies the product. This number is used when the customer orders the product. This is an AUTO_INCREMENT field, so MySQL assigns numbers to it sequentially when the product is added to the database. In some stores, a meaningful product ID number is assigned and entered, rather than just a sequential number.

The pix field has a default filename. If no filename is entered, a default image file (Missing.jpg) that says "image not available" is entered.

Building the Catalog database

The following SQL statement creates this database:

```
CREATE DATABASE FoodCatalog;
```

The following SQL statement creates the table:

```
CREATE TABLE Food (
  catalog_number  INT(6)        NOT NULL AUTO_INCREMENT,
  name            VARCHAR(20)   NOT NULL,
  added_date      DATE          NOT NULL,
  category        VARCHAR(20)   NOT NULL,
  type            VARCHAR(20)   NOT NULL,
  description     VARCHAR(255),
  price           DECIMAL(7,2)  NOT NULL,
  pix             VARCHAR(20)   NOT NULL DEFAULT "Missing.jpg",
PRIMARY KEY(catalog_number) );
```

Accessing the food database

PHP. provides MySQL functions for accessing your database from your PHP script. The MySQL functions are passed the information needed to access the database, such as a MySQL account name and password. This is not related to any other account name or password that you have, such as a password to log onto the system.

PHP provides two different sets of MySQL functions, as follows:

✔ mysql: MySQL functions developed for MySQL versions up to 4.0. Although you can continue to use these functions with newer versions of MySQL, you can't use some of the advanced features of MySQL. The functions are in the format mysql_*action*(), such as mysql_connect() and mysql_query(). Because you have used PHP and MySQL prior to reading this book, you should be familiar with these functions.

✔ `mysqli`: MySQL Improved functions developed to use the advanced features of MySQL 4.1 and later. The MySQL Improved extension is available only with PHP 5, not with PHP 4. The functions are in the format `mysqli_action()`, such as `mysqli_connect()` and `mysqli_query()`. In addition, the MySQL Improved extension includes some built-in classes, so you can use objects when working with your database.

Because MySQL 4.1 is now the recommended version on the MySQL Web site, I use the MySQL Improved functions in this chapter. I use the procedural functions when building the procedural programs. I use the object-oriented classes when building the object-oriented programs.

If you're using PHP 4 or for other reasons want to use the mysql functions — rather than the mysqli functions — you might need to make small changes to the syntax. The mysqli functions are very similar to the mysql functions, but some differences exist. The syntax differences are shown in Appendix C. More information about the functions is available in the PHP manual at `www.php.net/manual/en/ref.mysqli.php` and `www.php.net/manual/en/ref.mysql.php`.

In this application, I have stored the information needed by the PHP mysqli functions in a separate file called `Vars.inc`. This file is stored in a directory outside my Web space for security reasons. The file contains information similar to the following:

```php
<?php
        $host = "localhost";
        $user = "admin";
        $passwd = "xy.34W";
        $database = "FoodCatalog";
?>
```

Notice the PHP tags at the beginning (`<?php`) and the end (`?>`) of the file. If you don't include these tags, the information might display on the Web page for the whole world to see, which isn't what you want at all.

Adding data to the database

This database is intended to hold the information for all your products. You can enter the product information in any way you normally enter rows into your databases.

Building the Catalog Web Pages

The online catalog requires two types of Web pages. One page displays an index of product categories, where customers select the category that interests them. If your catalog has subcategories, you may display the index page more than once — once for each level of categories. The second type of page is the product page, which displays the product information for products in the selected category.

Designing the catalog Web pages

Online catalogs abound on the Web. You've undoubtedly seen many, each with a unique look and feel. However, different designs can provide the same functionality. You might already know exactly what design you want, but keep in mind that the most functional design for you depends a great deal on the type and quantity of products that you have in your catalog.

The catalog in this chapter offers foods. The information to be displayed for each product is the name, description, price, and a picture. The information fits easily on one or two lines across the screen. Other products might require more or less space on the screen. Some catalogs display one page per product.

You need to design two different types of pages: an index page that displays categories and a product page that displays the products in a category.

Designing the index page

The index page needs to display categories in a form so that users can select a category. In this design, the categories are displayed in a form with radio buttons. Figure 5-1 shows what the index page of the online catalog looks like when it's displayed in a browser.

Figure 5-1:
The index
page
displayed by
the online
catalog
application.

The code for the index page is stored in separate files that are included when the application needs to display the catalog index page. Thus, the code that defines the Web page is separate from the PHP code that provides the logic of the application.

The code for the catalog index page consists of two files: the code that defines the look and feel of the page and the code that provides the specific information for the page.

Designing the products page

The products page for a catalog needs to display products so that customers can see all the information about the product. If all the products don't fit on a page, the product page needs to display as many times as necessary to show the customer all the products in the category. Some catalogs display just a list of products with a link to a page containing more information, which can sometimes be a complete page about one product.

In this design for the Food Shop, the information for the product fits on a line or two so that several products can be displayed on a page. One page of products is displayed at a time. At the bottom of a page, a form is displayed with submit buttons that users can press to see the next page, a previous page, or to return to the categories page. Figure 5-2 shows the products page of the online catalog displayed in a browser.

The code for the products page is stored in separate files, just like the code for the index page: the file that defines the look and feel of the page and the file that provides the specific information for the page.

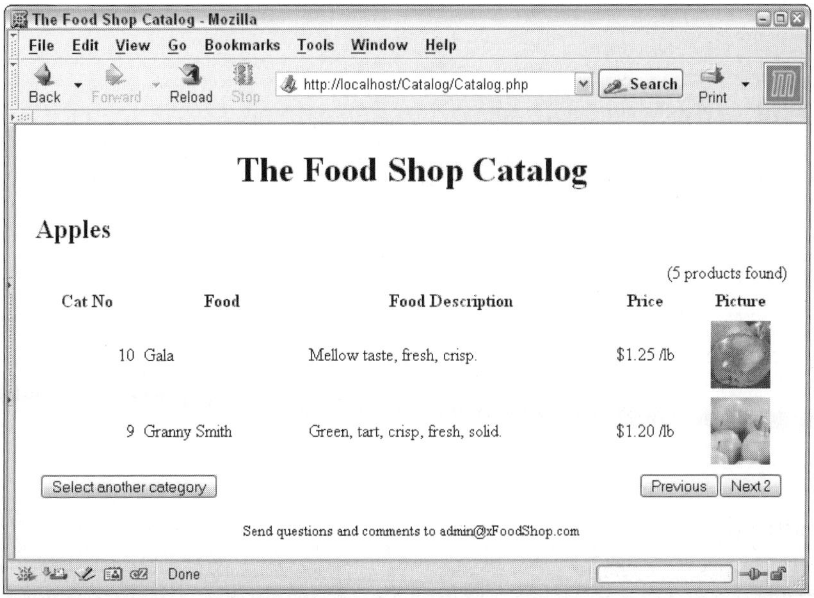

Figure 5-2: The products page displayed by the online catalog application.

Writing the code for the index page

The catalog index page provides a simple form that contains a list of categories. The Food Shop catalog contains two levels of categories. However, because the catalog doesn't have a lot of categories at this time, both levels of categories can be displayed on one index page. Some catalogs might have so many categories that only the top-level categories are displayed on one index page. The customer would need to click a top-level category to see the second-level categories. In the Food Shop catalog, however, displaying the category levels separately isn't necessary.

The code that creates the index page is in two separate files:

- ✔ `catalog_index_page.inc`: Contains the code that defines the look and feel of the Web page. It produces a Web page with a form that lists the categories. The first-level categories are headings. The second-level categories are listed under the related first-level category. Each second-level category is a radio button choice, so the customer can click the category of products he wants to see. This file doesn't include specific information, such as the category names displayed by the radio buttons. Another file must be used in conjunction with this file to create the Web page.

- ✔ `fields_index_page.inc`: Contains the specific information for the Catalog Index Web page. When used with `catalog_index_page.inc`, it displays a form where customers can select a category. A different file could be used with `catalog_index_page.inc` to create a different Web page.

The remainder of this section shows the details of these files. The second file is short and easier to understand, so I discuss it first, in Listing 5-1. Then, when explaining the first file, `catalog_index_page.inc` in Listing 5-2, I can refer to the information contained in `fields_index_page.inc`. The same two files are used for both the procedural and the object-oriented applications.

Writing fields_index_page.inc

The file shown in Listing 5-1 provides information specific to the Web page. For this page, only one array is needed. The `$page` array contains elements that are displayed at the top and bottom of the entire page.

Setting up your elements and fields in this separate file, rather than including them in the file with the HTML code for the form, greatly simplifies the design and maintenance of the form. You can easily see and edit the fields and elements in this separate file.

LISTING 5-1: THE FILE THAT CONTAINS THE ARRAYS NEEDED FOR THE INDEX PAGE

```php
<?php
   /* File:    fields_index_page.inc
    * Desc:    Builds the arrays needed to display the
    *          product categories for the catalog.
    */
   $page = array( "title" =>   "The Food Shop Catalog",
                  "top"   =>   "The Food Shop Catalog",
                  "bottom" => "Send questions and comments
                               to admin@xFoodShop.com",
                );
?>
```

Notice that the $page array is defined in a structured format. The array could be defined with much less space, but this format makes the values clear and easy to change if necessary.

Writing catalog_index_page.inc

This script contains the code that defines how the Web page looks. It includes HTML code for the forms and for tables to organize the page. The code includes variables where specific information is needed. The variable values are provided in the previous file, fields_index_page.inc. For example, the script includes the following line that defines the Web page title:

```
<head><title><?php echo $page['title']?></title></head>
```

The variable $page['title'] is found in the file fields_index_page.inc, where it is set to "The Food Shop Catalog".

LISTING 5-2: THE SCRIPT THAT DEFINES THE CATALOG INDEX PAGE

```php
<?php
   /* File:    catalog_index_page.inc
    * Desc:    Displays the categories for the catalog.
    */
?>
<html>
<head><title><?php echo $page['title'] ?></title></head>      #7
<body>
<?php
   /* Display text before form */
   echo "<div style='margin-left: .1in'>
   <h1 align='center'> {$page['top']}</h1><hr>";           #12
```

Continued

LISTING 5-2: *(Continued)*

```
    /* Create form containing selection list */
    echo "<form action='$_SERVER[PHP_SELF]' method='POST'>\n";
    foreach($food_categories  as $key => $subarray)          #16
    {
        echo "<h3>$key</h3>";
        echo "<ul>";
        foreach($subarray as $type)                           #20
        {
            echo "<input type='radio' name='interest'
                     value='$type'><b>$type</b><br>\n";
        }
        echo "</ul>";
    }                                                         #26
    echo "<p><input type='submit' name='Products'
             value='Select Category'>\n
        </form>\n";                                           #29
?>
</div>
<hr><font size="-1"><?php echo $page['bottom'] ?>             #32
</body></html>
```

The following numbers refer to the bold line numbers in Listing 5-2:

#7 Includes a short PHP section that echoes the title.

#12 Includes a short PHP section that echoes the top heading in the Web page.

#15 Echoes the HTML for the form tag that starts the form.

#16 Starts a `foreach` loop that loops through the `$food_categories` array. The loop displays the array. The outside loop displays the first-level categories. The loop ends at line 26.

> **#20** Begins an inside `foreach` loop that displays the second level categories.

#27 Lines 27 to 29 echo the HTML that displays the submit button and ends the form. The submit button is named Products because it's a button to display products.

#32 Displays the "bottom" element from the `$page` array.

Writing the code for the products page

The catalog products page displays a list of product information. Products are displayed one page at a time. A small form at the end of each page displays submit buttons for going to the next page, the previous page, and the index page.

The code that creates the products page is in two separate files:

- ✔ `catalog_product_page.inc`: Contains the code that defines the look and feel of the Web page. This file produces a Web page that lists the products in a table. After the tables, a small form is displayed with no fields, just the submit buttons. Hidden fields in the form pass needed information to the next page. This file doesn't include the product information. Another file must be used in conjunction with this file to create the Web page.

  This file is a little different for the procedural application and the object-oriented application. The differences are pointed out following the code listing.

- ✔ `fields_product_page.inc`: Contains the specific information for the Catalog Products Web page. When used with `catalog_product_page.inc`, this file displays the product information. A different file could be used with `catalog_product_page.inc` to create a Web page that displays different product information.

  This file is the same for the procedural application and the object-oriented application.

The remainder of this section shows the details of these files. The second file is short and easier to understand, so I discuss it first, in Listing 5-3. Then, when explaining the first file, `catalog_product_page.inc` in Listing 5-4, I can refer to the information contained in `fields_product_page.inc`.

Writing fields_product_page.inc

The file shown in Listing 5-3 builds three arrays that contain the specific information displayed in the product page. The arrays are:

- ✔ `$page`: Contains elements that are displayed at the top and the bottom of the entire page.
- ✔ `$table_heads`: Contains elements that provide the headings for the table that displays the products.

In this separate file, you can easily see and modify the fields and elements.

LISTING 5-3: THE FILE THAT CONTAINS THE ARRAYS NEEDED FOR THE PRODUCT PAGE

```php
<?php
   /* File:   fields_products_page.inc
    * Desc:   Builds the arrays needed to display the products
    *         page of the catalog.
    */
```

Continued

LISTING 5-3: *(Continued)*

```php
$page = array( "title"   => "The Food Shop Catalog",
               "top"     => "The Food Shop Catalog",
               "bottom"  => "Send questions and comments
                             to admin@xFoodShop.com",
             );
  $table_heads = array("catalog_number" => "Cat No",
                       "name"           => "Food",
                       "description"    => "Food Description",
                       "price"          => "Price",
                       "pix"            => "Picture",
                      );
?>
```

$page and $table_heads are created in structured array statements that are easy to see and maintain.

Writing catalog_product_page.inc

Listing 5-4 shows the code for catalog_product_page.inc. Like the catalog_index_page.inc file shown in Listing 5-2, this file defines the look and feel of the Web page. It includes the HTML code that displays the page. It also includes small sections that display the information from the file fields_products_page.inc.

Listing 5-4 shows the file used for the procedural application. After the listing, I discuss the changes that need to be made to use the file with the object-oriented application.

LISTING 5-4: THE SCRIPT THAT DEFINES THE CATALOG PRODUCT PAGE

```php
<?php
  /* File:  catalog_product_page.inc
   * Desc:  Displays the products in the catalog for the
   *        selected category.
   */
?>
<html>
<head><title><?php echo $page['title'] ?></title></head>
<body>
<?php
echo "<div style='margin-left: .1in; margin-right: .1in'>
      <h1 align='center'>{$page['top']}</h1>
      <p><font size='+2'><b>{$_POST['interest']}</b></font>";
echo  "<p align='right'>($n_products products found)";      #14
echo "<table border = '0' cellpadding = '3' width = '100%'>";
```

```
echo "<tr>";
foreach($table_heads as $heading)                            #17
{
    echo "<th>$heading</th>";
}
echo "</tr>";
for ($i=$n_start;$i<=$n_end;$i++)                             #22
{
    echo "<tr>";
    echo "<td
align='right'>{$products[$i]['catalog_number']}</td>";
    echo "<td>{$products[$i]['name']}</td>";
    echo "<td>{$products[$i]['description']}</td>";
    echo "<td style='text-align: center'>
                    \${$products[$i]['price']}/lb</td>";
    echo "<td style='text-align: center'>
             <img src='images/{$products[$i]['pix']}'
                   width='55' height='60'></td>";
    echo "</tr>";
}
echo "<form action='$_SERVER[PHP_SELF]' method='POST'>";     #35
echo "<input type='hidden' name='n_end' value='$n_end'>";
echo "<input type='hidden' name='interest'
             value='$_POST[interest]'>";
echo "<tr>
        <td colspan='2'>
            <input type='submit'
                    value='Select another category'></td>
        <td colspan='3' align='right'>";
        if($n_end > $n_per_page)                              #44
        {
            echo "<input type='submit' name='Products'
                        value='Previous'>";
        }
        if($n_end < $n_products)                              #49
        {
            echo "<input type='submit' name='Products'
                        value='Next $n_per_page'>";
        }
echo "</td></form></tr></table>";                            #54
echo "<p style='text-align: center; font-size: 75%'>
        {$page['bottom']}";
?>
</div></body></html>
```

The following numbers refer to the bold line numbers in Listing 5-4:

#8   Includes a short PHP section that echoes the title.

#11 Lines 11 to 14 display the top section of the Web page, including a line that shows the category being listed (lines 12 and 13) and a line that shows how many total products were found for the category (line 14).

#15 Displays the table tag that begins the product table.

#17 Starts a `foreach` loop that displays the table headers in the first row of the table.

#22 Starts a `for` loop that loops through all the products in the `$products` array. This loop creates a table row for each product.

#24 Lines 24 to 33 display each information item in the product row.

#35 Echoes the tag that starts the form. The form is the last row of the product table and holds the next, previous, and new category buttons.

#36 Lines 36 to 38 create hidden variables that pass the information needed on the next page: `$n_end` and the category being displayed.

#40 Creates a wide cell where the Select Another Category submit button is displayed. The button is not given a name.

#43 Creates a wide cell on the right where the Next and Previous submit buttons are displayed.

#44 Begins an `if` statement that displays the Previous button. If the page being displayed isn't the first page, the previous button is displayed. The Previous button is named Products.

#49 Begins an `if` statement that displays the Next button. If the last product isn't yet displayed, the Next button is displayed. The Next button is named Products. Because both the Next and Previous buttons are named Products, the application script can test for the value of Products when deciding which products to display on the product page.

#55 Displays information at the bottom of the page.

Changing catalog_product_page.inc for the object-oriented application

The code in Listing 5-4 displays the products Web page when used with the procedural code. The file needs changes to work correctly with the object-oriented code.

Lines 24 to 33 display the product information on each row. In Listing 5-4, the information is displayed from an array named `$products`. This array is built from the information in the database in the `Catalog.php` script, described in Listing 5-5. For the object-oriented application, these lines need to be changed to display the information from an object. The object is created in the script `Catalog-oo.php`, shown in Listing 5-8.

To use the file with the object-oriented application, change lines 24 to 33 in Listing 5-4 to the following lines and call the new file `catalog_product_page-oo.inc`.

```
echo "<tr>";
echo "<td align='right'>{$all[$i]->catalog_number}</td>\n";
```

```
echo "<td>{$all[$i]->name}</td>\n";
echo "<td>{$all[$i]->description}</td>\n";
echo "<td>\${$all[$i]->price} /lb</td>\n";
echo "<td><img src='images/{$all[$i]->pix}'></td>\n";
echo "</tr>";
```

Displaying the catalog Web pages

Two files are used in conjunction to display each Web page. The files `catalog_index_page.inc` and `fields_index_page.inc` display the category page; the files `fields_products_page.inc` and `catalog_product_page.inc` (or `catalog_product_page-oo.inc`) display the products page.

The index Web page is displayed with the following code:

```
include("fields_index_page.inc");
include("catalog_index_page.inc");
```

The products Web page is displayed in the procedural application with the following code:

```
include("fields_products_page.inc");
include("catalog_product_page.inc");
```

The product page is displayed in the object-oriented application with the following code:

```
include("fields_products_page.inc");
include("catalog_product_page-oo.inc");
```

The procedural script and the object-oriented script use slightly different code, but the same general approach. One file contains the code for the look and feel, appropriate for any catalog. The catalog-specific information is provided in a separate file that's included when the "look and feel" file is included.

Building the Online Catalog Application: Procedural Approach

The Catalog application has one main script. The script is organized into two basic sections: one section that displays the index page and one that displays the products page. The index page section displays when the application first runs, before any buttons have been clicked. When the user clicks a button, the script displays a Web page dependent on which button was pushed. The following is an overview of the structure of the script:

```
if (Button)

    The Product button was pushed,
        1 Test whether a category was selected. If
          not, redisplay the index page.
        2 Display the products page.

    The Product button was not pushed,
        1 Display the index page.
```

Listing 5-5 shows the code for the online catalog application script.

LISTING 5-5: THE ONLINE CATALOG CODE

```php
<?php
  /* Program: Catalog.php
   * Desc:    Displays a catalog of products. Displays two
   *          different pages: an index page that shows
   *          categories and a product page that is displayed
   *          when the customer selects a category.
   */
include("functions_main.inc");                          #8
$n_per_page = 2;                                        #9
if(isset($_POST['Products']))                           #10
{
  if(!isset($_POST['interest']))                        #12
  {
    header("location:  Catalog.php");
    exit();
  }
  else                                                  #17
  {
    if(isset($_POST['n_end']))                          #19
    {
      if($_POST['Products'] == "Previous")              #21
      {
        $n_start = $_POST['n_end']-($n_per_page);
      }
      else                                              #25
      {
        $n_start = $_POST['n_end'] + 1;
      }
    }
    else                                                #30
    {
      $n_start = 1;
    }
    $n_end = $n_start + $n_per_page -1;                 #35
    $connect = connect_to_db("Vars.inc");              #36
    $query_food = "SELECT * FROM Food WHERE
```

```
                    type='$_POST[interest]' ORDER BY name";
        $result = mysqli_query($connect,$query_food)
            or die ("query_food: ".mysqli_error($connect));      #39
        $n=1;
        while($row = mysqli_fetch_assoc($result))                #41
        {
            foreach($row as $field => $value)                    #43
            {
              $products[$n][$field]=$value;
            }
            $n++;
        }
        $n_products = sizeof($products);                         #49
        if($n_end > $n_products)
        {
          $n_end = $n_products;
        }
        include("fields_products_page.inc");                     #54
        include("catalog_product_page.inc");
    }
}
else                                                             #58
{
    $cxn = connect_to_db("Vars.inc");                           #60
    $query = "SELECT DISTINCT category,type FROM Food
                  ORDER BY category,type";
    $result = mysqli_query($cxn,$query)
            or die ("Couldn't execute query.
                  ".mysqli_error($cxn));                        #65
    while($row = mysqli_fetch_array($result))                   #66
    {
        $food_categories[$row['category']][]=$row['type'];
    }
    include("fields_index_page.inc");                           #70
    include("catalog_index_page.inc");
}
?>
```

The numbers in the following explanation refer to the line numbers in
Listing 5-5:

#8   Includes a file that contains the function Connect_to_db — a func-
         tion used throughout the book. In this script, the function is used on
         line 36 and line 60.

#9   Sets $n_per_page, the number of products to be displayed on a
         single page. $n_per_page is set to 2, an unusually low number. It's
         more common to set the number to 10, but it depends on how many
         products entries fit on a page. You can set this number to any integer.

#10 Begins an if statement that executes if the customer clicks the
         submit button named Products.

#12   Begins an `if` statement that executes if the customer did *not* select a category in the form. The category page is displayed again.

#17   Begins an `else` statement that executes if the customer selected a category in the form. The products page is displayed.

> **#19**   Begins an `if` statement that executes if this is not the first page displayed. It checks which button was pressed. If the Previous button was pressed, `$n_start` is set back to the beginning of the previous page. If the Next button was pressed, the `$n_start` is set to the product after the last product displayed on the last page.

> **#30**   Begins an `else` block that executes if this is the first time the product page is displayed. It sets `n_start` to 1.

> **#35**   Sets `$n_end` to `$n_start` plus the number of products to be displayed on the page, minus one.

> **#36**   Lines 36 to 39 build and execute a query that retrieves the product information for all the products in the selected category.

> **#40**   Lines 40 to 48 build an array named `$products` that contains all the selected product information.

> **#49**   Sets `$n_products` to the number of products in the category.

> **#50**   Begins an `if` statement that makes sure `$n_end` is higher than the number of products. If `$n_end` is more than the total number of products, `$n_end` is set to the last product.

> **#54**   Lines 54 to 55 display the product page.

#58   Starts an `else` block that executes if the Product button wasn't clicked. Either no button or the Select Another Category button was clicked. This block displays the·categories page.

> **#60**   Lines 60 to 65 build and execute a query that retrieves all the categories in the database.

> **#66**   Lines 66 to 69 create an array of food categories.

> **#70**   Lines 70 to 71 display the category page.

The online catalog application script calls a function to connect to the database. The `functions_main.inc` file, called on line 8, contains the function code. Listing 5-6 shows the function code.

LISTING 5-6: THE CONNECT_TO_DB FUNCTION

```php
<?php
/*  Function:    Connect_to_db
 *  Desc:        Connects to a MySQL database. The name of
 *               a file containing the database variables
```

```
     *              is passed to the function.
     */
     function Connect_to_db($filename)
     {
         include($filename);
         $cxn = mysqli_connect($host, $user,$passwd)
                 or die ("Couldn't connect to server.");
         $db = mysqli_select_db($cxn,$database)
                 or die ("Couldn't select database.");
         return $cxn;
     }
 ?>
```

This function gets the information it needs from a separate file. The filename is passed when the function is called. The file contents are something like the following:

```
<?php
$host = "localhost";
$user = "admin";
$passwd = "";
$database = "FoodCatalog"
?>
```

Store this file outside your Web space for security reasons. If you set your `include_path` in your `php.ini` file to a location outside your Web space, you can store files there and include them without using a complete path name.

Building the Online Catalog Application: The Object-Oriented Approach

Object-oriented programming requires that you create and use objects to provide the functionality of the application. You first identify the objects needed for the application. Then you write the classes that define the objects, including the methods that the application needs. When the objects are ready, you write the application script that creates and uses the objects.

Developing the Objects

The online catalog application needs to display information from a database. It needs to display two types of information from the database: a list of categories or a list of product information within a category. To display a catalog, the application needs only one object: a `Catalog` object. I discuss the details for the `Catalog` object in the following sections.

Writing the Catalog class

The definition for the `Catalog` object is coded in the `Catalog` class. This class is a general class that you can use to display any catalog, not just the food catalog used in this chapter.

The `Catalog` class maintains a connection to the database where the product information is stored and returns or displays product information as needed. The `Catalog` class contains five properties, a constructor, and five methods.

The properties

The Catalog properties store information needed to define and manage the form and its data. The properties are

```
private $cxn;
private $catalog_name;
private $host;
private $user;
private $password;
```

The first property is the connection to the MySQL database server. The second property is the catalog name, which is the name of the database where the product information is stored. The remaining properties are the information needed to access the database.

The code

Listing 5-7 contains the complete code for the `Catalog` class. I cover each method in detail after the code listing. Notice the line numbers at the ends of some of the lines of code. The discussion in the six subsections following the listing refers to the bold line numbers in Listing 5-7.

LISTING 5-7: THE CATALOG CLASS

```php
<?php
/*  Class:   Catalog
 *  Desc:    Class that contains product information.
 */
class Catalog
{
    private $cxn;
    private $catalog_name;
    private $host;
```

```
    private $user;
    private $password;
    function __construct($filename)
    {
      if(is_string($filename))
      {
        include("$filename");
      }
      else
      {
        throw new Exception("Parameter is not a filename");
      }
      $this->cxn = new mysqli($host,$user,$passwd);          #23
      if(mysqli_connect_errno())                              #24
      {
        throw new Exception("Database is not available.
                            Try again later.");
        exit();
      }
      $this->host = $host;
      $this->user = $user;
      $this->password = $passwd;
    }

    function selectCatalog($database)
    {
      $db = $this->cxn->select_db($database);                 #37
      if(mysqli_errno($this->cxn))                            #38
      {
        if(mysqli_errno($this->cxn) == 1049)                 #40
        {
          throw new Exception("$database does not exist");
          exit();
        }
        else
        {
          throw new Exception("Database is not available.
                                    Try again later");
          exit();
        }
      }
      $this->catalog_name = $database;
    }

    function getCategoriesAndTypes()
    {
      $sql = "SELECT DISTINCT category,type FROM Food
                    ORDER BY category,type";
      if(!$result = $this->cxn->query($sql))
      {
        throw new Exception(mysqli_error($this->cxn));
        exit();
      }
```

Continued

LISTING 5-7: *(Continued)*

```
    while($row=$result->fetch_array())
    {
        $array_cat_type[$row['category']][]=$row['type'];
    }
    return $array_cat_type;
}

function getAllofType($type)
{
    if(is_string($type))                                    #73
    {
        $sql = "SELECT * FROM Food WHERE type='$type'
                                ORDER BY name";
    }
    else
    {
        throw new Exception("$type is not a type.");
        exit();
    }
    if(!$result = $this->cxn->query($sql))                  #83
    {
        throw new Exception(mysqli_error($this->cxn));
        exit();
    }
    $n=1;
    while($row=$result->fetch_object())                     #89
    {
        $array_all[$n] = $row;
        $n++;
    }
    return $array_all;
}

function displayCategories()
{
    $food_categories = $this->getCategoriesAndTypes();
    include("fields_index_page.inc");
    include("catalog_index_page.inc");
}

function displayAllofType($type,$page)
{
    if(is_string($type))
    {
        $all = $this->getAllofType($type);
    }
    else
    {
        throw new Exception("$type is not a type.");
        exit();
    }
    if(is_int($page))
    {
```

```
                    $n_per_page = $page;
            }
            else
            {
                throw new Exception("$page is not an integer.");
                exit();
            }
            $n_products = sizeof($all);
            if(isset($_POST['n_end']))                           #125
            {
                if($_POST['Products'] == "Previous")             #127
                {
                    $n_start = $_POST['n_end']-($n_per_page);
                }
                else                                             #131
                {
                    $n_start = $_POST['n_end'] + 1;
                }
            }
            else                                                 #136
            {
                $n_start = 1;
            }
            $n_end = $n_start + $n_per_page -1;                  #140
            if($n_end >= $n_products)                            #141
            {
                $n_end = $n_products;
            }
            include("fields_products_page.inc");
            include("catalog_product_page-oo.inc");
        }
    }
    ?>
```

The constructor

The constructor creates a connection to the MySQL server. It gets the host-name, account name, and password for MySQL from a file; the filename is passed when the object is instantiated. The file can be stored in the include directory, as specified in the php.ini file. The constructor checks whether the information passed to the class is the correct type of data. If it is, it includes the file; if not, it throws an exception.

The constructor creates a connection to MySQL. The objects provided by the MySQL Improved (mysqli) extension are used. Line 23 creates a connection that is stored in the property $cxn. Line 24 begins an if statements that checks whether the connection was successful. If it failed, an exception is thrown.

The host name, account name, and password are stored in properties.

You can create a `Catalog` object with the following statement:

```
$food_catalog = new Catalog("Vars.inc");
```

selectCatalog

The `selectCatalog` method sets the database to be used when accessing MySQL. The database name is passed. The stored connection is used to set the current database.

> **#37** Sets the database.
>
> **#38** Starts an `if` block that executes if the database was not successfully selected. The block checks whether the error is Error 1049, which would signal that the database doesn't exist. If the error is 1049, an exception is created that informs the user that the database name given isn't a valid database. If the error number isn't 1049, an exception is created with a more generic error message.

This method can be used at any time to change the current database.

getCategoryAndTypes

The `getCategoryAndTypes` method gets all categories and types and returns them in a multidimensional array. It creates and executes the appropriate `SELECT` query. A `while` statement builds a multidimensional array from the result set. The method returns the array.

getAllofType

The `getAllofType` method gets all the product information for a given sub-category (type). The type is passed to the method.

> **#73** Begins an `if/else` block that checks whether the type name passed is a string. If so, the `if` block creates a `SELECT` query using the type passed. If not, the `else` block throws an exception.
>
> **#83** Executes the query. If the query fails, a new exception is thrown.
>
> **#89** Begins a `while` loop that builds an array of objects from the result set. Each product (row) is an object. The object properties are the field names and contain the information in the cell.

displayCategories

The `displayCategories` method displays the category Web page. A multi-dimensional array of product categories is created by using the method `getCategoriesAndTypes`. The method displays the category page by including two files: one file contains additional variables needed for the food catalog, and the other file contains the code that defines the look and feel of the Web page. I discuss these two files in the "Building the Catalog Web Pages" section.

displayAllofType

The `displayAllofType` method displays all the products for a given type. The method gets the product info using the method `getAllofType`. The method displays the products by including two separate files: one that provides some additional variables and one that provides the code to define the look and feel of the Web page. The two files are discussed in the "Building the Catalog Web Pages" section.

#125 Begins an `if` statement that executes if this is *not* the first page displayed. It sets `$n_start` to a value based on which button — Previous or Next — was pressed.

> **#127** Begins an `if` block that executes if the Previous button was clicked. `$n_start` is set back to the beginning of the previous page.

> **#131** Begins an `else` block that executes if the Previous button was not clicked. The Next button was pressed. The `$n_start` is set to the product after the last product displayed on the last page.

#136 Begins an `else` block that executes if this is the first time the product page is displayed. It sets `n_start` to 1.

#140 Sets `$n_end` to `$n_start` plus the number of products to be displayed on the page, minus one.

#141 Begins an `if` statement that makes sure `$n_end` is higher than the number of products. If `$n_end` is more than the total number of products, `$n_end` is set to the last product.

#145 Lines 145 to 146 display the product page.

Writing the catalog application script

After writing all the class code needed for the online catalog application, you write the application script that creates and uses the objects to provide the application functionality. The application script has the following general structure:

```
if (Button)

    The Products button was pushed,
        1 Test whether a category was selected. If
          not, redisplay the index page.
        2 Display the products page.

    The Products button was not pushed,
        1 Display the index page.
```

The second choice (the Products button was not pushed) means that this is either the first time the page is displayed or the user clicked the Select Another Category button.

The application program creates objects and uses their methods to perform the tasks that I describe in the preceding section that describes the structure. The application program script is shown in Listing 5-8.

LISTING 5-8: THE LOGIN APPLICATION SCRIPT

```php
<?php
  /* Program: Catalog-oo.php
   * Desc:    Displays a catalog of products. Displays two
   *          different pages: an index page that shows
   *          categories and a product page that is displayed
   *          when the customer selects a category.
   */
require_once("Catalog.class");
if(isset($_POST['Products']))                                  #9
{
   if(!isset($_POST['interest']))                              #11
   {
      header("location:  Catalog-oo.php");
      exit();
   }
   else                                                        #16
   {
      try
      {
         $foodcat = new Catalog("Vars.inc");                   #20
         $foodcat->selectCatalog("FoodCatalog");
         $foodcat->displayAllofType($_POST['interest'],2);
      }
      catch(Exception $e)
      {
         echo $e->getMessage();
         exit();
      }
   }
}
else                                                           #31
{
   try
   {
      $foodcat = new Catalog("Vars.inc");                      #35
      $foodcat->selectCatalog("FoodCatalog");                  #36
      $foodcat->displayCategories();                           #37
   }
   catch(Exception $e)
   {
      echo $e->getMessage();
      exit();
   }
}
?>
```

Notice that many of the statements in this script are enclosed in `try/catch` blocks. If a method throws an exception and the exception isn't caught, the following fatal error occurs:

```
Fatal error: Uncaught exception 'Exception' with message
'Database is not available.' in c:\Database.class:56
```

Therefore, you need to catch any exception thrown by a method either in the method itself or in the script that uses the method.

The following explanation of the script refers to the line numbers in Listing 5-8:

#9 Begins an `if` statement that executes if a button named Products was pushed.

> **#11** Begins an `if` block that executes if the customer did *not* check a product category. The customer is returned to the category Web page.

#16 Begins an `else` block that executes if the user selected a category.

> **#20** Lines 20 to 22 display the product Web page. Line 20 creates a new `Catalog` object, line 21 selects the catalog to use, and line 22 displays the products.

#31 Begins an `else` block that executes if the user did not click a button named Products. This block displays the categories page. It will display the first time the script is called, when the user hasn't clicked any button at all. It also executes when the user clicks the Select New Category button on the products page because that button is not named Products.

#35 Lines 35 to 37 display the categories Web page. Line 35 creates a new Catalog object, line 36 selects the catalog to use, and line 37 displays the categories.

Growing the Catalog class

The `Catalog` class in this chapter provides the essential features for the example application. However, you can easily see where additional methods would be very useful, perhaps even required. For instance, the class needs a method that gets individual fields for a particular food, so that you can retrieve the price for bermuda onions or delicious apples. Such a method might be called as follows:

```
getPrice("bermuda")
```

Other useful methods might include a method that adds a product to the catalog and another that removes products from the catalog.

One of the benefits of object-oriented programming is the ease of adding functionality to applications. Adding a method for new functionality is as simple as `eatFood("cake")`.

Chapter 6

Shopping Cart Application

*T*he Internet provides endless opportunities to buy things. In this chapter, I develop an online ordering system that provides product information in a catalog and a shopping cart to purchase the items. In Chapter 5, you see an online catalog application. The online catalog application provides information about products to potential customers. In this chapter, the shopping cart application provides the ability to buy the products in the catalog. The shopping cart does not stand alone. It needs the catalog to provide products for the customer to place in his or her shopping cart.

Designing the Shopping Cart Application

Shopping carts can be implemented in many ways. Your first task is to decide how to implement yours.

Basic application design decisions

You must make some fundamental programming design decisions before designing the user interface. Some basic considerations are:

✓ **Customer login:** Many stores require customers to register and log in before they can purchase products. Customer registration provides the store with information about its customers, such as phone numbers and e-mail addresses. Requiring logins also allows features that can't be provided without the login process. For instance, you can't provide a feature that allows customers to track their orders without requiring that the customer log in. If the customer isn't required to log in, nothing prevents customers from looking at each other's orders.

On the other hand, many customers avoid registrations. Some customers are suspicious that their information might be used for nefarious purposes, such as unwanted marketing calls or e-mails. Other customers are impatient with the process, flitting away to an easier site. Therefore, requiring a login might cost the store some sales.

The application in this chapter doesn't require customer login. Anyone can purchase the products. Chapters 3 and 4 provide login applications that you can add to this application if you desire a customer login.

✔ **Purchasing methods:** How may customers purchase the products? The easiest method is to send the order information in an e-mail to the sales department and invoice the customer. Or, to require a check from the user before shipping the products. However, most Web sites accept payment on the Web site. Web sites can quickly accept and approve credit card payments. Some sites accept PayPal payments, either in addition to or instead of credit card payments. PayPal is an Internet Web site that provides accounts that people can use to send or receive money over the Internet. For instance, a PayPal account can be used to pay for eBay purchases. In addition to providing account setup, the PayPal Web site provides merchant tools that you can use to accept payment easily via PayPal. See `www.paypal.com`.

The application in this chapter accepts only credit cards.

✔ **Credit card handling:** Accepting credit card payments raises security issues. If the customer is going to send you a credit card number, you need to implement SSL (Secure Socket Layers) for security, as I discuss in Chapter 2. If you store credit card numbers, you need to implement strong security. Storing credit card numbers allows quicker and easier purchasing for customers (because their credit information is on file) but increases the opportunity for bad guys to steal important information. In addition, some customers don't want their credit information stored on your Web site. One possible solution, used at some online stores, is to allow customers to decide whether you store their credit card information.

The application in this chapter doesn't save credit card information. The information is accepted, used, and then discarded, not stored in the database.

✔ **Shipping fees:** Sending purchases to customers costs you money. The easiest solution to implement is a single, standard shipping and handling fee. Adding one amount to the total is a simple program step. The more difficult solution is to try to compute the actual shipping charge, allowing the customer to select the type of shipping used and computing the shipping charge based on the distance from your zip code to the customer's zip code. The customers appreciate the more accurate cost, but the programming takes more time and effort.

The application in this chapter charges a shipping fee that is a flat fee per item.

✔ **Shopping cart:** You can use several mechanisms to store the shopping cart while the customer continues to shop, before the order is submitted. The customer needs to be able to add and remove items from the shopping cart while putting together the final order. The most common techniques for storing the shopping cart contents are

- **Database table:** More secure, but more overhead.
- **Cookies:** The customer might have cookies turned off.
- **Session variables:** Less secure on a shared server.
- **Text file:** Easy, but less secure.

Other, less common methods are sometimes used.

The application in this chapter stores the shopping cart two different ways. The procedural program stores the shopping cart items in the MySQL database. The object-oriented program stores the shopping cart items in a session variable.

Application functionality design

The basic function of the shopping cart application is to collect the information needed to complete a customer's purchase. The application should

✔ **Display the products so that the customer can select products to purchase.** This step is provided by the online catalog application, which I describe in detail in Chapter 5. However, you need to add some additional features to the catalog to allow online purchasing. I cover the additional features in this chapter.

✔ **Keep track of the products selected by the customer.** The customer should be able to see what he has already selected at any time. The customer should also be able to remove any selections.

✔ **Collect the information needed to ship the product to the customer.** You need the customer's name and address. Also, you need a phone number in case of delivery problems. An e-mail address is useful for communication. The application can also collect any information required to compute shipping charges.

✔ **Collect the information needed to charge the customer.** The application collects credit card information, a billing address, and the exact name associated with the credit card. In this chapter, the shipping and billing information are assumed to be the same. I do this to keep the example simple. However, for a real-world Web site, you can't assume this.

✔ **Provide feedback to the customer.** The customer needs to see the information that she entered at all steps along the way and be able to correct information. Not everyone has perfect typing skills.

Creating the Shopping Cart Database

The shopping cart database stores information about the orders. It stores general information about the order, such as the customers' names and addresses, and the items selected for each order. Another important detail to know is when the order was submitted. This application also requires that the order store the product information, which appears in the online catalog. The application in this chapter sells products from The Food Shop catalog, which I describe in Chapter 5.

Designing the shopping cart database

The sample application in this chapter uses a database named OnlineOrders. The database contains two tables. One table stores information general to the order, such as name and address, order number, and so on. The second table stores a row for each item ordered, linked to the first table by the order number.

In addition, because the application needs to display the products, it needs access to the catalog database.

Designing the Customer_Order table

The table named Customer_Order contains information related to the order as a whole, as shown in Table 6-1.

You can't name tables with MySQL-reserved words. This table seems like it ought to be named Order, but that's a MySQL-reserved word. If you name your table Order, it generates a MySQL syntax error and you can spend hours staring at the query, convinced that there's nothing wrong. You can see a list of reserved words at http://dev.mysql.com/doc/mysql/en/reserved-words.html.

Table 6-1	Database Table: Customer_Order	
Variable Name	**Type**	**Description**
order_number	INT(6)	Integer assigned by AUTO_INCREMENT (primary key)
order_date	DATE	Date when order was added to table
shipping_fee	DECIMAL(9,2)	Total shipping cost for the order
sales_tax	DECIMAL(9,2)	Total sales tax for the order

Variable Name	Type	Description
submitted	ENUM('yes', 'no')	Order status
ship_name	VARCHAR(50)	Ship to: name
ship_street	VARCHAR(50)	Street address
ship_city	VARCHAR(50)	City where the order is to be shipped
ship_state	CHAR(2)	Two-letter state code
ship_zip	CHAR(10)	Zip code. (Five numbers or zip+4)
email	CHAR(50)	Customer's e-mail address
phone	CHAR(20)	Customer's phone number

In this design, the order number is an integer assigned sequentially by MySQL. Some designs might use an order number with meaningful numbers and/or letters, such as dates or department codes.

The shipping fee and sales tax are stored in the order. Although they can be computed, the rates might change in the future. Therefore, when looking up an order, you want to know what the charges were at the time of the order.

Designing the Order_Item table

The table named Order_Item contains information on each item in the order, as shown in Table 6-2.

Table 6-2	Database Table: Order_Item	
Variable Name	**Type**	**Description**
order_number	INT(6)	Link to Customer_Order table (primary key 1)
item_number	INT(4)	Number assigned to each item (primary key 2)
catalog_number	INT(8)	Number assigned to the product in the catalog
quantity	DECIMAL(7,2)	Amount ordered
price	DECIMAL(9,2)	Price of the item

The `Order_Item` table has five fields. The first two fields together are the primary key. The price is stored so the actual price paid for this item can be recovered in the future, even if the price has changed.

Designing the Food table

The application uses the `Food` table from the online catalog that I design and explain in Chapter 5. (Specifically, check out Table 5-1.) The application could access the table from that database. However, I have added the `Food` table to the `OnlineOrders` database (which I design and explain in this chapter) to simplify the design.

Building the shopping cart database

You can create the MySQL database using any of the methods that I discuss in Chapter 1. The following SQL statement creates this database:

```
CREATE DATABASE OnlineOrders;
```

The following SQL statements create the tables:

```
CREATE TABLE Customer_Order (
  order_number    INT(6)          NOT NULL AUTO_INCREMENT,
  order_date      DATE            NOT NULL,
  shipping_fee    DECIMAL(9,2),
  sales_tax       DECIMAL(9,2),
  submitted       ENUM("yes",'no'),
  ship_name       VARCHAR(50),
  ship_street     VARCHAR(50),
  ship_city       VARCHAR(50),
  ship_state      VARCHAR(2),
  ship_zip        VARCHAR(10),
  email           VARCHAR(50),
  phone           VARCHAR(20),
PRIMARY KEY(order_number) );
```

All fields in the preceding code are required to complete the order processing. However, only the first two fields are declared NOT NULL. When the application first inserts the order into the database, values are inserted into only the first two fields. The remaining fields are blank at that time; the values for those fields are added later. Consequently, the remaining fields must be allowed to be blank. The PHP application script must ensure that the fields contain the appropriate information.

```
CREATE TABLE Order_Item (
  order_number    INT(6)          NOT NULL,
  item_number     INT(5)          NOT NULL,
  catalog_number  INT(6)          NOT NULL,
  quantity        DECIMAL(7,2)    NOT NULL,
  price           DECIMAL(9,2)    NOT NULL,
PRIMARY KEY(order_number,item_number) );
```

```
CREATE TABLE Food (
  catalog_number INT(6)        NOT NULL AUTO_INCREMENT,
  name           VARCHAR(20)   NOT NULL,
  added_date     DATE          NOT NULL,
  category       VARCHAR(20)   NOT NULL,
  type           VARCHAR(20)   NOT NULL,
  description    VARCHAR(255)  NOT NULL,
  price          DECIMAL(7,2)  NOT NULL,
  pix            VARCHAR(20)   NOT NULL DEFAULT
"Missing.jpg",
PRIMARY KEY(catalog_number) );
```

Accessing the shopping cart database

PHP provides MySQL functions for accessing your database from your PHP
script. The MySQL functions are passed the information needed to access the
database, such as a MySQL account name and password. This account name
and password is not related to any other account name or password that you
have, such as a password to log onto the system.

PHP provides two different sets of MySQL functions: mysql functions and
mysqli functions. The mysqli functions are provided for access to features
added in MySQL version 4.1. You can use the mysql functions with version
4.1, but you don't have access to the newer features. The mysql or mysqli
extension is activated when PHP is installed. You must use PHP 5 to use the
mysqli functions.

Because MySQL 4.1 is now the recommended version on the MySQL Web site,
I use the MySQL Improved (mysqli) functions in this chapter. I use the procedural functions when building the procedural programs. I use the object-
oriented classes when building the object-oriented programs.

If you're using PHP 4 or for other reasons want to use the mysql functions,
rather than the mysqli functions, you might need to make small changes to the
syntax. The mysqli functions are very similar to the mysql functions, but some
differences exist. The PHP and MySQL versions are explained in Chapter 1. The
syntax differences are shown in Appendix C. More information about the functions is available in the PHP manual at www.php.net/manual/en/ref.mysqli.
php and www.php.net/manual/en/ref.mysql.php.

Adding data to the shopping cart database

The Food table contains the product information. You add this data to the
database yourself, outside this application. To add items to the Food catalog,
you can use the mysql client installed with MySQL, any MySQL administration application (such as phpmyadmin [www.phpmyadmin.net] or MySQL
Administrator, which you can download from MySQL

[www.mysql.com/products/administrator/index.html]), or write your own application in PHP.

The order information is added to the database by the shopping cart application. When customers submit orders, the order and item information is added to the appropriate table.

Building the Shopping Cart Web Pages

The shopping cart application provides the customer with product information, displayed from an online catalog, similar to the online catalog application discussed in Chapter 5. The customer selects items from the catalog and puts them into a shopping cart. When the customer is satisfied with the contents of the shopping cart and submits the order, the application builds the order, collecting the shipping information and storing the chosen items.

Designing the shopping cart Web pages

The shopping cart application displays five Web pages, in the following order:

1. **Product information:** The application displays the product information from an online catalog, as I describe in Chapter 5. The catalog actually displays two different types of pages: the categories page and the product information page. The categories page is the same page designed in Chapter 5. The product page is similar, but has some added elements that are necessary for online purchasing.

2. **Shopping cart:** The shopping cart Web page displays the items that are currently in the shopping cart.

3. **Shipping form:** When the customer submits the order, the application displays a form to collect the shipping address and credit card information.

4. **Summary page:** The summary page displays all the order information, including the address.

5. **Confirmation page:** When the credit information is approved, the application displays a confirmation page, accepting the order and providing any information the customer needs. Alternatively, if the customer cancels the order, a cancellation page is displayed.

Designing the product information Web page

In Chapter 5, I describe the online catalog application that displays items from a catalog. The application in the current chapter also displays items from a catalog. Two types of pages are displayed. One page is the product categories page (refer to Figure 5-2). This page is the same for the shopping cart application as for the online catalog application.

The second type of page displays information for products in the selected category. The product page for the shopping cart application is similar to the product page described in the previous chapter (refer to Figure 5-2), but has some added components, as shown in Figure 6-1.

Notice the following additions on this page:

- **View Shopping Cart button:** A new submit button — View Shopping Cart — is added to the upper-right corner of the page that allows customers to view the current contents of their shopping carts. This button is also added to the categories page.

- **The lbs column:** This column allows customers to enter the quantity they want for each item. The food catalog allows users to specify the number of pounds desired. The items display with 0 (zero) pounds. The customer can change the amount.

- **Add Items to Shopping Cart button:** A new submit button — Add Items to Shopping Cart — is added.

The new elements on the page are added so the customer can select products to purchase.

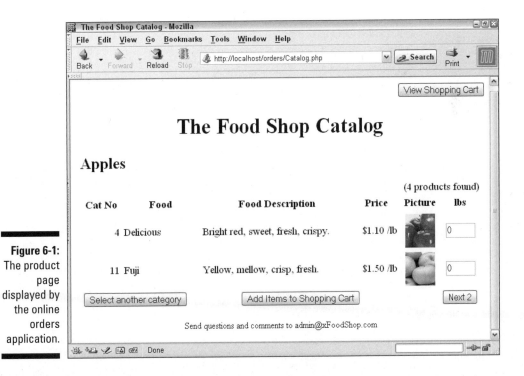

Figure 6-1:
The product page displayed by the online orders application.

Designing the shopping cart Web page

The application displays the items currently stored in the shopping cart, as shown in Figure 6-2.

The shopping cart provides three buttons that the customer can click:

- ✔ **Continue Shopping:** Returns the customer to the first catalog page.
- ✔ **Submit Order:** Submits an order for the items that are in the shopping cart.
- ✔ **Update Cart:** Allows the customer to change the items in the cart. The customer can change the number of pounds in the Amount column and click this button. The shopping cart is redisplayed with the changed amounts. If the number is changed to 0 (zero), the item is removed from the shopping cart.

Notice that three items are currently in the cart. Only two items were selected in the products page shown in Figure 6-1. The first item shown in the cart was stored in the cart previously; the two items were added.

Designing the shipping form Web page

The application collects the information needed to process and ship the order with the form shown in Figure 6-3.

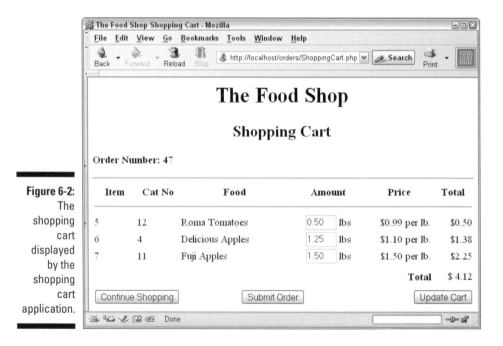

Figure 6-2: The shopping cart displayed by the shopping cart application.

I've simplified the shipping information form for this sample application. For your application, you will probably need to collect a billing name and address, as well as a shipping name and address as shown. You also might need to collect a shipping method and other information.

Designing the summary Web page

The application displays a summary of the order, so the customer can catch any errors and correct them, as shown in Figure 6-4.

The summary page provides four buttons that the customer can click:

- **Continue Shopping:** Returns the customer to the first catalog page while retaining the information in the order.

- **Edit Shipping Information:** Returns the customer to the shipping infor- mation form where the customer can change the shipping information as necessary.

- **Cancel Order:** Cancels the order.

- **Submit Order:** Submits the order on the summary page. The customer is unable to make changes after this final submission.

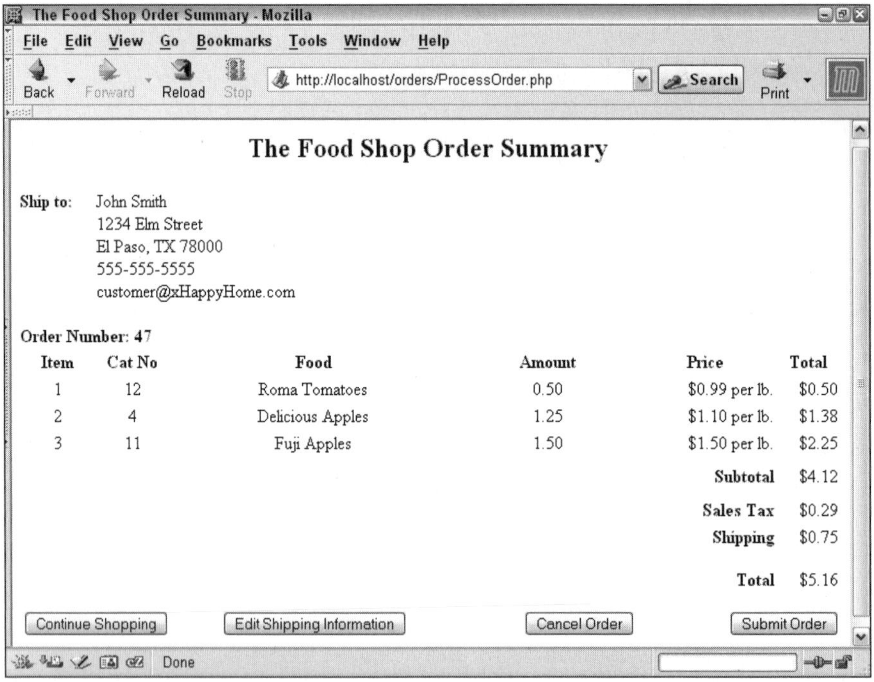

Figure 6-4:
The
summary
Web Page
displayed by
the online
orders
application.

The Food Shop must collect sales tax for customers living in Texas. Thus, the summary page shows sales tax. If the address were in a different state, no sales tax would be charged.

The Food Shop charges shipping at 25 cents per item. Thus, this three item order is charged 75 cents. This simple amount was chosen to simplify the example.

Designing the confirmation page

The confirmation page is specific to your store. It might simply be a repeat of the summary page. A confirmation page tells the customer that the order has been approved. It might also tell the customer when the order will be shipped and often provides the order number that the customer can use to track the order. I don't develop a specific confirmation or cancellation page in this chapter. I believe you can handle that without my help. I just show you how to display it.

Writing the code for the product information page

The catalog products page displays a list of product information. Products are displayed one page at a time. Each page displays submit buttons for next, previous, and return to the index page.

The code that creates the products page is in two separate files, as follows:

- ✔ `shopping_product_page.inc`: Contains the code that defines the look and feel of the Web page. It produces a page that lists the products in a table. Another file must be used in conjunction with this file to create the page. The other file contains the specific information for the page.

- ✔ `fields_products_page.inc`: Contains the specific information for the Catalog Products Web page. When used with `shopping_product_page.inc`, it displays the product information. A different file with different products could be used with `shopping_product_page.inc` (see Chapter 5) to create a page that displayed different products.

I describe these two files in detail in Chapter 5. For this chapter, I add some elements to the Web page to allow online orders. In this section, I describe the added elements only.

Writing fields_products_page.inc

The `fields_products_page.inc` file is almost the same file that I describe in Chapter 5. It builds two arrays that contain the specific information displayed in the product page. The arrays are

- ✔ `$page`: Contains elements that are displayed at the top and the bottom of the entire page.

- ✔ `$table_heads`: Contains elements that provide the headings for the table that displays the products.

The only difference between this file and the file of the same name in Chapter 5 is one additional element in the `$table_heads` array. The extra element is identified in the explanation following Listing 6-1.

The procedural and object-oriented files are the same.

LISTING 6-1: THE FILE THAT CONTAINS THE ARRAYS NEEDED FOR THE PRODUCT PAGE

```php
<?php
 /* File:    fields__products_page.inc
  * Desc:    Defines the variables and builds the arrays needed
  *          to display the products page of the catalog.
  */
$page = array( "title"   => "The Food Shop Catalog",
               "top"     => "The Food Shop Catalog",
               "bottom" => "Send questions and comments
                            to admin@xFoodShop.com",
             );
$table_heads = array("catalog_number"  => "Cat No",
                     "name"            => "Food",
                     "description"     => "Food Description",
                     "price"           => "Price",
                     "pix"             => "Picture",
                     "amount"          => "lbs",
                    );
?>
```

The products page has one additional column in the product information row. The new column allows customers to enter the amount of the product they want to order. Therefore, the new column is added to the `$table_heads` array. The new column is the amount column.

Writing shopping_product_page.inc

The `shopping_product_page.inc` and `shopping_product_page-oo.inc` files are very similar to the `catalog_product_page.inc` and `catalog_product_page-oo.inc` files in Chapter 5. However, a few additions are required that allow the customer to order online. The file with the additions is shown in Listing 6-2. I describe only the lines that are changed in this section. For a complete description of all the lines, see the section "Writing the code for the products page" in Chapter 5.

The file for the procedural application is slightly different than the file for the object-oriented application. I first show the procedural file, and then I describe the changes needed to use the file with the object-oriented application.

The file shown in Listing 6-2 defines the look and feel of the Product page.

LISTING 6-2: THE FILE THAT DEFINES THE PRODUCT PAGE

```php
<?php
 /* File:    shopping_product_page.inc
  * Desc:    Displays the products in the catalog for the
  *          selected category.
  */
```

```
?>
<html>
<head><title><?php echo $page['title'] ?></title></head>
<body>
<?php                                                            #10
 echo "<form action='ShoppingCart.php' method='POST'>\n
        <p style='text-align: right'>\n
        <input type='submit' name='Cart'
                        value='View Shopping Cart'>\n
        </form>\n";                                              #15
 echo "<div style='margin-left: .1in; margin-right: .1in'>\n
     <h1 style='text-align: center'>{$page['top']}</h1>\n
     <p style='font-size: 150%'><b>{$_POST['interest']}</b>";
 echo "<p align='right'>($n_products products found)\n";
 echo "<table border='0' cellpadding='5' width='100%'>\n";
 echo "<tr>";
 foreach($table_heads as $heading)
 {
     echo "<th>$heading</th>";
 }
 echo "</tr>\n";
 echo "<form action='$_SERVER[PHP_SELF]' method='POST'>\n";
 for($i=$n_start;$i<=$n_end;$i++)
 {
     echo "<tr>";
     echo "<td align='right'>
                 {$products[$i]['catalog_number']}</td>\n";
     echo "<td>{$products[$i]['name']}</td>\n";
     echo "<td>{$products[$i]['description']}</td>\n";
     echo "<td>\${$products[$i]['price']} /lb</td>\n";
     echo "<td>
        <img src='images/{$products[$i]['pix']}'></td>\n";   #37
     echo "<td style='text-align: center'><input type='text'
                 name='item{$products[$i]['catalog_number']}'
                 value='0' size='4'></td>\n";                    #40
     echo "</tr>";
 }
 echo "<input type='hidden' name='n_end' value='$n_end'>\n";
 echo "<input type='hidden' name='interest'
                 value='$_POST[interest]'>\n";
 echo "<tr>
         <td colspan='2'> <input type='submit'
                 value='Select another category'></td>\n";
 echo "<td colspan='2' style='text-align: center'>
         <input type='submit' name='Products'
                 value='Add Items to Shopping Cart'>";           #51
 echo "<td colspan='2' style='text-align: right'>\n";
         if($n_end > $n_per_page)
         {
             echo "<input type='submit' name='Products'
                         value='Previous'>\n";
         }
         if($n_end < $n_products)
```

Continued

```
LISTING 6-2: (Continued)

        {
            echo "<input type='submit' name='Products'
                value='Next $n_per_page'>\n";
        }
  echo "</td></form></tr></table>\n";
  echo "<p style='font-size: 75%; text-align: center'>
          {$page['bottom']}\n";
?>
</div></body></html>
```

The numbers in the following explanation refer to the line numbers in Listing 6-2. I discuss only the elements added to the file in this chapter. For information about the original file, see the discussion that follows Listing 5-4.

#11 Lines 11 to 15 add the View Shopping Cart button in the upper-right corner of the products page. The button displays the current contents of the shopping cart.

#38 Lines 38 to 40 add an input text field to each item where customers can enter an amount to purchase. The name of the field is built using the catalog number of the product. For instance, the name of the text field might be `item11` or `item4002`. The default value is 0 (zero). The customer can change the value to the desired quantity. The name of the field is passed in the `$_POST` array, along with the quantity, where the processing program can obtain the catalog number from the field name.

#49 Lines 49 through 51 add an extra button named Products to the product page, which is labeled Add Items to Shopping Cart.

Changing shopping_product_page.inc for use with the object-oriented application

The code in Listing 6-2 displays the products Web page when used with the procedural code. The file needs changes to work correctly with the object-oriented code.

Lines 30 to 41 display the product information on each row. In Listing 6-2, the information is displayed from an array named `$products`. This array is built from the information in the database in the `ShopCatalog.php` script, described in Listing 6-11. For the object-oriented application, these lines need to be changed to display the information from an object. The object is created in the script `Orders-oo.php`, shown in Listing 6-18.

To use the file with the object-oriented application, change lines 30 to 41 in Listing 6-2 to the following lines and call the new file `shopping_product_page-oo.inc`:

```
echo "<tr>";
     echo "<td align='right'>{$all[$i]- ⊃
          >catalog_number}</td>\n";
     echo "<td>{$all[$i]->name}</td>\n";
     echo "<td>{$all[$i]->description}</td>\n";
     echo "<td>\${$all[$i]->price} /lb</td>\n";
     echo "<td align='center'><img src='images/{$all[$i]- ⊃
          >pix}'></td>\n";
     echo "<td style='text-align: center'><input ⊃
          type='text'
          name='item{$all[$i]->catalog_number}'
          value='0' size='4'></td>\n";           #40
     echo "</tr>";
```

As you can see, the variables are changed from arrays (`$products[$i]['name']`) to objects (`$all[$i]->name'`).

Writing the code for the shopping cart Web page

The shopping cart page displays the items currently stored in the shopping cart. The customer can change the quantity ordered. The customer can return to the catalog to add more items or can submit the order.

In this chapter, the shopping cart is not implemented the same way in the procedural code and the object-oriented code. To show both methods, I implemented the shopping cart by storing the items in the MySQL table in the procedural code, but stored the items in a `SESSION` variable in the object-oriented code. As a result, the code that displays the Web pages is slightly different. The following sections show the code for both methods.

Writing the shopping cart Web page files: The procedural method

The code that creates the shopping cart page is in two separate files, as follows:

- `table_page.inc`: Contains the code that defines the look and feel of the Web page. It produces a page that lists the products in a table. Another file must be used in conjunction with this file to create the page. The other file contains the specific information for the page.

- `fields_cart.inc`: Contains the specific information for the shopping cart Web page. When used with `table_page.inc`, it displays the items stored in the shopping cart.

Writing fields_cart.inc

Listing 6-3 shows the file that defines the variables for the shopping cart Web page.

LISTING 6-3: THE FILE THAT CONTAINS THE VARIABLES FOR THE SHOPPING CART

```php
<?php
 /* File:    fields_cart.inc
  * Desc:    Provides the information needed to display the
  *          cart.
  */
$page = array("title"  => "The Food Shop Shopping Cart",
              "top"     => "The Food Shop",
              "top2"    => "Shopping Cart",
              "bottom" => "Send questions or problems to
                           admin@xFoodShop.com"
             );
$table_headers = array( "Item","Cat No","Food",
                        "Amount","Price","Total");
$order_number = $_SESSION['order_number'];                    #14
$table_name = $order_number;
$cxn = connect_to_db("Vars.inc");                             #16
$sql_1 = "SELECT * FROM order_item
          WHERE order_number='$order_number'";
$result = mysqli_query($cxn,$sql_1)
    or die("sql_1: ".mysqli_error($cxn));
$n_row = mysqli_num_rows($result);                           #21
if($n_row < 1)                                               #22
{
    echo "Shopping Cart is currently empty<br>\n
        <a href='ShopCatalog.php'>Continue Shopping</a>\n";
    exit();
}
$n=1;                                                        #28
while($row = mysqli_fetch_assoc($result))                    #29
{
    foreach($row as $field => $value)
    {
       if($field != "order_number")
       {
          $items[$n][$field]=$value;
          if($field == "catalog_number")
          {
             $sql_2 = "SELECT name,type FROM food WHERE
                    catalog_number = '$row[catalog_number]'";
             $result2 = mysqli_query($cxn,$sql_2)
                 or die("sql_2: ".mysqli_error($cxn));
```

```
                  $row = mysqli_fetch_row($result2);
                  $items[$n]["name"]=$row[0]." ".$row[1];
              }
          }
      }
      $n++;
  }
  ?>
```

The line numbers called out in Listing 6-2 correspond to the numbered explanations in the following bullets:

#14   Retrieves the order number from a session variable. The order number was stored in the session variable when the order was stored in the database, when the user clicked the Add Items to Shopping Cart button. The order number identifies this order in the database.

#16   Lines 16 to 20 retrieve all the items from the `order_item` table in the database. (In other words, these lines retrieve all the items currently stored in the shopping cart.)

#21   Sets `$n_rows` to the number of items found in the database for this order.

#22   Starts an `if` block that displays a message and a link when there are no items in the database for the specified order number.

#28   Sets a counter for the number of items.

#29   Starts a `while` loop that creates an array named `$items` that contains all the information about the items. The food name is retrieved from the catalog and added to the array.

Writing table_page.inc

Listing 6-4 shows the file that defines the look and feel of the shopping cart Web page.

LISTING 6-4: THE FILE THAT DISPLAYS THE SHOPPING CART

```
<?php
 /*File:    table_page.inc
  *Desc:    Defines an HTML page that displays items in a
  *         table of items with prices. A column named
  *         quantity and a column named price are multiplied
  *         together to get the item total price. The item
  *         totals are summed.
  */
```

Continued

LISTING 6-4: *(Continued)*

```php
echo "<html
      <head><title>{$page['title']}</title></head>\n
      <body>\n";
echo "<h1 style='text-align: center'>{$page['top']}</h1>\n";
echo "<h2 style='text-align: center'>{$page['top2']}</h2>\n";
echo "<p style='font-weight: bold'>
                Order Number: $table_name<hr>\n";
echo "<table border = '0' style='width: 100%'>\n";
echo "<form action='$_SERVER[PHP_SELF]' method='POST'>";
echo "<tr>";
foreach($table_headers as $header)
{
   echo "<th>$header</th>\n";
}
echo "</tr>";
echo "<tr><td colspan='6'><hr></td></tr>\n";
for($i=1;$i<=sizeof($items);$i++)                          #25
{
   echo "<tr>";
   echo "<td style='width: 10%'>
                   {$items[$i]['item_number']}\n";
   echo "<td style='width: 10%'>
                   {$items[$i]['catalog_number']}\n";
   echo "<td >{$items[$i]['name']}\n";
   echo "<td style='text-align: center; width: 20%'>
            <input type='text' name='quantity[]'
                   value='{$items[$i]['quantity']}'
                   size='4'> lbs</td>\n";
   $f_price = number_format($items[$i]['price'],2);
   echo "<td style='text-align: right; width: 17%'>$
                   $f_price per lb.</td>\n";
   $total = $items[$i]['quantity']*$items[$i]['price'];    #40
   $f_total = number_format($total,2);
   echo "<td style='text-align: right'>
                   $$f_total</td></tr>\n";
   @$order_total = $order_total + $total;                  #44
}
$f_order_total = number_format($order_total,2);
?>                                                          #47
<tr><td colspan='5' style='text-align: right;
        font-weight: bold'>Total</td>
    <td style='text-align: right; line-height: 200%'> $
        <?php echo $f_order_total ?></td></tr>
<tr><td colspan='2' style='text-align: left'>
       <input type='submit' name='Cart'
              value='Continue Shopping'></td>
<td colspan='2' style='text-align: center'>
       <input type='submit' name='Cart'
              value='Submit Order'></td>
<td colspan='2' style='text-align: right'>
       <input type='submit' name='Cart'
              value='Update Cart'></td>
</tr></table></form></body></html>
```

The numbered items in the following list refer to the line numbers in Listing 6-4:

#25 Starts a `for` loop that loops through the `$items` array, displaying each row in the shopping cart Web page. The loop ends on line 45.

> **#27** Lines 27 to 39 display each item in the row from the current `$item` element. The price is formatted as a dollar amount.

> **#40** Lines 40 to 43 display the total price. Line 40 computes the total cost, by computing price × quantity. Line 41 formats the total cost as a dollar amount. Line 42 to 43 display the line in the shopping cart Web page.

> **#44** Sums the item total to accumulate a total for the cart.

#48 Lines 48 to the end are HTML code that display the shopping cart total and the submit buttons.

Writing the shopping cart Web page files: The object-oriented method

The code that creates the shopping cart page is in two separate files, as follows:

✔ `table_page-oo.inc`: Contains the code that defines the look and feel of the Web page. It produces a page that lists the products in a table. Another file must be used in conjunction with this file to create the page. The other file contains the specific information for the page.

✔ `fields_cart-oo.inc`: Contains the specific information for the shopping cart Web page. When used with `table_page-oo.inc`, it displays the items stored in the shopping cart.

Writing fields_cart-oo.inc

Listing 6-5 shows the file that defines the variables for the shopping cart Web page.

LISTING 6-5: THE FILE THAT CONTAINS THE VARIABLES FOR THE SHOPPING CART

```php
<?php
  /* File:    fields_cart-oo.inc
   * Desc:    Builds the arrays needed to display the shopping
   *          cart.
   */
  $page = array("title"  => "Shopping Cart",
                "top"    => "The Food Shop",
                "top2"   => "Shopping Cart",
                "bottom" => "Send questions or problems
                             to admin@xFoodShop.com"
               );
  $table_headers = array( "Item","Cat No","Food",
                          "Amount","Price","Total");
?>
```

Writing table-page-oo.inc

Listing 6-6 shows the file that defines the variables for the shopping cart Web page.

LISTING 6-6: THE FILE THAT DISPLAYS THE SHOPPING CART

```php
<?php
 /*File:    table_page-oo.inc
  *Desc:    Defines an HTML page that displays items in a
  *         table of items with prices. A column named
  *         quantity and a column named price are multiplied
  *         together to get the item total price. The item
  *         totals are summed.
  */
echo "<html>
     <head><title>{$page['title']}</title></head>\n
     <body>\n";
echo "<h1 style='text-align: center'>{$page['top']}</h1>\n";
echo "<h2 style='text-align: center'>{$page['top2']}</h2>\n";
echo "<p style='font-weight: bold'>$this->message<hr>\n";
echo "<table border = '0' style='width: 100%'\n";
echo "<form action='$_SERVER[PHP_SELF]' method='POST'>";
if(sizeof($this->items) > 0)                                  #17
{
  echo "<tr>";
  foreach($table_headers as $header)
  {
     echo "<th>$header</th>\n";
  }
  echo "</tr>";
  echo "<tr><td colspan='6'><hr></td></tr>\n";
  for($i=0;$i<sizeof($this->items);$i++)                      #26
  {
    echo "<tr>";
    echo "<td width='5%'>".($i+1)."</td>\n";
    $cat = new catalog("Vars.inc");                           #30
    $cat->selectCatalog("OnlineOrders");
    $cat_no = $this->items[$i]->getCatalogNumber();
    $food_name = $cat->getName($cat_no);
    echo "<td width='5%'>$cat_no</td>\n";                     #34
    echo "<td>".$food_name."</td>\n";
    echo "<td width='20%' style='text-align: center'>
         <input size='4' type='text' name='item$cat_no'
           value='".$this->items[$i]->getQuantity().
                "'> lbs</td>\n";
    echo "<td width='10%' style='text-align: right'> $".
           number_format($this->items[$i]->getPrice(),2).
         " per lb</td>\n";
    $total = $this->items[$i]->getQuantity() *
             $this->items[$i]->getPrice();                    #44
    echo "<td style='text-align: right; width: 7%'> $".
           number_format($total,2)."</td>\n";
    @$order_total = $order_total + $total;
```

```
}                                                      #48
$f_order_total = number_format($order_total,2);
echo "<tr><td colspan='5'
        style='text-align: right;
        font-weight: bold'>Total</td>
          <td style='text-align: right;
            line-height: 200%'>$$f_order_total</td></tr>\n";
echo "<tr><td colspan='2' style='text-align: left'>
          <input type='submit'
                value='Continue Shopping'></td>\n";
echo "    <td colspan='2' style='text-align: center'>
          <input type='submit' name='Ship'
                value='Submit Order'></td>\n";
echo "    <td colspan='2' style='text-align: right'>
          <input type='submit' name='Cart'
                value='Update Cart'></td>\n";
echo "</tr>\n";
}
else                                                   #66
{
  echo "<hr>";
  echo "<tr><td colspan='5' style='text-align: left'>
          <input type='submit'
                value='Continue Shopping'></td>\n";
}
?>
</table></form>
```

The following numbers refer to the line numbers in Listing 6-5:

#17 Begins an `if` block that executes if there are one or more items in the shopping cart. The variable `$items` is an array of item objects, stored in the `ShoppingCart` class, which I discuss later in this chapter. The `ShoppingCart` class is created in the orders application script. The `if` block displays the shopping cart Web page. The `if` block ends on line 65.

#26 Begins a `for` loop that loops through the `$items` array and displays the information for each item on the Web page. The `for` loop ends on line 48.

#30 Lines 30 to 33 get some information using a `catalog` object. For instance, line 33 gets the name of the item by using the `getName` method in the `Catalog` class. Lines 34 to 35 display the information obtained.

#44 Lines 43 to 44 accumulate the total for the shopping cart.

#49 Lines 49 through the end display the shopping cart total and the shopping cart submit buttons.

#66 Begins an `else` block that executes when no items are stored in the shopping cart. The block displays a button that returns the customer to the catalog category page.

Writing the code for the shipping information form

The shipping information form collects the information needed to ship the product. It collects name, address, phone number, and other information. The code that displays the form is in two separate files, as follows:

- `single_form.inc`: Contains the code that defines the look and feel of the Web form. You must use another file in conjunction with this file to create the Web form. The other file contains the specific information such as the field names.

- `fields_ship_info.inc`: Contains the arrays and variables that are used by `single_form.inc` to display the shipping information Web form.

Writing fields_ship_info.inc

The `fields_ship_info.inc` file provides the information needed to display the shipping information Web form. The file shown in Listing 6-7 defines six arrays that contain the specific information displayed in the shipping information form. The arrays are

- `$page`: Contains elements that are displayed at the top and the bottom of the entire page.

- `$ship_info`: Contains elements that provide the field names and labels for the shipping information form. For instance, one field name is `email`. The associated label that displays by the field in the form is `Email Address`.

- `$cc_types`: Contains elements that provide the types of credit cards the form accepts. The credit card types are displayed in a drop-down list in the form.

- `$length`: Contains the lengths that are allowed for each field in the form.

- `$elements`: Contains elements that are displayed at the top and bottom of the form. This array contains only text to display on the submit button.

- `$months`: Contains the months of the year. The months are displayed in a drop-down list for the credit card expiration date.

In addition, the file sets a variable that contains the current date and several variables that contains the shipping information currently stored in the database, which is displayed in the fields of the form.

The file used with the procedural script is slightly different from the file used with the object-oriented script. Listing 6-7 shows the file to be used with in the procedural application. After the listing, you find the changes required to use this file in the object-oriented script.

LISTING 6-7: THE FILE THAT CONTAINS THE VARIABLES FOR THE SHIPPING INFORMATION FORM

```php
<?php
 /* File: fields_ship_info.inc
  * Desc: Contains arrays with the field names and form
  *       elements for the login Web page.
  */
$page = array( "title"   => "Food Shop Order: Shipping
                             Information",
               "top"     => "Food Shop Order: Shipping
                             Information",
               "top2"    => "Please fill in the
                             information below",
               "bottom"  => "Send questions and comments
                             to admin@xFoodShop.com",
             );
$ship_info =   array("email"         => "Email Address",
                     "ship_name"     => "Name",
                     "ship_street"   => "Street",
                     "ship_city"     => "City",
                     "ship_state"    => "State",
                     "ship_zip"      => "Zip",
                     "phone"         => "Phone",
                     "cc_type"       => "Credit Card Type",
                     "cc_number"     => "Credit Card Number",
                     "cc_exp"        => "Expiration Date"
                   );
$cc_types =    array("visa"          => "Visa",
                     "mc"            => "Master Card",
                     "amex"          => "American Express"
                   );
$length    =   array("email"         => "55",
                     "ship_name"     => "40",
                     "ship_street"   => "55",
                     "ship_city"     => "40",
                     "ship_zip"      => "10",
                     "phone"         => "15",
                     "cc_number"     => "20"
                   );
$elements =    array( "submit"       => "Continue");
$months   =    array (1=> "January", "February", "March",
                      "April", "May", "June", "July",
                      "August", "September",
```

Continued

LISTING 6-7: *(Continued)*

```
                              "October", "November", "December"
                        );
$today = time("Y-m-d");
if(!isset($_POST))
{
  $connect = connect_to_db("Vars.inc");                          #47
  $sql = "SELECT
          ship_name,ship_street,ship_city,ship_state,ship_zip,
          phone,email FROM Customer_Order WHERE
          order_number = '{$_SESSION['order_number']}'";
  $result = mysqli_query($connect,$sql)
          or die("Error: ".mysqli_error($connect));
  $n = mysqli_num_rows($result);                                 #54
  if($n > 0)                                                     #55
  {
    $row = mysqli_fetch_assoc($result);
    extract($row);
  }
}
?>
```

The numbers in the following explanation refer to the line numbers in Listing 6-7:

#45 Starts an if block that executes if no POST data exists. No post data exists when the user clicks the Edit Shipping Information button on the summary page. This block gets the shipping information from the database.

#47 Lines 47 to 53 create and execute an SQL query that selects the shipping information from the database. Connect_to_db is a function used frequently throughout this book and described in Chapter 3. The function is stored in a file named functions_ main.inc that is included in the three application scripts, described in the section "Building the Shopping Cart Application: The Procedural Approach."

#54 Tests whether any shipping information was found.

#55 Starts an if block that executes if shipping information was found. If so, the information is extracted into variables with the field names.

Changing fields_ship_info.inc for use in the object-oriented application

The first 44 lines of the file are the same for the procedural and object-oriented versions.

The variables created in the remaining lines of the file are created in a class in the object-oriented application, rather than in this file. Therefore, to use the file in the object-oriented application, you need to remove the remaining lines (45 to 57). Name the file with lines 45 to 57 removed `fields_ship_info-oo.inc`.

Writing single_form.inc

The `fields_ship_info.inc` or `fields_ship_info-oo.inc` file provides the information needed to display the shipping information Web form. The `single_form.inc` file defines the look and feel of the shipping form. Listing 6-8 shows the file. You use the same file for the procedural and object-oriented scripts.

LISTING 6-8: THE FILE THAT DEFINES THE SHIPPING INFORMATION FORM

```php
<?php
 /* File: single_form.inc
  * Desc: Contains the code for a Web page that displays
  *       an HTML form.
  */
include("functions.inc");
echo "<head><title> {$page['title']} </title></head>\n
     <h2 align='center'>{$page['top']} </h2>\n
     <p style='font-style: italic;
             font-weight: bold'>{$page['top2']}\n
     <form action='{$_SERVER['PHP_SELF']}' method='POST'>
     <table border='0' cellpadding='5' cellspacing='0'>\n";
if(isset($GLOBALS['message']))                                    #13
{
   echo "<tr>
           <td colspan='2'
               style=\"font-weight: bold; font-style: italic;
               font-size: 90%; color: red\">
               {$GLOBALS['message']}<p></td></tr>";
}
foreach($ship_info as $field => $value)                           #21
{
  if($field == "ship_state")                                      #23
  {
    echo "<tr><td style=\"text-align: right;
                 font-weight: bold\">State</td>
             <td><select name='ship_state'>";
    $stateName=getStateName();                                    #28
    $stateCode=getStateCode();
    for ($n=1;$n<=50;$n++)
```

Continued

LISTING 6-8: *(Continued)*

```php
        {
            $state=$stateName[$n];
            $scode=$stateCode[$n];
            echo "<option value='$scode'";
            if($scode == @$_POST['state'] ||
                $scode == @$ship_state)
                    echo " selected";
            echo ">$state\n";
        }
        echo "</select>";
    }
    elseif($field == "cc_type")                              #42
    {
        echo "<tr><td style=\"text-align: right;
                    font-weight: bold\">Credit Card Type</td>
                <td><select name='cc_type'>";
        foreach($cc_types as $field => $value)
        {
            echo "<option value='$field'";
            echo ">$value\n";
        }
        echo "</select>";
    }
    elseif($field == "cc_exp")                               #54
    {
        echo "<tr><td style=\"text-align: right;
                    font-weight: bold\">Expiration Date</td>
                <td><select name='cc_exp_mo'>";
                    for($n=1;$n<=12;$n++)
                    {
                        echo "<option
                                value='$n'>{$months[$n]}\n";
                    }
                    echo "</select>\n";
                    echo "<select name='cc_exp_da'>";
                    for($n=1;$n<=31;$n++)
                    {
                        echo " <option value='$n'>$n\n";
                    }
                    echo "</select>\n";
                    echo "<select name='cc_exp_yr'>";
                    $start_yr = date("Y",$today);
                    for($n=$start_yr;$n<=$start_yr+5;$n++)
                    {
                        echo " <option value='$n'>$n\n";
                    }
                    echo "</select>\n";
    }
    else                                                     #79
    {
        echo "<tr><td style=\"text-align: right;
```

```
                        font-weight: bold\">$value</td>
                <td><input type='text' name='$field'
                        value='".@$$field."'
                        size='{$length[$field]}'
                        maxsize='{$length[$field]}'>
                </td></tr>";
    }
}                                                                    #89
?>
<tr><td colspan="2" style="text-align: center">
        <p style="margin-top: .05in">
            <input type="submit" name="Summary"
                value="<?php echo $elements['submit']?>">
</td></tr></table></form></body></html>
```

The following numbers in the explanation refer to the line numbers in Listing 6-8:

#13 Starts an `if` block that checks whether a message is stored in the `$GLOBALS` array. If so, the block displays the message at the beginning of the form. The application script stores the message when an error condition is encountered.

#21 Begins a `foreach` loop that loops through the `$ship_info` array. The ship_info array is built in `fields_ship_info.inc`.

> **#23** Starts an `if` block that executes when the field name is `ship_state`. Lines 23 to 39 display a drop-down list containing the states. Lines 28 to 29 call functions stored in the file `functions.inc`, which in included in line 6.

> **#42** Starts an `elseif` block that executes when the field name is `cc_type`. Lines 41 to 52 create a drop-down list containing the types of credit cards the customer can select.

> **#54** Starts an `elseif` block that executes when the field name is `cc_exp`. (That field contains the credit card expiration date.) Lines 53 through 77 create a drop-down list of dates the user can select.

> **#79** Starts an `else` block that executes for any other fields. Text input lines are displayed in the form for all remaining fields.

#91 The first line of an HTML section that displays the submit button and the ending tags for the form.

Writing the code for the summary page

The summary Web page shows the final order to the customer. The customer can review the selected items and shipping information. The customer can submit the displayed order or change it. The code that displays the summary page is in two separate files, as follows:

- summary_form.inc: Contains the code that defines the look and feel of the summary page. Another file must be used in conjunction with this file to provide the specific information.

- fields_summary.inc: Contains the arrays and variables that are used by summary_form.inc to display the summary page.

Writing fields_summary.inc

The fields_summary.inc file provides the information needed to display the summary page. The file shown in Listing 6-9 defines two arrays that contain the specific information displayed in the summary page. The arrays are

- $page: Contains elements that are displayed at the top and the bottom of the entire page.

- $table_headers: Contains the column heads for the table that displays the order summary.

In addition, the file retrieves the order number from the session and stores it in $order_number, sets a variable with the shipping rate for the order, and sets a name for the table.

The file used with the procedural script is slightly different from the file used with the object-oriented script. Listing 6-9 shows the file to be used in the procedural application. After the listing, you find the changes required to use this file with the object-oriented script.

LISTING 6-9: THE FILE THAT PROVIDES THE INFORMATION FOR THE SUMMARY PAGE

```php
<?php
 /* File:   fields_summary.inc
  * Desc:   Builds the arrays needed to display a summary
  *         of the order.
  */
$page = array("title"  => "The Food Shop Order Summary",
              "top"    => "The Food Shop Order Summary",
              "top2"   => "Order Summary",
              "table"  => "Order Number: ",
              "bottom" => "Send questions or problems
                          to admin@xFoodShop.com"
             );
$table_headers = array( "Item","Cat No","Food",
                        "Amount","Price","Total");
$order_number = $_SESSION['order_number'];                    #15
$shipping_rate = .25;                                         #16
$table_name = $order_number;                                  #17
```

```
$cxn = connect_to_db("Vars.inc");                          #18
$sql_ord = "SELECT * FROM order_item
                    WHERE order_number='$order_number'";
$result = mysqli_query($cxn,$sql_ord)
    or die("sql_ord: ".mysqli_error($cxn));
$n_row = mysqli_num_rows($result);
if($n_row < 1)                                             #24
{
    echo "Shopping Cart is currently empty<br>\n
            <a href='ShopCatalog.php'>Continue Shopping</a>\n";
    exit();
}
$n=1;                                                      #30
while($row = mysqli_fetch_assoc($result))
{
    foreach($row as $field => $value)
    {
        if($field != "order_number")
        {
            $items[$n][$field]=$value;
            if($field == "catalog_number")
            {
              $sql_name = "SELECT name,type FROM food WHERE
                    catalog_number = '$row[catalog_number]'";
              $result2 = mysqli_query($cxn,$sql_name)
                  or die("sql_name: ".mysqli_error($cxn));
              $row = mysqli_fetch_row($result2);
              $items[$n]["name"]=$row[0]." ".$row[1];
            }
        }
    }
    $n++;
}
?>
```

The following numbers in the explanation refer to the line numbers in
Listing 6-9:

#15 Retrieves the order number from the session and stores it in
$order_number.

#16 Stores the shipping rate in a variable.

#17 Stores a table name that is displayed in the summary page.

#18 Lines 18 to the end create an array of order information that is displayed in the summary form. Lines 18 to 22 connect to the order
database and select all the items currently in the order. Line 23 sets
$n_row to the number of items returned.

#24 Starts an `if` block that executes if no items were found. The block displays a message and provides a link that returns the user to the catalog.

#30 Lines 30 to 50 create the `$items` array that contains all the item information.

Changing fields_summary.inc for use in the object-oriented application

The first 17 lines of the file are the same for the procedural and object-oriented versions.

The variables created in the remaining lines of the file are created in a class in the object-oriented application, rather than in this file. Therefore, to use the file in the object-oriented application, you need to remove the remaining lines (18 to 50). Name the file `fields_summary-oo.inc` after you remove lines 18 to 50.

Writing summary_page.inc

The `summary_page.inc` file displays the summary Web page (see Listing 6-10). You use the same file with the procedural and object-oriented scripts.

LISTING 6-10: THE FILE THAT DEFINES THE SUMMARY PAGE

```php
<?php
 /*File:    summary_page.inc
  *Desc:    Defines an HTML page that displays a summary
  *         of the order.
  */
echo "<html>
     <head><title>{$page['title']}</title></head>\n
     <body>\n";
echo "<h2 style='text-align: center'>{$page['top']}</h2>\n";
echo "<p style='position: absolute; margin-top: .25in;
               font-weight: bold'>Ship to:</p>";                    #11
echo "<p style='position: absolute; margin-top: .25in;
               margin-left: .75in'>$ship_name<br>";
echo "$ship_street<br>
     $ship_city, $ship_state $ship_zip<br>
     $phone<br>
     $email<br>";                                                  #17
echo "<div style='margin-top: 1.5in'>";
echo "<p style='font-weight: bold'>
               <b>{$page['table']}</b> $table_name\n";
echo "<table border = '0' style='width: 100%'>\n";
echo "<form action='$_SERVER[PHP_SELF]' method='POST'>";
echo "<tr>";
foreach($table_headers as $header)
{
```

```
        echo "<th>$header</th>\n";
}
echo "</tr>";
for($i=1;$i <=sizeof($items);$i++)                          #29
{
    echo "<tr>";
    echo "<td width='10%'>$i</td>";
    echo "<td width='10%'>
            {$items[$i]['catalog_number']}</td>";
    echo "<td>{$items[$i]['name']}</td>";
    echo "<td>{$items[$i]['quantity']}</td>";
    $f_price = number_format($items[$i]['price'],2);
    echo "<td style='text-align: right; width: 17%'>
            $$f_price per lb.</td>\n";
    $total = $items[$i]['quantity'] * $items[$i]['price'];
    $f_total = number_format($total,2);
    echo "<td style='text-align: right'>$$f_total</td>\n";
    echo "</tr>";
    @$order_subtotal = $order_subtotal + $total;
}
$f_order_subtotal = number_format($order_subtotal,2);       #46
if(substr($ship_zip,0,5) > 75000
            && substr($ship_zip,0,5) < 80000)               #48
{
    $taxrate = .0700;
}
else
{
    $taxrate = 0.0;
}                                                           #55
$sales_tax = $order_subtotal * $taxrate;                    #56
$f_sales_tax = number_format($sales_tax,2);
$shipping = $shipping_rate * sizeof($items);                #58
$f_shipping = number_format($shipping,2);
$order_total = $order_subtotal+$sales_tax+$shipping;        #60
$f_order_total = number_format($order_total,2);             #61
echo "<tr><td colspan='5' style='text-align: right;
                font-weight: bold'>Subtotal</td>
        <td style='text-align: right; line-height: 200%'>
            $$f_order_subtotal</td></tr>\n";
echo "<tr><td colspan='5'
        style='text-align: right; font-weight: bold'>
            Sales Tax</td>
        <td style='text-align: right; line-height: 50%'>
            $$f_sales_tax</td></tr>\n";
echo "<tr><td colspan='5' style='text-align: right;
                font-weight: bold'>Shipping</td>
        <td style='text-align: right; line-height: 50%'>
            $$f_shipping</td></tr>\n";
echo "<tr><td colspan='5'
        style='text-align: right; font-weight: bold'>
            Total</td>
        <td style='text-align: right; line-height: 300%'>
```

Continued

LISTING 6-10: *(Continued)*

```
                $$f_order_total</td></tr>\n";
echo "<tr><td colspan='2' style='text-align: left'>
                <input type='submit'
                        value='Continue Shopping'></td>\n";
echo "      <td colspan='1' style='text-align: center'>
                <input type='submit' name='Ship'
                        value='Edit Shipping Information'></td>\n";
echo "      <td colspan='1' style='text-align: right'>
                <input type='submit' name='Final'
                        value='Cancel Order'></td>\n";
echo "      <td colspan='2' style='text-align: right'>
                <input type='submit' name='Final'
                        value='Submit Order'></td>\n";
echo "</tr></table></form>\n";
?>
```

The numbers in the following explanation refer to the line numbers in Listing 6-10:

#10 Lines 10 to 17 display the shipping information at the top of the summary page.

#18 Lines 18 to 28 display the top of the form and the table column names.

#29 Lines 29 to 45 display the order items on the summary page.

#47 Begins an if/else statement that sets the tax rate. Sales tax is charged for shipping addresses in Texas only. The tax rate is set by zip code. For orders with a Texas zip code, the tax rate is 0.07. Otherwise, the tax rate is 0 (zero).

#55 Sales tax is computed by multiplying the total cost of the items by the tax rate.

#58 The shipping cost is set by multiplying the number of items times the shipping rate per item.

#60 The order total is computed by summing the item total, the sales tax, and the shipping cost.

#62 The remaining lines display the item total, shipping cost, sales tax, order total, and then display the four submit buttons.

Building the Shopping Cart Application: The Procedural Approach

The shopping cart application has three application scripts, as follows:

- ✔ `ShopCatalog.php`: Manages and displays the catalog Web pages. When the customer clicks the Add Items to Shopping Cart button, the item information is stored in the database and the shopping cart is displayed.

- ✔ `ShoppingCart.php`: Manages and displays the shopping cart. Updates the shopping cart when the customer clicks the Update Cart button. When the customer clicks the Submit Order button, the application script displays the shipping information form.

- ✔ `ProcessOrder.php`: Processes the shipping information form, stores order information in the database, and displays the summary form. It processes the credit card and order information when the customer clicks the Submit Order button.

Writing ShopCatalog.php

The first script for the shopping cart application displays the catalog and stores the customer selections in the Shopping Cart. `ShopCatalog.php` is organized in nested `if` statements, based on which submit button the customer clicked, if any. The following is an overview of the structure of the script:

```
if (button named Products was clicked)

   if (button = "Add Items to Shopping Cart")
      1. Determine the order number
            If current order exists, get the number. If not,
            create a new order in the database and set the
            new order number to be the current order number.
      2. Store selected items in the database.
      3. Pass control to ShoppingCart.php, which displays
         the shopping cart.
   else (if button is not Add Items to Shopping Cart)
      Display catalog product page

else (button named Products was not clicked)
   display catalog categories page
```

This script runs when any of the following events happens:

- ✔ **The customer enters the URL for `ShopCatalog.php` in the browser.**
  Because this is the first script for the application, it runs correctly when started in the browser. In this case, no button is clicked, so the script drops to the final `else` statement and displays the catalog index page.

✔ **The customer clicks the Add Items to Shopping Cart button.** This button is named Products, so the script enters the first if block. The second if checks the value of the button. The button matches so the script enters the second if block, where it adds the items to an existing order or creates a new order if no current order exists. It then starts the second script, ShoppingCart.php, which displays the shopping cart.

✔ **The customer clicks Next or Previous.** These buttons are named Products, so the script enters the first if block. However, the button value doesn't match the inner if statement, so the script enters the inner else block where it displays the next or previous items in the catalog product page.

✔ **The customer clicks the Select Another Category button.** This button has no name, so the script drops to the final else statement and displays the catalog index page.

Listing 6-11 shows the code for ShopCatalog.php — the first application script in the online orders application.

LISTING 6-11: THE FIRST APPLICATION SCRIPT FOR SHOPPING CART

```php
<?php
 /* Program:  ShopCatalog.php
  * Desc:     Displays a catalog of products. Displays two
  *           different pages: an index page that shows
  *           categories and a product page that is displayed
  *           when the customer selects a category. This
  *           version is used with a shopping cart for
  *           purchasing items.
  */
$n_per_page = 2;

session_start();
include_once("functions_main.inc");
if(isset($_POST['Products']) &&
   isset($_POST['interest']))                               #15
{
  if($_POST['Products'] == "Add Items to Shopping Cart")
  {
    if(!isset($_SESSION['order_number']))                   #19
    {
      $connect = connect_to_db("Vars.inc");
      $today = date("Y-m-d");
      $sql_order = "INSERT INTO Customer_Order (order_date)
                    VALUES ('$today')";
      $result = mysqli_query($connect,$sql_order)
         or die("sql_order".mysqli_error($connect));
      $order_number = mysqli_insert_id($connect);
      $_SESSION['order_number'] = $order_number;
      $n_items = 0;
```

```
        }
        else                                                    #31
        {
            $order_number = $_SESSION['order_number'];
            $n_items = $_SESSION['n_items'];
        }
        foreach($_POST as $field => $value)                      #36
        {
            if(substr($field,0,4) == "item" && $value > 0)       #38
            {
                $n_items++;
                $catalog_number =
                        substr($field,4,strlen($field)-4);       #42
                $connect = connect_to_db("Vars.inc");
                $sql_price = "SELECT price FROM Food WHERE
                        catalog_number='$catalog_number'";
                $result = mysqli_query($connect,$sql_price)
                    or die("sql_price: ".mysqli_error($connect));
                $row = mysqli_fetch_assoc($result);              #49
                $sql_item = "INSERT INTO Order_Item
                        (order_number,item_number,catalog_number,
                        quantity,price) VALUES
                        ($order_number,$n_items,$catalog_number,
                        $value,{$row['price']})";
                $result = mysqli_query($connect,$sql_item)
                    or die("sql_item: ".mysqli_error($connect));
            }
        }
        $_SESSION['n_items'] = $n_items;                         #58
        header("Location: ShoppingCart.php");
        exit();
    }
    else                                                        #62
    {
        if(isset($_POST['n_end']))                              #64
        {
            if($_POST['Products'] == "Previous")                #66
            {
                $n_start = $_POST['n_end']-($n_per_page);
            }
            else                                                #70
            {
                $n_start = $_POST['n_end'] + 1;
            }
        }
        else                                                    #75
        {
            $n_start = 1;
        }
        $n_end = $n_start + $n_per_page -1;                     #79
        $connect = connect_to_db("Vars.inc");                  #80
        $query_food = "SELECT * FROM Food WHERE
                type='$_POST[interest]' ORDER BY name";
```

Continued

LISTING 6-11: *(Continued)*

```
    $result = mysqli_query($connect,$query_food)
        or die ("query_food: ".mysqli_error($connect));      #84
    $n=1;
    while($row = mysqli_fetch_assoc($result))                #86
    {
        foreach($row as $field => $value)                    #88
        {
            $products[$n][$field]=$value;
        }
        $n++;
    }
    $n_products = sizeof($products);                          #94
    if($n_end > $n_products)
    {
        $n_end = $n_products;
    }
      include("fields_products_page.inc");
      include("shopping_product_page.inc");
  }
}
else
{
    $connect = connect_to_db("Vars.inc");                    #105
    $sql_cat = "SELECT DISTINCT category,type FROM Food
                ORDER BY category,type";
    $result = mysqli_query($connect,$sql_cat)
        or die("sql_cat: ".mysqli_error($connect));
    while($row = mysqli_fetch_array($result))                #110
    {
        $food_categories[$row['category']][]=$row['type'];
    }
    include("fields_index_page.inc");
    include("catalog_index_page.inc");
}
?>
```

The following explains the line numbers that appear in Listing 6-11:

#10 Sets the number of items to be displayed on a page.

#12 Opens a session. The customer remains in a session throughout the online ordering process.

#14 Lines 14 to 15 start an `if` block that executes if the products button is found in the `$_POST` array and if the customer selected a category. The `if` block continues to line 102.

#17 Begins an `if` block that executes when the user clicks the Add Items to Shopping Cart button. The `if` block continues to line 61.

#19 Starts an `if/else` statement that sets the order number and the number of items in the cart. If no order number is found in the session, the if block inserts a new order into the database. The current date is inserted. MySQL inserts a sequential order number. Line 27 stores the order number for the new order in `$order_number`. Line 28 stores the new order number in the session. No items have yet been added to the order, so `$n_items` is set to 0 (zero). If an order number is found, the else block retrieves the order number and the number of items currently in the cart from the session.

#36 Starts a `foreach` loop that loops through the `$_POST` array. The loop ends on line 57.

#38 Begins an `if` block that executes for any fields in the array that contain the substring `"item"` in them and that have a value greater than 0. The value is the quantity the user entered. The field name contains the catalog number of the item. The `if` block enters the items into the `order_item` table. On line 37, the catalog number is extracted from the field name. The price is obtained from the catalog. The item information is inserted into the database. The `if` block ends on line 56.

#58 Stores the new number of items in the session.

#59 Runs the `ShoppingCart.php` script, which displays the shopping cart.

#62 Starts an `else` block that executes when the value of the Products button isn't Add Items to Shopping Cart. The value of the button is Previous or Next. The block sets the item numbers for the first and last items to be displayed and builds an array that contains the product information (`$products`). The products page is displayed.

#103 Starts an `else` block that executes when the Products button isn't clicked. The user clicks either no button or a button with a different name or no name. The catalog index page is displayed.

Writing ShoppingCart.php

The second script for the shopping cart application manages and displays the shopping cart. The user can change the quantity for the displayed items. If the quantity is changed to 0 (zero), the item is removed from the cart. The script is organized by a `switch` statement, executing code depending on the value of the button that the customer clicked. The following is an overview of the structure of the script:

```
if (no order number exists in session)
     Display message that cart is empty and a link that
```

returns the user to the catalog index page.

```
switch (value of button named Cart)
   case: Cart = "Continue Shopping"
      start ShopCatalog.php, which will display
         the first catalog index page.
   case: Cart = Update Cart
      1. Update quantities in the database.
      2. Delete any items with 0 quantity.
      3. Renumber the items with sequential numbers.
      4. Redisplay the shopping cart.
   case: Cart = Submit Order
      Run the script ProcessOrder.php, which displays the
      shipping information form
   default:
      display shopping cart
```

Listing 6-12 shows the code for ShoppingCart.php — the second application
script in the shopping cart application.

LISTING 6-12: THE SHOPPINGCART APPLICATION SCRIPT FOR SHOPPING CART

```php
<?php
 /* Program: ShoppingCart.php
  * Desc:    Manages and displays the Shopping Cart.
  */
session_start();                                              #5
include("functions_main.inc");
if(!isset($_SESSION['order_number'])
   or empty($_SESSION['order_number']))                       #8
{
   echo "Shopping Cart is currently empty<br>\n
         <a href='ShopCatalog.php'>Continue Shopping</a>\n";
   exit();
}
switch (@$_POST['Cart'])                                      #14
{
   case "Continue Shopping":                                  #16
      header("Location: ShopCatalog.php");
      break;
   case "Update Cart":                                        #19
      $connect = connect_to_db("Vars.inc");
      $order_number = $_SESSION['order_number'];
      $n = 1;
      /* Update quantities in database */                     #23
      foreach($_POST['quantity'] as $field => $value)
      {
         $sql_quant = "UPDATE Order_Item SET quantity='$value'
                       WHERE item_number= '$n'
                       AND order_number='$order_number'";
         $result = mysqli_query($connect,$sql_quant)
             or die("sql_quant: ".mysqli_error($connect));
         $n++;
```

```
                }
            /* Delete any items with zero quantity */              #33
       $sql_del = "DELETE FROM Order_Item
                   WHERE quantity= '0.00'
                   AND order_number='$order_number'";
       $result = mysqli_query($connect,$sql_del)
          or die("sql_del: ".mysqli_error($connect));
  /* Renumber items in database. First, put items in an
     array. Next, delete all items from the database. Then,
     re-insert items with new item numbers. */                    #41
       $sql_getnew = "SELECT * from Order_Item
                      WHERE order_number='$order_number'";
       $result = mysqli_query($connect,$sql_getnew)
          or die("sql_getnew: ".mysqli_error($connect));
       $n_rows = mysqli_num_rows($result);
       if($n_rows < 1)                                             #47
       {
          echo "Shopping Cart is currently empty<br>\n
          <a href='Catalog'>Continue Shopping</a>\n";
          exit();
       }
       while($row = mysqli_fetch_assoc($result))                  #53
       {
          $items_new[]=$row;
       }                                                          #56
       $sql_del2 = "DELETE FROM Order_Item
                    WHERE order_number='$order_number'";
       $result = mysqli_query($connect,$sql_del2)
          or die("sql_del2: ".mysqli_error($connect));
       for($i=0;$i<sizeof($items_new);$i++)                       #61
       {
          $sql_ord = "INSERT INTO Order_Item
                      (order_number,item_number,catalog_number,
                       quantity,price) VALUES
                      ($order_number,$i+1,
                         {$items_new[$i]['catalog_number']},
                         {$items_new[$i]['quantity']},
                         {$items_new[$i]['price']})";
          $result = mysqli_query($connect,$sql_ord)
             or die("sql_ord: ".mysqli_error($connect));
       }                                                          #72
       $_SESSION['n_items'] = $i;                                 #73
       include("fields_cart.inc");                                #74
       include("table_page.inc");
       break;
    case "Submit Order":                                          #77
       header("Location: ProcessOrder.php?from=cart");
       exit();
       break;
    default:                                                      #81
       include("fields_cart.inc");
       include("table_page.inc");
       break;
}
?>
```

In the following discussion, the numbers refer to line numbers in Listing 6-12:

#5 Starts a session, maintaining the order for the user.

#7 Begins an `if` block that executes when no current order exists, displaying a message and a link to the catalog index page.

#14 Starts a `switch` statement for the values of a button named Cart.

#16 Begins the `case` block that executes if the button is Continue Shopping. The block displays the catalog index page.

#19 Begins the `case` block that executes if the button is Update Cart.

> **#23** Starts a `foreach` loop that updates the quantities for each item in the database.
>
> **#33** Lines 33 to 38 delete all the items in the database with 0 quantity.
>
> **#42** Lines 42 to 46 select the remaining items from the database.
>
> **#47** Starts an `if` block that executes when no items were found in the database. The `if` block displays a message and a link to the catalog.
>
> **#53** Starts a `while` loop that creates a new array (`$items_new`) containing the remaining items retrieved from the database.
>
> **#57** Deletes all the items from the database for the current order.
>
> **#61** Begins a `for` loop that inserts all the items in the new array (`$items_new`), created on line 53, into the database with sequential item numbers. The loop ends on line 72.
>
> **#73** Stores the current number of items in the session.
>
> **#74** Lines 74 and 75 display the shopping cart.

#77 Begins the `case` block that executes when the button value is Submit Order. The block runs the third shopping cart application script: `ProcessOrder.php`.

#81 Begins the `default` case block. The block displays the shopping cart.

Writing ProcessOrder.php

The third application script for the shopping cart application processes the order when the customer submits it. The script collects the shipping information, verifies the information that the customer enters, and displays the summary form. When the customer clicks a button on the summary form, the script accepts and processes the order and displays a confirmation page. The script is organized by a series of `if/elseif` statements, executing code depending on the name and value of the button that the customer clicked. The following is an overview of the structure of the script:

```
if (no order number exists in session)
   Display message that cart is empty and a link that
   returns the user to the catalog index page.

if (script started from shopping cart)
  Display shipping information form
elseif (button name = "Summary")
  1. Check form for blank fields. If blanks are found,
     redisplay the form.
  2. Check format of form fields. If invalid data is found,
     redisplay the form.
  3. Insert shipping information into the order database.
  4. Display the summary form.
elseif (button name = "Ship")
     1. Update quantities in the database
     2. Delete any items with 0 quantity.
     3. Renumber the items with sequential numbers
     4. Redisplay the shopping cart
elseif (Button name = "Final")
  switch (Button value)
     case: "Continue Shopping"
        Run ShopCatalog.php
     case: Cancel Order
        Display cancellation Web page
        Destroy session
     case: Submit Order
        Set order status to submitted
        Process credit information
        Send order to be filled
        Display order confirmation Web page
```

Listing 6-13 shows the code for `ProcessOrder.php` — the third application script in the online orders application.

LISTING 6-13: THE PROCESSORDER APPLICATION SCRIPT FOR SHOPPING CART

```php
<?php
 /* Program name:  ProcessOrder.php
  * Description:   Processes order when it's been submitted.
  */
 session_start();                                          #5
 include("functions_main.inc");
 if(!isset($_SESSION['order_number']))                     #7
 {
    echo "No order number found<br>\n";
    header("Location: ShopCatalog.php");
    exit();
 }
```

Continued

LISTING 6-13: *(Continued)*

```
if(@$_GET['from'] == "cart")                                    #13
{
    include("fields_ship_info.inc");
    include("single_form.inc");
    exit();
}
elseif(isset($_POST['Summary']))                                #19
{
    foreach($_POST as $field => $value)                         #21
    {
        if ($value == "")
        {
            $blanks[] = $field;
        }
    }
    if(isset($blanks))
    {
        $message = "The following fields are blank.
                    Please enter the required information:  ";
        foreach($blanks as $value)
        {
            $message .="$value, ";
        }
        extract($_POST);
        include("fields_ship_info.inc");
        include("single_form.inc");
        exit();
    }
    foreach($_POST as $field => $value)                         #41
    {
      if($field != "Summary")
      {
        if(eregi("name",$field))
        {
          if (!ereg("^[A-Za-z' -]{1,50}$",$value))
          {
             $errors[] = "$value is not a valid name.";
          }
        }
        if(eregi("street",$field)or eregi("addr",$field) or
           eregi("city",$field))
        {
          if(!ereg("^[A-Za-z0-9.,' -]{1,50}$",$value))
          {
             $errors[] = "$value is not a valid address
                          or city.";
          }
        }
        if(eregi("state",$field))
        {
          if(!ereg("[A-Za-z]",$value))
          {
             $errors[] = "$value is not a valid state.";
```

```
         }
      }
      if(eregi("email",$field))
      {
         if(!ereg("^.+@.+\\..+$",$value))
         {
            $errors[]="$value is not a valid email address.";
         }
      }
      if(eregi("zip",$field))
      {
         if(!ereg("^[0-9]{5,5}(\-[0-9]{4,4})?$",$value))
         {
            $errors[] = "$value is not a valid zipcode.";
         }
      }
      if(eregi("phone",$field))
      {
         if(!ereg("^[0-9](xX -]{7,20}$",$value))
         {
            $errors[]="$value is not a valid phone number. ";
         }
      }
      if(eregi("cc_number",$field))
      {
         $value = trim($value);
         $value = ereg_replace(' ','',$value);
         $value = ereg_replace('-','',$value);
         $_POST['cc_number'] = $value;
         if($_POST['cc_type'] == "visa")
         {
            if(!ereg("^[4]{1,1}[0-9]{12,15}$",$value))
            {
               $errors[]="$value is not a valid Visa number. ";
            }
         }
         elseif($_POST['cc_type'] == "mc")
         {
            if(!ereg("^[5]{1,1}[0-9]{15,15}$",$value))
            {
               $errors[] = "$value is not a valid
                           MasterCard number. ";
            }
         }
         else
         {
            if(!ereg("^[3]{1,1}[0-9]{14,14}$",$value))
            {
               $errors[] = "$value is not a valid
                           American Express number. ";
            }
         }
      }
      $$field = strip_tags(trim($value));
```

Continued

LISTING 6-13: *(Continued)*

```
        }
      }
      if(@is_array($errors))
      {
         $message = "";
         foreach($errors as $value)
         {
            $message .= $value." Please try again<br />";
         }
         include("fields_ship_info.inc");
         include("single_form.inc");
         exit();
      }                                                           #132
       /* Process data when all fields are correct */
      foreach($_POST as $field => $value)                         #134
      {
         if(!eregi("cc_",$field) && $field != "Summary" )         #136
         {
            $value = addslashes($value);
            $updates[] = "$field = '$value'";
         }
      }
      $update_string = implode($updates,",");                     #142
      $sql_ship = "UPDATE Customer_Order SET $update_string
            WHERE order_number='{$_SESSION['order_number']}'";
      $cxn = connect_to_db("Vars.inc");
      $result = mysqli_query($cxn,$sql_ship)
                  or die(mysqli_error($cxn));
      extract($_POST);                                            #148
      include("fields_summary.inc");
      include("summary_page.inc");
   }
   elseif(isset($_POST['Ship']))                                  #152
   {
      include("fields_ship_info.inc");
      include("single_form.inc");
   }
   elseif(isset($_POST['Final']))                                 #157
   {
      switch ($_POST['Final'])                                    #159
      {
         case "Continue Shopping":                                #161
            header("Location: ShopCatalog.php");
            break;
         case "Cancel Order":                                     #164
            #include("fields_cancel.inc");
            #include("cancel_message.inc");
            unset($_SESSION['order_number']);
            session_destroy();
            exit();
            break;
         case "Submit Order":                                     #171
            $cxn = connect_to_db("Vars.inc");
```

```
        $sql = "UPDATE Customer_Order SET submitted='yes'
          WHERE order_number='{$_SESSION['order_number']}'";
        $result = mysqli_query($cxn,$sql)
            or die("Error: ".mysqli_error($cxn));
        #processCCInfo();                                    #177
        #sendOrder();
        #include("fields_accept.inc");                       #179
        #include("accept_message.inc");
        #email();                                            #181
        session_destroy();                                   #182
        break;
      }
  }
  ?>
```

In the following list, I explain the designated lines in Listing 6-12:

#5   Starts a session for the current order.

#7   Begins an `if` block that executes if there is no current order. It displays a message and a link to the catalog.

#13   Begins an `if` block that executes when the user clicks the Submit Order button in the shopping cart. The block displays the shipping information form.

#19   Begins an `elseif` block that executes when the user clicks the button named summary, which is the button that displays Continue in the shipping information form. The `elseif` block processes the information from the shipping information form. Lines 21 to 132 check the form fields. (I discuss form fields in more detail in Chapter 4.)

    #21   Lines 21 to 40 checks for blank fields and redisplays the form if blanks are found.

    #41   Lines 41 to 132 check the format of the information entered by the user. The form is redisplayed with an error message if any invalid formats are found.

#134 Starts a `foreach` loop that creates an array, called `$update`, that contains the shipping information. This array is used later to build the SQL statement that adds the shipping information to the database.

    #136 Begins an `if` block that executes if the field doesn't contain credit card information. This application doesn't store the credit card information in the database. Consequently, the customer needs to reenter the credit card information if it's needed again.

#142 Creates a string containing the shipping information.

#143 Lines 143 to 147 create and execute the SQL statement that adds the shipping information to the database.

#148 Lines 148 to 150 display the summary Web page.

#152 Begins an `elseif` block that executes when the button is named Ship. This condition is true when the user clicks the Edit Shipping Information button on the summary page. The block displays the shipping information form with the shipping information that is currently stored in the database.

#157 Begins an `elseif` block that executes when the user clicks a button named Final. These buttons are displayed on the summary Web page.

> **#159** Starts a `switch` statement based on which Final button the user clicks.
>
> **#161** Starts the `case` block that executes when the value of the Final button is Continue Shopping. The block runs the `ShopCatalog.php` script, which displays the catalog index page.
>
> **#164** Starts the `case` block that executes when the value of the Final button is Cancel Order. The block displays a cancellation Web page, by including two files, and destroys the session. Notice that the two include statements have a comment mark (#) at the beginning of the line. These two statements are commented out because the cancellation Web page isn't provided in this chapter, in the interests of saving space. You need to develop a cancellation page that is specific to your order process.
>
> **#171** Starts the `case` block that executes when the value of the Final button is Submit Order. The block sets the order status to `Submitted='yes'`.
>
> **#177** Calls a function that processes the credit card information. I don't provide this function because it depends on which credit card processing company you use. The company will provide you with the information needed to write the function. In general, the function sends the credit information to the company and receives a code from them that either accepts or rejects the credit charge. Notice that the statement in the listing has a comment mark (#) at the beginning of the line so that it doesn't actually execute. It's just there to show you a possible statement to use.
>
> **#178** Calls a function that sends the order information to the person/department responsible for filling and shipping the order. This function depends on your internal procedures. The function might send an e-mail notice to the shipping department, or your process might be altogether different. This statement is also commented out because I don't provide the function.
>
> **#179** Displays an order confirmation (or not accepted) Web page by including two files. The files are not provided, so the include statements are commented out. You need to write your own files to include at this location.

#181 Calls a function that sends an e-mail to the customer. This function call is commented out, because I don't provide the `email` function. You need to write a function that creates and sends an e-mail message specific to your business. Sending an e-mail is shown in detail in Chapter 4.

#182 Destroys the session. The user can't make any changes to the order after clicking the Submit Order button on the summary page.

Building the Shopping Cart Application: The Object-Oriented Approach

Object-oriented programming requires that you create and use objects to provide the functionality of the application. You first identify the objects needed for the application. Then you write the classes that define the objects, including the methods that the application needs. When the objects are ready, you write the application script that creates and uses the objects.

Developing the objects

The shopping cart application needs to display products from the catalog. It stores the customer's choices in a shopping cart. It stores the order shipping information and the items ordered in a database. The following list of objects reflects the tasks this application needs to perform:

- `Catalog`: The `Catalog` class returns and displays product information as needed.

- `Database`: The application stores the product information in a database. The `Database` class provides the container that stores the data.

- `Item`: The customer orders items. The items are stored in the shopping cart and stored in the order database. The `Item` class stores and retrieves information about the item.

- `ShoppingCart`: The shopping cart holds the items currently selected by the customer. The customer can add items to and delete items from the cart.

- `Order`: The shipping and credit information for the order needs to be associated with the items in the order. The `Order` class stores and retrieves all the information about the order that is stored in the database.

✔ WebForm: A form is used to collect the shipping and credit information from the customer. The WebForm class provides the form for the application. It collects and processes the information typed by the customer.

✔ WebPage: The WebPage class displays a Web page that includes information from PHP variables. The WebPage class is used frequently throughout this book whenever a Web page needs to be displayed.

✔ Email: The application sends an e-mail to customers when they order, letting them know that the order has been accepted and other information about their orders. The Email class contains and manages the e-mail message.

I discuss the details for each class in the following sections.

Writing the Catalog class

The Catalog class maintains a connection to the database where the product information is stored. The Catalog class returns or displays product information as needed. I develop the Catalog class in Chapter 5. I add two additional methods to the class for the shopping cart application. (Refer to Listing 5-7 for the Catalog class code.) I describe the new methods, getName and getPrice, later in this section.

The methods provided by the Catalog class are:

✔ **The constructor:** Creates a connection to a MySQL database. The constructor expects to be passed a filename of the file that contains the hostname, account name, and password necessary to access MySQL. The following statement creates a Database object:

```
$db = new Database("Vars.inc");
```

✔ useDatabase: Selects a database and stores the database name. The method expects to be passed a database name. It checks whether the database exists and returns a message if the database doesn't exist.

✔ getConnection: Returns the connection that is established and stored in the constructor.

✔ getName: Returns the product name. This method expects to be passed a catalog number. This method is added in this chapter. The code is shown in Listing 6-14.

✔ getPrice: Returns the price. This method expects to be passed a catalog number. This method is added in this chapter. The code is shown in Listing 6-14.

The code for the getName and getPrice methods is shown in Listing 6-14.

```php
function getName($catalog_number)
{
   if(ereg("[0-9]*",$catalog_number))
   {
      $sql = "SELECT name,type FROM Food
            WHERE catalog_number='$catalog_number'";
   }
   else
   {
      throw new Exception("$catalog_number is not a
                           catalog number.");
      exit();
   }
   if(!$result = $this->connection->query($sql))
   {
      throw new Exception(mysqli_error($this->connection));
      exit();
   }
   $name = $result->fetch_assoc();
   return "{$name['name']}"." {$name['type']}";
}

function getPrice($catalog_number)
{
if(ereg("[0-9]*",$catalog_number))
{
   $sql = "SELECT price FROM Food
         WHERE catalog_number='$catalog_number'";
}
else
{
   throw new Exception("$catalog_number is not a
                        catalog number.");
   exit();
}
if(!$result = $this->connection->query($sql))
{
   throw new Exception(mysqli_error($this->connection));
   exit();
}
   $price = $result->fetch_assoc();
   return "{$price['price']}";
}
```

The getName method

The getName method returns the product name, formatted as name-space-type. For instance, in this application, the method returns Delicious Apple or Mandarin Orange.

The method tests that the catalog number passed to it contains only numbers. For other applications, the catalog number might have a different format that contains letters or other characters. The `if` statement needs to test the format of the catalog number in as much detail as possible.

If the catalog number has the correct format, an SQL query is built to select the needed information from the database. The query is executed. The information returned by the query is added to a string with the correct format. The formatted information is returned. You can call the method as follows:

```
$product_name = $catalog->getName("1004");
```

where `"1004"` is the catalog number for the product.

The getPrice method

The `getPrice` method returns the product price. An SQL query is built to select the price from the database and executed. The method returns the price. The syntax for calling the method is shown here:

```
$product_price = $catalog->getPrice($catalog_number);
```

Writing the Item class

The `Item` class is a fundamental class. The customer orders items. The item object stores and retrieves the information about an item that the customer selected.

The properties

The `Item` properties store information about the item. The properties are:

```
private $catalog_number;
private $quantity;
private $name;
private $price;
```

The first property is the number needed to locate the item in the catalog database. The second property is the quantity of the item entered by the customer. The remaining properties are the name and the price for the item, information obtained from the catalog.

The code

Listing 6-15 contains the complete code for the `Item` class. After the code listing you can find details about each method.

LISTING 6-15: THE ITEM CLASS

```php
<?php
 /* Name: Item.class
  * Desc: Represents an item in the order.
  */
 class Item
 {
    private $catalog_number;
    private $quantity;
    private $name;
    private $price;

    function __construct($cat_no,$quantity)
    {
      if(is_string($cat_no) && is_numeric($quantity))
      {
         $this->quantity = $quantity;
         $this->catalog_number = $cat_no;
         $cat = new Catalog("Vars.inc");
         $cat->selectCatalog("OnlineOrders");
         $this->name = $cat->getName($cat_no);
         $this->price = $cat->getPrice($cat_no);
      }
      else
      {
         throw new Exception("Parameter is not a valid
                               catalog number and quantity");
      }
    }

    function getCatalogNumber()
    {
       return $this->catalog_number;
    }

    function getQuantity()
    {
       return $this->quantity;
    }

    function getPrice()
    {
       return $this->price;
    }

    function getName()
    {
       return $this->name;
    }
 }
?>
```

The constructor

The constructor collects and stores the information for the item. the catalog number and the quantity are passed when a new Item is created. The constructor stores the catalog number and quantity in the `Item` properties. The constructor retrieves the remaining two properties from the catalog database and stores them in the `Item` properties.

An item is created as follows:

```
$item1 = new Item(5007,3)
```

getCatalogNumber, getQuantity, getPrice, getName

These methods return the specified item information. The methods are used as follows:

```
$price = getPrice();
```

Writing the ShoppingCart class

The shopping cart is a major component of the shopping cart application. It holds the items currently selected by the customer.

The properties

The shopping cart properties store the items in the shopping cart, along with information needed by the shopping cart to display the cart correctly.

```
private $items = array();
private $message;
private $n_items = 0;
```

The first property is an array of objects that contains the items currently stored in the shopping cart. The second property is a message that appears when the shopping cart is displayed. The third property is the number of items currently stored in the cart.

The code

Listing 6-16 contains the complete code for the ShoppingCart class. I cover each method in detail after the code listing.

LISTING 6-16: THE SHOPPINGCART CLASS

```php
<?php
 /* Name: ShoppingCart.class
  * Desc: Creates a shopping cart--a structure that
  *       holds items.
  */
class ShoppingCart
{
   private $items = array();
   private $message;
   private $n_items = 0;

   function __construct()
   {
      if(isset($_SESSION['items']))
      {
         $this->items = $_SESSION['items'];
         $this->n_items = sizeof($this->items);
      }
      $this->message = "Shopping Cart contains
                       {$this->n_items} items.";
   }

   function addItem(Item $item)
   {
      $this->items[] = $item;
      $_SESSION['items'] = $this->items;
      $this->n_items++;
      $this->message = "Shopping Cart contains
                       {$this->n_items} items.";
   }

   function getAllItems()
   {
      return $this->items;
   }

   function getMessage()
   {
      return $this->message;
   }

   function displayCart($file_fields,$file_page)
   {
      include($file_fields);
      include($file_page);
   }

   function updateCart($new_array)
   {
      if(is_array($new_array))
      {
```

Continued

```
LISTING 6-16: (Continued)

        foreach($new_array as $field => $value)
        {
            if(ereg("item",$field) && $value > 0)          #51
            {
                $cat_no = substr($field,4);
                $items_new[] = new Item($cat_no,$value);
            }
        }
        $this->items = @$items_new;
        $_SESSION['items'] = $this->items;
        $this->n_items = sizeof($this->items);
        $this->message = "Shopping Cart contains
                          {$this->n_items} items.";
    }
    else
    {
        throw new Exception("Parameter is not an array");
    }
  }
}
?>
```

The constructor

The constructor sets the three properties. The default values set an empty array and the number of items is 0. The constructor looks for an array of items in the session. If it finds it, it stores it in the $items property and sets the number of items to the size of the array. If no items are stored in the session, the properties retain the default settings for an empty cart. The third property, $message, is set to a string of text that shows the number of items in the cart.

The object is created without passing any arguments, as follows:

$cart = new ShoppingCart();

When the shopping cart is created, either it is new and empty or it contains the items stored for the session.

addItem

The addItem method adds an item to the cart. It expects to receive an item object. It adds the item to the item array and stores the new array in the session variable. This method also increments the number of items stored and updates the message with the new number of items. You use the method as follows:

$cart->addItem($item5);

where the $item5 variable contains an item object.

getAllItems, getMessage

The getAllItems and getMessage methods get the specified properties. The getAllItems method returns the array of item objects stored in the cart properties. The getMessage method returns the stored message. Neither method expects an argument to be passed.

displayCart

The displayCart method displays the shopping cart on a Web page. The names of the files that provide the fields and define the page are passed to the method. You can use the methods as follows:

```
$cart = new ShoppingCart();
$cart->displayCart("fields_cart-oo.inc","table_page.inc");
```

updateCart

The updateCart method updates an existing cart. It expects an array containing the information for all the items to be in the updated cart. The method replaces the existing array of items with the a new array of items created from the information passed to the method.

The array passed to the method should contain keys in the format item*nnnn* where *nnnn* is the catalog number of an item. The value is the quantity for the item. A sample array might contain the following:

```
$item_array[item1003] = 1
$item_array[item27] = 2.5
$item_array[item673] = 1.7
```

The $_POST array (which is sent when the user clicks the submit button in the shopping cart Web page) contains similar elements, such as:

```
$item_array[item1003] = 1
$item_array[item27] = 2.5
```

For each element in the array, the method extracts the catalog number from the key, passes the catalog number and the quantity to create an item object, and adds the new item object to an array of objects. When all the elements have been added to the new array of objects, the new array is stored in the object property $items and in the session variable. The number of items is incremented and stored.

Writing the Database class

The Database class provides the connection to the database where the customer information is stored. I develop the Database class in Chapter 3. See Listing 3-4 for the Database class code.

The methods provided by the `Database` class are:

✔ **The constructor:** Creates a connection to a MySQL database. The constructor expects to be passed a filename where the hostname, account name, and password necessary to access MySQL are stored. A Database object is created with the following statement:

```
$db = new Database("Vars.inc");
```

✔ `useDatabase`: Selects a database and stores the database name. The method expects to be passed a database name. It checks whether the database exists and returns a message if the database doesn't exist.

✔ `getConnection`: Returns the connection that is established and stored in the constructor.

Writing the Order class

The order contains all the information needed to complete the customer's purchase. It contains the shipping and credit information and the item information for each item ordered. The order information is stored in a database.

The properties

The `Order` properties store information about the order. The properties are:

```
private $order_number;
private $cxn;
private $table;
```

The first property is the number needed to identify the order in the database. The remaining two properties contain the information needed to access the order in the database.

The code

Listing 6-17 contains the complete code for the `Order` class. After the code listing, you can find a discussion about each method.

LISTING 6-17: THE ORDER CLASS

```php
<?php
 /* Class: Order
  * Desc:  Class that holds orders.
  */

class Order
{
  private $order_number;
```

```php
private $order_info;
private $order_items=array();
private $cxn;
private $table;

function __construct(mysqli $cxn,$table)
{
    $this->cxn = $cxn;
    if(is_string($table))
    {
        $this->table = $table;
    }
    else
    {
        throw new Exception("$table is not a
                             valid table name.");
    }
}

function createOrder()
{
    $today = date("Y-m-d");
    $sql = "INSERT INTO $this->table
            (order_date) VALUES ('$today')";
    if($result = $this->cxn->query($sql))
    {
        $this->order_number = $this->cxn->insert_id;
        $_SESSION['order_number'] = $this->order_number;
    }
    else
    {
        throw new Exception("Database is not available.
                             Try again later");
    }
}

function getOrderNumber()
{
    return $this->order_number;
}

function addCart(ShoppingCart $cart)
{
    foreach($cart->getAllItems() as $n => $item)
    {
        $cat_no = $item->getCatalogNumber();
        $quantity = $item->getQuantity();
        $price = $item->getPrice();
        $sql = "INSERT INTO Order_Item
                (order_number,catalog_number,
                 quantity,item_number,price)
                  VALUES
                ($this->order_number,$cat_no,
                 $quantity,($n+1),$price)";
```

Continued

LISTING 6-17: *(Continued)*

```php
        $result = $this->cxn->query($sql);
    }
}

function selectOrder($order_number)
{
    if(is_int($order_number))
    {
    $this->order_number = $order_number;
    }
    else
    {
        throw new Exception("$order_number
                            is not an integer.");
    }
}

function getOrderInfo()
{
    $sql = "SELECT * FROM $this->table
            WHERE order_number='$this->order_number'";
    if($result = $this->cxn->query($sql))
    {
        return $result->fetch_assoc();
    }
    else
    {
        throw new Exception("Database is not available.
                            Try again later");
    }
}

function getItemInfo()
{
    $sql = "SELECT item_number,catalog_number,quantity,price
            FROM order_item
            WHERE order_number='$this->order_number'";
    if($result = $this->cxn->query($sql))
    {
      $n=1;
      while($row=$result->fetch_assoc())
      {
        foreach($row as $field => $value)
        {
            $item[$n][$field] = $value;
        }
        $cat = new Catalog("Vars.inc");
        $cat->selectCatalog("OnlineOrders");
        $item[$n]['name'] =
            $cat->getName($item[$n]['catalog_number']);
        $n++;
      }
```

```
        return $item;
      }
      else
      {
        throw new Exception("Database is not available.
                             Try again later");
      }
   }

   function updateOrderInfo($data)
   {
      if(!is_array($data))
      {
        throw new Exception("Data must be in an array.");
        exit();
      }
      $sql = "UPDATE $this->table SET ";
      foreach($data as $field => $value)
      {
         if(ereg("ship",$field) || $field == "phone"
                  || $field == "email")
         {
            $data_array[] = "$field='$value'";
         }
      }
      $sql .= implode($data_array,',');
      $sql .= "WHERE order_number='$this->order_number'";
      if(!$result = $this->cxn->query($sql))
      {
         throw new Exception("Database is not available.
                             Try again later");
      }
      return true;
   }

   function displayOrderSummary($field_info,$field_page)
   {
     $data = $this->getOrderInfo();
     $items = $this->getItemInfo();
     extract($data);
     if(is_string($field_info) and is_string($field_page))
     {
       include($field_info);
       include ($field_page);
     }
     else
     {
        throw new Exception("Requires two valid filenames.");
     }
   }
}
?>
```

The constructor

The constructor stores the information needed to connect to the database. It expects to be passed a connection and a table name. The connection is a database connection provided by a `Database` object. The constructor stores the information in the `Order` properties.

You can create an `Order` object as follows:

```
$db = new Database("Vars.inc");
$db->selectDatabase("OnlineOrders");
$order = new Order($db->getConnection(),"Customer_Order");
```

createOrder

The `createOrder` method inserts a new order into the order database using an SQL query. Today's date is stored. The MySQL `AUTO_INCREMENT` feature creates the order number. The new order number is stored in the order property and in a session variable. The method returns `true` if the order is successfully created.

selectOrder

The `selectOrder` method sets the order number in the `Order` to the order number passed to it. Any information retrieved later from the database is retrieved based on the order number property.

addCart

The `addCart` method adds all the items in a shopping cart to the order. The method expects to be passed a `ShoppingCart` object. The method uses a `foreach` loop to loop through all the items in the shopping cart. The information from each item object is used to build an SQL query that inserts the item into the `order_item` table.

getOrderInfo

The `getOrderInfo` method returns an associative array containing all the information from the `customer_order` table. It includes the name and address, phone, date created, and other order-level information. It creates an SQL `SELECT` query that selects all the information. No parameter is expected.

getItemInfo

The `getItemInfo` method returns a multidimensional array containing all the information for all the items in the order. The information for each item in the array includes all the fields from the `order_item` table in the database, plus the product name retrieved from the catalog.

The method executes a query that gets all the information from the order_ item table. A while loop processes each item row in turn. A foreach loop runs for each row, adding each field to the array element resulting in a multi-dimensional array. After the foreach loop finishes, the method retrieves the product name from the catalog and adds it to the array.

updateOrderInfo

The updateOrderInfo method updates the shipping information in the customer_order table of the database. The method expects an array of shipping information, such as the $_POST array from the shipping information form. An SQL UPDATE query is created from the data in the $data array.

The query is built with an opening section and phrases for each field, such as ship_name=John Smith. Each update phrase is added to a new array, $data_array. After all fields have been processed and added to the new array, the implode function is used to convert the array into a string suitable for use in the query. The WHERE clause is then added to the end of the query.

The method can be used with a statement similar to the following:

```
$order->updateOrderInfo($_POST);
```

updateOrderInfo returns true when the information is updated successfully.

displayOrderSummary

The displayOrderSummary method displays a summary of the order. The names of the two files that define the summary page are passed. The summary page is displayed by including the two files.

Writing the WebForm class

The WebForm is used to display and process the shipping information form. I create and explain the WebForm class in Chapter 4. The class is shown in Listing 4-6.

The methods in the WebForm class that the shopping cart application script uses are:

- ✔ **The constructor:** Stores the properties needed to display the form correctly. Two files — an information file and a file that defines the look and feel — are required. The two filenames are passed when the WebForm object is created and stored in two properties. The data for the form fields can be passed, but can be left out and the form fields will be blank. You can create the object by using either of the following statements:

```
$form = new WebForm("file1.inc","file2.inc",$_POST);
$form = new WebForm("file1.inc","file2.inc");
```

✔ `displayForm`: This method displays the form. It extracts the data from the `$data` property where it is stored. An `@` is used to suppress the error messages so that the form can be displayed without any data. The form is displayed by including the two files that define the form. These two files can define any type of form, with fields and elements you want to use. For this application, I use the files I describe earlier in this chapter — `fields_ship_info-oo.inc` and `single_form.inc` — which define the shipping information form.

✔ `checkForBlanks`: Checks each field in the form to see whether it contains information. If the method finds invalid blank fields, it returns an array containing the field names of the blank fields.

✔ `verifyData`: This method checks each field to ensure that the information submitted in the field is in a reasonable format. For instance, you know that "hi you" is not a reasonable format for a zip code. This method checks the information from specific fields against regular expressions that match the information allowed in that field. If invalid data is found in any fields, the method returns an array containing messages that identify the problems.

✔ `trimData`, `stripTagsFromData`: A PHP function is applied to each value in the `$data` property. The resulting values are stored in `$data`. The `trim` function removes leading and trailing blanks from a string. The `strip_tags` function removes any HTML tags from the string, important for security.

Writing the WebPage class

I use the `WebPage` class throughout this book whenever I need to display a Web page. The `WebPage` object is a Web page that displays information in PHP variables, along with HTML code. The code that defines the Web page is in a separate file. You include the file to display the Web page. I develop and explain the `WebPage` class in Chapter 3. You can see the `WebPage` class listing in Listing 3-6.

The `WebPage` class includes the following methods:

✔ **The constructor:** Stores a filename and the data needed to display the page. Expects to be passed the filename of the file that contains the HTML code that defines the Web page. It also expects to be passed an array containing any data that needs to be displayed in the page. A WebPage object can be created with a statement similar to the following:

```
$web_page1 = new WebPage("define_page.inc",$data);
```

✔ `displayPage`: Displays the Web page. The method extracts the information in the `$data` array and includes the HTML file.

Writing the Email Class

After a customer successfully submits an order, the application sends a confirmation e-mail message to the e-mail address provided by the customer. (You can find out about the Email class in Chapter 4, and the code is shown in Listing 4-9.)

Writing the shopping cart application script

After writing all the class code needed for the shopping cart application, you write the application script that creates and uses the objects to provide the application functionality. The application script is organized as an if statement with nested if statements. The if statements execute based on the name and value of the submit buttons. Table 6-3 shows the buttons used throughout the application. The table shows the text displayed on the button, the Web page where the button appears, and the name given to the button in the input tag.

Table 6-3	Buttons Displayed by the Shopping Cart Application	
Displays	*Web Page*	*Name*
Select a Category	Catalog index	Products
Continue Shopping	Catalog Product	(No name)
Continue Shopping	Shopping Cart	(No name)
Continue Shopping	Summary	(No name)
Add Items to Cart	Catalog Product	Cart
Previous	Catalog Product	Cart
Next	Catalog Product	Cart
Submit Order	Shopping Cart	Ship
Update Cart	Shopping Cart	Cart
Continue	Shipping information form	Summary
Edit Shipping Info	Summary	Ship
Submit Order	Summary	Final
Cancel Order	Summary	Final

The following text gives a general overview of the application script:

```
if (Button name = Products)
   Display catalog products page for the category selected.
elseif (Button name = Cart)
    if (Button = Update Cart)
          1. Update items and quantities in shopping cart.
          2. Display cart.
      elseif (Button = Add Items to Cart)
          1. Add the selected items to shopping cart.
          2. Display shopping cart.
elseif (Button name = Ship)
      1. If current order exists, get order number from the
         session variable. If not, create a new order.
      2. Display shipping information form.
elseif (Button name = Summary)
      1. Check form information for blanks. If blanks found,
         redisplay form with error message.
      2. Check form information for correct format. If
         invalid information found, redisplay form with error
         message.
      3. Add shipping information from form to database.
      4. Add the items in the shopping cart to the database.
      5. Display summary form.
elseif (Button name = Final)
    if (Button = "Submit Order")
          1. Update order status to submitted.
          2. Process credit card information.
          3. Submit order to be filled and shipped.
          4. Send confirmation email to customer.
          5. Display confirmation Web page.
      elseif (Button = "Cancel Order")
          1. Update order status to cancelled.
          2. Display cancellation Web page.
          3. Destroy session.
else
      Display catalog index page
```

The application program creates objects and uses their methods to perform the tasks that I describe in the preceding application overview. You see the application program script in Listing 6-18.

LISTING 6-18: THE SHOPPING CART APPLICATION SCRIPT

```php
<?php
/* Program: Orders-oo.php
 * Desc:    Handles all functions of the Online Orders
 *          application. The submit button name is tested
 *          to determine which section of the program
 *          executes.
 */
require_once("Item.class");
require_once("Catalog.class");
```

```
require_once("ShoppingCart.class");
require_once("WebForm.class");
require_once("WebPage.class");
require_once("Order.class");
require_once("Database.class");
include("functions_main.inc");
session_start();                                               #16
if(isset($_POST['Products']) && isset($_POST['interest']))
{
   try
   {
      $catalog = new Catalog("Vars.inc");
      $catalog->selectCatalog("OnlineOrders");
      $catalog->displayAllofType($_POST['interest'],2);
   }
   catch(Exception $e)
   {
       echo $e->getMessage();
       exit();
   }
}
elseif(isset($_POST['Cart']))                                  #31
{
   $cart = new ShoppingCart();
   if($_POST['Cart'] == "Update Cart")                         #34
   {
     try
     {
       $cart->updateCart($_POST);
     }
     catch(Exception $e)
     {
        echo $e->getMessage();
        exit();
     }
   }
   elseif($_POST['Cart'] == "Add Items to Cart")               #46
   {
     foreach($_POST as $field => $value)                       #48
     {
        if(ereg("item",$field) && $value > 0)
        {
           try
           {
             $cat_no = substr($field,4);                       #54
             $item = new Item($cat_no,$value);
             $cart->addItem($item);
           }
           catch(Exception $e)
           {
               echo $e->getMessage();
               exit();
           }
```

Continued

LISTING 6-18: *(Continued)*

```php
            }
        }
    }
    try
    {
        $cart->displayCart("fields_cart-oo.inc",
                "table_page-oo.inc");                              #69
    }
    catch(Exception $e)
    {
        echo $e->getMessage();
        exit();
    }
}
elseif(isset($_POST['Ship']))                                      #77
{
    try
    {
        $db = new Database("Vars.inc");
        $db->useDatabase("OnlineOrders");
        $order = new Order($db->getConnection(),
                        "Customer_Order");
        if(isset($_SESSION['order_number']))                      #85
        {
            $order->selectOrder($_SESSION['order_number']);
        }
        else
        {
            $order->createOrder();
        }
        $ord = $order->getOrderNumber();
        $info = $order->getOrderInfo();
        $form = new WebForm("single_form.inc",
                "fields_ship_info.inc",$info);
        $form->displayForm();
    }
    catch(Exception $e)
    {
        echo $e->getMessage();
        exit();
    }
}
elseif(isset($_POST['Summary']))                                  #105
{
    try
    {
        $form = new WebForm("single_form.inc",
                        "fields_ship_info-oo.inc",$_POST);
        $blanks = $form->checkForBlanks();
    }
    catch(Exception $e)
```

```
                {
                   echo $e->getMessage();
                }
                if(is_array($blanks))                              #117
                {
                    $GLOBALS['message'] = "The following required fields
                                          were blank. Please enter the
                                          required information:  ";
                    foreach($blanks as $value)
                    {
                      $GLOBALS['message'] .="$value, ";
                    }
                    $form->displayform();
                    exit();
                }
                $form->trimData();                                 #129
                $form->stripTagsFromData();
                try
                {
                    $errors = $form->verifyData();
                }
                catch(Exception $e)
                {
                    echo $e->getMessage();
                }
                if(is_array($errors))
                {
                    $GLOBALS['message'] = "";
                    foreach($errors as $value)
                    {
                        $GLOBALS['message'] .="$value<br> ";
                    }
                    $form->displayForm();
                    exit();
                }
                try
                {
                  $db = new Database("Vars.inc");                  #151
                  $db->useDatabase("OnlineOrders");
                  $order =
                      new Order($db->getConnection(),"Customer_Order");
                  $order->selectOrder($_SESSION['order_number']);

          // Add shipping form info to db
                  $order->updateOrderInfo($_POST);

          // Add items to db
                  $cart = new ShoppingCart();                      #161
                  $order->addCart($cart);

          // display summary form
                  $order->displayOrderSummary("fields_summary-oo.inc",
                                              "summary_page.inc");
```

Continued

LISTING 6-18: *(Continued)*

```
        }
      catch(Exception $e)
      {
        echo $e->getMessage();
      }
  }
  elseif(isset($_POST['Final']))                                    #173
  {
     if($_POST['Final'] == "Submit Order")                         #175
     {
        $db = new Database("Vars.inc");
        $db->useDatabase("OnlineOrders");
        $order = new Order($db->getConnection(),
                           "Customer_Order");
        $order->selectOrder($_SESSION['order_number']);
        if(processCC())                                            #182
        {
           $order->setSubmitted();                                 #184
           $order->sendToShipping();                               #185
           $order->sendEMailtoCustomer();                          #186
           $confirm = new webPage("confirm_page.inc",$data);
           $confirmpage->displayPage();                            #188
        }
        else                                                       #190
        {
           $order->cancel();
           $unapp = new webPage("not_accepted_page.inc",$data);
           $unapp->displayPage();
           unset($_SESSION['order_number']);
           unset($_SESSION);
           session_destroy();
        }
     }
     else                                                          #200
     {
           $order->cancel();
           $cancel = new webPage("cancel.inc",$data);
           $cancel->displayPage();
           unset($_SESSION['order_number']);
           unset($_SESSION);
           session_destroy();
     }
  }
  else                                                             #210
  {
     $catalog = new Catalog("Vars.inc");
     $catalog->selectCatalog("OnlineOrders");
     $catalog->displayCategories();
  }
  ?>
```

The following numbered items discuss the numbered lines in Listing 6-18:

#16 Opens an existing session or, if no session exists, opens a new session.

#17 Begins an `if` block that executes when the user clicks the Products button with a product category selected. The block displays the catalog product page for the selected category.

#31 Begins an `elseif` block that executes when the user clicks the Cart button.

> **#33** Creates a `ShoppingCart` object. The `ShoppingCart` class constructor looks for items in the session. If existing items are found in the session variable `$items`, they are loaded into the cart object. If `$items` isn't found in the session, the cart is set up empty.
>
> **#34** Begins an `if` block that executes when the user clicks the Update Cart button. The block updates the quantities and items in the shopping cart.
>
> **#46** Begins an `elseif` block that executes when the user clicks the Add Items to Cart button. Line 48 starts a `foreach` loop the loops through the `$_POST` array. When an array element key contains `item` and the quantity is greater than 0, the catalog number is extracted from the field name (line 54) and an item object is created (line 55) and added to the cart (line 56).
>
> **#68** Lines 68 to 69 display the shopping cart.

#77 Begins an `elseif` block that executes when the user clicks the Ship button. This block displays the shipping information form.

> **#81** Lines 81 to 84 create an order object.
>
> **#85** Starts an `if/else` statement that sets the order number. If the order number is found in a session variable, the order property is set to the session order number. If not, a new order is created with a new order number.
>
> **#93** Lines 93 to 97 display the shipping information form, with the shipping information from the order database.

#105 Begins an `elseif` block that executes when the user clicks the Summary button. This block processes the information from the shipping information form.

> **#109** Lines 109 to 128 check the `$_POST` array for blank form fields. If blanks are found, the form is redisplayed with an error message.
>
> **#129** Lines 129 to 148 check the format of the data in the elements in the `$_POST` array. If invalid data is found, the form is redisplayed with an error message.

#151 Lines 151 to 158 add the shipping information to the database. This line is not reached until the shipping information has been validated.

#161 Lines 161 to 162 add the items in the shopping cart to the order database.

#165 Lines 165 to 166 get the information from the database and display the summary Web page.

#173 Starts an `elseif` block that executes when the user clicks the Final button. This block processes the final order. The customer can cancel or submit the order. If submitted, the order is either approved or not approved.

#175 Starts an `if` block that executes when the user clicks the Submit Order button. The block creates an order object.

#182 Starts an `if` block that executes when the credit card processing company approves the credit charge. The function `processCC` isn't included in this chapter. You must write this function yourself because it is different for different credit processing companies. The company tells you what the function needs to do. In general, you send the credit information to the company computer, which processes the credit charge. A code for success or failure is returned to your function.

#184 Sets the status of the order in the database to be approved.

#185 Sends the order to be filled and shipped. This method isn't included in the `Order` class in this chapter. You need to write the method to fulfill orders per your company procedures.

#187 Lines 187 and 188 display a confirmation Web page. You need to write `confirmation_page.inc` to include the information that you want your customers to know, such as shipping date, shipping method, and so on.

#190 Starts an `else` block that executes when the credit charge is not approved. The block cancels the order, displays a not approved Web page, and destroys the session. The file `not_accepted_page.inc` is not provided in this chapter. You need to write the HTML for this file with the information you want the customer to have.

#200 Starts an `else` block that executes when the customer clicks the Cancel Order button. The block cancels the order, displays a cancellation page, and destroys the session. You need to write the file, `cancel_page.inc` yourself.

#210 Begins an `else` block that executes when the user clicks no button or a button without a name. The block displays the catalog index page.

Adding Features to the Application

The shopping cart application in this chapter provides basic online ordering functionality. However, you can add even more features. Some common features of a shopping cart applications that aren't provided in this chapter include

- ✔ **Login:** As I discuss at the beginning of this chapter, many online merchants require customers to log in before they can order. You can add this feature with the login application provided in Chapter 4.

  Some sites allow customers to purchase items without logging in, but offer them the option of saving their information for faster checkout during their next order.

  This application doesn't save the credit card information. Some users trust well-known merchants to store their credit card numbers. It provides faster checkout. It's more trouble, but more customer friendly, to make credit card storage optional. Customers will be happier if you ask their permission before storing their credit card numbers.

- ✔ **Order Tracking:** Customers appreciate the opportunity to track their orders. It's difficult to provide this feature without a login. If you allow a customer to see the details of an order by simply entering the order number, there's really nothing to prevent that customer from looking at any order number in your system.

- ✔ **Inventory:** For some companies, the database that holds information about the product also keeps track of the inventory of products. Customers receive immediate information regarding the availability of an item. The database can also let purchasing know when the quantity of a product is low.

You can add these common features or other features that are very specific to your Web site. I suggest that you get the application working as it is first. Then, when it's working, you can add features one at a time. Don't change too many things at once. It's easiest to troubleshoot one feature at a time.

In general, adding features to the object-oriented application is easier than adding to the procedural application. One of the strengths of object-oriented programming is that you can add code without needed to change the existing code. If you believe your application is likely to grow in the future, building with the object-oriented application would be wise.

Part IV
Building Other Useful Applications

The 5th Wave   By Rich Tennant

"The engineers lived on Jolt and cheese sticks putting this product together, but if you wanted to just use 'cola and cheese sticks' in the Users Documentation, that's okay too. We're pretty loose around here."

In this part . . .

In this part, I provide two independent applications. The first application, discussed in Chapter 7, is a Content Management System (CMS) that allows users to post their documents on a Web site. The second application, discussed in Chapter 8, is a Forum application that allows users to read and post messages on a public bulletin board.

Chapter 7

Building a Content Management System

A *content management system* (CMS) is a general term for a Web site that can have its content, flow, and/or look and feel managed by using an administrative, Web-based interface. A CMS allows a non-technical user to update a Web site's content with ease. This alleviates the need to have a programmer present to change code for each piece of content the user wishes to publish. A CMS won't put programmers out of work, but a properly constructed CMS can make their lives easier because they won't be needed for every little change to the site content. By enabling the Web site's users to maintain the content for the site, maybe you'll finally be able to take that vacation! Before you buy that plane ticket and pack your scuba gear, however, take a look at this chapter, in which I show you how to build a CMS.

Designing the CMS Application

Before you design the user interface, you must make some fundamental programming design decisions, such as

▸ **Content types:** The goal of a CMS is to make Web site content totally user-driven, alleviating the need for programmers to make code changes to change the Web site. However, the designer of a CMS will have to decide how robust the CMS should be. Some CMS systems provide a WYSIWYG editor and a complex hierarchy for organizing sections of the Web site. In this chapter I show you a sample intranet CMS. It provides an area for each department in a company. Each department's area of the Web site will have a section for News, Events, Meeting Materials, and FAQ. Therefore, the hierarchy and the types of content the Web site will manage are somewhat limited, but the design of the CMS makes it easy to add a new department or to add a new content type (with no additional code).

✔ **Permissions:** A CMS usually needs to know who is using the Web site so that appropriate menus are displayed. An *intranet* is usually a set of internal Web applications that allow a company to share information within the organization. In the example CMS in this chapter, any member of a given department can create or modify content for that department. A user cannot edit content for a department in which the user does not belong. For instance, an employee in the Sales Department cannot edit content in the Information Technology Department's section of the Web site. So, the CMS application needs to have a login screen. The user accounts need to identify which department the user is in. I develop the login program used for this application in Chapter 4, and I describe the issues and code in that chapter as well. Using the login program in this application requires some minor changes, which I detail later in this chapter.

✔ **Handling Uploads:** Intranets are valuable tools because of the information that is available on them. To allow users to share documents, you need to provide a way for the users to upload files. In the sample CMS in this chapter, the user can upload documents. The CMS simply keeps track of the filename and the content to which it is associated. For example, if a user wants to post an FAQ where the question being posed is "How do I sign up for the 401K?", the user posting the FAQ will be able to answer the FAQ and also post related documents, perhaps forms that the people browsing the Web site will find useful.

Creating the CMS Database

The database stores information about users, departments, content types, content items, and downloads. The user table helps you determine the department to which a user belongs. The department table gives you information about a department, such as its name and a description of what the department does. The content type table defines the types of content that the Web site can accommodate. The content and download tables store the details that the users will be interested in. The CMS can determine whether a user is allowed to modify or edit content if the user belongs to the department in which the user is browsing.

Designing the CMS database

The sample application in this chapter uses a database named IntranetCMS. The database needs tables that contain the user, department, and content data. The database contains the following five tables:

- ✔ Dept_User: Stores information about the users, including which department they work in.

- ✔ Department: Stores a name and description for each department.

- ✔ Content_Type: Stores an ID and description for each type of content that the user can store.

- ✔ Content: Stores information about a content item, such as title and description, date created, who created it, and other information.

- ✔ Content_Download: Stores the filenames of any documents that can be downloaded. Each item is connected to an item in the Content table.

Auto increment columns in each of the tables help to tie all the information together. The dept_id column is used in the Department, Dept_User, and Content tables. The content_id (the auto increment column of the Content table) ties a piece of content to any associated downloads, stored in the Content_Download table.

Designing the Dept_User Table

The Dept_User table, shown in Table 7-1, contains user information, including the dept_id that will tie each user to a specific department.

Table 7-1	Database Table: Dept_User	
Variable Name	*Type*	*Description*
user_name	VARCHAR(255)	User identifier (primary key)
dept_id	INT	Department identifier (see Table 7-2)
first_name	VARCHAR(255)	User's first name
last_name	VARCHAR(255)	User's last name
password	VARCHAR(255)	User's password
create_date	TIMESTAMP	Date (and time) user's record was created
email	VARCHAR(255)	E-mail address

The `user_name` and `password` will be used to gain access to the site. The `dept_id` column will be useful when the CMS needs to decide whether a user can add or modify content in a section of the Web site.

Designing the Department table

The `Department` database table, shown in Table 7-2, is a simple table that stores the name and a short description for a department. The `dept_id` column is an identity column that is also used in other tables, allowing content and users to be associated with a department.

Table 7-2	Database Table: Department	
Variable Name	*Type*	*Description*
dept_id	SERIAL	Department's unique ID (primary key)
name	VARCHAR(255)	Department's name
description	VARCHAR(255)	Long description of what the department does in the company

What kind of column is `SERIAL`? `SERIAL` is a built-in alias for `BIGINT UNSIGNED NOT NULL AUTO_INCREMENT`. Save your fingers from typing that and use the alias to build an auto increment column. However, keep in mind that the storage required for a `BIGINT` is 8 bytes whereas the storage for an `INT` is 4 bytes. Storage requirements for MySQL data types are found here: `http://dev.mysql.com/doc/mysql/en/storage-requirements.html`.

The department list in the example CMS could have been hard-coded into the PHP code, but what if the company you work for merges with another company and suddenly a bunch of new departments exist? By storing the department information in the database, you can make the Web site more manageable. Isn't that the goal of a content *management* system? You want the users and the system — not the programmers — to manage information. The more the CMS can manage itself, the more opportunities you will find to build more and more exiting applications. If you had to do all the content maintenance for the Web sites you build, you might find yourself continuously changing little pieces of the Web site for your clients or end users.

Designing the Content_Type table

Table 7-3 shows the table structure that will allow the CMS to keep track of the different types of content that can be posted on the Web site.

Table 7-3	Database Table: Content_Type	
Variable Name	**Type**	**Description**
type_id	SERIAL	Content type identifier (primary key)
name	VARCHAR(255)	Description of the content type

The list of content types could have been hard-coded into the Web site's PHP code, but, again, by making this kind of information database-driven you make the Web site flexible enough to accommodate many future content types.

Designing the Content table

The Content table is a generic table for keeping any type of content. In a more complex CMS, this task might not be feasible with a single table, but it does the trick for this example application. Table 7-4 shows the columns for the Content table. A simple piece of content has a number of attributes associated with it, such as the date and time at which the content item was created and the date and time at which the content item was last modified.

Table 7-4	Database Table: Content	
Variable Name	**Type**	**Description**
content_id	SERIAL	Content identifier (primary key).
dept_id	INT	This column identifies the department to which this content belongs (see Table 7-2).
content_type	INT	This column identifies the type of content being stored in this record (see Table 7-3).
title	VARCHAR(255)	Short description for the content.
description	TEXT	Long description for the content.
content_date	DATE	Date when the content is relevant or when some event occurs.
create_date	TIMESTAMP	Date content item was created.
created_by	VARCHAR(255)	User name of the user who created this content item.

(continued)

Table 7-4 (continued)

Variable Name	Type	Description
last_upd_date	TIMESTAMP	Date content item was last modified.
last_upd_by	VARCHAR(255)	User name of the user that last modified this content item.

The Content table uses a TEXT column for the long description because the VARCHAR and CHAR data types have a length limit of 255 (in MySQL 4.x and previous versions). Using a TEXT column type, if the content is very verbose, it won't get cut off because a TEXT column can handle up to $2 + 2^{16}$ bytes. The description is the bulk of the content item, and it is displayed by using a TEXTAREA element in the HTML form when the user has edit permissions.

Designing the Content_Download table

A list of downloadable documents might be associated with each content item from the Content table (shown in Table 7-4). Table 7-5 shows the simple table that essentially ties a document with a content item. The name of the file will be used in the display.

Table 7-5   Database Table: Content_Download

Variable Name	Type	Description
download_id	SERIAL	Download identifier, primary key.
content_id	INT	This column identifies the content item to which this download belongs (see Table 7-4).
name	VARCHAR(255)	The name of the uploaded file.

The Content_Download table is very simple in the sample CMS implemented in this chapter. If you want to make the download functionality more robust, you can also keep track of the size of the file, the file type, and so on. In the sample application, I implement a simple upload and download capability.

Building the CMS database

The following SQL statement creates this database:

```
CREATE DATABASE IntranetCMS;
USE IntranetCMS;
```

The following SQL statements create the tables:

```
DROP TABLE IF EXISTS Department;

CREATE TABLE Department (
  dept_id        SERIAL,
  name           VARCHAR(255)  NOT NULL,
  description    VARCHAR(255) NOT NULL,

  PRIMARY KEY (dept_id)
);

DROP TABLE IF EXISTS Content_Type;

CREATE TABLE Content_Type (
  type_id        SERIAL,
  name           VARCHAR(255) NOT NULL,

  PRIMARY KEY (type_id)
);

DROP TABLE IF EXISTS Content;

CREATE TABLE Content (
  content_id     SERIAL,
  dept_id        INT            NOT NULL,
  content_type   INT            NOT NULL,
  title          VARCHAR(255)   NOT NULL,
  description    TEXT           NOT NULL,
  content_date   DATE,
  create_date    TIMESTAMP
                 DEFAULT now() NOT NULL,
  created_by     VARCHAR(255)   NOT NULL,
  last_upd_date  TIMESTAMP      NOT NULL,
  last_upd_by    VARCHAR(255)   NOT NULL,

  PRIMARY KEY(content_id)
);

DROP TABLE IF EXISTS Dept_User;

CREATE TABLE Dept_User (
  user_name      VARCHAR(255)
                          UNIQUE NOT NULL,
  dept_id        INT            NOT NULL,
  first_name     VARCHAR(255)   NOT NULL,
  last_name      VARCHAR(255)   NOT NULL,
  password       VARCHAR(255)   NOT NULL,
  create_date    TIMESTAMP
                 DEFAULT now() NOT NULL,
  email          VARCHAR(255),
```

```
    PRIMARY KEY(user_name)
);

DROP TABLE IF EXISTS Content_Download;

CREATE TABLE Content_Download (
   download_id   SERIAL,
   content_id    INT(6)       NOT NULL,
   file_name     VARCHAR(255) NOT NULL
);
```

Why drop tables before creating them? Well, when I'm developing a new Web site, I find it helpful to have a file that I can use to quickly re-create the database structure all at once. I can then use all or part of this "script" as I fine-tune the structure of the database. The `drop table if exists` statement in the file just saves me some time while I copy and paste the *data definition language* (DDL) into the MySQL client window. DDL statements are a subset of SQL statements that are used to create or modify database objects and their structure.

The following SQL statements fill the `Content_Type` table with the content types that are to appear in the CMS:

```
INSERT Content_Type (name) values ("News");
INSERT Content_Type (name) values ("Events");
INSERT Content_Type (name) values ("FAQ");
INSERT Content_Type (name) values ("Meeting Materials");
```

The following SQL statements fill the `Department` table with the departments in the fictitious company in this chapter's CMS example:

```
INSERT Department (name, description)
   values ("Human Resources",
     "Bringing the right people together to get the job
        done.");

INSERT Department (name, description)
   values ("Sales",
     "Our experienced sales team markets our great products
          to the public.");

INSERT Department (name, description)
   values ("Distribution", "We get the goods to the
           customers.");

INSERT Department (name, description)
   values ("Information Technology",
     "Building the applications that give us the edge.");
```

Accessing the CMS database

In the sample CMS in this chapter, as in previous chapters, the database credentials are stored in a file named `Vars.inc`. The contents of this file contain your account and password, similar to the following:

```php
<?php
        $host = "localhost";
        $user = "admin";
        $passwd = "";
        $database = "IntranetCMS";
?>
```

Designing the CMS Web Pages

The CMS application has a login page and content pages that have five levels of browsing, as follows:

1. **Login:** The CMS application requires users to register and log in before they can browse content. I took the login page for this application from Chapter 4 and slightly modified it; I describe the changes in Listing 7-1.

2. **Home page:** The home page simply displays a list of the departments that make up the company's intranet. The department descriptions are displayed in the main body of the page; along the left side of the page are links to the departments in the intranet. See Figure 7-1.

3. **Department page:** From the home page, the user clicks a single department. At the department-level page, the content types are listed in the main section of the page and on the left, as shown in Figure 7-2.

4. **Content List page:** From the Department page, the user clicks a content area, such as New, Events, or FAQ. The content area contains a list of items for the department and content type that the user selected. In Figure 7-3, the FAQs are listed for the Human Resources Department. If the user browsing this page isn't a member of the Human Resources Department, she won't see the Edit or Delete links. (The Edit and Deleted links are located in the far right column.)

5. **Content Detail page:** From the Content List page, the user can view the details of a single content item, including any downloads. The left side of the page lists any available downloads associated with the content item, and the main body of the page includes the details of the content item, including the creation date and creator of the content item. In Figure 7-4, a single FAQ's details are displayed for the Human Resources department. This shows a user that is part of the Human Resources department. If she weren't a Human Resources employee, she would see a read-only view of the content, like the one shown in Figure 7-5.

Figure 7-1:
The Intranet
home page,
where the
departments
in the
company
are listed.

Figure 7-2:
The content
types are
listed for the
Human
Resources
Department
page.

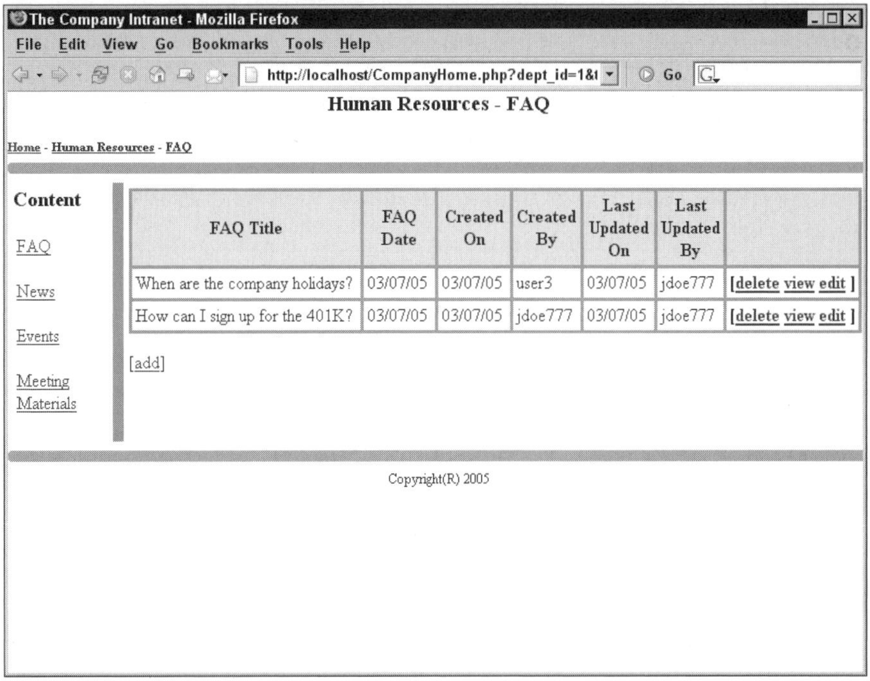

Figure 7-3:
The Human
Resources
FAQ List
page.

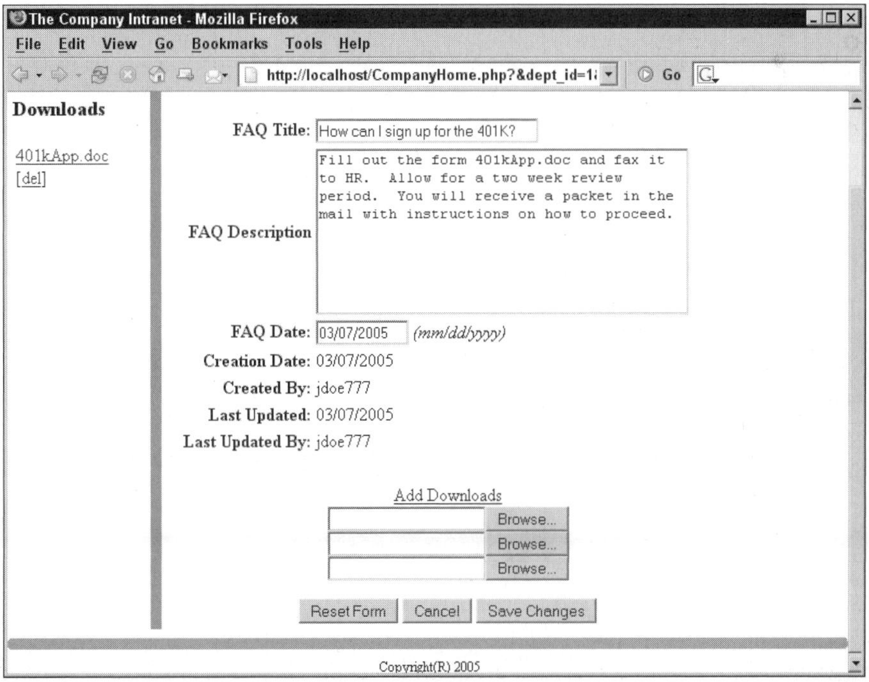

Figure 7-4:
The Human
Resources
FAQ Detail
page.

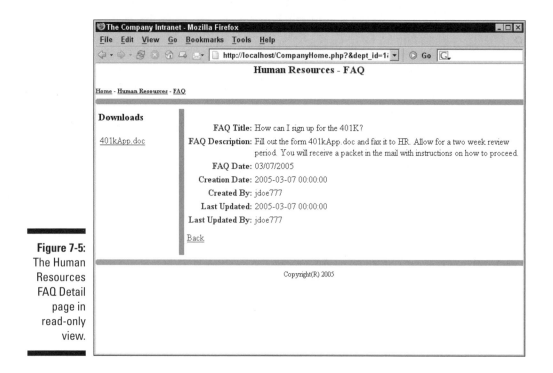

Building the CMS Application: Procedural Approach

The `CompanyHome.php` file contains the logic for organizing the data for the main display of the CMS. It figures out whether the user is looking at the main page, a department-level page, a content list page, or a detail page. It fills in elements of the `$page` array. The `$page` array is used in the `company.inc` program to construct the HTML display. This CMS intranet Web site requires that the people browsing it are registered users who have logged in to the system. Some intranet sites require only a login to gain access to administrative parts of the Web site. In the example in this chapter, the Web site requires users to be logged in to browse any of the content. The include file `company.inc` does the HTML work with the data that was set up by `CompanyHome.php`.

Writing the login code

The example in this chapter uses a very simple login and authentication scheme. The application assumes that the users that belong in a department have permission to create, edit, or delete any of the content for that department. Furthermore, the application allows the users signing up to choose the department in which they work. In a real-world application, this is quite a leap of faith. If you create a CMS system, you should implement a system that can appropriately identify users and apply the appropriate entitlements. To keep things simple in this chapter, you reuse the Login.php code from Chapter 4, Listing 4-4. A few modifications are needed, however; I identify those changes in Listing 7-1.

LISTING 7-1: LOGIN.PHP CHANGES

```
$table_name = "Dept_User";                              #11
$next_program = "CompanyHome.php";                      #12

$sql = "SELECT user_name,dept_id FROM $table_name       #25

$_SESSION['user_dept'] = $row['dept_id'];               #33
$_SESSION['user_name'] = $row['user_name'];             #34


$_SESSION['user_dept'] = $dept_id;                      #192
$_SESSION['user_name'] = $user_name;                    #193
```

Following is a description of the lines changed from the Login.php found in Chapter 4:

#11 The database tables used in the CMS application are different from the database tables used in Chapter 4. You change line 11 to use the Dept_User table designed earlier in this chapter.

#12 The page to which Login.php will redirect the user upon a successful login or registration is changed to the home page for the CMS application, CompanyHome.php.

#25 The application stores the user name and department ID in the session to use later in the application. The field dept_id is added to the SELECT query started on this line so that the department ID can be stored in the session.

#33 Stores the department ID in the session.

#34 Stores the user name in the session. Lines 33 and 34 stored different bits of information on these lines in Login.php in Chapter 4.

#192 [and **#193**] Chapter 4 stored a flag in the session to indicate that the user had been authenticated (auth), and it stored the user's ID (logname). The CMS application in this chapter stores the user name (user_name) and department identifier (dept_id) in the session variable. The user_name comes in handy when the CMS needs to store information about the person adding or changing content in the system. The department ID (dept_id) helps the CMS keep track of the department for which the user has permission to add or modify content.

The file in Listing 7-2 is copied from Chapter 4 (specifically, from Listing 4-1) and is also altered a bit to meet the needs of the CMS application in this chapter. The biggest difference is that the list of departments is constructed by connecting to the database and querying the Department table. The list of departments is needed for the Department drop-down list on the login page, thus allowing the user to select the department in which he is a member.

LISTING 7-2: THE FILE THAT CONTAINS THE ARRAYS NEEDED FOR THE LOGIN PAGE

```php
<?
 /* File: fields_login.inc
  * Desc: Contains arrays with the field names and form
  *       elements for the login Web page.
  */
include_once("functions_main.inc");

$page = array( "title"  => "Login Page",
               "top"    => "",
               "bottom" => "Send questions and comments
                            to admin@ourplace.com",
             );

$elements_1 = array( "top" => "Returning Home:
                              <span style=\"font-size: 80%;
                              font-weight: 100%\">
                              <i>Login here</i></span>",
                    "bottom" => "",
                    "submit" => "Login"
                   );
$elements_2 = array("top" => "New Users:
                              <span style=\"font-size: 80%;
                              font-weight: 100%\">
                              <i>Register here</i></span>",
                    "bottom" => "",
                    "submit" => "Register"
                   );

$fields_1 =   array("fusername" => "User Name",
                    "fpassword" => "Password"
                   );
$length_1 =   array("fusername" => "10",
                    "fpassword" => "10"
                   );
$types_1 =    array("fusername"     => "text",
                    "fpassword"     => "password"
                   );

$fields_2 =   array("user_name"     => "User Name",
                    "password"      => "Password",
                    "email"         => "Email Address",
                    "first_name"    => "First Name",
                    "last_name"     => "Last Name",
```

```
                            "dept_id"           => "Department"
                        );
$types_2 =      array("user_name"           => "text",
                      "password"            => "password",
                      "email"               => "text",
                      "first_name"          => "text",
                      "last_name"           => "text",
                      "dept_id"             => "select"
                    );
$length_2 =     array("user_name"           => "20",
                      "password"            => "8",
                      "email"               => "55",
                      "first_name"          => "40",
                      "last_name"           => "40",
                    );

$options =      array();

$connection = Connect_to_db("Vars.inc");
$results = mysqli_query($connection, "SELECT dept_id, name
                                      FROM Department
                                      ORDER BY name");
while($row = mysqli_fetch_assoc($results)) {
  $options['dept_id'][$row['dept_id']] = $row['name'];
}

?>
```

The `double_form.inc` file in Listing 7-3 was copied from Chapter 4, Listing 4-2, and was altered a bit, too. The biggest difference is that there is now code that builds the department drop-down list, starting at line 85.

LISTING 7-3: DEFINING TWO SIDE-BY-SIDE HTML FORMS

```
<?php
 /* File: double_form.inc
  * Desc: Contains the code for a Web page that displays
  *       two HTML forms, side by side in a table.
  */
 ?>
<head><title><?php echo $page['title']?></title></head>
<body style="margin: 0">
<h1 align="center"><?php echo $page['top'] ?></h1>
<hr size="10" noshade>

<table border="0" cellpadding="5" cellspacing="0">
<?php
```

Continued

Listing 7-3: *(Continued)*

```php
    #############
    ##  Form 1  #
    #############
?>
    <tr>
       <td width="33%" valign="top">
          <p style="font-size: 110%; font-weight: bold">
              <?php echo $elements_1['top']?></p>
          <!-- Beginning of form 1 (left) -->
          <form action=<?php echo $_SERVER['PHP_SELF']?>
                   method="POST">
          <table border="0">
<?php
    if (isset($GLOBALS['message_1']))                        #27
    {
       echo "<tr>
                <td colspan='2'
                    style=\"font-weight: bold;
                     font-style: italic;
                     font-size: 90%; color: red\">
                      {$GLOBALS['message_1']}<p></td></tr>\n";
    }
    foreach($fields_1 as $field => $value)                   #36
    {
      $type = $types_1[$field];
      echo "<tr><td style=\"text-align: right;
                    font-weight: bold\">$value</td>
                 <td><input type='$type' name='$field'
                            value='".@$$field."'
                            size='{$length_1[$field]}'
                            maxsize='{$length_1[$field]}'>
                 </td></tr>\n";
    }                                                        #46
?>
            <tr>
              <td colspan="2" style="text-align: center" >
              <br />
              <input type="submit" name="Button"
                  value="<?php echo $elements_1['submit']?>">
              </td></tr>
       </table>
       </form>
    </td>

    <!-- Column that separates the two forms -->
    <td style="background-color: gray"></td>
<?php
    #############
    ##  Form 2  #
    #############                                            #63
?>
    <td width="67%">
       <p style="font-size: 110%; font-weight: bold">
```

```php
                <?php echo $elements_2['top']?>
        <!-- Beginning of Form 1 (right side) -->
        <form action=<?php echo $_SERVER['PHP_SELF']?>
                method="POST">
        <p>
        <table border="0" width="100%">
<?php
  if (isset($GLOBALS['message_2']))                              #74
  {
    echo "<tr>
            <td colspan='2'
                style=\"font-weight: bold; font-style: italic;
                font-size: 90%; color: red\">
                {$GLOBALS['message_2']}<p></td></tr>";
  }
  foreach($fields_2 as $field => $value)                         #82
  {
    $type = $types_2[$field];
    if($type == "select")                                        #85
    {
      echo "<tr><td style=\"text-align: right;
                  font-weight: bold\">$fields_2[$field]</td>
            <td><select name='$field'>";
      foreach ($options[$field] as $opt_id => $opt_name)
      {
        echo "<option value='$opt_id'";
        if (@$_GET[$field] == $opt_id)
          echo " selected";
        echo ">$opt_name\n";
      }
      echo "</select>";
    }
    else
    {
      echo "<tr><td style=\"text-align: right;                   #101
                  font-weight: bold\">$value</td>
            <td><input type='$type' name='$field'
                      value='".@$$field."'
                      size='{$length_2[$field]}'
                      maxsize='{$length_2[$field]}'>
            </td></tr>";
    }
  }                                                              #109
?>
      <tr>
        <td colspan="2" style="text-align: center">
            <p style="margin-top: .05in">
            <input type="submit" name="Button"
                value="<?php echo $elements_2['submit']?>">
        </td></tr>
      </table>
      </form>
      </td>
```

Continued

LISTING 7-3: *(Continued)*

```
    </tr>
  </table>
  <hr size="10" noshade>
  <div style="text-align: center; font-size: 75%">
  <?php echo $page['bottom']?>
  </body></html>
```

Following is a description of the numbered lines of code that appear in `double_form.inc`, in Listing 7-3:

#27 Checks for the existence of an error message that is stored in the `$_GLOBALS` array. If it is set, the error message is displayed.

#36 For each element in the `$fields_1` array, which is used in the login form, a form input element is constructed.

#48 At line 48, the submit button is displayed. This button, if clicked, will make the form submit to `Login.php` and the user's user name and password will be evaluated.

#63 The form created after line 63 is the registration form.

#74 The `isset` function call checks for the existence of an error message that is stored in the `$_GLOBALS` array. If set, the error message is displayed.

#82 The `foreach` statement starts a loop through the elements that should be displayed on the registration form, as defined by the `$fields_2` array. Line 84 looks up the HTML element type for the field in the `$types_2` array (that is defined in `fields_login.inc`).

#85 This block of code creates the drop-down list of departments. In a real-life CMS, you will probably find tighter security. In the CMS example in this chapter, the user is trusted to choose her department. Remember, a user associated with a certain department has administrative rights for that department. A real-life CMS should include another layer of administration where a "super-user" can grant or revoke administrative privileges.

#101 In the HTML around line 101, a form input element is constructed. The length of the element is defined in the `$length_2` array (found in `fields_login.inc`).

#111 At line 111, the submit button is displayed. This button, if clicked, will make the form submit to `Login.php`, and `Login.php` will process registration information. If the validation succeeds the user will be forwarded on to the Intranet home page. If there is an error found while validating the registration information, the login page will be redisplayed and the errors will be noted on the screen in red text.

Writing CompanyHome.php, a data retrieval file

CompanyHome.php is responsible for setting up the data elements used by company.inc, a file that will display the HTML interface. CompanyHome.php is structured as a switch statement, with case blocks for each browse level. The browse level reflects the level in the site hierarchy at which the user is browsing, starting at the home page and drilling down to the content detail level. The browse level is passed in the URL. The switch statement tests the browse level and executes the appropriate case block. The following is an overview of the structure of the script:

```
switch (browse_level)

    case "home":
        1 Get the list of departments from the Department
            database table.
        2 Use the list of departments to build left-hand
            links to the departments.
        3 Use the list of departments to build the main body
            text of the Web page that will include the
            department description text.

    case "department":
        1 Get the list of content types supported in the CMS
            from the Content_Type database table.
        2 Use the list of content types to build left-hand
            links to the content type pages for the selected
            department.
        3 Use the list of content types to build main body
            text of links to the content type pages for the
            selected department.

    case "content":
        1 Get the list of content items based on the
            department and content type that the user has
            selected.
        2 If no content items exist, display a message
            indicating this.
        3 If content items exist, list the items in a table.
        4 If the user has administrative permissions in this
            department, display links that allow the user to
            add or edit the content item.

    case "details":
        1 Get the list of content details based on the
            department, content type, and content item that
            the user has selected.
        2 If the user is an administrator, show a form that
            includes elements that allow the user to upload
            files.
        3 Show any downloadable files in the left-hand
            section of the Web page.
```

Listing 7-4 contains the PHP code that sets up data elements that are going to be used to display the Web pages.

LISTING 7-4: GETTING THE DEPARTMENT AND CONTENT DATA FROM MYSQL

```php
<?php
  /* Program: CompanyHome.php
   * Desc:    Displays a Web page that has four levels:
   *          1) the home page, 2) a department page, 3) a
   *          content list page, and 4) a detail page.
   */
if (!isset($_SESSION))                                           #7
  session_start();

include_once("functions_main.inc");

$page = array(                                                   #12
  "title"         => "The Company Intranet",
  "header"        => "The Company Intranet",
  "bottom"        => "Copyright(R) 2005",
  "left_nav_links" => array(),
  "body_links"    => array(),
  "col_headers"   => array(),
  "data_rows"     => array(),
);

$admin = FALSE;
$base_url = "CompanyHome.php";
$trail = "<a href='$base_url'>Home</a>";                         #24

if (!isset($_SESSION['user_name']))
  header("Location: Login.php");                                 #27
else
{
  if (isset($_SESSION['user_dept'])
      && isset($_GET['dept_id']))
  {                                                              #32
    $admin = $_SESSION['user_dept'] == $_GET['dept_id'];
  }

  $cxn = Connect_to_db("Vars.inc");
  $left_nav_links = array();
  $page["browse_level"] =                                        #38
    isset($_GET['browse_level']) ?
      $_GET['browse_level'] : "home";

  switch ($page["browse_level"])                                 #42
  {
    case "home":
      $sql = "SELECT name, dept_id, description
              FROM Department
              ORDER BY name";
      $results = mysqli_query($cxn, $sql);
```

```php
      $body_links = "";
      while($row = mysqli_fetch_assoc($results))          #50
      {
        $link = "$base_url?dept_id=" . $row['dept_id']
          . "&browse_level=department";
        $page["left_nav_links"][$link] = $row['name'];
        $body_links .= "<li><a href=\"" . $link
          . "\">" . $row['name'] . "</a> - "
          . $row['description'];
      }
      $page["left_nav_header"] = "Departments";        #59
      $page["top"] = "Welcome to our Intranet";
      $page["body_text"] = "Welcome to our Intranet "
        . "where each department shares content with "
        . "the whole company.  You can update your "
        . "own departments content too with our simple "
        . "interface.<p>Vist the departments' "
        . "home pages: $body_links";

      break;

    case "department":                                 #70
      $dept_id = $_GET['dept_id'];
      $sql = "SELECT name, dept_id, description
              FROM Department
              WHERE dept_id = $dept_id ORDER BY name";
      $results = mysqli_query($cxn, $sql);
      $row = mysqli_fetch_assoc($results);
      $dept_name = $row['name'];
      $dept_desc= $row['description'];

      $page["left_nav"] = "$dept_name Content";
      $page["body_text"] = "$dept_name - $dept_desc";
      $sql = "SELECT a.name, a.type_id,
                     count(b.content_id)
              FROM Content_Type a
              LEFT OUTER JOIN Content b on
                   a.type_id = b.content_type
                   and b.dept_id = $dept_id
              GROUP BY a.name, a.type_id ORDER BY name";
      $results = mysqli_query($cxn, $sql);

      $body_links = "";
      while($row = mysqli_fetch_assoc($results))          #92
      {
        $link = "$base_url?dept_id=$dept_id"
          . "&type_id=" . $row['type_id']
          . "&browse_level=content";
        $page["left_nav_links"][$link] = $row['name'];
        $body_links .= "<li><a href=\"" . $link
          . "\">" . $row['name'] . "</a>";
      }
      $page["left_nav_header"] = "Content Index";
```

Continued

LISTING 7-4: *(Continued)*

```
    $page["top"] = $dept_name;
    $page["body_text"] = "$dept_name - $dept_desc "
      . "<p>Vist the departments' "
      . "areas: $body_links";
    $trail .= " - <a href='$base_url?dept_id=$dept_id"
          .   "&browse_level=department'>$dept_name</a>";
    break;

  case "content":                                        #110
    $dept_id = $_GET['dept_id'];
    $type_id = $_GET['type_id'];
    $sql = "SELECT a.name, a.type_id, b.title,
               b.description, b.content_date,
               b.create_date, b.created_by,
               b.last_upd_date, b.last_upd_by,
               c.name as dept_name, content_id
            FROM Content_Type a, Department c
            LEFT OUTER JOIN Content b on
               a.type_id = b.content_type
               and a.type_id = b.content_type
               and b.dept_id = $dept_id
               and b.content_type = $type_id
            WHERE c.dept_id = $dept_id
            ORDER BY content_date DESC";
    $results = mysqli_query($cxn, $sql);

    $body_links = "";
    $content_count = 0;
    $page["body_text"] = "";

    while($row = mysqli_fetch_assoc($results))           #132
    {
      if (!isset($area_name) && $type_id == $row["type_id"])
      {
        $area_name = $row["name"];
        $dept_name = $row["dept_name"];
      }
      $link = "$base_url?dept_id=$dept_id"
        . "&type_id=" . $row['type_id']
        . "&browse_level=content";
      $page["left_nav_links"][$link] = $row['name'];

      if (!isset($row["content_id"]))                    #144
        continue;

      $content_id = $row["content_id"];

      $content_count++;
      $link = "$base_url?dept_id=$dept_id"
        . "&type_id=$type_id&browse_level=content";
      $page["left_nav_links"][$link] = $row['name'];
```

```
      $page["data_rows"][] = $row;

   }
   if ($content_count == 0)                              #156
   {
      $page["body_text"] = "There are no $area_name
         content items for $dept_name";
   }
   if ($admin)                                           #161
   {
      $page["body_text"] .= "<p>[<a
               href='$base_url?dept_id=$dept_id"
            . "&browse_level=details&type_id=$type_id"
            . "&content_id='>add</a>]";
   }
   $page["col_headers"]["title"] = "$area_name Title";
   $page["col_headers"]["content_date"] = "$area_name
           Date";
   $page["col_headers"]["create_date"] = "Created On";
   $page["col_headers"]["created_by"] = "Created By";
   $page["col_headers"]["last_upd_date"] =
      "Last Updated On";
   $page["col_headers"]["last_upd_by"] =
      "Last Updated By";

   $page["left_nav_header"] = "Content";                 #176
   $page["top"] = "$dept_name - $area_name";
   $trail .= " - <a href='$base_url?dept_id=$dept_id"
         .   "&browse_level=department'>$dept_name</a>";
   $trail .= " - <a href='$base_url?dept_id=$dept_id"
         .   "&browse_level=content"
         .   "&type_id=$type_id'>$area_name</a>";
   break;

case "details":                                          #185
   $dept_id = $_GET['dept_id'];
   $type_id = $_GET['type_id'];

   $sql = "SELECT a.name as dept_name, b.name
           FROM Department a, Content_Type b
           WHERE b.type_id = $type_id
             and a.dept_id = $dept_id
           ORDER BY name";
   $results = mysqli_query($cxn, $sql);
   $body_links = "";
   $content_count = 0;

   while($row = mysqli_fetch_assoc($results))            #198
   {
      $area_name = $row["name"];
      $dept_name = $row["dept_name"];

      if (!isset($row["content_id"]))                    #203
         continue;
```

Continued

LISTING 7-4: *(Continued)*

```
      $content_count++;
      $link = "$base_url?dept_id=$dept_id"
        . "&type_id=".$row['type_id']
        . "&browse_level=content";
      $page["left_nav_links"][$link] = $row['name'];
      $body_links .= "<li><a href=\"" . $link
        . "\">" . $row['name'] . "</a>";
    }
    $create_date = date("m/d/y", time());
    $created_by = $_SESSION["user_name"];
    $last_upd_by = $_SESSION["user_name"];

    $content_id = $_GET["content_id"];
    $edit = $admin && (@$_GET["edit"] == "true"
                        || $content_id == "");

    if ($content_id != "")                              #222
    {
      Connect_to_db("Vars.inc");
      $sql = "SELECT content_id, dept_id, content_date,
                content_type as type_id, title,
                description, create_date,
                created_by, last_upd_date, last_upd_by
            FROM Content
            WHERE content_id = $content_id";
      $results = mysqli_query($cxn, $sql);
      if ($row = mysqli_fetch_assoc($results))
      {
        foreach ($row as $key => $value)
          $$key = $value;
      }
      $sql = "SELECT download_id, file_name
            FROM Content_Download
            WHERE content_id = $content_id";

      $results = mysqli_query($cxn, $sql);
      while($row = mysqli_fetch_assoc($results))        #242
      {
        $download_id = $row["download_id"];
        $file_name = $row["file_name"];
        $link = "files/$download_id/$file_name";
        $page["left_nav_links"][$link] = $file_name;

        if ($edit)                                      #249
          $page["left_nav_links"][$link] .= "</a>
          [<a href=\"Admin.php"
            . "?action=DeleteDownload&download_id=$down⤸
                    load_id\"
          >del</a>]";
      }
    }

    foreach ($_GET as $name => $value)                  #257
```

```
                $$name = $value;

        $edit = $admin && (@$_GET["edit"] == "true" || $con⤴
                          tent_id == "");

        $page["top"] = "$dept_name - $area_name";

        if ($edit)                                          #264
        {
          $page["body_text"] = "<center><u>Add Downloads</u>";
          for ($i = 0; $i < 3; $i++)
          {
            $page["body_text"] .=
              "<br><input type='file' name='upload_file$i'>";
          }

          $page["body_text"] .= "
            </center> <p />
            <center>
              <input type='reset' name='action'
                value ='Reset Form'>
              <input type='submit' name='action'
                value ='Cancel'>
              <input type='submit' name='action'
                value ='Save Changes'>
            </center>";

          $page["top"] .= " Edit/Create";
        }
        else
        {
          $page["body_text"] =
            "<a href='javascript:history.go(-1)'>Back</a>";
        }

        $page["left_nav_header"] = "Downloads";
        $trail .= " - <a href='$base_url?dept_id=$dept_id"
              . "&browse_level=department'>$dept_name</a>";
        $trail .= " - <a href='$base_url?dept_id=$dept_id"
              . "&browse_level=content"
              . "&type_id=$type_id'>$area_name</a>";

        break;

  }

  include("company.inc");
}
?>
```

Following is a description of the numbered lines of code that appear in `CompanyHome.php`, shown in Listing 7-4:

#7 Lines 7 and 8 ensure that a session has been started. The `isset` call at line 7 is used because `Admin.php`, which also has a `session_start` call, uses this file in an include call. Without the isset check for the `$_SESSION` variable, a notice might be displayed, like this: "Notice: A session had already been started — ignoring `session_start()`." This notice would display on your PHP page if the `error_reporting` level (set in the `php.ini` file) includes the `E_NOTICE` level.

#12 Lines 12 to 19 set up some strings and arrays that will be used in `company.inc` to display the Web page. You can change the title, header, and bottom variables to reflect the name of your company. The `left_nav`, `body_links`, `col_headers`, and `data_rows` elements are actually lists of data elements.

#24 Here a variable named `$trail` is defined. This string will be used to build a trail of links that will represent the hierarchy of the site that the user has traversed. In Figure 7-3 earlier in this chapter, you see the trail includes Home, the department being browsed (Human Resources), and the content area being browsed (FAQ).

#27 Line 27 and 28 check that the user is registered and has logged in. You can remove these lines if you want to open up the Web site to unregistered users. Some intranet Web sites don't require a login unless the user is trying to enter an administrative part of the site.

#32 Lines 30 to 34 set the `$admin` variable to either `TRUE` or `FALSE`. The `$admin` variable, defined at line 22, is used to determine whether a user has administrative privileges to the area of the Web site that the user is browsing.

#38 Lines 38 to 40 set up the `browse_level` variable (really an element in the `$page` array). The browse level determines whether the user is looking at

- The company's home page (`browse_level` of `"home"`)
- A department's home page (`browse_level` of `"department"`)
- A content item list (`browse_level` of `"content"`)
- The detailed view of a single content item (`browse_level` of `"details"`)

#42 Line 42 contains a switch statement that executes a block of code that depends on the level of hierarchy at which the user is browsing.

#50 Line 50 gathers the departments that make up the company's intranet. The design of the Department table (Table 7-2) enables flexible addition of new departments (or removal of departments that have been axed).

#59 Lines 59 to 66 fill in some page-level variables. The "home" `browse_level` represents the main home page (as seen in Figure 7-1). At this level, the departments are listed. The `left_nav_header`, top, and `body_text` elements of the `$page` array are set here. To make the CMS more managed (and less programmer-dependant), you can have the CMS get these strings from the database. Of course, to make the CMS truly user-managed, you have to build an interface to change these strings.

#70 Lines 70 to 88 are used to build the department-level display as shown in Figure 7-2 (shown earlier). The SQL that ends at line 88 uses an OUTER JOIN clause to make sure that all the content types are retrieved from the `Content_Type` table. If a regular join (INNER JOIN) were used here, then if there were no content items in the Content table for the department, no rows would get returned. The OUTER JOIN clause gets the content types (from the `Content_Type` table) regardless of if no content items exist (in the Content table).

#92 Begins a loop through the list of content types. At lines 94 to 96, the link to the content list is constructed.

#110 Begins a block of code that builds the content-level display, as shown in Figure 7-3, earlier in the chapter.

#132 Begins a loop through the list of content items. When the execution is at this point in the code, the program knows the department and content type in which the user is browsing.

#144 At line 144, a check for `content_id` is done. If `content_id` isn't set, the loop continues its next iteration. The `content_id` variable can be null because of the LEFT OUTER JOIN clause in the SQL. The code constructs the left-hand links to the content types regardless of whether there are items in the Content table. Line 153 assigns the `data_rows` element of the `$page` array to the results of the query.

#156 Line 156 checks the number of content items processed in the previous loop. If there are no content items, a message is displayed so that the user doesn't simply see a blank page.

#161 Begins a block of code that will add an administrative "add" link if the user is an administrator of the department being browsed.

#176 Lines 176 and 177 set up some display items to let the user know that the level of data being browsed is the content level. Lines 178 to 181 set up the trail of links that helps the user determine where in the Web site hierarchy she is browsing.

#185 Begins a block of code that builds the content detail-level display, as shown in Figure 7-4 and Figure 7-5.

#198 Begins a loop through the list of content items. When the execution is at this point in the code, the program knows the department, the content type, and the exact content item to which the user has browsed.

#203 At line 203 (like at line 144), a check for content_id is done. If the content_id variable isn't set, the loop continues its next iteration.

#222 If the $content_id contains a value, the code knows that the user is editing an existing content item. If this $content_id variable is empty, then the user is creating a new item.

#242 Begins a block of code that builds the list of downloads for a content item. In Figure 7-5, shown earlier, you can see in the left area of the Web page that one download is available.

#249 Begins a block of code that will add an administrative "del" link if the user is an administrator of the department being browsed. The "del" link will allow the user to delete the specific download item.

#257 Begins a loop through the $_GET array and sets up variables based on submitted HTML form elements.

#264 Begins a block of code used to build links for administrative actions. Users who aren't administrators in a department in which they are browsing won't see any administrative links and will be restricted to a read-only view of the data.

#297 This is the end of the CompanyHome.php script. At this point in the program's execution, the data needed to construct the HTML has been set up. Now, the company.inc file is included to actually build the HTML display.

Writing company.inc, the main HTML display file

The preceding code file, CompanyHome.php (shown in Listing 7-4), does most of the work of determining where the user is in the hierarchy of the Web site, if the user is an administrator, and what the title is of the Web page. The next code file, company.inc — shown in Listing 7-5 — does the display work. It parses the data lists set up in CompanyHome.php and builds the HTML.

LISTING 7-5: BUILDING THE HOME AND DEPARTMENT HTML DISPLAY

```php
<?php
 /* File: company.inc
  * Desc: Contains the code for a Web page that displays
  *       company and department data.
  */
include_once("functions_main.inc");                              #6
?>
<html>
```

```
<head><title><?php echo $page['title']?></title></head>
<body style="margin: 0">
<h3 align="center"><?php echo $page['top'] ?></h3>
<div style="font-size: 70%; font-weight: bold">
   <?php echo $trail ?></div>
<hr size="10" noshade>
<table border="0" cellpadding="5" cellspacing="0">
<?php
   ############
   ## Left Nav #
   ############                                              #16
?>
   <tr>
     <td width="20%" valign="top" >
       <p style="font-size: 110%; font-weight: bold">
            <?php echo $page['left_nav_header']?></p>
       <table border="0">
<?php
   foreach($page["left_nav_links"] as $link => $label)        #27
   {
     echo "<tr><td >"
       . "<a href=\"$link\">$label<p><p></td></tr>\n";
   }
   if (sizeof($page["left_nav_links"]) == 0)
     echo "<i>no items yet</i>";
?>
       </table>
     </td>

     <!-- Column that separates the two forms -->
     <td style="background-color: gray"></td>
<?php
   ##################
   ##  Main Content  #
   ##################
?>
     <td width="80%" valign="top">
       <form method="POST" action="Admin.php"
       enctype="multipart/form-data">
<?php

if ($page["browse_level"] == "details")                     #50
{
  include("fields_content.inc");
  include("content_form.inc");
}
else if (@$content_count > 0)                                #55
{
  echo "<table cellspacing='3' cellpadding='3'
    width='100%'bgcolor='gray'>
```

Continued

LISTING 7-5: *(Continued)*

```php
           <tr bgcolor='lightgray'>\n";
   foreach ($page["col_headers"] as $key => $display)
   {
     echo "<th >$display</th>\n";cl
   }
   echo "<th nowrap> </th>\n";
   echo "</tr>\n";
   foreach ($page["data_rows"] as $row)                          #66
   {
     echo "<tr bgcolor=white>\n";
     foreach ($page["col_headers"] as $key => $display)
     {
       if (ereg("date", $key))
         $row[$key] = date("m/d/y", strtotime($row[$key]));
       echo "<td nowrap>".$row[$key]."</th>\n";
     }
     echo "<th nowrap>[";
     if ($admin)                                                 #76
     {
       echo "<a href=\"Admin.php?action=delete"
         . "&dept_id=$dept_id&type_id=$type_id&content_id="
         . $row["content_id"] . "\">delete</a>\n";
     }
     echo "<a href=\"CompanyHome.php?"
       . "&dept_id=$dept_id&type_id=$type_id&content_id="
       . $row["content_id"] . ⤸
              "&browse_level=details&edit=false\">"
       . "view</a>\n";
     if ($admin)                                                 #86
     {
       echo "<a href=\"CompanyHome.php?"
         . "&dept_id=$dept_id&type_id=$type_id&content_id="
         . $row["content_id"] . ⤸
                "&browse_level=details&edit=true\">"
         . "edit</a>\n";
     }
     echo "]</th></tr>\n";
   }
   echo "</table>\n";
}

echo $page["body_text"];
?>
      </form>
     </td>
   </tr>
</table>
<hr size="10" noshade>
<div style="text-align: center; font-size: 75%">
<?php echo $page['bottom']?>
</body>
</html>
```

Following is a description of the lines of numbered code that appear in `company.inc`, shown in Listing 7-5:

#6   Line 6 ensures that the file that has the code for connecting to the database in included once.

#16   Begins an HTML row and the left column that contains either the departments (when the user is at the home page), the content types (when the user is at a department page), or the available downloads (when the user is viewing a content item's details).

#27   Begins the loop of the links on the left. If no links exist, a `no items yet` message is displayed.

#50   If the user is looking at a specific content item, the HTML is built by the included files.

#55   If more than one content item is listed, an HTML table listing the content items is constructed. Lines 57 to 65 set up the beginning of the HTML table.

#66   Begins the loop that builds a row in the HTML table for each content item.

#76   If the user is an administrator, a link to delete the content item is added to the display.

#86   If the user is an administrator, a link to edit the content item is added to the display.

Writing the content detail code

The Web site is designed in such a way that the user will drill down to the details. The home page and the department page don't list the full details of a single content item. The content detail page has all the information related to a single content item.

Writing fields_content.inc, setting up fields for the detail page

This next file — `fields_content`, shown in Listing 7-6 — sets up the elements to display on the content item form. The `$fields` associative array maps the form element IDs to display names. Some form names are left blank because they are hidden.

LISTING 7-6: SETTING UP ELEMENTS AND TYPES USED TO BUILD DISPLAY

```php
<?php
/* File: fields_content.inc
 * Desc: Contains arrays with the field names and form
 *       elements for the content pages.
 */
include_once("functions_main.inc");

$fields =   array("content_id"     => "",
                  "dept_id"        => "",
                  "type_id"        => "",
                  "title"          => "$area_name Title",
                  "description"    =>
                    "$area_name Description",
                  "content_date"   => "$area_name Date",
                  "create_date"    => "Creation Date",
                  "created_by"     => "Created By",
                  "last_upd_date"  => "Last Updated",
                  "last_upd_by"    => "Last Updated By"
                  );

$types =    array("content_id"     => "hidden",
                  "dept_id"        => "hidden",
                  "type_id"        => "hidden",
                  "content_date"   => "date",
                  "title"          => "text",
                  "description"    => "textarea",
                  "create_date"    => "datelabel",
                  "created_by"     => "label",
                  "last_upd_date"  => "datelabel",
                  "last_upd_by"    => "label"
                  );

$length =   array("content_date"   => "10",
                  "title"          => "30");
?>
```

The `$fields` associative array sets up the key to display mapping. The values of this associative array will be used in the labels on the HTML form. The `$types` associative array sets up the key to HTML type mapping. The values of this associative array determine the type of HTML element to use in the HTML form. The `$length` array maps an element key to the length of the HTML text box to be used in the display.

Writing content_form.inc, the content item detail display code

This next file — `content_form`, shown in Listing 7-7 — works as a form for editing data for a content item and also as a read-only view of a content item. If the user is an administrator, the form is shown, but non-administrators see only a read-only view of the data.

LISTING 7-7: BUILDING THE CONTENT DETAIL HTML DISPLAY

```php
<?php
 /* File: content_form.inc
  * Desc: Contains the display code for a content item.
  */
?>
<p>
<table border="0" width="100%">
<?php

  if (isset($GLOBALS['message_2']))                          #10
  {
    echo "<tr>
            <td colspan='2' style=\"font-weight: bold;
              font-style: italic;
              font-size: 90%; color: red\">
              {$GLOBALS['message_2']}<p></td></tr>";
  }

  $edit = $admin && (@$_GET["edit"] == "true"                #19
                    || @$content_id == "");
  foreach($fields as $field => $value)                       #21
  {
    $type = $types[$field];
    if ($type != "hidden" && !$edit)
    {
      $type = $type == "date" ? "datelabel" : "label";
    }
    switch ($type) {                                         #28
      case "hidden":
        echo "<input type='hidden' "
          . "name=\"$field\" value=\"".@$$field."\">";
        break;

      case "datelabel":
        if (!isset($$field) || $$field == "")
          break;
        $$field = date("m/d/Y", time($$field));

      case "label":
        echo "<tr><td nowrap valign=top
                    style=\"text-align: right;
                    font-weight: bold\">$value:</td>
                <td valign=top>".@$$field."</td></tr>";
        break;

      case "date":
        if (isset($$field) && $$field != "")
          $$field = date("m/d/Y", time($$field));

      case "text":
        echo "<tr><td valign=top nowrap
                    style=\"text-align: right;
```

Continued

LISTING 7-7: *(Continued)*

```
                        font-weight: bold\">$value:</td>
                <td valign=top>
                    <input type='$type'
                            name='$field'
                            value='".@$$field."'
                            size='{$length[$field]}'
                            maxsize='{$length[$field]}'>";

        if ($type == "date")
           echo " <i>(mm/dd/yyyy)</i>";
        echo "</td></tr>";
        break;

     case "textarea":
        echo "<tr><td nowrap style=\"text-align: right;
                        font-weight: bold\">$value</td>
                <td><textarea name='$field' cols=40 rows=8>"
            . @$$field
            . "</textarea>
                    </td></tr>";
  }
 }
?>
<input type="hidden" name="browse_level" value="details">
    <tr><td colspan="2" style="text-align: center">
            <p style="margin-top: .05in">
</table>
```

Following is a description of the numbered lines that appear in content_
form.inc, shown in Listing 7-7:

#10 Begins a block of code that, if message_2 is set in the $_GLOBALS array, displays the error text that is stored in the array element.

#19 The $edit variable gets set to either TRUE or FALSE. If the user is an administrator and the user clicked the Edit link to get to the detail page, $edit is set to TRUE and the page shows up in the edit mode. Otherwise, $edit is set to FALSE and the page appears in a read-only view.

#21 Begins a loop through the form elements. HTML is constructed based on the attributes set in the $types array and whether the user can edit the content item.

#28 Begins a switch statement that looks at the type of the element and builds the HTML based on that type.

Writing Admin.php, the data manipulation code

When writing code that is going to make changes to data, you can never be too careful when validating that the user has proper access to modify data, that the data being submitted is valid, and that related data relationships are valid. In the CMS example in this chapter, some validation is done, but for simplicity's sake only a couple checks are in place. Ideally, you should look at every line of code and ask yourself whether someone could in any way maliciously (or accidentally) reach an invalid state in the code. You can use the built-in `assert` function while debugging your code to check any code assumptions.

The brains of the CMS reside in the `Admin.php` file. Items are added, deleted, and modified in this code file. The form built in the `content_form.inc` file will post its form elements to `Admin.php`. `Admin.php` has to validate data, redirect the user to the next display, and save the data to the database.

Here is the basic flow of the administrative PHP file (`Admin.php`), which is shown in its entirety in Listing 7-8:

Loop through the submitted form elements.

Examine the action that the user is performing:

switch (action)

    case "delete":
       1 Delete the content details from the Content table for the content item that the user is trying to delete.
       2 Delete any download items from the Content_Download table that are associated with the content item that the user is deleting.

    case "Save Changes":
       1 Organize and validate the form elements being submitted.
       2 If the user is saving a new content item, insert a new row into the Content database table.
       3 If the user is saving an existing content item, update a row in the Content database table.
       4 Loop through the files that have been uploaded and add their details to the Content_Download table.

    case "DeleteDownload":
       1 Delete from the Content_Download table a single item.

LISTING 7-8: UPDATING THE DATABASE AND SAVE UPLOADED FILES

```php
<?php
 /* File:    Admin.php
  * Desc:    Perform any data manipulation tasks, like
  *          creating, editing, or deleting content items.
  */
session_start();
include_once("functions_main.inc");

foreach ($_POST as $name => $value)                      #9
  $$name = $value;
foreach ($_GET as $name => $value)                       #11
  $$name = $value;

if (!isset($action))                                     #14
  header("Location: CompanyHome.php");

if (!isset($create_date))                                #17
  $create_date = date("Y-m-d", time());
else
  $create_date = time($create_date);
if (!isset($content_date))
  $content_date = date("Y-m-d", time());
else
  $content_date = strtotime($content_date);

$content_date = date("Y-m-d", $content_date);
$last_upd_date = date("Y-m-d", time());

if (!isset($created_by))
  $created_by = $_SESSION["user_name"];

$last_upd_by = $_SESSION["user_name"];

$cxn = Connect_to_db("Vars.inc");
switch ($action)                                         #35
{
  case "delete":                                         #37
    $sql = "DELETE FROM Content
            WHERE content_id=$content_id";

    mysqli_query($cxn, $sql);
    $sql = "DELETE FROM Content_Download
            WHERE content_id=$content_id";
    mysqli_query($cxn, $sql);

    break;

  case "Save Changes":                                   #48
    $message_2 = "";

    if ($content_date <= 0)
      $message_2 = "<li>Invalid Content Date";
```

```php
      if ($title == "")
        $message_2 .= "<li>Title cannot be left blank";

      if ($message_2)
        $message_2 = "Please correct these errors: $message_2";

      if ($message_2 != "")
      {
        include("CompanyHome.php");
        exit();
      }
      if ($content_id)                                          #65
      {
        $sql = "UPDATE Content
                   SET title = '$title',
                   description = '$description',
                   content_date = '$content_date',
                   last_upd_date = '$last_upd_date',
                   last_upd_by = '$last_upd_by'
                 WHERE content_id = $content_id";
      }
      else                                                      #75
      {
        $sql = "INSERT Content (dept_id, content_type,
                   title, description, content_date,
                   create_date, created_by,
                   last_upd_date, last_upd_by)
                 VALUES ($dept_id, $type_id, '$title',
                   '$description', '$content_date',
                   '$create_date', '$created_by',
                   '$last_upd_date', '$last_upd_by')";
      }

      Connect_to_db("Vars.inc");                                #87

      mysqli_query($cxn, $sql);

      if (!$content_id)
        $content_id = mysqli_insert_id($cxn);                   #92

      foreach ($_FILES as $file)                                #94
      {
        $file_name = $file["name"];
        if ($file["size"] <= 0)
          continue;

        $sql = "INSERT Content_Download (content_id, file_name)
                 VALUES ($content_id, '$file_name')";
        mysqli_query($cxn, $sql);
        $file_id = mysqli_insert_id($cxn);                      #103
        $dest_dir = "files".DIRECTORY_SEPARATOR.$file_id;
        $dest_file = $dest_dir.DIRECTORY_SEPARATOR.$file_name;
```

Continued

LISTING 7-8: *(Continued)*

```
      if(!file_exists($dest_dir))                            #107
      {
        if(!mkdir($dest_dir, 0700, TRUE))
          die ("Can't archive attachments to $dest_dir");
      }

      if (!file_exists($dest_file))                          #113
      {
        if (!move_uploaded_file($file["tmp_name"], ⤶
          $dest_file))
          die ("Can't archive attachments to $dest_dir");
      }
    }

    break;
  case "DeleteDownload":                                     #121
    $sql = "SELECT a.dept_id, a.content_type
            FROM Content a, Content_Download b
            WHERE b.download_id=$download_id
              AND a.content_id = b.content_id";

    $results = mysqli_query($cxn, $sql);

    $row = mysqli_fetch_assoc($results);
    $dept_id = $row["dept_id"];
    $type_id = $row["content_type"];
                                                             #132
    $sql = "DELETE FROM Content_Download
            WHERE download_id=$download_id";
    mysqli_query($cxn, $sql);

    break;
  case "Cancel":
    break;
}

$query_str = "browse_level=content"                          #142
  . "&dept_id=$dept_id&type_id=$type_id";
header("Location: CompanyHome.php?$query_str");
?>
```

Following is a description of the numbered lines that appear in `Admin.php`, shown in Listing 7-8:

#9   Begins a loop through the form elements that have been submitted to `Admin.php` by using the POST form method.

#11   Begins a loop through the form elements that have been submitted to `Admin.php` by using the GET form method.

#14 When the form from `content_form.inc` is submitted to `Admin.php`, it should supply an action. Without an action (that gets set in the `$action` variable), the code won't know whether the user is trying to add, delete, or modify a content item. Therefore, if no action has been supplied, the user is sent back to the home page by the header directive. The `"Location: pathname"` header directive tells the user's browser to go to another location. There are other headers that are useful when designing dynamic Web sites. The `"Pragma: no-cache"` header directive tells the user's browser how to manage caching. The `"Expires: GMT time"` header directive can help make sure timely content is refreshed. (Note that these are not used in this chapter.)

#17 For new content items, the creation date is created from scratch by using the `time()` function. In this file, you see the `time`, `strtotime`, and `date` functions used. The `time` function creates an integer storing the milliseconds since January 1, 1970, GMT, also known as the UNIX Epoch. The `strtotime` function is used to parse a generic date string in an attempt to retrieve a real-time value. (A –1 returned from this function means that PHP cannot determine the time value of the string passed in as a variable.) The `date` function will take a `time` variable and apply a formatting to it.

#35 Begins a `switch` block that examines the action that the user wants to take for a content item. The user might be adding a new content item, adding a new download item, deleting a content item, deleting a download item, or editing a content item's details.

#37 Begins a block of code that deletes a content item. Associated download items are also deleted in lines 42 to 44.

#48 Begins a block of code that saves changes to a content item. Lines 49 to 58 validate some of the submitted form elements. At line 63, if there are any problems found while validating the submitted form, the user is sent to back to the content details page.

#65 At lines 65 to 74, SQL is constructed for updating an existing content item that the user is attempting to update. The code knows that this is an item to edit (as opposed to being a new item) because the check for the `$content_id` variable passes.

#75 At lines 75 to 85, SQL is constructed for a creating a new content item.

#87 Lines 87 to 89 connect to the database and execute the SQL that will either create or update a content item.

#92 Lines 91 and 92 will fill in the `$content_id` variable if the item is a new item. The `mysql_insert_id` function will retrieve from the database the value of the identity column from the most recently inserted row.

#94 Begins a loop that will save each uploaded file that the user has attached. In Figure 7-4 (shown earlier), you see an Add Downloads section of the Web page where, using the Browse button, the user can upload a file. Three downloads are shown by default, but you can add more after saving the content item details if the user returns to the edit view of the content item.

#103 The file is stored in the file system by using a path that includes the identifier of the row ($file_id) in the Content_Download table. Notice the DIRECTOR_SEPARATOR constant. This built-in constant helps ensure that your code is portable across different operating systems. If you were to hard-code a backslash (\) as the directory separator (like C:\www\files), then if you ever had to relocate your code to a UNIX or Mac server you might find that your code failed when trying to access an invalid file path.

#107 Checks for the existence of the destination directory. This directory should be unique, so you could insert additional error checking code here to display a system error if the $dest_dir directory already exists. The directory is created at line 109.

#113 Checks for the existence of the destination file. It shouldn't already exist, but your PHP code should never assume too much about the state of the system. At line 115, the file that was uploaded by the user is moved to the destination that the CMS has constructed, the $dest_dir directory. The move_uploaded_file function call is necessary because PHP will eventually remove any uploaded files that it stored in the temporary file location (determined by the upload_tmp_dir value in the php.ini file). The PHP code in the example in this chapter does not restrict the file upload size. You can restrict the size of uploaded files in one of two ways:

- Change the upload_max_filesize setting in the php.ini file.

- Add a hidden input field to the HTML form named MAX_FILE_SIZE and enter a value (in bytes) in the HTML input's value field.

#121 At line 121 is a block of code for is deleting a download item. The first SQL query retrieves the dept_id and type_id values from the database for the download item that is being deleted. This is done so that the next page being displayed has enough information to maintain the user's place in the hierarchy of the Web site being browsed.

#132 Delete the database information pertaining to the download item. Notice that the file hasn't been deleted from the file system. To do this, the code would need to retrieve the path of the download item (before the database row is deleted) and then use the unlink function to delete the actual file.

#142 At this point in the code's execution, all data manipulation has been done, and the code redirects the user (via the Location header directive) to the home page.

Building the CMS Application: Object-Oriented Approach

When designing an objected-oriented system, designers can define the object model first — including the properties, methods, and constructors of the objects — without filling in all the code that will eventually reside in the objects. By first designing the high-level objects, designers, programmers, and users can conceptually view a system and hopefully find any holes in the design before writing a bunch of code. Furthermore, with an object model design in place, the coding tasks can be broken up among multiple programmers. As long as the programmer knows the methods of an object, she can write code that uses objects that someone else coded. For more information on designing an object-oriented system, check out *An Introduction to Object-Oriented Analysis: Objects and UML in Plain English,* 2nd Edition, by David William Brown (Wiley).

Writing the object model

In the section "The objects" I tell you about the classes that make up the object model for the CMS in this chapter. The object-oriented code is functional and reuses much of the procedural code. The biggest difference between the procedural code and the object-oriented code is that a set of objects have been created to encapsulate the underlying data objects.

If you look at the DDL defined earlier in this chapter (in the "Designing the Content_Type table" section), you see a direct correlation between the underlying database tables and the following classes. The object models that you design for other applications might not always reflect your database structure.

The CMS example in this chapter consists of departments, content areas, content items, and downloads. Each of these things can be represented using objects. For instance, a `Department` object has methods that reveal the name and description of a department.

The objects

The `Department`, `ContentType`, `ContentItem`, and `ContentDownload` classes are used in this chapter and help to make up the object model for the CMS. I describe them here, along with a couple other classes:

- `Department`: This class represents a department within a company's organization. The CMS application in this chapter cares only about the department's name, description, and its underlying ID in the database. This class has only read-only methods because the CMS application has no mechanism for modifying the department list. The department list is driven by the contents of the `Department` table. A possible enhancement to the CMS example in this chapter would be an administrative module that would allow administrators to add new departments to the system.

✔ `ContentType`: Within the CMS, a user can browse a number of content types, such as New, Events, and FAQs. The `ContentType` class helps the CMS categorize the content data. The class contains only an ID and a name. The content type list is driven by the contents of the `Content_Type` table. A possible enhancement to the CMS example in this chapter would be an administrative module that would allow administrators to add new content types to the system.

✔ `ContentItem`: This class is the workhorse of the CMS. This class encapsulates the data that users are creating or editing. The underlying data is stored in the `Content` table in the database. This class has `save` and `delete` functions so that changes to the object can be reflected in the database.

✔ `ContentDownload`: This class, representing data stored in the `Content_Download` table, simply exposes a filename and ID. The `save` and `delete` functions allow the PHP code to persist the object's details to the database.

✔ `BaseInfo`: The classes outlined in the preceding bullets have a couple things in common: a name and an identifier. The `BaseInfo` class is the common denominator among the other classes. This class allows you to simplify all the other classes because the common code has been centralized in one class.

✔ `Database`: This class encapsulates the setup of the database connection. The `getConnection` function is used by consumers of this object to get the database connection. A benefit of object-oriented programming (OO programming) is that implementation details can be in a *black box*. In other words, code that uses the `Database` class doesn't need to know how the class sets up database connections. Consumer code cares only about the methods that objects make available.

✔ `WebForm`: The `WebForm` class provides forms for the application. It collects and processes the information typed by a user.

Creating static finder methods

How do you get data from the database into an object representation in your PHP code? There are several approaches to this. You could build a single PHP file to search for data and instantiate the appropriate objects. You could put the object instantiation code wherever the need for objects arises. In the example in this chapter, the factory approach is used. A *factory method* is responsible for taking some search parameters and returning the desired object or objects. Factory methods have a simple, straightforward job: They just churn out objects. The *finder methods* have static scope. This means that the factory methods do not require an instantiated object to execute. For regular class methods, the object has to be instantiated (created) with the new keyword before its methods can be used. Static methods do not need to be executed within an object context.

The static finder methods for the objects in the object model in this chapter reside in the objects' code. Therefore, each class is responsible for locating the underlying data from the database and instantiating the objects that represent the data. For instance, the Department object has a method, findAll, that returns an array of Department objects. The findById method returns a single object (or NULL if no data is found in the database for the ID that is supplied as a parameter to the method call). The name of each of the finder method begins with find.

A static method is called by using the format ClassName::staticMethod Name(). This is different from an object method call, which looks like $variableNam->methodName(). Here are some more illustrations of code that use object methods versus static method calls:

```
# Object instantiation
$object_instance = new MyObject();

# Object method call
echo $object_instance->getDescription();

# Static method call, returns an array of objects
$object_array = MyObject::findAllData();

# Static method call, returns a single object
$object_instance = MyObject::findById($id);

# Object method call
echo $object_instance->getName();
```

Creating getter and setter methods

Objects reveal their details through *getter methods*. These methods, usually with a name beginning with get, return an object's attributes. If you were designing an Employee object, you might implement these getter methods: getFirstName, getLastName, getIdNumber, getAge, and so on. *Setter methods*, on the other hand, are methods that enable consumers of the objects to set an object's attributes. Some setter methods of an Employee object might include setFirstName, setLastName, setDepartment, setAge, and so on.

Writing a basic data class

When creating an object model, you can often *factor out* (or *generalize*) common attributes and functions into a base class. In the CMS in this chapter, each of the data objects has an identifier and a name. These properties, along with a static helper function to retrieve a database connection, will make up the base class, BaseInfo.class.

The properties

The `BaseInfo` properties store the ID and name of an item. The properties are:

```
protected $id;
protected $name;
```

The first property, `$id`, is the underlying identifier of the column. The `$name` property is a displayable name or title for the item. Notice that these properties are *protected*, which means that the properties cannot be accessed from consumers of the object. However, subclasses do have access to these properties.

The code

Listing 7-9 contains the complete code for the `BaseInfo` class. I discuss each method in detail after the code listing.

LISTING 7-9: THE BASEINFO CLASS

```php
<?php
 /* Name: BaseInfo.class
  * Desc: Base Class from which the data objects can
  *       extend.  The ID and name are common among
  *       all the data objects.  Also, the database
  *       connection can be obtained from this class.
  */
include_once("Database.class");

class BaseInfo
{
  protected $id;
  protected $name;

  function __construct($id, $name)
  {
    $this->id = $id;
    $this->name = $name;
  }

  protected static function getConnection()
  {
    $db = new Database("Vars.inc");
    $db->useDatabase("IntranetCMS");
    return $db->getConnection();
  }

  public function getId()
  {
    return $this->id;
```

```
   }

   public function getName()
   {
     return $this->name;
   }

 }
 ?>
```

The constructor

The constructor requires an identifier and a name. These parameters are used to assign values to the properties of the object.

getConnection

This method simply instantiates a `Database` object and uses its `get Connection` method to return the database connection. The method is static because the finder methods, which are static too, need to obtain a database connection to perform a search.

getId, getName

The `$id` value is exposed by the `getId` function. In object-oriented programming, you should try to declare functions to get and set internal attributes instead of exposing class variables by making them public. This helps to ensure that a class strictly controls its internal state. The `getName` method returns the name of the object.

Writing the Department class

The `Department` class encapsulates the information that makes up a department within the organization. This includes the department name, description, and the department ID.

The properties

The `Department` object's properties store information about a single department within the organization. The properties are:

protected $description;

Notice that this class defines one property, but the class really has three properties. The other two properties (`ID` and `name`) are defined in the `BaseInfo` class. Because the `Department` class is a subclass of the `BaseInfo` class, the `Department` class has inherited the `BaseInfo` class's properties.

The code

Listing 7-10 contains the complete code for the Department class. I discuss each method in detail after the code listing.

LISTING 7-10: THE DEPARTMENT CLASS

```php
<?php
 /* Name: Department.class
  * Desc: Class containing details for a department
  *       and the content within the department.
  */
include_once("BaseInfo.class");

class Department extends BaseInfo
{
  protected $description;                                    #10

  function __construct($id, $name, $desc)
  {
     parent::__construct($id, $name);                        #14
     $this->description = $desc;
  }

  public function getDescription()                           #18
  {
     return $this->description;
  }

  public static function findAll()
  {
     $cxn = parent::getConnection();                         #25
     $sql = "SELECT dept_id, name, description
                FROM Department
               ORDER BY name";
     $results = $cxn->query($sql);
     if (!$results)
     {
        throw new Exception("Problem getting data: " +
                          $cxn->error);
     }
     $depts = array();
     while ($row = $results->fetch_assoc())                  #36
     {
        $depts[] = new Department($row['dept_id'],
          $row['name'], $row['description']);
     }
     return $depts;
  }

  public static function findById($id)
  {
     $cxn = parent::getConnection();
```

```
      $sql = "SELECT dept_id, name, description
              FROM Department
              WHERE dept_id = $id";
      $results = $cxn->query($sql);
      if (!$results)
      {
        throw new Exception("Problem getting data: " +
                            $cxn->error);
      }
      if ($row = $results->fetch_assoc())
      {
        return new Department($row['dept_id'],
          $row['name'], $row['description']);
      }
      return NULL;
    }

  }

  ?>
```

The constructor

The base class doesn't have all the properties needed to represent a department, so an additional property is declared to represent the long description for a department at line 10. Remember that the $id and $name properties from the base class, BaseInfo, are also accessible in this class. The constructor is needed to handle the additional $description property. The parent class's constructor is called on line 14 so that the $id and $name properties get set.

getDescription

This new method at line 18 exposes the $description property.

findAll, findById

These methods are static finder functions. In the object model in this design, the code that does the searching resides in the classes themselves. The findAll function will return an array of instantiated objects that meet the search parameters. At line 25, a database connection is retrieved by using a function defined in the parent class. At line 36 is a loop that will fill the return array with new Department objects. findById will return a single object for the search if there is a matching row in the database for the identifier.

Writing the ContentType class

This class is very simple. It represents a content type available in the CMS. A content type has only an ID and a name. These properties were already coded in the base class, so the only other code that needs to go in this class is the code that will handle the searching and instantiating of ContentType objects.

The properties

The ContentType class doesn't define any properties, but it will use the properties that are defined in the *super class* (also called the *parent class*), the $id and $name properties.

The code

Listing 7-11 contains the complete code for the ContentType class. I discuss each method in detail after the code listing.

LISTING 7-11: THE CONTENTTYPE CLASS

```php
<?php
/* Name: ContentType.class
 * Desc: Class containing details for a content type
 *       available in the CMS.
 */
include_once("BaseInfo.class");

class ContentType extends BaseInfo
{

  public static function findAll()                          #11
  {
    $cxn = parent::getConnection();
    $sql = "SELECT type_id, name
            FROM Content_Type
            ORDER BY name";
    $results = $cxn->query($sql);
    if (!$results)
    {
      throw new Exception("Problem getting data: " +
                          $cxn->error());
    }
    $types = array();
    while ($row = $results->fetch_assoc())
    {
      $types[] = new ContentType($row['type_id'],
        $row['name']);
    }
    return $types;
  }

  public static function findById($id)                       #32
  {
    $cxn = parent::getConnection();
    $sql = "SELECT type_id, name
```

```
               FROM Content_Type
               WHERE type_id = $id";
    $results = $cxn->query($sql);
    if (!$results)
    {
      throw new Exception("Problem getting data: " +
                          $cxn->error());
    }
    if ($row = $results->fetch_assoc())
    {
      return new ContentType($row['type_id'], $row['name']);
    }
    return NULL;
  }

}
?>
```

The constructor

This class doesn't explicitly define a constructor because the one defined in the parent class (`BaseInfo.class`) meets the needs of this class too. So there's no code for a constructor in this class file.

findAll, findById

These methods are static finder functions. `findAll` at line 11 returns an array of objects, and `findById` at line 32 returns a single object (if the search yields a row in the database).

Writing the ContentItem class

The `ContentItem` class is the base class representing the different types of content items available in the CMS. This class can be extended because some content items might have more or fewer details tied to the content item. For instance, in Listing 7-13 the `FAQ` class is defined. The `showColumn` function returns `FALSE` when the `content_date` string is passed in as a parameter. For an `FAQ` content item, this `content_date` isn't relevant for the end user, therefore the overridden class will enable the display interface to ignore the field.

The properties

The `Department` object's properties store information about a single department within the organization. The properties are

```
protected $description;
protected $content_date;
protected $create_date;
```

```
    protected $created_by;
    protected $last_upd_date;
    protected $last_upd_by;
```

The properties $id and $name are inherited from the BaseInfo class, so they aren't redefined here. The $description property is a string that represents the main body of a content item. The $content_date property reflects that date on which a content item is relevant; in the case of an event content item, the $content_type property is used to signify the date of the listed event. The $created_by, $create_date, $last_upd_date, and $last_upd_by properties are used for basic auditing the content item.

The code

Listing 7-12 contains the complete code for the ContentItem class. I discuss each method in detail after the code listing.

LISTING 7-12: THE CONTENTITEM CLASS

```php
<?php
/* Name: ContentItem.class
 * Desc: Class containing details for a single
 *       content item.
 */
include_once("BaseInfo.class");

class ContentItem extends BaseInfo
{
    protected $description;                              #10
    protected $content_date;
    protected $create_date;
    protected $created_by;
    protected $last_upd_date;
    protected $last_upd_by;

    function __construct($id, $title, $desc,             #17
        $content_date, $created_on, $created_by,
        $last_upd_on, $last_upd_by)
    {
        parent::__construct($id, $title);

        $this->description = $desc;
        $this->content_date = $content_date;
        $this->create_date = $created_on;
        $this->created_by = $created_by;
        $this->last_upd_date = $last_upd_on;
        $this->last_upd_by = $last_upd_by;
    }

    public function setName($name)                       #31
```

```php
{
  $this->name = $name;
}

public function getDescription()                                    #36
{
  return $this->description;
}

public function setDescription($desc)
{
  $this->description = $desc;
}

public function getContentDate()
{
  return date("m/d/y", strtotime($this->content_date));
}

public function setContentDate($content_date)
{
  $this->content_date = strtotime($content_date);
}

public function getCreationDate()
{
  return date("m/d/y", strtotime($this->create_date));
}

public function setCreationDate($create_date)
{
  $this->create_date = strtotime($create_date);
}

public function getCreatedBy()
{
  return $this->created_by;
}

public function getLastUpdDate()
{
  return date("m/d/y", strtotime($this->last_upd_date));
}

public function getLastUpdBy()
{
  return $this->last_upd_by;
}

public function setLastUpdBy($last_upd_by)
{
  $this->last_upd_by = $last_upd_by;
}
```

Continued

LISTING 7-12: *(Continued)*

```
public static function findById($content_id)                    #86
{
  $cxn = parent::getConnection();
  $sql = "SELECT content_id, title, description,
          content_date, create_date,
          created_by, last_upd_date, last_upd_by
      FROM Content
      WHERE content_id = $content_id";

  $results = $cxn->query($sql);
  if (!$results)
  {
    throw new Exception("Problem getting data: " +
                        $cxn->error);
  }
  $row = $results->fetch_assoc();

  return ContentItem::getContentItem($row);                     #103
}

public static function findByDeptType($dept_id,
                                      $content_type)
{
  $cxn = parent::getConnection();
  $sql = "SELECT content_id, title, description,
          content_date, create_date,
          created_by, last_upd_date, last_upd_by
      FROM Content
      WHERE content_type = $content_type
          and dept_id = $dept_id";
  $results = $cxn->query($sql);
  if (!$results)
  {
    throw new Exception("Problem getting data: " +
                        $cxn->error);
  }
  $ret_array = array();
  while ($row = $results->fetch_assoc())                        #123
    $ret_array[] = ContentItem::getContentItem($row);

  return $ret_array;
}

public static function getContentItem($row)                     #129
{
  if (!$row)
    return NULL;

  return new ContentItem($row['content_id'], $row['title'],
    $row['description'], $row['content_date'],
    $row['create_date'], $row['created_by'],
```

```
      $row['last_upd_date'], $row['last_upd_by']);
}

public function save($dept_id = NULL, $type_id = NULL)    #140
{
  if (isset($this->id))                                    #142
  {
    $sql = "UPDATE Content
                SET title = '$this->name',
                description = '$this->description',
                content_date = '$this->content_date',
                last_upd_date = now(),
                last_upd_by = '$this->last_upd_by'
            WHERE content_id = $this->id";
  }
  else                                                     #152
  {
    $sql = "INSERT Content (dept_id, content_type,
                title, description, content_date,
                create_date, created_by,
                last_upd_date, last_upd_by)
            VALUES ($dept_id, $type_id,
                '$this->name',
                '$this->description', '$this->content_date',
                now(), '$this->created_by',
                now(), '$this->last_upd_by')";
  }

  $cxn = parent::getConnection();
  $cxn->query($sql);

  if (!isset($this->id))
    $this->id = $cxn->insert_id;

  return $this->id;
}

public function delete()                                   #174
{
  if (!isset($this->id))
    return;

  $sql = "DELETE FROM Content
          WHERE content_id = $this->id";
  $cxn = parent::getConnection();
  $results = $cxn->query($sql);
  if (!$results)
  {
    throw new Exception("Problem deleting data: " +
                        $cxn->error);
  }
                                                           #188
  $sql = "DELETE FROM Content_Download
```

Continued

```
LISTING 7-12: (Continued)

            WHERE content_id = $this->id";
    $results = $cxn->query($sql);
    if (!$results)
    {
      throw new Exception("Problem deleting data: " +
                          $cxn->error);
    }
  }

}
?>
```

The constructor

The constructor sets up the properties of the ContentItem class at line 17. Remember, the $id and $name properties aren't defined in this class because they have already been defined in the parent class. Within the constructor the parent class's constructor is also called so that the base class's properties get set properly.

setName, setDescriptionn, setContentDate, setCreationDate, setLastUpdBy

The setter methods change the object's internal state. For instance, a call to setName at line 31 changes the $name property, which is actually defined in the BaseInfo class. These setter functions don't persist the data changes to the database. That is the responsibility of the save and delete functions.

getContentDate, getCreationDate, getLastUpdBy, getLastUpDate

The getter methods expose the properties of the object. Without these methods, the outside world wouldn't be able to retrieve the details of the object's properties. The getDescription method at line 36 will return the long description of the content item.

findById, findByDeptType

Line 106 begins the definition of a function that returns an array of ContentItem objects for a given department and content type, whereas the findById method at line 86 returns a single ContentItem object based on the ID of the content item.

save, delete

The save function is responsible for saving a new or modified ContentItem object to the database, whereas the delete function removes its details from the database. At line 142, the isset function call helps the save function decide whether the ContentItem object ($this) is a new or existing object in the database. If the ID hasn't yet been set in the object, the code considers the `ContentItem` to be a brand new content item.

getContentItem

The `getContentItem` function is used by the finder functions to instantiate a single `ContentItem` object from a single row returned from the database, like at line 103. The `getContentItem` function simplifies the code that instantiates a new object.

Writing the ContentDownload class

This is another simple object that represents a single row in the database. In this case, a `ContentDownload` item represents a row in the `Content_Download` table. Notice that this object doesn't define a constructor because the constructor defined in the parent class fits the needs of this class. Just some additional finder functions are needed along with the data manipulation methods.

The properties

The `ContentDownload` class doesn't define any properties, but it will use the properties that are defined in the parent class: the `$id` and `$name` properties.

The code

Listing 7-13 contains the complete code for the `ContentDownload` class. I discuss each method in detail after the code listing.

LISTING 7-13: THE CONTENTDOWNLOAD CLASS

```php
<?php
 /* Name: ContentDownload.class
  * Desc: Class containing details for a
  *       content item's downloadable file.
  */
include_once("BaseInfo.class");

class ContentDownload extends BaseInfo
{
   public static function findByContentId($content_id)          #10
   {
     $ret_arr = array();

     $cxn = parent::getConnection();
     $sql = "SELECT download_id, file_name
```

Continued

LISTING 7-13: *(Continued)*

```php
                    FROM Content_Download
            WHERE content_id = $content_id";
    $results = $cxn->query($sql);
    if (!$results)
    {
      throw new Exception("Problem getting data: " +
                          $cxn->error);
    }
    while($row = $results->fetch_assoc())
    {
      $download_id = $row["download_id"];
      $file_name = $row["file_name"];

      $ret_arr[] =
        new ContentDownload($download_id, $file_name);
    }

    return $ret_arr;
  }

  public static function findById($file_id)                  #36
  {
    $ret_arr = array();

    $cxn = parent::getConnection();
    $sql = "SELECT download_id, file_name
            FROM Content_Download
            WHERE download_id = $file_id";
    $results = $cxn->query($sql);
    if (!$results)
    {
      throw new Exception("Problem getting data: " +
                          $cxn->error);
    }
    if ($row = $results->fetch_assoc())
    {
      $download_id = $row["download_id"];
      $file_name = $row["file_name"];

      return new ContentDownload($download_id, $file_name);
    }

    return NULL;
  }

  public function save()                                     #61
  {
    $sql = "INSERT Content_Download (content_id, file_name)
            VALUES ($this->id, '$this->name')";

    $cxn = parent::getConnection();
    $results = $cxn->query($sql);
```

```
      if (!$results)
      {
        throw new Exception("Problem saving data: " +
                        $cxn->error);
      }

      $this->id = $cxn->insert_id;                        #74

      return $this->id;
   }

   public function delete()                               #79
   {
      $sql = "DELETE FROM Content_Download
              WHERE download_id=$this->id";

      $cxn = parent::getConnection();
      $results = $cxn->query($sql);
      if (!$results)
      {
        throw new Exception("Problem deleting data: " +
                        $cxn->error);
      }
    }
  }
}
?>
```

The constructor

This class doesn't explicitly define a constructor because the one defined in the parent class (BaseInfo.class) meets the needs of this class too. You can save a lot of typing when writing object-oriented code.

findByContentId, findById

These methods are static finder functions. The findByContentId method at line 10 returns an array of objects, and findById at line 36 returns a single object (if the search yields a row in the database).

save, delete

The save (line 61) and delete (line 79) methods ensure that data is either saved to the database or removed from the database.

Writing the Database class

The Database class provides the connection to the database where the user, department, and content data are stored. I develop the Database class in Chapter 3. See Listing 3-4 for the Database class code.

The methods provided by the `Database` class are:

✔ **The constructor:** This method creates a connection to a MySQL database. It also expects to be passed the hostname, account name, and password necessary to access MySQL. A `Database` object is created with the following statement:

```
$db = new Database($host,$user,$password);
```

✔ `useDatabase`: This method selects a database and stores the database name. It expects to be passed a database name. It also checks whether the database exists and returns a message if the database doesn't exist.

✔ `getConnection`: This method returns the connection that is established and stored in the constructor.

Writing the WebForm class

The `WebForm` class is used to display the page with the login and registration forms. I create and explain the `WebForm` class in Chapter 4. The class is shown in Listing 4-6.

The methods in the `WebForm` class that are used in this application are:

✔ **The constructor:** The constructor stores the properties needed to display the form correctly. Two files — an information file and a file that defines the look and feel — are required. The two filenames are passed when the `WebForm` object is created and stored in two properties. The data for the form fields can be passed, but can be left out, and the form fields will be blank. You can create the object by using either of the following statements:

```
$form = new WebForm("file1.inc","file2.inc",$_POST);
$form = new WebForm("file1.inc","file2.inc");
```

✔ `displayForm`: This method displays the form. It extracts the data from the `$data` property where it is stored.

✔ `checkForBlanks`: This method checks each field in the form to see whether it contains information. If invalid blank fields are found, it returns an array containing the field names of the blank fields.

✔ `verifyData`: This method checks each field to ensure that the information submitted in the field is in a reasonable format. If invalid data is found in any field, the method returns an array containing messages that identify the problems.

✔ `trimData, stripTagsFromData`: A PHP function is applied to each value in the `$data` property. The resulting values are stored in `$data`. The trim function removes leading and trailing blanks from a string. The `strip_tags` function removes any HTML tags from the string, which is important for security.

Writing the code for the login page

The object-oriented login page — Login-OO.php — from Chapter 4 (Listing 4-10) is modified here to deal with the tables and PHP files in this chapter. Listing 7-14 highlights the changes.

Login-OO.php requires three additional classes that are not used by other programs in the CMS application: Account.class, Session.class, and Email.class. I don't describe these classes in this chapter. For more information on these classes and how they are used in the login application, see the object-oriented application section in Chapter 4.

LISTING 7-14: LOGIN-OO.PHP CHANGES

```
Line 38:
$db->useDatabase("intranetCMS");                                    #38
Line 39:
$acct = new Account($db->getConnection(),"Dept_User");
Lines 83 and 174:
header("Location: CompanyHome-OO.php");
Line 154:
$sess->storeVariable("user_name",$newdata['user_name']);
$sess->storeVariable("user_dept",$newdata['dept_id']);
```

Following is a description of the lines that were changed from the Login-OO.php file in Chapter 4:

#38 Changes the name of the database.

#39 The name of the database table that stored user details has been changed to use the Dept_User table.

#83 [and **#174**] Upon successful login or registration, the user's browser is redirected to the application's main display PHP, CompanyHome-OO.php. The header directive sends a command to the user's browser. If you have HTML being sent to the browser before a header directive has been sent, the directive call will create an error because all headers must be sent before any content is displayed.

#154 Chapter 4 stored a flag in the session to indicate that the user had been authenticated ("auth"), and it stored the user's ID ("logname"). The CMS application in this chapter stores the user name ("user_name") and department identifier ("dept_id") in the session variable.

Writing fields_content.inc and content_form.inc

The `fields_content.inc` (refer to Listing 7-6) and `content_form.inc` (refer to Listing 7-7) files from the procedural code section can be reused for the object-oriented approach to coding the CMS application.

Writing the display code

`CompanyHome-OO.php` is very similar to `CompanyHome.php` defined earlier in this chapter (in Listing 7-4). The only real difference is that the object model defined in the "Writing the Object Model" section is leveraged. Because the object code handles the database retrieval and persistence details, the display code is alleviated from needing to know about the database structure. This is the beautiful thing about OO code: You can create layers of abstraction that can make it possible to change the internals of objects without having to change the consumers of the objects in the object model.

Writing CompanyHome-OO.php

`CompanyHome-OO.php` — shown in Listing 7-15 — is responsible for setting up the data elements used by `company-OO.inc`, a file that will display the HTML interface.

LISTING 7-15: SETTING UP DISPLAY DATA, COMPANYHOME-OO.PHP

```php
<?php
  /* Program: CompanyHome-OO.php
   * Desc:    Displays a Web page that has four levels:
   *          1) the home page, 2) a department page, 3) a
   *          content list page, and 4) a detail page.
   */
if (!isset($_SESSION))
  session_start();

include_once("functions_main.inc");
include_once("Department.class");                          #11
include_once("ContentType.class");
include_once("ContentItem.class");
include_once("ContentDownload.class");                     #14

$page = array(
  "title"          => "The Company Intranet",
  "header"         => "The Company Intranet",
  "bottom"         => "Copyright(R) 2005",
```

```php
  "left_nav_links" => array(),
  "body_links"     => array(),
  "col_headers"    => array(),
  "data_rows"      => array(),
);

$admin = FALSE;
$base_url = "CompanyHome-OO.php";
$trail = "<a href='$base_url'>Home</a>";

if (!isset($_SESSION['user_name']))
  header("Location: Login-OO.php");                         #31
else
{
  if (isset($_SESSION['user_name'])
      && isset($_GET['dept_id']))
  {
    $admin = $_SESSION['user_dept'] == $_GET['dept_id'];
  }

  $left_nav_links = array();

  $page["browse_level"] =
    isset($_GET['browse_level']) ?
      $_GET['browse_level'] : "home";

  switch ($page["browse_level"])
  {
    case "home":                                            #48
      try
      {
        $departments = Department::findAll();               #51
      }
      catch(Exception $e)
      {
        echo $e->getMessage();
        exit();
      }
      $body_links = "";
      foreach ($departments as $department)                 #59
      {
        $link = "$base_url?dept_id=" . $department->getId()
          . "&browse_level=department";
        $page["left_nav_links"][$link] =
          $department->getName();
        $body_links .= "<li><a href=\"" . $link
          . "\">" . $department->getName() . "</a> - "
          . $department->getDescription();
      }
      $page["left_nav_header"] = "Departments";
      $page["top"] = "Welcome to our Intranet";
```

Continued

LISTING 7-15: (Continued)

```
      $page["body_text"] = "Welcome to our Intranet "
        . "where each department shares content with "
        . "the whole company.  You can update your "
        . "own departments content too with our simple "
        . "interface.<p>Vist the departments' "
        . "home pages: $body_links";
    break;

  case "department":                                        #79
    $dept_id = $_GET['dept_id'];
    try
    {
      $department = Department::findById($dept_id);          #83
    }
    catch(Exception $e)
    {
      echo $e->getMessage();
      exit();
    }
    $dept_name = $department->getName();                     #90
    $dept_desc= $department->getDescription();

    $page["left_nav"] = "$dept_name Content";
    $page["body_text"] = "$dept_name - $dept_desc";

    $body_links = "";
    $content_types = ContentType::findAll();                 #97
    foreach ($content_types as $content_type)                #98
    {
      $link = "$base_url?dept_id=$dept_id"
        . "&type_id=" . $content_type->getId()
        . "&browse_level=content";
      $page["left_nav_links"][$link] =
        $content_type->getName();
      $body_links .= "<li><a href=\"" . $link
        . "\">" . $content_type->getName() . "</a>";
    }
    $page["left_nav_header"] = "Content Index";
    $page["top"] = $dept_name;
    $page["body_text"] = "$dept_name - $dept_desc "
      . "<p>Vist the departments' "
      . "areas: $body_links";
    $trail .= " - <a href='$base_url?dept_id=$dept_id"
          . "&browse_level=department'>$dept_name</a>";
    break;

  case "content":                                           #117
    $dept_id = $_GET['dept_id'];
    $type_id = $_GET['type_id'];
    try
    {
```

```
    $department = Department::findById($dept_id);        #122
}
catch(Exception $e)
{
  echo $e->getMessage();
  exit();
}
$dept_name = $department->getName();
$body_links = "";
$page["body_text"] = "";
try
{
  $content_types = ContentType::findAll();             #134
}
catch(Exception $e)
{
  echo $e->getMessage();
  exit();
}
foreach ($content_types as $content_type)
{
  $link = "$base_url?dept_id=$dept_id"
    . "&type_id=" . $content_type->getId()
    . "&browse_level=content";
  $page["left_nav_links"][$link] =
    $content_type->getName();
  if ($content_type->getId() == $type_id)
    $area_name = $content_type->getName();
}
$page["data_rows"] =                                    #151
  ContentItem::findByDeptType($dept_id, $type_id);
if (sizeof($page["data_rows"]) == 0)                    #153
{
  $page["body_text"] = "There are no $area_name
    content items for $dept_name";
}
if ($admin)
{
  $page["body_text"] .=
          "<p>[<a href='$base_url?dept_id=$dept_id"
        . "&browse_level=details&type_id=$type_id"
        . "&content_id='>add</a>]";
}
$page["col_headers"]["title"] = "$area_name Title";
$page["col_headers"]["content_date"] =
                                "$area_name Date";
$page["col_headers"]["create_date"] = "Created On";
$page["col_headers"]["created_by"] = "Created By";
$page["col_headers"]["last_upd_date"] =
  "Last Updated On";
$page["col_headers"]["last_upd_by"] =
```

Continued

LISTING 7-15: *(Continued)*

```
      "Last Updated By";
    $page["left_nav_header"] = "Content";
    $page["top"] = "$dept_name - $area_name";
    $trail .= " - <a href='$base_url?dept_id=$dept_id"
           . "&browse_level=department'>$dept_name</a>";
    $trail .= " - <a href='$base_url?dept_id=$dept_id"
           . "&browse_level=content"
           . "&type_id=$type_id'>$area_name</a>";
    break;

  case "details":                                          #183
    $dept_id = $_GET['dept_id'];
    $type_id = $_GET['type_id'];
    $department = Department::findById($dept_id);          #186
    $dept_name = $department->getName();
    $content_type = ContentType::findById($type_id);
    $area_name = $content_type->getName();
    $body_links = "";
    $create_date = date("m/d/y", time());
    $created_by = $_SESSION["user_name"];
    $last_upd_by = $_SESSION["user_name"];
    $content_id = $_GET["content_id"];
    $edit = $admin && (@$_GET["edit"] == "true"
                       || $content_id == "");
    if ($content_id != "")
    {                                                      #198
      $content_item = ContentItem::findById($content_id);
      $title = $content_item->getName();                  #200
      $content_date = $content_item->getContentDate();
      $description = $content_item->getDescription();
      $create_date = $content_item->getCreationDate();
      $created_by = $content_item->getCreatedBy();
      $last_upd_date = $content_item->getLastUpdDate();
      $last_upd_by = $content_item->getLastUpdBy();
      $downloads =                                         #207
        ContentDownload::findByContentId($content_id);
      foreach($downloads as $download)                    #209
      {
        $download_id = $download->getId();
        $file_name = $download->getName();
        $link = "files/$download_id/$file_name";
        $page["left_nav_links"][$link] = $file_name;
        if ($edit)
          $page["left_nav_links"][$link] .= "</a>
          [<a href=\"Admin-OO.php" .
        "?action=DeleteDownload&download_id=$download_id&"
            . "dept_id=$dept_id&type_id=$type_id\"
          >del</a>]";
      }
    }
    foreach ($_GET as $name => $value)
```

```php
        $$name = $value;
      $edit = $admin && (@$_GET["edit"] == "true" ||
                          $content_id == "");
      $page["top"] = "$dept_name - $area_name";
      if ($edit)
      {
        $page["body_text"] = "<center><u>Add Downloads</u>";
        for ($i = 0; $i < 3; $i++)
        {
          $page["body_text"] .=
            "<br><input type='file' name='upload_file$i'>";
        }
        $page["body_text"] .= "
          </center> <p />
          <center>
            <input type='reset' name='action'
              value ='Reset Form'>
            <input type='submit' name='action'
              value ='Cancel'>
            <input type='submit' name='action'
              value ='Save Changes'>
          </center>";
        $page["top"] .= " Edit/Create";
      }
      else
      {
        $page["body_text"] =
          "<a href='javascript:history.go(-1)'>Back</a>";
      }
      $page["left_nav_header"] = "Downloads";
      $trail .= " - <a href='$base_url?dept_id=$dept_id"
              . "&browse_level=department'>$dept_name</a>";
      $trail .= " - <a href='$base_url?dept_id=$dept_id"
              . "&browse_level=content"
              . "&type_id=$type_id'>$area_name</a>";

      break;
  }
  include("company-OO.inc");
}
?>
```

Following is a description of the numbered lines of code that appear in
CompanyHome-OO.php, shown in listing 7-15:

#11   Lines 11 to 14 ensure that the class definitions are included so that
the object model outlined earlier can be put into action.

#31   Here the OO login application from Chapter 4 is leveraged.

#48   The home page display is handled in this block of the switch
statement.

#51 The static method call finds all the departments in the intranet. The array returned from this function contains `Department` objects.

#59 Each `Department` object is examined in this loop so that the department name and description can be displayed on the home page.

#79 The department-level display is handled in this block of the `switch` statement.

#83 At this point in the program's execution, the user has clicked a specific department. The `$department` variable becomes an instantiation of the `Department` class when the `findById` function returns.

#90 Lines 90 and 91 retrieve some details about the department.

#97 Line 97 gets the list of content types in the CMS, each content type being represented by a `ContentType` object.

#98 Begins a loop through all the `ContentType` objects. The objects' details will be used to build the links to the content areas for the selected department.

#117 The content list display is handled in this block of the `switch` statement.

#122 This static function call retrieves an object representing the selected department.

#134 The static function call will find all the content types in the system.

#151 At line 151 the list of content items is added to a page-level variable so that `company-OO.inc` will be able to build the display of all the objects' data.

#153 Begins a block of code that will display an informational message if there are no content items for the selected department and content type.

#183 The block of code executed when a user is looking at the details for a single content item.

#186 Lines 186 to 189 get details for the display from objects.

#198 If the `$content_id` variable contains a value, the details of the content item are retrieved by using the finder function at line 199.

#200 Lines 200 to 206 show the details of the content item being extracted from the object using the getter functions.

#207 The downloadable files associated with the selected content item are retrieved.

#209 Begins the loop that builds links to the downloadable files by using the details from the `ContentDownload` objects.

Writing company-OO.inc, the main display code

Here the objects set up in CompanyHome-OO.php — the file shown in Listing 7-16 — are leveraged to build the HTML display. Other than the use of these objects, not much else is different from the procedural version of this file, company.inc.

LISTING 7-16: BUILDING THE HTML DISPLAY

```php
<?php
 /* File: company-OO.inc
  * Desc: Contains the code for a Web page that displays
  *        company and department data.
  */
include_once("functions_main.inc");
?>
<html>
<head><title><?php echo $page['title']?></title></head>
<body style="margin: 0">
<h3 align="center"><?php echo $page['top'] ?></h3>
<div style="font-size: 70%; font-weight: bold">
   <?php echo $trail ?></div>
<hr size="10" noshade>
<table border="0" cellpadding="5" cellspacing="0">
<?php
   #############
   ## Left Nav #
   #############
?>
   <tr>
     <td width="20%" valign="top" >
       <p style="font-size: 110%; font-weight: bold">
            <?php echo $page['left_nav_header']?></p>
       <table border="0">
<?php
   foreach($page["left_nav_links"] as $link => $label)
   {
     echo "<tr><td >"
       . "<a href=\"$link\">$label<p><p></td></tr>\n";
   }
   if (sizeof($page["left_nav_links"]) == 0)
     echo "<i>no items yet</i>";
?>
       </table>
     </td>

     <!-- Column that separates the two forms -->
     <td style="background-color: gray"></td>
<?php
```

Continued

LISTING 7-16: *(Continued)*

```
    ####################
    ##  Main Content  #
    ####################
?>
    <td width="80%" valign="top">
      <form method="POST" action="Admin-OO.php"
      enctype="multipart/form-data">
<?php

if ($page["browse_level"] == "details")
{
  include("fields_content.inc");
  include("content_form.inc");
}
else if (sizeof($page["data_rows"]) > 0)
{
  echo "<table cellspacing='3' cellpadding='3'
    width='100%'bgcolor='gray'>
      <tr bgcolor='lightgray'>\n";
  foreach ($page["col_headers"] as $key => $display)
  {
    echo "<th >$display</th>\n";
  }
  echo "<th nowrap> </th>\n";
  echo "</tr>\n";
  foreach ($page["data_rows"] as $content_item)
  {
    echo "<tr bgcolor=white>\n";                                    #68
    echo "<td nowrap>" . $content_item->getName() . "</th>\n";
    echo "<td nowrap>" . $content_item->getContentDate()
      . "</th>\n";
    echo "<td nowrap>" . $content_item->getCreationDate()
      . "</th>\n";
    echo "<td nowrap>" . $content_item->getCreatedBy()
      . "</th>\n";
    echo "<td nowrap>" . $content_item->getLastUpdDate()
      . "</th>\n";
    echo "<td nowrap>" . $content_item->getLastUpdBy()
      . "</th>\n";                                                  #79

    echo "<th nowrap>[";
    if ($admin)
    {
      echo "<a href=\"Admin-OO.php?action=delete"
        . "&dept_id=$dept_id&type_id=$type_id&content_id="
        . $content_item->getId() . "\">delete</a>\n";
    }
    echo "<a href=\"CompanyHome-OO.php?"
      . "&dept_id=$dept_id&type_id=$type_id&content_id="
      . $content_item->getId() .
                      "&browse_level=details&edit=false\">"
      . "view</a>\n";
```

```
      if ($admin)
      {
        echo "<a href=\"CompanyHome-OO.php?"
          . "&dept_id=$dept_id&type_id=$type_id&content_id="
          . $content_item->getId() . ⤴
                          "&browse_level=details&edit=true\">"
          . "edit</a>\n";
      }
      echo "]</th></tr>\n";
    }
    echo "</table>\n";
  }

  echo $page["body_text"];
?>
        </form>
      </td>
    </tr>
</table>
<hr size="10" noshade>
<div style="text-align: center; font-size: 75%">
<?php echo $page['bottom']?>
</body>
</html>
```

Following is a description of the numbered lines of code that appear in
CompanyHome-OO.php (shown in Listing 7-16):

#68   Lines 68 to 79 show the use of the objects to get the content item
details. For each column displayed in the HTML table, a different function is used to get the value. Keep in mind that the data in this object
maps back to data stored in the database. However, this display code
doesn't know about the data, how it is stored, or how it is retrieved. As
long as the objects can be leveraged, the display can be constructed.

Writing fields_content.inc and content_form.inc

The fields_content.inc and content_form.inc files from the procedural
code section can be reused for the object-oriented approach to coding the
CMS application.

Writing Admin-OO.php, the data manipulation code

The data manipulation code is simpler than the procedural code in this
chapter because the SQL code isn't executed in the administrative PHP
code. Instead, the administrative PHP, Admin-OO.php, operates on objects.

The `save` and `delete` functions of the objects are used to modify the underlying data. This differs from the procedural `Admin.php` file, where SQL to manipulate the data is defined within the PHP itself. The OO code removes the need to have SQL in the administrative PHP file. In Listing 7-17, the PHP code simply uses method calls to manipulate the underlying data.

LISTING 7-17: UPDATING THE DATABASE AND SAVING UPLOADED FILES

```php
<?php
/* File:   Admin-OO.php
 * Desc:   Perform any data manipulation tasks, like
 *         creating, editing, or deleting content items.
 */
session_start();
include_once("functions_main.inc");
include_once("ContentItem.class");                          #8
include_once("ContentDownload.class");

foreach ($_POST as $name => $value)
  $$name = $value;
foreach ($_GET as $name => $value)
  $$name = $value;
if (!isset($action))
  header("Location: CompanyHome-OO.php");

if (!isset($create_date))
  $create_date = date("Y-m-d", time());
else
  $create_date = strtotime($create_date);
if (!isset($content_date))
  $content_date = date("Y-m-d", time());
else
  $content_date = strtotime($content_date);

$content_date = date("Y-m-d", $content_date);
$last_upd_date = date("Y-m-d", time());

if (!isset($created_by))
  $created_by = $_SESSION["user_name"];

$last_upd_by = $_SESSION["user_name"];

switch ($action)
{
  case "delete":                                            #37
    $content_item = ContentItem::findById($content_id);
    if (isset($content_item))
      try
      {
        $content_item->delete();
      }
      catch(Exception $e)
      {
```

```
            echo $e->getMessage();
            exit();
        }

    break;

case "Save Changes":
    $message_2 = "";
    if ($content_date <= 0)
        $message_2 = "<li>Invalid Content Date";
    if ($title == "")
        $message_2 .= "<li>Title cannot be left blank";
    if ($message_2)
        $message_2 = "Please correct these errors: $message_2";
    if ($message_2 != "")
    {
        include("CompanyHome-OO.php");
        exit();
    }
    if ($content_id)                                        #65
    {
        try
        {
            $content_item = ContentItem::findById($content_id);
        }
        catch(Exception $e)
        {
            echo $e->getMessage();
            exit();
        }
        $content_item->setName($title);
        $content_item->setDescription($description);
        $content_item->setLastUpdBy($last_upd_by);
        $content_id = $content_item->save();
    }
    else                                                    #81
    {
        $content_item = new ContentItem(NULL,
            $title, $description, $content_date,
            $create_date, $created_by,
            $last_upd_date, $last_upd_by);
        $content_id = $content_item->save($dept_id, $type_id);
    }
    foreach ($_FILES as $file)                              #89
    {
        $file_name = $file["name"];
        if ($file["size"] <= 0)
            continue;
        $download = new ContentDownload($content_id,
                                        $file_name);
        $file_id = $download->save();
```

Continued

LISTING 7-17: *(Continued)*

```php
      $dest_dir = "files".DIRECTORY_SEPARATOR.$file_id;
      $dest_file = $dest_dir.DIRECTORY_SEPARATOR.$file_name;
      if(!file_exists($dest_dir))
      {
        if(!mkdir($dest_dir, 0700, TRUE))
          die ("Can't archive attachments to $dest_dir");
      }
      if (!file_exists($dest_file))
      {
        if (!move_uploaded_file($file["tmp_name"],
                                $dest_file))
          die ("Can't archive attachments to $dest_dir");
      }
    }

    break;

  case "DeleteDownload":                                   #114
    try
    {
      $download = ContentDownload::findById($download_id);
      $download->delete();
    }
    catch(Exception $e)
    {
      echo $e->getMessage();
      exit();
    }

    break;

  case "Cancel":
    break;
}

$query_str = "browse_level=content"
  . "&dept_id=$dept_id&type_id=$type_id";
header("Location: CompanyHome-OO.php?$query_str");
?>
```

Following is a description of the numbered lines in `Admin-OO.php`, shown in Listing 7-17:

> **#8**   The two types of data that can be changed by users of the CMS, represented by the `ContentItem` and `ContentDownload` classes, are used in `Admin-OO.php`.

#37   The block of code beginning at line 37 uses the `ContentItem` class's static finder function to get the single content item object that the user wishes to delete. The object's `delete` function is called to remove the underlying data from the database. `Admin-OO.php` doesn't need to know how this is accomplished because the object-oriented approach allows such details to be encapsulated in the class's code.

#65   Begins a block of code that updates an existing content item.

#81   Begins a block of code that creates a new content item.

#89   Begins a loop that saves any uploaded files to the database. Again, the details of how the information is saved to the database is abstracted from the code in `Admin-OO.php`.

#114 This is where the details for a single downloadable file are looked up. After the information is located, it's removed via the `ContentDownload` object's `delete` function.

Enhancing the Content Management System

The CMS you see in this chapter is very generic. It supports a number of content types, but the user interface, the data, and the object model don't differ much for each content type. The object model could be further developed so that, perhaps, a `News` object and an `Event` object would have more attributes that are relevant to the object model's specific content type. For instance, an `Event` content type could be implemented so that users could register for one or more events.

A well-designed CMS should organize content so that, if the volume of data grows, browsing through and searching for content doesn't become tedious. Paging is a useful feature for simplifying navigation through long lists of content items. Also, a keyword search is a nice tool that enables users to quickly locate a number of related but distinct content items.

Chapter 8

Hosting Discussions with a Web Forum

* * *

* * *

A *Web forum* is a popular way to let your Web site visitors communicate with you and with each other. A forum is like a community bulletin board where one visitor can leave a message and other visitors can read that message and reply to it with messages of their own. In a lively forum, you can typically find questions (and answers); tips and techniques; reviews (for products, books, restaurants, and so on); and links to other resources.

Designing the Forum Application

The basic function of a Web forum is to store, organize, and display messages. When you navigate to a forum site (by using a Web browser, such as Firefox or Konqueror), you see a page that displays a list of forums. For example, if the site hosts discussions related to household pets, you might see forums named Cats, Dogs, Reptiles, and Others. Underneath each forum, you might see a list of topics *owned by* the forum. Within the Cats forum, for example, you might see topics such as Cat Breeds, Health Issues, Feeding, and Bad Habits. The Dogs forum might hold a similar set of topics. If you look inside the Reptiles forum, you might find Amphibians, Snakes, Lizards, Housing, and Feeding.

When you click a topic, your browser moves to a new page that displays a list of the *threads* owned by the topic. A thread is a collection of messages, all of which share the same topic. From this page, you can click a thread to display the messages owned by that thread or you can click the Start a New Thread button to create a new thread. When you navigate to a specific thread, you see a list of all the messages in that thread. Each message displays the author (that is, the e-mail address of the user who posted the message); the date/time that the message was posted; and the body of the message. To reply to a message, just click the Reply button next to that message.

The heart of the forum application is a set of tables that organize the messages created by your users. When a user *posts* a new message, the text of the message is stored as a single row in a table that I call Post. Each Post contains a bit of bookkeeping information (such as the author of the message, the date the message was posted, and so on). To organize the messages in your forum, you can add a few layers on top of the Post table to group messages into similar areas of discussion. Each Post belongs to a single Thread. Each Thread belongs to a single Topic. Each Topic belongs to a single Forum. All together, you need four tables to organize messages the way I describe: Forum, Topic, Thread, and Post.

Forums and topics are different from threads and posts in several respects. You, the forum administrator, create the forums and topics. Your users create threads and posts. To create a new forum, you simply add a row to the Forum table. To create a new topic, add a row to the Topic table. When a user posts a message, he can start a new thread or reply to an existing thread. To start a new thread, the user clicks the Start a New Thread button, types in a subject for the thread, and types in the body of the message. When he clicks the Post Message button, a new row is inserted into the Thread table and a new row is inserted into the Post table. To add a message to an existing thread, the user clicks the Reply To button and types in the body of the message. (Note that he doesn't have to enter a subject for the message — the subject is inherited from the message that he's replying to.) When he clicks the Post Reply button, a new row is inserted into the Post table (and the related Thread is updated to indicate the date of the most recent message).

You need to consider the security of your forum. Will you allow *any* visitor to start new threads? Must a user register (and log in) before she can reply to an existing thread? The forum application that you develop in this chapter takes a middle-of-the-road approach to security. Only a forum administrator can add new forums and new topics. Anyone can start a new thread or reply to an existing one. Throughout this chapter, I point out a few changes that you can make to adjust the security policy to fit your needs.

Creating the Forum Database

This application has four layers of organization. Looking from the top down, you start with a forum, which contains one or more topics. Each topic contains a collection of zero or more threads. (A topic is empty until someone starts a thread.) Each thread contains a collection of one or more posts, all sharing the same subject. Looking at the forum structure from the bottom up, each message is owned by a single thread, each thread is owned by a single topic, and each topic is owned by a single forum.

Designing the Forum database

The sample application in this chapter uses a database named Forum. The forum application defines four tables: Forum, Topic, Thread, and Post. Each table contains an id column — every row is uniquely identified by its id. To link the tables together into a hierarchy, every Post, Thread, and Topic contains the unique identifier of its parent. For example, a Post is owned by a Thread: If you look inside a Post, you see a column named parent_thread that contains the id of the parent Thread. In a similar fashion, each Thread contains a parent_topic and each Topic contains a parent_forum.

Designing the Forum table

The Forum table contains information about each forum. Table 8-1 shows the layout of the Forum table.

Table 8-1	Database Table: Forum	
Variable Name	*Type*	*Description*
id	INTEGER UNSIGNED	Unique identifier for forum (primary key)
name	VARCHAR(100)	Forum name
description	TEXT	Description of forum

The Forum table is straightforward; it exists only to organize similar topics into meaningful groups. Each row contains a unique identifier (id), a name, and a description. The id column is defined as an auto_increment column so that the MySQL server assigns a unique value to each row. The forum name is required, but the description is optional.

Designing the Topic table

The Topic table contains information about each topic. Table 8-2 shows the layout of the Topic table.

Table 8-2	Database Table: Topic	
Variable Name	*Type*	*Description*
parent_forum	INTEGER UNSIGNED	Forum to which this topic belongs
id	INTEGER UNSIGNED	Unique identifier for topic (primary key)
name	VARCHAR(100)	Topic name
description	TEXT	Description of topic

The `Topic` table is very similar to the `Forum` table; the `Topic` table exists only to organize similar threads into meaningful groups. Every row in the `Topic` table belongs to some row in the `Forum` table. The `parent_forum` in any given `Topic` identifies the owner of the `Topic` (that is, `Topic.parent_forum` will contain the `Forum.id` value of the `Forum` that owns the `Topic`). The `id` column serves as a unique identifier for the `Topic` and, like the `Forum.id` column, the MySQL server assigns a value to this column each time you add a new `Topic`. `Topic.name` is required and `Topic.description` is optional.

Designing the Thread table

The `Thread` table contains information about each thread. The `Thread` table is shown in Table 8-3.

Table 8-3	Database Table: Thread	
Variable Name	*Type*	*Description*
parent_topic	INTEGER UNSIGNED	Topic to which this thread belongs
id	INTEGER UNSIGNED	Unique identifier for thread (primary key)
subject	TEXT	Subject for all messages in this thread
replies	INTEGER UNSIGNED	Number of replies in this thread
last_post	TIMESTAMP	Date (and time) of most recent post in this thread

The Thread table is a bit more complex than the Forum and Topic tables. Each Thread belongs to a Topic and the Thread.parent_topic column contains the Topic.id of the owner. Like the Forum and Topic tables, each Thread is uniquely identified by a server-assigned id. When a user starts a new Thread, she must provide a subject. The replies column contains a count of the number of messages in the thread (minus one — the first message in a thread doesn't count as a reply). The last_post column contains the time and date of the most recent message added to any given Thread. You add a new record to the Thread table each time a user starts a new discussion. You update Thread.replies and Thread.last_post each time a message is added to the thread.

Designing the Post table

The Post table contains information about each post. The Post table is shown in Table 8-4.

Table 8-4	Database Table: Post	
Variable Name	**Type**	**Description**
parent_thread	INTEGER UNSIGNED	Thread to which this post belongs.
in_reply_to	INTEGER UNSIGNED	If this message is the first message in a thread, in_reply_to is NULL; otherwise, in_reply_to contains the ID of some other Post.
Id	INTEGER UNSIGNED	Unique identifier for post (primary key).
author	VARCHAR(100)	Name of user who posted this message.
date	TIMESTAMP	Date that this message was posted.
body	TEXT	Text of message.

Each message is stored as a single row in the Post table. Notice that you aren't storing a subject with each Post — instead, the subject is stored in the Thread that *owns* the Post. The in_reply_to column contains the id of another Post. If a Post is the first message in a Thread, in_reply_to will be NULL; otherwise, the Post must be a reply to some other message. The author column contains the name of the user who posted the message. The date column stores the time and date that the message was added — the MySQL server automatically timestamps each row when it is added it to the table.

The `parent_thread`, `parent_topic`, and `parent_forum` columns link the forum tables together into a hierarchy.

You can find the thread that owns a given post by executing a query such as `SELECT * FROM Thread WHERE Thread.id = Post.parent_thread`.

Similarly, you can find the topic that owns a thread with the query `SELECT * FROM Topic WHERE Topic.id = Thread.parent_topic`.

You can find the forum that owns a topic with the query `SELECT * FROM Forum WHERE Forum.id = Topic.parent_forum`.

To find all the topics belonging to a forum, use `SELECT * FROM Topic WHERE Topic.parent_forum = Forum.id`.

To find all the threads belonging to a topic, use `SELECT * FROM Thread WHERE parent_topic = Topic.id`.

To find all messages that belong to a thread, use a query such as `SELECT * FROM Thread, Post WHERE parent_thread = Thread.id`.

If you want to tighten the security policy for your site, you must create an additional table that keeps track of registered users. The Login application that you develop in Chapter 4 provides everything you need to register and authenticate visitors.

Building the forum tables

The following SQL query creates this database:

CREATE DATABASE Forum

The following `CREATE TABLE` statements create all the tables you need for the forums application.

```
CREATE TABLE Forum (
   id            INTEGER UNSIGNED NOT NULL auto_increment,
   name          VARCHAR(100) NOT NULL,
   description   TEXT,
PRIMARY KEY(id) );

CREATE TABLE Topic (
   parent_forum  INTEGER UNSIGNED NOT NULL,
   id            INTEGER UNSIGNED NOT NULL auto_increment,
   name          VARCHAR(100) NOT NULL,
   description   TEXT,
PRIMARY KEY(id) );
```

```
CREATE TABLE Thread (
  parent_topic  INTEGER UNSIGNED NOT NULL,
  id            INTEGER UNSIGNED NOT NULL auto_increment,
  subject       TEXT NOT NULL,
  replies       INTEGER UNSIGNED,
  last_post     TIMESTAMP,
PRIMARY KEY(id) );

CREATE TABLE Post (
  parent_thread INTEGER UNSIGNED NOT NULL,
  in_reply_to   INTEGER UNSIGNED,
  id            INTEGER UNSIGNED NOT NULL auto_increment,
  author        VARCHAR(100) NOT NULL,
  date          TIMESTAMP,
  body          TEXT,
PRIMARY KEY(id) );
```

Accessing the forum tables

To interact with the MySQL server, your PHP scripts use the mysql (or mysqli) API that comes with PHP. By using the mysql functions, you can connect to a MySQL server, execute queries and other SQL statements, and retrieve results from the server. When you *fetch* (or retrieve) a row of data from the MySQL server, you can ask PHP to deliver the row in many different forms. If you call the `mysql_fetch_array` function, you get an array of values, indexed by column number. If you call `mysql_fetch_assoc`, you get an associative array, indexed by column name. You can also ask mysql to return a row in the form of an object. (The resulting object has one field for each column in the row. The name of the field corresponds to the name of the column.)

In this application, I fetch each row of data into an associative array. An associative array offers three advantages over an enumerated array:

- ✔ **When you access a member of an associate array, your code is self-documenting.** `$thread['parent_topic']` is much more descriptive than `$thread[2]`.

- ✔ **Your code is self-maintaining.** If you change the SELECT statement that creates a result set, `$thread['parent_topic']` always refers to a `parent_topic`, but `$thread[2]` might refer to the wrong column. (Consider what would happen if you add a column to the beginning of the SELECT list.)

- ✔ **You can easily convert an associative array into a set of "normal" variables by using the `extract` function.** For example, if you have an associative array that contains columns named `parent_topic`, `name`, and `description`, you can *extract* the array, and you'll have three new variables: `$parent_topic`, `$name`, and `$description`.

PHP provides two different sets of MySQL functions: mysql functions and mysqli functions. The mysqli functions were developed to allow the use of features that were added in MySQL version 4.1. You can use the mysql functions with version 4.1, but you don't have access to the newer features. The mysql or mysqli extension is activated when PHP is installed. You must use PHP 5 to use the mysqli functions.

Because MySQL 4.1 is now the recommended version on the MySQL Web site, I use the MySQL Improved (mysqli) functions in this chapter. I use the procedural functions when building the procedural programs. I use the object-oriented classes when building the object-oriented programs.

If you're using PHP 4 or for other reasons want to use the mysql functions — rather than the mysqli functions — you might need to make small changes to the syntax. The mysqli functions are very similar to the mysql functions, but some differences exist. I explain the PHP and MySQL versions in Chapter 1. The syntax differences are shown in Appendix C. More information about the functions is available in the PHP manual at `www.php.net/manual/en/ref.mysqli.php` and `www.php.net/manual/en/ref.mysql.php`.

In this application, I have stored the information needed by the PHP mysql functions in a separate file called `forumVars.inc`. This file is stored in a directory outside my Web space, for security reasons. The file contains information similar to the following:

```php
<?php
        $host = "localhost";
        $user = "admin";
        $passwd = "";
        $database = "Forum";
?>
```

Notice the PHP tags at the beginning (`<?php`) and the end (`?>`) of the file. If you forget those tags, a visitor to your Web site will see the username and password required to log into your MySQL server, which is not at all what you want.

Adding data to the database

To cut down on the number of forms required by this application, you need to maintain two of these tables (`Forum` and `Topic`) directly. Visitors to your site maintain the other two tables (`Thread` and `Post`) by using the forms that I describe later in this chapter.

To create a new forum, simply insert (by using an `INSERT` query) a new row into the `Forum` table, like this:

```
INSERT INTO Forum (name, description)
  VALUES ('Cats', 'All things kitty');
```

Notice that you can omit the id column and MySQL will assign a unique number for you. If you let MySQL assign an id for your Forum, you can find the value that the server chose by calling the LAST_INSERT_ID function. To create a new topic, you need to know the id of the Forum that should own the topic. Creating a new topic is almost as easy as creating a new forum; just insert (INSERT) a new row into the Topic table:

```
INSERT INTO Topic (parent_forum, name, description )
  VALUES ( 1, 'Cat Breeds', 'Discussions regarding
    different breeds' );
INSERT INTO Topic (parent_forum, name, description )
  VALUES ( 1, 'Health Issues', 'Keeping your felines
    healthy and happy' );
```

You must create at least one Forum and one Topic before your forum site will be usable.

Building the Forum Web Pages

A visitor interacts with your forum application through a series of HTML Web pages. Some of the pages display simple HTML tables; others display HTML forms that the user must complete in order to proceed to the next page. Each page is *dynamically created,* which means that the data displayed to the user comes from one or more tables stored in the MySQL server.

Designing the Forum Web pages

The forum application displays the following five Web pages:

- ✔ **Forums:** This page lists all the forums and the topics available in each forum.

- ✔ **Threads:** This page lists all the threads in the selected topic. This page is displayed when the user clicks a Topic link in the Forums page.

- ✔ **Messages:** This page displays all the messages in a thread. This page is displayed when the user clicks a thread link in the Threads page.

- ✔ **New Message:** This page displays a form where the user can create and post a message. This page is displayed when the user clicks the Start a New Thread link.

- ✔ **Reply:** This page displays a form where the user can reply to a message. This page is displayed when the user clicks the reply button.

The same files are used in both the procedural and object-oriented code to display all five pages. The next few sections describe the pages and the files that display the pages.

Designing the Forums page

The Forums page displays all the forums and topics available. Figure 8-1 shows the Forums page.

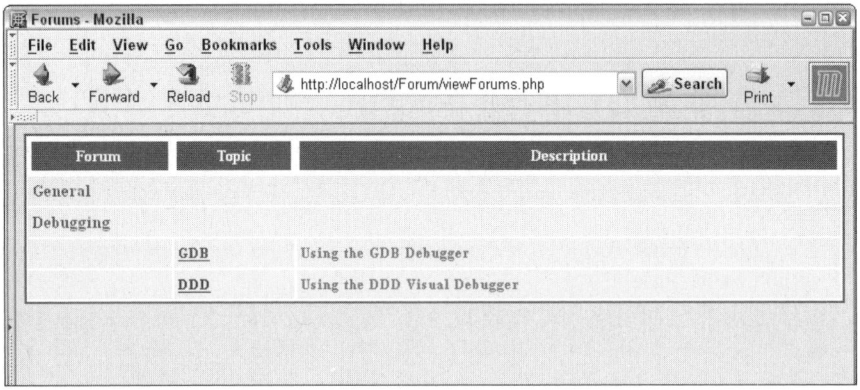

Figure 8-1:
The Forums
page
displayed by
the forum
application.

The Forums page displays the names of the forums. In this case, two forums are displayed: General and Debugging. The name and description of topics within the forums are displayed. In this case, the Debugging forum has two topics: GDB and DDD.

Designing the Threads page

The Threads page (see Figure 8-2) displays all the threads available for a topic. This page is displayed when the user clicks a topic name on the forums page.

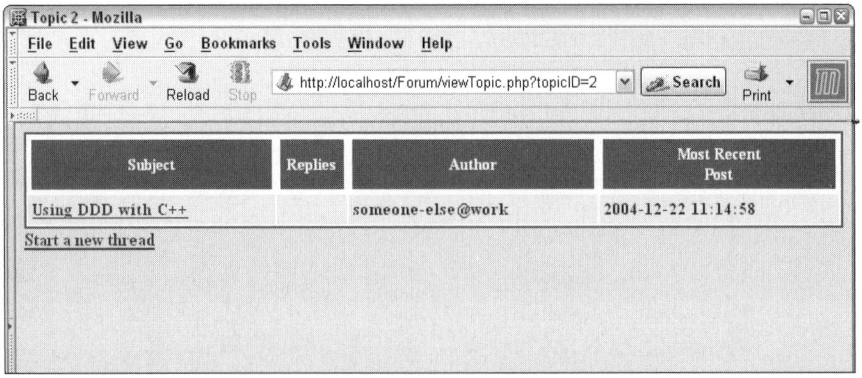

Figure 8-2:
The Threads
page
displayed by
the forum
application.

The Threads page displays the subject, number of replies, author, and date and time of the most recent reply. Below the list of threads is a link that allows the user to create a new thread.

Designing the Messages page

The Messages page (see Figure 8-3) displays all the messages in a thread. This page is displayed when the user clicks a thread subject on the Threads page.

The Messages page displays all the messages in a thread. The display has two columns: Author and Message. The e-mail address of the author and the date and time the message was posted are displayed in the first column. A link that allows the user to reply to the message is also displayed in the first column. The second column displays the contents of the message. If the user clicks the Reply link next to a message, a page with a form where the user can post a reply is displayed.

Designing the New Message page

The New Message page (see Figure 8-4) displays a form where the user can enter a new message. This page is displayed when the user clicks the Start a New Thread link on the Threads page.

The New Message page displays a form with three fields for users to enter their e-mail address, the subject of the message, and the message contents. The user clicks the Post Message button when finished typing the message. The message posts and returns the user to the Threads page, where the new message now appears in the list.

Designing the Reply page

The Reply page (see Figure 8-5) displays a form where the user can reply to a message. This page is displayed when the user clicks the Reply link next to any message on the Messages page.

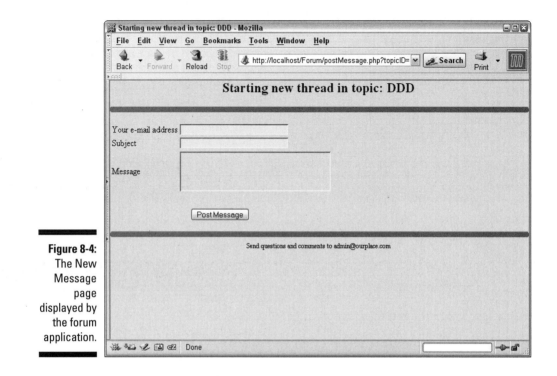

Figure 8-4:
The New
Message
page
displayed by
the forum
application.

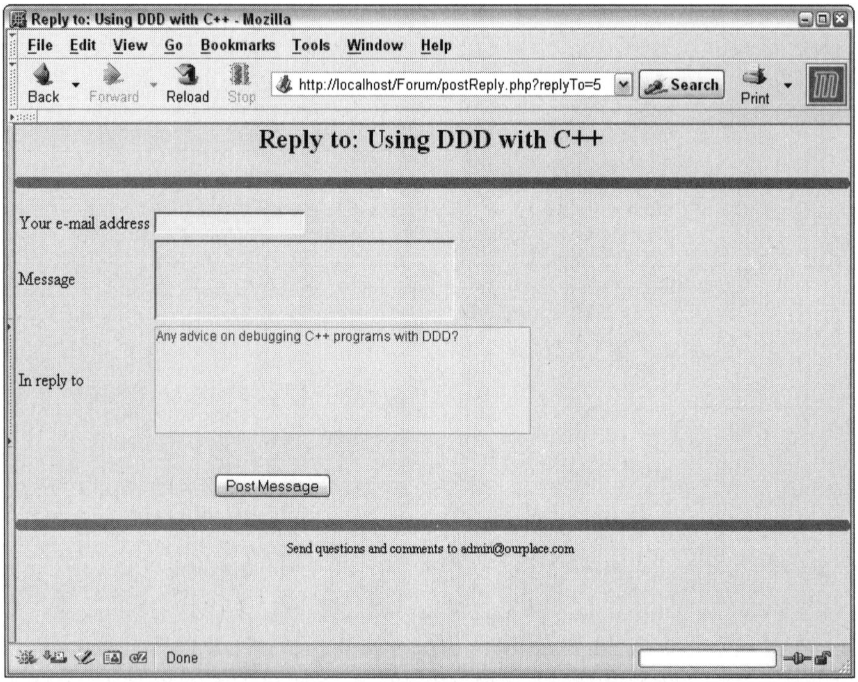

Figure 8-5:
The Reply
page
displayed by
the Forum
application.

The Reply page displays a form with two fields for users to enter their e-mail addresses and their reply contents. The subject of the message that the user is replying to is displayed. The user clicks the Post Message button when finished typing the message. The message posts and returns the user to the Messages page, where the reply now appears in the list.

Writing the code for the Forums page

The Forums page is the first page displayed when the application starts. It displays a list of all the forums and topics available. The user can click any topic to display a page showing a list of threads available in the topic.

The code that displays the forums page is shown in Listing 8-1.

LISTING 8-1: THE FILE THAT DEFINES THE FORUMS PAGE

```php
<?php
/* Program: viewForums.inc
 * Desc:     Program that displays all forums and the topics
 *           within each forum. Each topic displays a link to
 *           the threads within that topic.
 */

  include("functions_viewforums.inc");
?>
<html>
<head><title>Forums</title>
  <link rel="stylesheet" href="Forums.css"
        type="text/css"></head>
<body>
<?php
  $cxn = Connect_to_db("forumVars.inc" );                    #16
  $result = mysqli_query($cxn,"SELECT * FROM Forum");        #17
  if ($result == 0)
  {
    echo "<b>Error ";
    echo mysqli_errno($cxn).": ".mysqli_error($cxn);
    echo "</b>";
  }
  else
  {
    echo "<table width=\"100%\"
                  class=\"forumline\"cellpadding=\"4\"";
    echo " cellspacing=\"2\" border=\"0\" align=\"center\">";
    echo "<tbody>";
    DisplayForumsHeader();
    for( $i = 0; $i < mysqli_num_rows( $result ); $i++ )      #31
```

Continued

LISTING 8-1: *(Continued)*

```
    {
      $forum = mysqli_fetch_assoc( $result );
      echo "<tr>";
      echo '  <td class="forumTitle" ⤷
            colspan="5">'.$forum['name']."</td>";
      echo "</tr>\n";
      DisplayTopics($forum['id'],$cxn,"viewTopic.php");    #38
    }
    echo "</tbody></table>";
  }
?>
```

The numbers in the following list refer to the line numbers in Listing 8-1:

#16 Connects to the MySQL server with a function called `Connect_to_db`. The function is in the file `functions_main.inc` that is included in the `viewForums.php` application script. The function code is shown in Listing 8-15.

#17 Executes a query that returns all rows in the `Forum` table.

#18 If the query in line 17 fails, an error message is displayed.

#26 If the query in line 17 succeeds, the program displays the table with the forums and topics and continues to line 21. The call to `DisplayForumsHeader` (which I describe in the next section) writes the HTML column headers to the Web page.

#31 The loop at lines 31 through 39 reads through each row in the `Forum` table, displays the forum name, and calls the `DisplayTopics` function to display each topic belonging to the forum. As you will see in `functions_viewforums.inc`, the `DisplayTopics function` also contains a loop that reads through a MySQL result set. You commonly see this *nested loop* structure when you're dealing with tables that are related to each other in a parent/child relationship. The outer loop reads through the rows in the parent table and the inner loop reads through the details rows in the child table.

Listing 8-2 shows the supporting functions (`DisplayForumsHeader` and `DisplayTopics`) that `viewForums.inc` uses.

LISTING 8-2: SUPPORTING FUNCTIONS FOR VIEWFORUMS.INC

```php
<?php
/* File: functions_viewforums.inc
 * Desc: Supporting functions for the viewForums.inc file.
 */

function DisplayForumsHeader()
{
  echo '
  <tr>
    <th colspan="2" class="forumHeader" height="25"
          nowrap="nowrap">Forum</th>
    <th class="forumHeader" nowrap="nowrap">Topic</th>
    <th class="forumHeader" nowrap="nowrap">Description</th>
  </tr>';
}

function DisplayTopics($forumID,$cxn,$linkTarget)          #17
{
  $sql = "SELECT * FROM Topic
                    WHERE parent_forum = ".$forumID;
  $result = mysqli_query($cxn,$sql);

  for( $i = 0; $i < mysqli_num_rows( $result ); $i++ )     #21
  {
    echo '<tr>';
    $topic = mysqli_fetch_assoc( $result );
    echo '<td class="topicFiller" colspan="2"> </td>';

    echo '<td class="topicLink">';                         #29
    echo   '<a href="' . $linkTarget. '?topicID=' .
              $topic['id'] . '">';
    echo   $topic['name'];
    echo   '</a>';
    echo '</td>';
    echo '<td class=topicDesc>'.
              $topic['description']. '</td>';               #36
    echo "</tr>\n";
  }
}
?>
```

The following is a description of the numbered lines of code that appear in
functions_viewforums.inc in Listing 8-2:

#6   The DisplayForumsHeader function creates column headers for this
         Web page.

#16 `DisplayTopics` is called (by `viewForums.inc`) once for each forum. This function displays all topics owned by a single forum — the `$forumID` argument contains the ID of the parent forum.

#21 The `for` loop beginning at line 21 reads through each `Topic` owned by the given `$forumID`. For each topic, the page displays (from left to right) a blank column that indents the each topic to the right of its parent forum, the topic name, and the topic description.

#27 The first `<td>` item for each topic is a non-breaking space that fills the leftmost column.

#29 The second `<td>` item contains a link to another page (`viewTopic`) that displays the threads owned by a topic. The user sees the name of the topic. The link points to a parameterized Web page and looks something like `viewTopic.php?topicID=id` (where *id* identifies the topic you want to view).

#35 Finally, `DisplayTopics` displays the topic description in the right-most column and then terminates the HTML table row.

Writing the code for the Threads page

The Threads page displays when the user clicks a topic link on the Forums page. It displays a list of all the threads available for the selected topic. The user can click any thread to show all the messages available for the thread. The page also displays a Start a New Thread link, which, when clicked, displays a page where the user can post a new message. The code that displays the page is shown in Listing 8-3.

LISTING 8-3: THE FILE THAT DISPLAYS THE THREADS PAGE

```php
<?php
/* Program: viewTopic.inc
 * Desc:     Program that displays the discussion threads
 *           within a selected topic. Each thread displays
 *           a link to the posts within that thread.
 */


  include("functions_viewtopics.inc");
  echo '<html>';
  echo '<head>';
  echo '<title>Topic ' . $_GET['topicID'] .'</title>';        #12
  echo '<link rel="stylesheet" href="Forums.css"  ↩
                 type="text/css"></head>';
  echo '<body>';
  $connect = Connect_to_db("forumVars.inc");                  #15
  $query = "SELECT Thread.*, date, author
```

```
              FROM Thread, Post
              WHERE
                 parent_topic    =" . $_GET['topicID'] . " AND
                 parent_thread  = Thread.id AND
                 in_reply_to     IS NULL";
   $result = mysqli_query( $connect, $query );                    #22
   if ($result == 0)
   {
     echo "<b>Error: ";
     echo mysqli_error($cxn)."</b>";
   }
   else                                                           #28
   {
     echo "<table width=\"100%\"
                 class=\"forumline \"cellpadding=\"4\"";
     echo " cellspacing=\"2\" border=\"0\" align=\"center\">";
     echo "<tbody>";
     DisplayThreadsHeader();
     for( $i = 0; $i < mysqli_num_rows( $result ); $i++ )   #35
     {
       $thread = mysqli_fetch_assoc( $result );
       echo "<tr>\n";
       echo '<td class="threadSubject">';                        #39
       echo '<a href="viewThread.php?threadID='.
                    $thread['id'] . '">';
       echo   $thread['subject'];
       echo   '</a>';
       echo "  </td>\n";
       AddField( $thread, "replies",   "threadFiller" );         #45
       AddField( $thread, "author",    "threadFiller" );
       AddField( $thread, "last_post", "threadFiller" );
       echo "</tr>\n";
     }
     echo "</tbody></table>";
     echo '<b><a href="postMessage.php?topicID='.
                           $_GET['topicID]. '">';
     echo "Start a new thread</a></b>";
   }
?>
</body></html>
```

The following is a description of the lines of code that appear in Listing 8-3:

#12 The Web page produced by this script displays all threads belonging to a particular topic. The forwarding page (that is, the page that you're coming from) includes a topic ID in the URL for this page. You can find that ID in the variable $_GET['topicID']. Line 12 displays the topic ID in the browser's title bar — if you prefer, you could write code to look up the topic name in the database and display that instead.

#15 Connects to the MySQL server with the connection options specified in `forumVars.inc`. `Connect_to_db` is a function defined in the file `functions_main.inc` that is included in the `viewTopic.php` script.

#16 The query built on lines 16 to 21 reads all threads belonging to the given topic. It also reads author and original posting date from the first message in each thread. (Remember, you can find the first message in a thread by looking for a `Post` whose `in_reply_to` column is `NULL`.) The query is executed on line 22.

#23 Begins an `if` block that executes if no threads were found. An error message is displayed.

#28 Begins an `else` block that executes if a thread is found. This block displays the thread information in a table.

#34 The `DisplayThreadsHeader` function creates the column headers for the HTML table.

#35 Starts a loop that reads through each `Thread` that belongs to the topic of interest. As the loop reads each `Thread`, it creates a new row in the HTML table. Each row displays the subject under discussion, the number of replies, the author of the first message in the thread, and the date and time of the most recent message.

#39 The subject is actually a link to a another page that displays all of the messages within that thread. The users sees the thread subject, the URL contains the thread ID as a parameter and looks something like `viewThread.php?threaded=47`.

#45 You see three calls to the `AddField` function (which you see in the next section). `AddField` creates a styled `<td>` (table data) element by extracting a column from the `$thread` associative array — when you call `AddField`, you provide an associative array, a column name, and a style name; `AddField` does the rest. In this case, `AddField` displays `Thread.replies`, `Post.author`, `Thread.last_post`.

The `DisplayThreadsHeader` and `AddField` functions are defined in a separate include file, `functions_viewtopic.inc`, shown in Listing 8-4.

LISTING 8-4: SUPPORTING FUNCTIONS FOR VIEWTOPIC.INC

```php
<?php
/* File: functions_viewtopic.inc
 * Desc: Supporting functions for the viewTopic.inc file.
 */

/*  Function: DisplayThreadsHeader
 *  Desc:      Displays the column headers
```

```
    */
function DisplayThreadsHeader()                                    #9
{
  echo '
  <tr>
    <th class="threadHeader" height="25"
        nowrap="nowrap">Subject</th>
    <th class="threadHeader" nowrap="nowrap"
        width="50">Replies</th>
    <th class="threadHeader" nowrap="nowrap"
        width="50">Author</th>
    <th class="threadHeader"
        nowrap="nowrap">Most Recent<br>Post</th>
  </tr>';
}
/*  Function:  AddField
 *  Desc:       Generates a TD (table data) element
 *              by extracting the given column from
 *              an associative array.  The resulting
 *              value is displayed in the $style
 *              provided by the caller
 */
function AddField( $assoc, $column, $style )                       #30
{
  echo '   <td class="'. $style . '">'
                 . $assoc[$column] . "</td>\n";
}
?>
```

Following is a description of the lines of code numbered in Listing 8-4:

#9   The `DisplayThreadsHeader` function creates the column headers for an HTML table. This particular table contains a list of the discussion threads within a specific topic, so you see labels for `Subject`, `Replies`, `Author`, and `Most Recent Post`.

#30 The `AddField` function creates a `<td>` (table data) element. The caller provides an associative array (presumably a row produced by a MySQL query), a column name, and a CSS style name. `AddField` extracts the desired value from the array and generates a `<td>` element that will be displayed in the requested style. `AddField` is a simple but useful function: If you want to use it in your own applications, you might want to add some extra error checking (for example, you might want to ensure that the column named by the caller actually exists in the associative array).

Writing the code for the Messages page

The Messages page displays when the user clicks a thread link on the Threads page. All the messages for the selected thread are displayed, one row per message. The author, the date and time the message was posted, and the message content are shown for each message. The user can click the Reply link for any message to display the reply page, where the user can create and post a reply. If you want to enforce a tighter security policy in your forum so that only properly authenticated users can post messages, simply omit (or disable) the Reply link unless the user has logged in. See Chapter 4 for more information regarding user registration and authentication.

The code that displays the page is shown in Listing 8-5.

LISTING 8-5: THE FILE THAT DISPLAYS THE MESSAGES PAGE

```php
<?php
/* Program: viewThread.inc
 * Desc:     Program that displays a thread of discussion.
 */


include("functions_viewthread.inc");
?>
<html>
<head>
<?php
  echo '<title>Thread ' . $_GET['threadID'] .'</title>';      #12
  echo '<link rel="stylesheet" href="Forums.css
            type="text/css"></head>';
  echo '<body>';
  $cxn = Connect_to_db("forumVars.inc");                       #16
  $query = "SELECT id, author, date, body
            FROM Post
            WHERE parent_thread = ". $_GET['threadID'];
  $result = mysqli_query( $cxn, $query );                      #20
  if ($result == 0)
  {
    echo "Error: " . mysqli_error($cxn);
  }
  else                                                         #25
  {
    echo "<table width=\"100%\"
                class=\"forumline \"cellpadding=\"4\"";
    echo " cellspacing=\"2\" border=\"0\" align=\"center\">";
    echo "<tbody>";
    DisplayPostsHeader();                                      #31
    for( $i = 0; $i < mysqli_num_rows( $result ); $i++ )       #32
    {
```

```
        $post = mysqli_fetch_assoc( $result );
        echo "<tr>\n";
        echo '<td class=postFiller>';                              #36
        echo   '<span class=postAuthor>'. $post['author'] .
               "</span><br>";
        echo   "<span class=postDate>".$post['date']."</span>";
        echo   "<span class=postReply>";
        echo   '<a href="postReply.php?replyTo='.$post['id'].
               '">';
        echo   '<img src="reply.gif" border="0"/>Reply</a>';
        echo   "</span>";
        echo   "</td>\n";
        echo '  <td class="postText">'.$post['body']."</td>\n";
        echo "</tr>\n";
      }
    echo "</tbody></table>";
  }
?>
</body></html>
```

Following is a description of the lines of code in Listing 8-5:

#12   This script produces a Web page that displays all messages (posts) belonging to a given thread. Line 12 displays the thread ID in the title bar. The thread ID is passed in the URL to identify which thread should be displayed. For example, the URL for this page is similar to: `viewThread.php?threadID=47`. The script retrieves the thread ID from the variable `$_GET['topicID']`.

#16   Connects to the database. The `Connect_to_db` function is stored in the file `functions_main.inc`, which is included in the `viewThread.php` script.

#17   The query built on lines 17 to 19 selects the `author`, `id`, `date`, and `body` from every message belonging to the selected thread. The author, date, and body are displayed. The ID values is used to generate a Reply To link. The query is executed on line 20.

#21   Begins an `if` block that displays an error message when no messages are found for the thread.

#25   Begins an `else` block that executes when messages are found for the thread. The block displays an HTML table with each message shown on a separate row.

#31   The call to `DisplayPostsHeader` creates the column headers for the HTML table. (I show you `DisplayPostsHeader` in the `functions_viewthread.inc` code listing.)

#36 The Reply To button links to another Web page (produced by the `postReply.php` script shown later in this chapter). The URL for the Reply To button includes a message ID and looks like this: `postReply.php?replyTo=52`.

#37 Begins a `for` loop that loops through the result set and displays each Post in a separate row. Each `Post` is displayed in two columns. The first column contains the message author's name, the post date, and a Reply To button. The author name is displayed above the other elements and each element is assigned its own CSS style so that you can easily customize the look and feel by changing the corresponding styles (`postAuthor`, `postDate`, and `postReply`) in the style sheet.

The `DisplayPostsHeader` function is defined in `functions_viewthread.inc`, shown in Listing 8-6.

LISTING 8-6: SUPPORTING FUNCTIONS FOR VIEWTHREAD.INC

```php
<?php
/* File: functions_viewthread.inc
 * Desc: Supporting functions for the viewThread.php program.
 */


/*  Function: DisplayPostsHeader
 *  Desc:     Displays the column headers for the table that
 *            shows the Post information
 */
function DisplayPostsHeader()
{
  echo '
  <tr>
    <th class="postHeader" height="25" ⮐
              nowrap="nowrap">Author</th>
    <th class="postHeader" nowrap="nowrap">Message</th>
  </tr>';
}
?>
```

The `DisplayPostHeader` function creates the column headers for an HTML table that displays each message in a thread. `viewThread.inc` calls this function after starting the HTML table.

Writing the code for the New Message page

The New Message page provides a form where the user can create and post a new message. The code that creates the new message page is in two separate files, as follows:

- ✔ `messageForm.inc`: Contains the code that defines the look and feel of the Web page. It produces a form that lets users post a new message. Another file must be used in conjunction with this file to create the page. The other file contains the specific information for the page. This file is used to display both the New Message page and the Reply page. The pages are different because different files are used in conjunction with this file.

- ✔ `messageFields.inc`: Contains the specific information for the New Message page. When used with `messageForm.inc`, it displays the New Message page. A different file with different information could be used with `messageForm.inc` to create a page that displayed a different form.

These two files are the same for the procedural application and the object-oriented application. I describe the two files in the following sections.

Writing messageFields.inc

The `messageFields.inc` file provides the specific information for the new message page. This file defines five arrays that, when interpreted by `messageForm.inc` (which I cover in Listing 8-7), are translated into HTML elements. The arrays are

- ✔ `$page`: This array stores the elements displayed in the browser's titlebar (`$page['title']`), at the top of the page (`$page['top']`), and at the bottom of the page (`$page['bottom']`).

- ✔ `$elements`: This array contains the elements displayed at the top and bottom of the form (and the label to display on the submit button). The members of the `$page` array form a visual frame around the members of the `$elements` array. This arrangement is a matter of preference and you can adjust the layout to fit your own personal style.

- ✔ `$fields`: Each member of this array describes a field that is displayed on the form. The key defines the name of the field and the value provides a label that is displayed to the left of the field.

- ✔ `$types`: This array defines the type of HTML control used to display each field in the `$fields` array. For example, the `$fauthor` field is displayed in an `input` control while `$fbody` is displayed in a `textarea` control.

✔ `$styles`: Defines the style assigned to each field in the `$fields` array. Because the Web pages utilize a CSS (cascading style sheet), most of the names you see in the `$styles` array refer to a CSS style. (The exception is `$styles['ftopicID']`, which creates a hidden HTML control.)

Listing 8-7 shows the `messageFields.inc` file.

LISTING 8-7: THE FILE THAT PROVIDES THE ARRAYS FOR THE NEW MESSAGE FORM

```php
<?php
 /* File: messageFields.inc
  * Desc: Contains arrays with the field names and form
  *       elements for the forum post form.
  */
$page = array( "title"  => "Starting new thread in topic:
                              $ftopic",
                "top"    => "Starting new thread in topic:
                              $ftopic",
                "bottom" => "Send questions and comments
                              to admin@ourplace.com",
             );

$elements = array( "top" => "",
                   "bottom" => "",
                   "submit" => "Post Message"
                 );

$fields    =   array( "author"   => "Your e-mail address",
                      "subject"  => "Subject",
                      "body"     => "Message",
                      "ftopicID" => "",
                    );

$types = array( "author"   => 'input type="text" size="30"',
                "subject"  => 'input type="text" size="30"',
                "body"     => 'textarea rows="5" cols="60"',
                "ftopicID" => 'input type="hidden"'
              );

$styles    =   array( "author"   => "postAuthor",
                      "subject"  => "postSubject",
                      "body"     => "postBody",
                      "ftopicID" => "hidden"
                    );
?>
```

Writing messageForm.inc

Listing 8-8 shows the `messageForm.inc` file. `messageForm.inc` converts the form description (see Listing 8-7) into an HTML form and displays that form to the user.

LISTING 8-8: THE FILE THAT DISPLAYS THE NEW MESSAGE AND REPLY PAGES

```php
<?php
/* File: messageForm.inc
 * Desc: Displays a Web page that lets the user post a
 *       reply to a new message.
 */                                                              #5
?>
<head><title><?php echo $page['title']?></title>
    <link rel="stylesheet" href="Forums.css" type="text/css">
</head>
<body style="margin: 0">
<h2 align="center"><?php echo $page['top'] ?></h2>
<hr size="10" noshade>
<p style="font-size: 110%; font-weight: bold">
<?php echo $elements['top']?></p>
<form action=<?php echo $_SERVER['PHP_SELF']?> method="POST">
<table border="0">
<?php                                                           #17
if (isset($GLOBALS['message_2']))
{
  echo "<tr>
        <td colspan='2'
            style=\"font-weight: bold; font-style: italic;
            font-size: 90%; color: red\">
            {$GLOBALS['message_2']}<p></td></tr>";
}
foreach($fields as $field => $value)                            #26
{
  echo "<tr>\n";
  DisplayField($value, $field, @$$field, $types[$field],
               $styles[$field]);
  echo "</tr>\n";
}                                                               #32
?>
<tr>
  <td colspan="2" style="text-align: center" >
    <br>
    <input type="submit" name="Button"
     value="<?php echo $elements['submit']?>">
  </td>
</tr>
</table></form>
<hr size="10" noshade>
<div style="text-align: center; font-size: 75%">
  <?php echo $page['bottom']?>
</div></body></html>
```

This script translates the $page, $elements, $fields, $types, and $styles associative arrays into an HTML page.

The following numbers correspond to the lines in Listing 8-8:

#7   Displays `$page['title']` in the browser title bar.

#11   The `$page['top']` element is centered across the top of the Web page.

#14   Displays the `$elements['top']` string value. The `postFields.inc` file puts an empty string into `$elements['top']`, but you can add your own message there if you like.

#16   Begins a table. The HTML controls defined by `postFields.inc` are displayed inside an HTML table so that the labels and controls line up nicely.

#26   Begins a `foreach` loop that loops through each field in the `$fields` array and creates a new row in the HTML table for each element in the array. To actually create the table elements, this script calls the `DisplayField` function (see Listing 8-16). `DisplayField` expects five arguments: a label, a field name, a value, a control type, and a style name.

       For example, the first element in the `$fields` array is `"fauthor"` => `"Your e-mail address"`. `DisplayField` paints the element value (`"Your e-mail address"`) as a label and uses element key (`fauthor`) to create an HTML control named `fauthor`. The value of the field is found by dereferencing `$field`. In other words, if `$field` is set to `fauthor` and `$fauthor` contains `me@home`, then `$$field` evaluates to the string `me@home`. The control type (`textarea`, `input`, and so on) is found by using the field name (`fauthor`, `fbody`, and so on) as an index into the `$types` array. Similarly, the style is found by using the field name as an index into the `$styles` array.

#37   The last row in the HTML table contains the submit button. The button label is derived from `$element['submit']`. (In this case, the button is labeled Post Message.)

Writing the code for the Reply page

The Reply page provides a form where the user can reply to a post. The code that creates the reply page is in two separate files, as follows:

- ✔ `messageForm.inc`: Contains the code that defines the look and feel of the Web page. It produces a form that lets users post a reply. Another file must be used in conjunction with this file to create the page.

- ✔ This is the same file used to produce the post message page, described in the previous section. It produces the reply page, rather than the post message page, because a different file is used in conjunction with it. To produce the reply page, this file is used with the `replyFields.inc` file. In the previous section, this file was used in conjunction with the `messageFields.inc` file to product the post message page.

✔ `replyFields.inc`: Contains the specific information for the reply page. When used with `messageForm.inc`, it displays the Reply page. A different file, with different information, is used with `messageForm.inc` to create a page that displays a different form, such as the post message page described in the previous section.

These two files are the same for the procedural application and the object-oriented application. I describe the `replyFields.inc` file in the following section.

Writing replyFields.inc

The `replyFields.inc` file provides the specific information for the Reply page. This file also defines five arrays that, when interpreted by the file `messageForm.inc` (which I cover in Listing 8-8), are translated into HTML elements. The arrays are

✔ `$page`: This array stores the elements displayed in the browser's title bar (`$page['title']`), at the top of the page (`$page['top']`), and at the bottom of the page (`$page['bottom']`).

✔ `$elements`: This array contains the elements displayed at the top and bottom of the form (and the label to display on the submit button). The members of the `$page` array form a visual frame around the members of the `$elements` array. This arrangement is a matter of preference and you can adjust the layout to fit your own personal style.

✔ `$fields`: Each member of this array describes a field that is displayed on the form. The key defines the name of the field and the value provides a label that is displayed to the left of the field.

✔ `$types`: This array defines the type of HTML control used to display each field in the `$fields` array. For example, the `$fauthor` field is displayed in an `input` control while `$fbody` is displayed in a `textarea` control.

✔ `$styles`: Defines the style assigned to each field in the `$fields` array. Because the Web pages utilize a CSS, most of the names you see in the `$styles` array refer to a CSS style. (The exception is `$styles['ftopicID']`, which creates a hidden HTML control.)

Listing 8-9 shows the `replyFields.inc` file. This file defines the content of the HTML form displayed to the user and, together with the `Forums.css` stylesheet, defines the appearance of each element in the form.

LISTING 8-9: THE PAGE THAT PROVIDES THE ARRAYS FOR THE REPLY PAGE

```php
<?php
 /* File: replyFields.inc
  * Desc: Contains arrays with the field names and form
  *       elements for the forum post form.
  */
$page = array( "title"  => "Reply to: " . $_POST['subject'],
               "top"    => "Reply to: " . $_POST['subject'],
               "bottom" => "Send questions and comments
                           to admin@ourplace.com",
           );

$elements = array( "top" => "",
                   "bottom" => "",
                   "submit" => "Post Message"
               );

$fields    =    array( "author"    => "Your e-mail address",
                       "body"      => "Message",
                       "fresponse" => "In reply to",
                       "freplyto"  => "",
                       "fsubject"  => "",
                   );

$types = array( "author"    => "input",
                "body"      => 'textarea rows="5" cols="60"',
                "fresponse" => 'textarea readonly rows="5"
                               cols="60"',
                "freplyto"  => 'input type="hidden"',
                "fsubject"  => 'input type="hidden"',
            );

$styles    =    array( "author"    => "postAuthor",
                       "body"      => "postBody",
                       "fresponse" => "postResponse",
                       "freplyto"  => "hidden",
                       "fsubject"  => "hidden",
                   );
?>
```

The $fields, $types, and $styles arrays describe five HTML controls:

✔ author: An input field where you expect the user to enter his or her e-mail address.

✔ body: A text area where you expect the user to type in the text of the message.

✔ fresponse: A text area that displays the text of the message that the user is replying to.

✔ `freplyto`: A hidden field that contains the ID of the message that the user is replying to. This field is used to forward the message ID from one phase to the next.

✔ `fsubject`: A hidden field that contains the subject of the message that the user is replying to.

Building the Forum Application: Procedural Approach

The Forum application has five application scripts, as follows:

✔ `viewForums.php`: Displays the forums Web page, which displays a list of the forums and topics available.

✔ `viewTopic.php`: Displays the threads Web page, which displays a list of the threads in a topic.

✔ `viewThread.php`: Displays the messages Web page, which displays a list of the messages in a thread.

✔ `postMessage.php`: Builds, displays, validates, and processes an HTML form using the strategies outlined in Chapters 3 and 4. When the user creates a new thread, the Web server runs `postReply.php` twice. The first time through, `postMessage.php` displays a form that shows the topic that will own the new thread and a number of empty fields. When the user completes the form and clicks the Post Message button, `postMessage.php` executes again — this time it validates the input and, if everything looks okay, writes the new message to the database.

✔ `postReply.php`: Builds, displays, validates, and processes the HTML form used in the reply page. The script is similar to the post Message script. However, `postMessage` creates both a message and thread, while `postReply` creates a message but updates an existing thread. This script runs when the user clicks a Reply link in the messages page. The thread ID is passed to this script in the URL.

Writing viewForums.php

The `viewForums.php` script (shown in Listing 8-10) is very simple. It simply includes the `viewForums.inc` file that displays the Web page. This script is run first, starting the application by displaying the forums Web page. Other scripts run when links or buttons are clicked.

LISTING 8-10: THE SCRIPT THAT DISPLAYS THE FORUMS PAGE

```php
<?php
/* Program: viewForums.php
 * Desc:     Displays the forums page.
 */
include("functions_main.inc");
include("viewForums.inc");

?>
```

The script includes a file containing functions needed by the `viewForums.inc` file and then includes `viewForums.inc`.

Writing viewTopic.php

The `viewTopic.php` script is the same as the `viewForums.php` script, except that it includes the `viewTopic.inc` file that displays the Threads Web page. This script runs when the user clicks a topic name in the forums page. Listing 8-11 shows `viewTopic.php`.

LISTING 8-11: THE SCRIPT THAT DISPLAYS THE FORUMS PAGE

```php
<?php
/* Program: viewTopic.php
 * Desc:     Displays the threads page.
 */
include("functions_main.inc");
include("viewTopic.inc");

?>
```

The script includes a file containing functions needed by the `viewTopic.inc` file and then includes `viewTopic.inc`.

Writing viewThread.php

The `viewThread.php` script is the same as the `viewForums.php` script, except that it includes the `viewThread.inc` file that displays the Messages Web page. This script runs when the user clicks a thread name in the threads page. Listing 8-12 shows `viewThread.php`.

LISTING 8-12: THE SCRIPT THAT DISPLAYS THE FORUMS PAGE

```php
<?php
/* Program: viewThread.php
 * Desc:    Displays the messages page.
 */
include("functions_main.inc");
include("viewThread.inc");

?>
```

The script includes a file containing functions needed by the `viewForums.inc` file and then includes `viewforums.inc`.

Writing postMessage.php

The `postMessage.php` script starts when the user clicks the Start a New Thread link. The `postMessage.php` script builds, displays, validates, and processes an HTML form. The following is an overview of the structure of the script:

```
switch (Button)

    case "Post Message":
        Save new message in thread

    case default:
        Show HTML form for creating new messages.
```

Listing 8-13 shows the `postMessage.php` program.

LISTING 8-13: POSTMESSAGE.PHP

```php
<?php
/*  Program: postMessage.php
 *  Desc:    Displays and validates a form that starts a new
 *           thread and posts a message to that thread.
 */
include("functions_main.inc");
include("functions_post.inc");

switch( @$_POST['Button'])                                      #9
{
  case "Post Message":                                         #11
  {
```

Continued

LISTING 8-13: *(Continued)*

```
$cxn = Connect_to_db("forumVars.inc");
// Create the new Thread                                       #14
$sql  = "INSERT INTO Thread(parent_topic,subject) ";
$sql .= "VALUES( ";
$sql .= $_POST['ftopicID'] . ","."'";
$sql .= addslashes(htmlentities($_POST['subject'])).."')";
if(!mysqli_query($cxn, $sql))
{
    echo "Error: ".mysqli_error($cxn);
}
$parentThread = mysqli_insert_id($cxn);                        #23
// Encode any quote characters                                 #24
$author = strip_tags($_POST['author']);
$author = mysqli_real_escape_string($cxn,$author);
$body = htmlentities($_POST['body']);
$body = mysqli_real_escape_string( $cxn, $body );
// And add the new message to the Post table                   #29
$query = "INSERT INTO Post (parent_thread,author,body)";
$query .= "VALUES( ";
$query .=    $parentThread . ",";
$query .=    "'" . $author . "',";
$query .=    "'" . $body. "')";
$result = mysqli_query( $cxn, $query );
if( $result == 0 )
  echo "Error: ".mysqli_error($cxn);
else
{
  echo '<meta http-equiv="Refresh" content="3;';            #40
  echo 'url=viewTopic.php?topicID=';
  echo $_POST['ftopicID'] . '"/>';
  echo "<b>Your message has been posted. In a moment you
          will be automatically returned to the
          topic.</b>";
}
break;
}

default:                                                       #50
{
  $parentTopic = $_GET['topicID'];
  $cxn = Connect_to_db("forumVars.inc");
  $sql = "SELECT name FROM Topic WHERE id = $parentTopic";
  $result = mysqli_query($cxn, $sql);
  if( $result == 0 )
  {
      echo "Error: ".mysqli_error($cxn);
      exit();
  }
  $topic = mysqli_fetch_assoc($result);
  $author   = "";                                             #62
  $subject  = "";
  $body     = "";
```

```
    $ftopic    = $topic['name'];
    $ftopicID  = $parentTopic;
    include( "messageFields.inc" );            #67
    include( "messageForm.inc" );
    break;
  }
}
?>
```

The following numbered items refer to the line numbers in Listing 8-13:

#9 The `switch` statement detects which phase the script is running in. If the user has filled in the form and clicked the Post Message button, `$_POST['Button']` is set to `Post Message`. If the user has not yet seen the form, `$_POST['Button']` is undefined (in fact, the entire `$POST` superglobal array is undefined).

#11 The `case` statement executes when the user completes the form and clicks Post Message.

#15 Lines 15 to 18 build an `INSERT` query that creates a new row in the `Thread` table. The `htmlentities` function is used on line 18 to convert any HTML tags in the subject to entities. This protects against dangerous text entered into the form by bad guys. The `addslashes` function is used to escape any quotes in the subject.

#23 If the `INSERT` statement succeeds, you can call the `mysqli_insert_id` function to retrieve the auto-generated ID of the new thread.

#25 Lines 25 to 28 prepare the input data for insertion into the database. You see two calls to the `mysqli_real_escape_string` function. The first call escapes any quotes that the user typed into the `author` field. The second takes care of any quotes in the `body` field. You might be wondering why you need to prepare the text entered by the user. Consider a simple `INSERT` statement that adds a single piece of data to a MySQL table:

```
INSERT INTO myTable VALUES( '$userData' );
```

Assume that a Web user provided the value for `$userData` by filling in a form. If the user typed in a value in the form that you're expecting, say "Good kitty", the `INSERT` statement translates to:

```
INSERT INTO myTable VALUES( 'Good kitty' );
```

But consider what would happen if, instead, the user typed in the value "There's a good kitty". If you simply plug this text into the `INSERT` statement, the embedded quote mark will produce a syntax error:

```
INSERT INTO myTable VALUES( 'There's a good kitty' );
```

As far as the MySQL server is concerned, the string begins at the first quote and ends at the second quote — the rest of the text between the parentheses is a syntax error. A call to `mysqli_real_escape_ string` will translate "There's a good kitty" into "There\'s a good kitty", making it safe to use in a MySQL statement.

#29 Lines 30 to 35 build and execute the `INSERT` query that inserts the new message into the `Post` table.

#40 By the time you reach line 40, all of the necessary database updates have completed and the new message has been posted. The only thing left to do is to send the user somewhere useful. The `<meta>` tag you produce at line 40 automatically redirects the browser back to the `viewThread` page after a delay of three seconds, giving the user a chance to read the "post successful" message. Using an automatic refresh this way means that the user still gets some feedback (the "post successful" message), but won't have to click another button to get back to the thread display.

#50 The `default case` executes when the user first navigates to this Web page. The code in this section prepares the form and displays it to the user.

#62 After retrieving the topic name from the `Topic` table, the fields that are about to be displayed to the user are initialized. In this case, the user must enter a value for `$author`, `$subject`, and `$body` so those fields are initialized to empty strings. (**Note:** If you decide to add user registration and authentication to your forum application, you should set the user's e-mail address in the `$author` field and disable that control.) The `$ftopic` variable displays the name of the topic that owns the new thread. `$ftopicID` is a hidden control that shuttles the topic ID from one phase to the next.

#67 The two `include` directives that you see at lines 67 and 68 display the new message page. I describe the files `messageFields.inc` and `messageForm.inc` in the earlier section "Writing the code for the new message page."

Writing postReply.php

The `postReply.php` script starts when the user clicks the Reply link for any message. The `postReply.php` script builds, displays, validates, and processes an HTML form. The ID of the post the user is replying to is passed in the URL. The following is an overview of the structure of the script:

```
switch (Button)

    case "Post Message":
        Get parent id
        Save new reply in thread
```

```
        Update thread

    case default:
        Show HTML form for creating reply.
```

Listing 8-14 shows the postReply.php script.

LISTING 8-14: POSTREPLY.PHP

```php
<?php
 /* Program: postReply.php
  * Desc:    Script that posts a reply to a message.
  */
include("functions_main.inc");                              #5
include("functions_post.inc");

switch( @$_POST['Button'])                                  #8
{
  case "Post Message":                                      #10
  {
    $cxn = Connect_to_db("forumVars.inc");                  #12

  // Find the parent_thread of the message that the user
  // is replying to
    $query  = "SELECT parent_thread FROM Post
                  WHERE id = " . $_POST['freplyto'];        #17
    $result = mysqli_query( $cxn, $query );
    $thread = mysqli_fetch_assoc( $result );
    // Encode any quote characters                          #20
  $author = strip_tags($_POST['author']);
  $author = mysqli_real_escape_string($cxn,$author);
  $body = htmlentities($_POST['body']);
  $body = mysqli_real_escape_string( $cxn, $body );
    // And add the new message to the Post table            #25
    $query  = "INSERT INTO Post
                  (parent_thread, in_reply_to, author, body) ";
    $query .= "VALUES( ";
    $query .=    $thread['parent_thread'] . ",";
    $query .=    $_POST['freplyto'] . ",";
    $query .=    "'$author',";
    $query .=    "'$body')";
    $result = mysqli_query( $cxn, $query );
    if( $result == 0 )
      echo "Error: ".mysqli_error($cxn);
    else
    {                                                       #37
      $query = "SELECT replies FROM Thread
                  WHERE id = $thread[parent_thread]";
      $result = mysqli_query($cxn,$query);
      $reps = mysqli_fetch_assoc($result);
      $query  = "UPDATE Thread SET last_post = now(),
```

Continued

LISTING 8-14: *(Continued)*

```
                        replies = {$reps['replies']}+1
                        WHERE id = $thread[parent_thread]";
      $result = mysqli_query( $cxn, $query );               #45
      if( $result == 0 )
        echo "Error: ".mysqli_error($cxn);
      else
      {
        echo '<meta http-equiv="Refresh" content="3;';     #50
        echo 'url=viewThread.php?threadID=';
        echo $thread['parent_thread']. '"/>';
        echo "<B>Your message has been posted. In a moment
                    you will be
                    automatically returned to the thread.</b>";
      }
    }
    break;
  }

  default:                                                   #61
  {
    $cxn = Connect_to_db("forumVars.inc");                   #63
    $query = "SELECT author, date, body, subject
                    FROM Post,Thread
                  WHERE Post.id = " . $_GET['replyTo'] . "
                    AND Thread.id = Post.parent_thread";
    $result = mysqli_query( $cxn, $query );
    $_POST    = mysqli_fetch_assoc( $result );
    $fresponse = $_POST['body'];                             #70
    $fsubject  = $_POST['subject'];
    $body      = "";
    $author    = "";
    $freplyto  = $_GET['replyTo'];
    include( "replyFields.inc" );                            #75
    include( "messageForm.inc" );
    break;
  }
}
?>
```

Following is a description of the lines of code in Listing 8-14:

#8   The switch statement detects which phase the script is running in. If the user has filled in the reply form and clicked the Post Message link, $_POST['Button'] is set to Post Message. If the user hasn't yet seen the form, $_POST['Button'] is undefined.

#10 The first case statement executes after the user has completed the form and clicked the Post Message button.

#16   Every post is owned by a single thread, and a new message is owned by the same thread that owns the message to which the user is replying. Lines 16 to 17 build the query that retrieves the ID of the thread that owns the original message. You could also include the parent thread ID as a second parameter in the URL, like this postReply.php?replyTo=47&parentThread=52.

#21   Lines 21 to 24 prepare the input data for insertion into the database. The strip_tags and htmlentities functions remove or convert HTML tags. The mysqli function escapes any quotes.

#25   After the user-entered data has been made safe, you can insert the new message into the Post table. Lines 26 to 33 build and execute the INSERT query.

#38   If the new message is successfully added to the Post table, lines 38 to 45 build and execute an UPDATE query that modifies last_post date and the number of replies in the parent thread.

#50   The <meta> tag you see automatically redirects the browser back to the viewThread page after a delay of three seconds.

#61   This case statement (the default case) executes when the user first navigates to this Web page. The code in this section displays a form to the user.

#63   When you display the reply form to the user, you want the user to see the subject and content of the message that he's replying to. That information is stored in two places: The subject is found in the parent thread, and the message content is stored in the original post. The Connect_to_db function that connects to the database on line 58 is stored in the functions_main.inc file included at line 5.

#64   Lines 59 to 63 build and execute the query that retrieves the subject and contents of the message being replied to.

#70   The form displayed to the user contains five fields (which I explain in the next section). The code starting at line 65 defines the data displayed to the user by assigning initial values to those five fields.

#75   The two include directives that you see at lines 70 and 71 display the reply page. The files replyFields.inc and messageForm.inc are described in the earlier sections "Writing the code for the new message page" and "Writing the code for the reply page."

Writing the supporting functions

The scripts in this application make use of a small set of functions stored in separate files. All the scripts use the function Connect_to_db stored in the file functions_main.inc. The two scripts that post messages — postMessage.php and postReply.inc — include the file functions_post.inc that defines a function used to display the forms.

Writing functions_main.inc

This file contains one function used by all the scripts. Listing 8-15 shows the file.

LISTING 8-15: THE FUNCTION THAT CONNECTS TO THE DATABASE

```php
<?php
/*  File:       functions_main.inc
 *  Function:   Connect_to_db
 *  Desc:       Connects to a MySQL database. The name of
 *              a file containing the database variables
 *              is passed to the function.
 */
function Connect_to_db($filename)
{
    include($filename);
    $cxn = mysqli_connect($host, $user,$passwd)
        or die ("Couldn't connect to server.");
    $db = mysqli_select_db($cxn,$database)
        or die ("Couldn't select database.");
    return $cxn;
}
?>
```

The `Connect_to_db` function that you see here is identical to the `Connect_to_db` function you see throughout the book. The call must provide the name of a file (`$filename`) that defines a set of connection options (`$host`, `$user`, `$passwd`, and `$database`). Given the name of a file that contains connection options, `Connect_to_db` connects to a MySQL server and returns a connection handle.

Writing functions_post.inc

This file contains one function that adds an HTML field to a form. Listing 8-16 shows the file.

LISTING 8-16: THE FILE THAT DEFINES THE DISPLAYFIELD FUNCTION

```php
<?php
/*  File: functions_post.inc
 *  Desc: Supporting functions for postMessage and postReply.
 */

function DisplayField( $label,$field,$value,$type,$style )
{
   $typeTags    = explode(" ", $type );
   $controlType = $typeTags[0];
```

```
     $result  = '  <td style="formLabel">';
     $result .= $label;
     $result .= "</td>\n";
     if( ereg("input", $controlType ))                         #16
     {
       $result .= "  <td><$type class='$style' name='$field'
                              value='$value'></td>\n";
     }
     else
     {
       $result .= "<td>";
       $result .= "<$type name='$field' class=\"$style\">";
       $result .= $value;
       $result .= "</$controlType></td>\n";
     }
     echo $result;
   }
?>
```

The caller provides a string ($label) that displays to the left of the field, a
name for the field ($field), an initial value ($value), a field type ($type),
and the name of a display style ($style).

The only tricky part of this function is that when you're creating an <input>
element the initial value (the value displayed to the user) is specified as an
attribute. When you're creating a <textarea> element, the initial value is
specified as the value of the element. In other words, if you're creating an
<input> element, you specify the value like this:

<input name="fieldName" value="initial value">

But if you're creating a <textarea> element, you specify the value like this:

<textarea name="fieldName">initial value</textarea>

This part of the function is handled by an if/else statement that begins on
line 16.

Building the Forum Application: The Object-Oriented Approach

From the user's perspective, the forum application behaves the same way
whether you've written it in a procedural fashion or you've used an object-
oriented approach. A visitor to your Web site sees the same HTML tables and
HTML forms regardless of which method you've chosen. The object-oriented

version of this application uses the same set of tables as the procedural version and produces the same set of Web pages.

Object-oriented programming requires that you create and use objects to provide the functionality of the application. You first identify the objects needed for the application. Then you write the classes that define the objects, including the methods that the application needs. When the objects are ready, you write the application script that creates and uses the objects.

Developing the objects

The Forum application stores and displays messages that are posted by users. It displays lists of forums, topics, and threads, so that the user can view and reply to any posted messages. The following list of objects reflects the tasks this application needs to perform.

- ✔ TableAccessor: A class that provides a means to retrieve data from a given table. This is a master class, providing general methods for accessing all types of tables. The Post class and the Thread class are subclasses that extend the TableAccessor class, providing methods for accessing specific types of tables.

- ✔ Post: The Post class provides a simple interface to the Post table. The Post class extends the TableAccessor class by adding two methods and overriding one of the methods defined in TableAccessor.

- ✔ Thread: The Thread class provides a convenient interface to the Thread table. The Thread class extends the TableAccessor class by adding two methods.

- ✔ Database: The application stores the forum information in a database. The Database class provides the container that stores the data.

- ✔ WebForm: A form is central to this application. The form allows customers to register or to enter their usernames and passwords if they're already registered. The WebForm class provides the form for the application. It collects and processes the information typed by a user.

The first three classes are developed to access the forum database. To interact with a MySQL table from a PHP program, you need to

1. Connect to the database.

2. Select the data that you need.

3. Access the values that you select.

4. Process any error messages you might encounter.

Those operations are pretty much the same regardless of which table you're dealing with.

Instead of creating separate classes that contain nearly identical code, I show you how to create a single class, TableAccessor, that defines a common set of methods required to access any table. Next, you *extend* the TableAccessor class, creating a Thread class that adds the methods that you need in order to interact with the Thread table. (The keyword *extend* indicates that the class being defined inherits from the other class.) When you create an object of type Thread, because of inheritance you're also creating an object of type TableAccessor — anything that you can do with a TableAccessor object you can also do with a Thread object. You then extend the TableAccessor to create a Post class that provides access to the Post table. The postReply script accesses two tables (Thread and Post), so I don't create Forum or Topic classes, but you could do that in a similar manner if those classes were needed.

Writing the TableAccessor class

Instead of interacting with the MySQL server directly, the TableAccessor class provides a more convenient way to retrieve data from a given table.

The properties

The TableAccessor properties store connection, table, and row information. The properties are

```
protected $cxn;
protected $table_name;
protected $message;
protected $currentRow;
```

The $cxn property is a database connection handle, the $table_name property represents the name of a MySQL table, and the $currentRow property holds the resultset contents. The $message property is used to convey any error messages.

The code

Listing 8-17 contains the complete code for the TableAccessor class. After the code listing you can find a discussion about each method. Notice the line numbers at the ends of some of the lines of code. The discussion following the listing refers to the line number.

LISTING 8-17: TABLEACCESSOR.CLASS

```php
<?php
class TableAccessor
{
  protected $cxn;
  protected $table_name;
  protected $message;
  protected $currentRow;

  function __construct(mysqli $cxn,$table)
  {
    $this->cxn = $cxn;                                        #11
    if(is_string($table))                                    #12
    {
      $sql = "SHOW TABLES LIKE '$table'";
      $table_res = mysqli_query($cxn,$sql);
      $nrow = mysqli_num_rows($table_res);
      if($nrow > 0)                                          #17
      {
        $this->table_name = $table;
      }
      else                                                   #21
      {
        throw new Exception("$table is not a table
                                  in the database");
        return FALSE;
      }
    }
    else                                                     #28
    {
      throw new Exception("Second parameter is not a
                                valid table name");
      return FALSE;
    }
  }

  function selectByID($id)                                   #36
  {
    $id = trim($id);
    $sql = "SELECT * FROM $this->table_name
                   WHERE id = $id";                          #40
    if(!$result = mysqli_query($this->cxn,$sql))
    {
      throw new Exception("Couldn't execute query: "
                            .mysqli_error($this->cxn));
      return FALSE;
    }
    if( mysqli_num_rows($result) > 0 )
    {
      $this->currentRow = mysqli_fetch_assoc($result);       #49
      return TRUE;
    }
    else
```

```
     {
       $this->message = "$this->table_name $id
                                    does not exist!";     #55
       unset($this->currentRow);
       return FALSE;
     }
   }

   function getValues($fieldNames)                          #61
   {
     if(!isset($fieldNames))                                #63
     {
       return $this->currentRow;
     }
     else if(is_array($fieldNames))                         #67
     {
       foreach($fieldNames as $name)
         $result[$name] = $this->currentRow[$name];
       return $result;
     }
     else
     {
       return $this->currentRow[$fieldNames];              #75
     }
   }

   function getMessage()
   {
       return $this->message;
   }

   function getConnection()
   {
       return $this->cxn;
   }
 }
?>
```

The constructor

The constructor tests the connection and the table name that are passed to
it to ensure that the parameters are in the proper format and stores them in
properties. There is no default for these values; the values must be passed
when the Account object is created.

#11 Stores the database connection in the property.

#12 Begins an if block that executes if the table name passed is a string.
The table name is checked to see whether it exists.

   #14 Lines 14 to 15 create and execute an SQL query that tests
   whether a table exists with the name that was passed to the
   constructor.

#17 Begins an `if` block that executes if the table exists. The table name is stored in the `$table` property.

#21 Begins an `else` block that executes when the table does not exist. The script throws an exception with a message and returns `FALSE`.

#28 Begins an `else` block that executes if the table name is not a string. The script throws an exception with a message and returns `FALSE`.

selectByID

This method retrieves a single row from the table. The row is identified by its `id` column. `selectByID` doesn't return the content of the row, it returns `TRUE` or `FALSE` to indicate whether the requested row was found. If the `selectByID` function can't find the row that is being looked up, it stores a message in the object explaining that no such object exists in the data — that can be retrieved by calling the `getMessage` method. The following numbers refer to line number in Listing 8-17.

#38 Because all the forum tables contain a column named `id`, you can simply hard-code a `SELECT` statement in this method. If you want to extend `TableAccessor` to access a table that doesn't contain a column named `id` (or if you need to access the table by some other set of columns), you can override the `selectByID` method in your own class. (In fact, you do just that when you create the `Post` class a little later.)

#48 If `selectByID` finds the requested row, it stores the row values in `$this->currentRow` (which is a protected member of the `TableAccessor` class) and returns `TRUE` to indicate success.

#54 If `selectByID` can't find the requested row, it stores a message in `$this->message` and returns `FALSE`.

getValues

Returns one or more values from the current row. How many values are returned depends on the type of argument passed to the method. The following numbers refer to line numbers in Listing 8-17:

#62 If you call this method with a `NULL` argument (or with no arguments), `getValues` returns the current row.

#66 If you want to retrieve a specific set of columns from the current row, call `getValues` with an array that contains the names of the columns that you want. `getValues` returns the requested values in the form of an associative array.

#74 You can also call `getValues` with the name of a single column, and it returns the value in that column.

getMessage
Returns the text of the most recent error message.

getConnection
Returns the database connection stored inside this object.

Writing the Thread class

The Thread class provides a convenient interface to the Thread table. After you create a Thread object, you can use it to call any of the methods defined by class Thread or by class TableAccessor. That means, for example, that you can retrieve a specific row in the Thread table by calling $thread->selectByID (assuming that $thread is an object of type Thread). The Thread class extends TableAccessor by adding two methods: updateTimeStamp and createNew.

The code
The complete code for the Thread class is shown in Listing 8-18. After the code listing you can find a discussion about each method. Notice the line numbers at the ends of some of the lines of code. The discussion following the listing refers to the line numbers.

LISTING 8-18: THE THREAD CLASS

```php
<?php
 /* Class:   Thread
  * Desc:    Represents a thread.
  */
  require_once("TableAccessor.class");

class Thread extends TableAccessor
{
   function updateTimeStamp($threadID)                          #9
   {
     $sql = "UPDATE Thread SET last_post = now()
             WHERE id = $threadID";
     return(mysqli_query($this->cxn,$sql));
   }

   function createNew($topic,$subject)                          #16
   {
     $subject=mysqli_real_escape_string($this->cxn,$subject);
     $sql = "INSERT INTO Thread(parent_topic, subject)
             VALUES( $topic, '$subject' )";
```

Continued

LISTING 8-18: *(Continued)*

```
    if(mysqli_query($this->cxn,$sql))                           #21
    {
       return $this->cxn->insert_id;
    }
    else
    {
       throw new Exception("Can't execute query insert: "
                             .mysqli_error($this->cxn));
       return NULL;
    }
 }
    function updateReplies($threadID)
    {
       $query = "SELECT replies FROM Thread
                 WHERE id = $threadID";
       $result = mysqli_query($this->cxn,$query);
       $reps = mysqli_fetch_assoc($result);
       $query = "UPDATE Thread
                 SET replies = {$reps['replies']}+1
                 WHERE id = '$threadID'";
       $result = mysqli_query( $this->cxn, $query );
       return($result);
 }
 ?>
```

updateTimeStamp

This method executes a single UPDATE statement that assigns the value
now() (a function executed by the MySQL server) to Thread.last_post. If
the UPDATE statement succeeds, updateTimeStamp returns TRUE; otherwise,
it returns FALSE.

createNew

This method inserts a new row into the Thread table. The caller provides the
ID of the parent topic and a string containing the subject of the thread. The
Thread.replies and Thread.last_post columns are set to NULL. Thread.
id is defined as an auto_increment column so the MySQL server will assign
a unique identifier to the new Thread. At line 21, if the new INSERT statement succeeds, createNew returns the id of the new thread. The mysqli
package makes it easy to find the auto-generated id value — just look in the
connection->insert_id property.

updateReplies

This method adds 1 to the replies field in the Thread table of the database. It
gets the number of replies currently in the database. It then updates the field,
setting the new value to the current (retrieved) value plus 1.

Writing the Post class

Like the `Thread` class, the `Post` class provides a simple interface to a MySQL table. The `Post` class extends the `TableAccessor` class by *adding* two methods (`postReply` and `postMessage`) and re-implementing, or *overriding,* one of the methods defined by the master class (`selectByID`).

When you select a row from the `Post` table, it's often convenient to retrieve the subject of the parent thread as well: The `selectByID` method implemented by the `Post` class does just that. The `selectByID` method offered by the base class (`TableAccessor`) doesn't know how to join two tables, so the `Post` class must override the `selectByID` method simply by supplying its own version.

The `postReply` and `postMessage` methods both add a new row to the `Post` table: `postReply` adds a message to an existing thread and `postMessage` creates a new message *and* a new thread.

The code

The complete code for the `Post` class is shown in Listing 8-19. After the code listing you can find a discussion about each method. Notice the line numbers at the ends of some of the lines of code. The discussion following the listing refers to the line numbers.

LISTING 8-19: THE POST CLASS

```php
<?php
 /* Class: Post
  * Desc:  Stores a post.
  */
require_once("TableAccessor.class");
require_once("Thread.class");

class Post extends TableAccessor
{
  function selectByID($id)                                      #10
  {
    $id = trim($id);
    $sql = "SELECT date,body,subject,parent_thread
            FROM Post,Thread WHERE Post.id = $id
                AND Thread.id = Post.parent_thread";
    if(!$result = mysqli_query($this->cxn,$sql))
    {
      throw new Exception("Couldn't execute query: "
                          .mysqli_error($this->cxn));
      return FALSE;
    }
    if( mysqli_num_rows($result) > 0 )
```

Continued

LISTING 8-19: *(Continued)*

```php
        {
$this->currentRow = mysqli_fetch_assoc($result);
        return TRUE;
      }
      else
      {
        $this->message = "Post $id does not exist!";
        return FALSE;
      }
    }

    function postReply($parent,$replyTo,$author,$body)          #34
    {
      // Encode any quote characters
      $author = mysqli_real_escape_string($this->cxn,$author);
      $body   = mysqli_real_escape_string( $this->cxn, $body );
      $sql = "INSERT INTO Post
                (parent_thread, in_reply_to, author, body)
                VALUES($parent, $replyTo, '$author', '$body')";
      if(mysqli_query($this->cxn,$sql))
      {
        return $this->cxn->insert_id;                          #44
      }
      else
      {
        throw new Exception("Can't execute query insert: "
                            .mysqli_error($this->cxn));
        return NULL;
      }
    }


    function postMessage($topic,$subject,$author,$body)         #54
    {
      $thread = new Thread($this->getConnection(),"Thread");
      $parent_thread = $thread->createNew($topic,$subject);
     // Encode any quote characters
      $author = mysqli_real_escape_string($this->cxn,$author);
      $body = mysqli_real_escape_string( $this->cxn, $body );
      $sql = "INSERT INTO Post (parent_thread, author, body)
                VALUES($parent_thread,'$author', '$body')";
      if(mysqli_query($this->cxn,$sql))
      {
        return $this->cxn->insert_id;
      }
      else
      {
        throw new Exception("Can't execute query insert: "
                            .mysqli_error($this->cxn));
        return NULL;
      }
    }
  }
?>
```

selectByID

This method overrides the `selectByID` method defined by class `TableAccessor`. When you call `selectByID` through a `Post` object, you're calling the method defined at line 10 in Listing 8-19. On the other hand, if you call `selectByID` through a `Thread` object, you're calling the `selectByID` defined in class `TableAccessor` (because class `Thread` does *not* override `selectByID`). The `selectByID` method defined by `Post` is very similar to the `selectByID` defined by `TableAccessor`. In fact, the only difference is that this version joins the `Post` and `Thread` tables rather than selecting from a single table.

postReply

This method adds a new message to the `Post` table. This method runs when a user replies to an existing message. The caller provides the ID of the parent thread, the ID of the message that the user is replying to, the author, and the body of the new message. As always, you should use `mysqli_real_escape_string` to clean up any data that comes from the outside world (that is, from the user's Web browser). At line 44, if the message is successfully added to the `Post` table, `postReply` returns the auto-generated ID of the new row.

postMessage

Like `postReply`, `postMessage` adds a new message to the `Post` table. This method is invoked when a user starts a new thread of discussion. The caller must provide the ID of the topic that the thread belongs to, the subject of the thread, the author, and the body of the message. At line 56, `postMessage` must create a new row in the `Thread` table. Rather than dealing directly with the `Thread` table, `postMessage` creates a `Thread` object and asks that object to create a new row. The `$thread->createNew` method returns the ID of the new thread. After you have the ID of the parent thread, you can `INSERT` a new row into the `Post` table. Notice that the `INSERT` statement omits the `in_reply_to`, `id`, and `date` columns. The new row contains a `NULL` `in_reply_to` value to indicate that it is the first message in a new thread (that is, the new message isn't a reply to some other message). The MySQL server automatically assigns values to the `date` and `id` columns. Like `postReply`, `postMessage` returns the ID of the newly created `Post`.

Writing the Database class

The `Database` class provides the connection to the database where the customer information is stored. I develop the `Database` class in Chapter 3. See Listing 3-4 for the `Database` class code.

The methods provided by the `Database` class are:

- ✔ **The constructor:** Creates a connection to a MySQL database. The constructor expects to be passed a filename where the hostname, account name, and password necessary to access MySQL are stored. A Database object is created with the following statement:

  `$db = new Database("forumVars.inc");`

- ✔ `useDatabase`: Selects a database and stores the database name. The method expects to be passed a database name. It checks whether the database exists and returns a message if the database doesn't exist.

- ✔ `getConnection`: Returns the connection that is established and stored in the constructor.

Writing the WebForm class

The `WebForm` is used to display and process the new message and reply forms. I create and explain the `WebForm` class in Chapter 4. The class is shown in Listing 4-6.

The methods in the `WebForm` class that this application uses are:

- ✔ **The constructor:** Stores the properties needed to display the form correctly. Two files — an information file and a file that defines the look and feel — are required. The two filenames are passed when the `WebForm` object is created and stored in two properties. The data for the form fields can be passed, but can be left out and the form fields will be blank. You can create the object by using either of the following statements:

  `$form = new WebForm("file1.inc","file2.inc",$_POST);`
  `$form = new WebForm("file1.inc","file2.inc");`

- ✔ `displayForm`: This method displays the form. It extracts the data from the `$data` property where it is stored. An @ to suppress the error messages so that the form can be displayed without any data. The form is displayed by including the two files that define the form. These two files can define any type of form, with fields and elements you want to use. For this application, I use the files I describe earlier in this chapter — `replyFields.inc`, `messageFields.inc`, and `messageForm.inc`.

- ✔ `checkForBlanks`: Checks each field in the form to see whether it contains information. If it finds invalid blank fields, it returns an array containing the field names of the blank fields.

- ✔ `verifyData`: This method checks each field to ensure that the information submitted in the field is in a reasonable format. For instance, you know that "hi you" is not a reasonable format for a zip code. This method checks the information from specific fields against regular expressions that match the information allowed in that field. If invalid data is found in any fields, the method returns an array containing messages that identify the problems.

✔ `trimData`, `stripTagsFromData`: A PHP function is applied to each value in the `$data` property. The resulting values are stored in `$data`. The `trim` function removes leading and trailing blanks from a string. The `strip_tags` function removes any HTML tags from the string, important for security.

Writing the Forum application scripts

The Forum application has five application scripts, as follows:

✔ `viewForums-OO.php`: Displays the forums Web page, which displays a list of the forums and topics available.

✔ `viewTopic-OO.php`: Displays the threads Web page, which displays a list of the threads in a topic.

✔ `viewThread-OO.php`: Displays the messages Web page, which displays a list of the messages in a thread.

✔ `postMessage-OO.php`: Builds, displays, validates, and processes the HTML form used on the new message page.

✔ `postReply-OO.php`: Builds, displays, validates, and processes the HTML form used in the reply page. The script is similar to the `postMessage-OO` script. However, `postMessage` creates both a message and thread, while `postReply` creates a message but updates an existing thread. This script runs when the user clicks a Reply link in the messages page. The thread ID is passed to this script in the URL.

Writing viewForums-OO.php

The `viewForums-OO.php` script simply includes the `viewForums.inc` file that displays the Web page. This script is run first, starting the application by displaying the forums Web page. Other scripts run when links or buttons are clicked. Listing 8-20 shows `viewForums-OO.php`.

LISTING 8-20: THE SCRIPT THAT DISPLAYS THE FORUMS PAGE

```php
<?php
/* Program: viewForums-OO.php
 * Desc:    Displays the forums page.
 */
include("functions_main.inc");
include("viewForums.inc");

?>
```

The script includes a file containing functions needed by the `viewForums.inc` file and then includes `viewForums.inc`. The `viewForums.inc` file is the same file used for the procedural application, shown in Listing 8-1, with the exception of line 38. The following two lines show the line to be changed. The first line is the line from the procedural application; the second line is the line as needed for the object-oriented application.

```
DisplayTopics($forum['id'],$cxn,"viewTopic.php");#38
DisplayTopics($forum['id'],$cxn,"viewTopic-OO.php");#38
```

Writing viewTopic-OO.php

The `viewTopic-OO.php` script is the same as the `viewForums-OO.php` script, except that it includes the `viewTopic.inc` file that displays the Threads Web page. This script runs when the user clicks a topic name in the forums page. Listing 8-21 shows `viewTopic-OO.php`.

LISTING 8-21: THE SCRIPT THAT DISPLAYS THE THREADS PAGE

```php
<?php
/* Program: viewTopic-OO.php
 * Desc:    Displays the threads page.
 */
include("functions_main.inc");
include("viewTopic.inc");

?>
```

The script includes a file containing functions needed by the `viewTopic.inc` file and then includes `viewTopic.inc`. The `viewTopic.inc` file is the same file used for the procedural application, shown in Listing 8-3, with the exception of two lines. The first line that must be changed is line 40, shown here:

```
echo '<a
    href="viewThread.php?threadID='.$thread['id'].'">';
```

In this line, `viewThread.php` needs to be changed to `viewThread-OO.php`. The second line that needs to be changed is line 51, shown here:

```
echo '<b><a
    href="postMessage.php?topicID='$_GET['topicID'].'">';
```

In this line, `postMessage.php` needs to be changed to `postMessage-OO.php`.

Writing viewThread-OO.php

The viewThread-OO.php script is the same as the viewForums-OO.php script, except that it includes the viewThread.inc file that displays the Messages Web page. This script runs when the user clicks a thread name in the threads page. Listing 8-22 shows viewThread-OO.php.

LISTING 8-22: SCRIPT THAT DISPLAYS THE MESSAGES PAGE

```php
<?php
/* Program: viewThread-OO.php
 * Desc:    Displays the messages page.
 */
include("functions_main.inc");
include("viewThread.inc");

?>
```

The script includes a file containing functions needed by the viewForums. inc file and then includes viewforums.inc. The viewTopic.inc file is the same file used for the procedural application, shown in Listing 8-3, with the exception of line 41, shown here:

```
echo    '<a href="postReply.php?replyTo='.$post['id'].
```

In this line, postReply.php needs to be changed to postReply-OO.php.

Writing the postMessage-OO application script

The postMessage-OO program is invoked when you click the Start a New Thread link on the Threads page. postMessage-OO creates and displays an HTML form and waits until you click the submit button (which, in this case, is labeled Post Message). After you click the submit button, the postReply-OO program re-invokes itself — the $_POST[] array contains the data that you entered. The second time around, postReply-OO validates the data that you entered and, if everything looks okay, writes your new message to the MySQL database.

Listing 8-23 shows the postReply-OO.php script.

LISTING 8-23: THE SCRIPT THAT POSTS A NEW MESSAGE

```php
<?php
/* Program: postMessage-OO.php
 * Desc:    Program that posts a new message and starts
 *          a new thread.
 */
require_once("WebForm.class");                                    #6
require_once("Database.class");
require_once("TableAccessor.class");
require_once("Post.class");
require_once("functions_post-OO.inc");
require_once("forumVars.inc");

try
{
  if(!isset($_POST['Button']))                                    #15
  {
    $parentTopic = $_GET['topicID'];                              #17

    $db = new Database("forumVars.inc");
    $db->useDatabase("forumTest");
    $topic = new TableAccessor($db->getConnection(),
                  "Topic" );
    if( !$topic->selectByID($parentTopic))
    {
      echo $topic->getMessage()."<br>";
      exit();
    }
    $_POST['author']    = "";                                     #28
    $_POST['subject']   = "";
    $_POST['body']      = "";
    $_POST['ftopic']    = $topic->getValues( "name");
    $_POST['ftopicID']  = $parentTopic;
  }
  $form = new WebForm("messageForm.inc",
                      "messageFields.inc", $_POST);
}
catch(Exception $e)
{
  echo $e->getMessage();
  exit();
}
if(!isset($_POST['Button']))                                      #42
{
  $form->displayForm();
  exit();
}
else                                                              #47
{
  if( !validate($form))
  {
    $form->displayform();
```

```
     exit();
   }
$newdata = $form->getAllFields();                          #54
@extract( $newdata );                                      #55
$db = new Database("forumVars.inc");                       #56
$db->useDatabase("forumTest");
$post = new Post($db->getConnection(),  "Post");           #58
$newMessage =
     $post->postMessage($ftopicID,$subject,$author,$body);
if( $newMessage == NULL )
{
  echo "Couldn't post new message.
        Try again later.";
  exit();
}
else
{
  echo '<meta http-equiv="Refresh" content="3;';          #69
  echo   "url=viewTopic-OO.php?topicID=$ftopicID";
  echo '"/>';
  echo "<B>Your message has been posted. In a moment you
        will be
        automatically returned to the topic</b>";
}
}
?>
```

The following numbers refer to the line numbers in Listing 8-23.

#6   Includes the files needed by this application script. The classes are included, including the `WebForm` and `Database` classes that are developed and explained in Chapters 3 and 4.

#15   Begins an `if` block that executes if the user did not click the submit button. This means that the user clicked the Start a New Thread link. The blank form should be displayed.

#17   Gets the topic ID that was passed in the URL.

#19   Lines 19 to 32 set up the default values to be displayed in the new message form.

#34   Creates a `WebForm` object with the default values.

#42   Starts an `if` block that executes if the user did not click the Post Message button. The form is displayed with the default values.

#47   Starts an `else` block that executes if the user clicked the Post Message button. The information the user enters in the form is validated, to determine if reasonable information was submitted. If the information is not valid data, the form is redisplayed with an error message. If the information is valid, the new message is stored in the database.

#69   Returns the user to the messages Web page.

Writing the postReply-OO application script

The postReply-OO program is invoked when the user clicks the Reply To button to reply to an existing message. postReply-OO creates and displays an HTML form and waits until the user clicks the submit button (which, in this case, is labeled Post Message). After the user clicks the submit button, the postReply-OO program starts again — the $_POST[] array contains the data that the user entered. The second time around, postReply-OO validates the data that the user entered and, if everything looks okay, writes the new message to the MySQL database.

Listing 8-24 shows the postReply-OO.php script.

LISTING 8-24: THE SCRIPT THAT POSTS A REPLY TO A MESSAGE

```php
<?php
/* Program: postReply-OO.php
 * Desc:     Program that posts a reply to an existing
 *           message.  This program displays a form to
 *           the user and processes the form when the
 *           user clicks the submit button.
 */
require_once("WebForm.class");                              #8
require_once("Database.class");
require_once("Post.class");
require_once("Thread.class");
require_once("functions_post-OO.inc");
require_once("forumVars.inc");

try
{
  if(!isset($_POST['Button']))                              #17
  {
    $replyTo = $_GET['replyTo'];                            #19
    $db = new Database("forumVars.inc");                    #20
    $db->useDatabase("Forum");
    $post = new Post($db->getConnection(), "Post");
    if( !$post->selectByID($replyTo))                       #23
    {
      echo $post->getMessage()."<br>";
      exit();
    }
    $postData = $post->getValues(array("body","subject"));
    $_POST['author']    = "";                               #29
    $_POST['body']      = "";
    $_POST['fsubject']  = $postData['subject'];
    $_POST['fresponse'] = $postData['body'];
    $_POST['freplyto']  = $replyTo;
    $_POST['subject']   = $postData['subject'];
  }
  $form = new WebForm("messageForm.inc",
                      "replyFields.inc",$_POST);
```

```
}
catch(Exception $e)
{
  echo $e->getMessage();
  exit();
}
if(!isset($_POST['Button']))                              #44
{
  $form->displayForm();
  exit();
}
else
{
  if( !validate($form))                                   #51
  {
    $form->displayform();
    exit();
  }
  $newdata = $form->getAllFields();                       #56
  @extract( $newdata );                                   #57
  $db = new Database("forumVars.inc");                    #58
  $db->useDatabase("Forum");
  $post    = new Post($db->getConnection(),  "Post");
  if( !$post->selectByID($_POST['freplyto']))
  {
    echo $post->getMessage()."<br>";
    exit();
  }
  $parent_thread = $post->getValues("parent_thread");     #66
  $newMessage = $post->postReply($parent_thread,
                        $_POST['freplyto'], $author, $body);
  if( $newMessage == NULL )
  {
    echo "Couldn't post new message.
            Try again later.";
    exit();
  }
  else
  {
    $thread = new Thread($db->getConnection(),"Thread");
    $thread->updateTimestamp( $parent_thread );           #78
    $thread->updateReplies( $parent_thread );             #79
    echo '<meta http-equiv="Refresh" content="3;';        #80
    echo    "url=viewThread-OO.php?threadID=$parent_thread";
    echo '"/>';
    echo "<B>Your message has been posted. In a moment you
            will be automatically returned to the
            thread.</b>";
  }
}
?>
```

Following is a description of the numbered lines of code that appear in postReply-OO.php in Listing 8-24:

#8 This program uses the Database and WebForm classes that you develop in Chapters 3 and 4 (respectively); refer to those chapters for full details.

#17 *Remember:* This program runs in two distinct phases. In the first phase, it builds (and displays) an HTML form and waits for the user to click the submit button. In the second phase, the user has (presumably) completed the form and postReply-OO should process the values provided by the user. To distinguish between the two phases, you test the $_POST['Button'] variable — if that variable is undefined (not set), you're running in the first phase. If $_POST['Button'] *is* defined, the user has completed the form and $_POST contains the data entered.

#19 Arriving at line 19 means that this form is being displayed to the user for the first time. Lines of code fill in the initial values that will be displayed on the form.

#20 When the reply form displays, the user should see the subject of the message to which she is replying, as well as an editable text area for the body of the reply message. To find the subject, postReply-OO creates a Database object (calling the constructor with the login parameters imported from forumVars.inc) and a Post object.

#23 The Post class provides a number of useful methods that make it easy to work with the Post table. The first method, selectByID, executes a SELECT statement that retrieves the Post whose ID matches $replyTo. selectByID does *not* return the values retrieved; it merely stores them inside the $post object. If selectByID can't find the requested Post, it stores an error message in $post and makes that message accessible through the getMessage method.

#28 The Post class also provides a method that lets you access the values retrieved by selectByID: getValues. You can call getValues three ways. If you call getValues with the name of a column, getValues returns the value of that column (as retrieved by selectByID). If you call getValues with an array of column names, getValues returns an associative array containing the values that you requested. If you call getValues without any arguments (or with a NULL argument), it returns the entire row (in the form of an associative array) retrieved by selectByID. Line 28 extracts the body and subject values from $post.

#29 postReply-OO uses the WebForm class to display an HTML form to the user. The initial values displayed on that form are found in the $_POST array. Lines 29 through 34 store the appropriate values in $_POST. The user is expected to fill in the author and body so those fields are blanked out. The fsubject and fresponse fields are initialized to the values found in the original message. freplyto is initialized to the message ID found in the forwarding URL.

#36 By the time the program arrives at line 35, the `$_POST` array contains the values displayed on the form. If the form is being shown for the first time, `$_POST` contains the initial values that will be displayed to the user. If the user has already completed the form (and clicked the Submit button), `$_POST` contains the values that the user typed into the form.

#44 Now that the form has been created and prepared, an `if/else` statement determines how to display the form, depending on the value of the button. If the user hasn't yet seen the form, `$_POST['Button']` will be undefined, `$form->displayForm` will be called and the program will `exit`. If the user has completed the form, `$_POST['Button']` is set and the program jumps down to line 48.

#49 Begins the `else` statement that executes if the user clicked the submit button. The call to `validate($form)` checks the content entered by the user and returns either `TRUE` or `FALSE`. If the data fails verification, `validate` returns `FALSE` — in that case, simply display the form again. (The `$form` object stores an error message that it displays to the user.)

#56 If `validate` succeeds (implying that the data entered by the user looks okay), you can call `$form->getAllFields` to retrieve those values. As I show you in Chapter 4, `getAllFields` returns an associative array that contains both the field names (the keys) and the field values.

#57 The `$newdata` array contains elements such as `author=>"bruce@example.com"` and `body=>"This is my message"`. The call to `extract` creates a new variable for each member of the `$newdata` array. The name of the variable matches the key and the value of the variable matches the value of the array element. For example, `extract` would create two new variables: `$author` and `$body`. `$author` would hold the string `"bruce@example.com"`, and `$body` would be set to `"This is my message"`. After you extract the values in `$newdata`, you have (at least) five new variables: `$author`, `$body`, `$fsubject`, `$fresponse`, and `$freplyto`.

#58 At this point, most of the information needed to create a new message in the `Post` table has been obtained. The one last piece is the ID of the parent thread. The forwarding page provided the original message ID in the URL, but the message needs to be looked up in the database to find out which thread it belonged to. First, a database connection is established by using the login parameters found in `forumVars.inc`. Then a new `Post` object is instantiated and `selectByID` is called to retrieve the original message.

#66 The call to `getValues` grabs the `parent_thread` from the row retrieved by `selectByID`. Now a new message can be saved to the `Post` table by calling `$post->postReply`. If successful, `postReply` returns the auto-generated ID of the new message. If `postReply` fails, it returns `NULL`.

#78 If `postReply` succeeds, the `last_post` timestamp in the parent thread is updated. The `Thread` class defines a method (`update Timestamp`) that does just that — you provide the thread ID, and `updateTimestamp` does the rest.

#79 If `postReply` succeeds, the `replies` field in the parent thread is updated. The `Thread` class defines a method (`updateReplies`) that does just that — you provide the thread ID and `updateReplies` does the rest.

#80 The only thing left to do is to send the user somewhere useful. The `<meta>` tag redirects the browser back to the `viewThread-OO` page after a delay of three seconds, giving the user a chance to read the "post successful" message.

Writing the supporting functions

The scripts in this application make use of a small set of functions stored in separate files. All the scripts use the function `Connect_to_db` stored in the file `functions_main.inc`. The two scripts that post messages — `postMessage.php` and `postReply.inc` — include the `functions_post.inc` file that defines a function used to display the forms.

Writing functions_main.inc

This file contains one function used by three of the scripts. Listing 8-25 shows the file.

LISTING 8-25: THE FUNCTION THAT CONNECTS TO THE DATABASE

```php
<?php
/*  File:       functions_main.inc
 *  Function:   Connect_to_db
 *  Desc:       Connects to a MySQL database. The name of
 *              a file containing the database variables
 *              is passed to the function.
 */
function Connect_to_db($filename)
{
    include($filename);
    $cxn = mysqli_connect($host, $user,$passwd)
        or die ("Couldn't connect to server.");
    $db = mysqli_select_db($cxn,$database)
        or die ("Couldn't select database.");
    return $cxn;
}
?>
```

The `Connect_to_db` function that you see here is identical to the `Connect_to_db` function you see throughout the book. The call must provide the name of a file (`$filename`) that defines a set of connection options (`$host`, `$user`, `$passwd`, and `$database`). Given the name of a file that contains connection options, `Connect_to_db` connects to a MySQL server and returns a connection handle.

Writing functions_post-00.inc

This file contains one function that adds an HTML field to a form. Listing 8-26 shows the file.

LISTING 8-26: THE FILE THAT DEFINES TWO FUNCTIONS NEEDED BY THE SCRIPTS

```php
<?php
/*  File: functions_post-00.inc
 *  Desc: Supporting functions for postMessage-OO and
 *        postReply-OO.
 */

function DisplayField( $label,$field,$value,$type,$style )
{
  $typeTags    = explode(" ", $type );
  $controlType = $typeTags[0];
  $result   = '  <td style="formLabel">';
  $result .= $label;
  $result .= "</td>\n";
  if( ereg("input", $controlType ))                          #14
  {
    $result .= "  <td><$type class='$style' name='$field'
                           value='$value'></td>\n";
  }
  else
  {
    $result .= "<td>";
    $result .= "<$type name='$field' class=\"$style\">";
    $result .= $value;
    $result .= "</$controlType></td>\n";
  }
  echo $result;
}

function validate( $form )                                   #29
{
  try
  {
    $blanks = $form->checkForBlanks();                       #33
  }
  catch(Exception $e)
  {
```

Continued

LISTING 8-26: *(Continued)*

```php
      echo $e->getMessage();
   }
   if(is_array($blanks))                                    #39
   {
      $GLOBALS['message_2'] =
        "The following required fields were blank.
            Please enter the required information:  ";
      foreach($blanks as $value)
      {
         $GLOBALS['message_2'] .="$value, ";
      }
      return FALSE;
   }
   $form->trimData();                                       #50
   $form->stripTagsFromData();
   try
   {
      $errors = $form->verifyData();                        #54
   }
   catch(Exception $e)
   {
      echo $e->getMessage();
   }
   if(is_array($errors))                                    #60
   {
      $GLOBALS['message_2'] = "";
      foreach($errors as $value)
      {
         $GLOBALS['message_2'] .="$value<br> ";
      }
      return FALSE;
   }
   return TRUE;                                             #69
}

?>
```

This file contains two functions needed by the postMessage-OO and post
Reply-OO scripts. The first function is DisplayFields. The calling statement
provides a string ($label) that displays to the left of the field, a name for the
field ($field), an initial value ($value), a field type ($type), and the name of
a display style ($style).

The only tricky part of this function is that, when you're creating an <input>
element, the initial value (the value displayed to the user) is specified as an
attribute. When you're creating a <textarea> element, the initial value is
specified as the value of the element. In other words, if you're creating an
<input> element, you specify the value like this:

```
<input name="fieldName" value="initial value">
```

But if you're creating a `<textarea>` element, you specify the value like this:

```
<textarea name="fieldName">initial value</textarea>
```

This part of the function is handled by an `if/else` statement that begins on line 16.

The second function is `Validate`, which processes the information typed into the form by the user.

#29 The calling statement passes an array of data to this function.

#33 Checks for blank fields that should contain data.

#39 Begins an `if` block that executes if blank fields are found. The form is re-displayed with an error message.

#50 Processes the data entered by a user. Removes blank spaces from the beginning and end. The script doesn't reach this line unless no blank fields are found.

#51 Removes any HTML tags from the data.

#54 Checks the data for valid formats.

#60 Begins an `if` block that executes if information was found with an invalid format. The form is re-displayed with an error message.

#69 Returns `true` when the data is all okay — no blanks and no invalid format found.

Possible Enhancements

If you've made it to this point, you have a complete Web forum application. Invite a few visitors to your site, and you'll have lively discussions popping up in no time. To wrap up this chapter, here are a few enhancements that you might want to consider:

- **User registration/authentication:** You can easily integrate the Login application that you develop in Chapter 3 if you want to require visitors to register (and log in) at your site before they can post new messages.

- **Threading:** Some forums *thread* messages together to make the relationship between message and reply easier to see. When the user clicks the Reply button in this application, the system keeps track of the relationship between the existing messages that have been created and the message that the user is replying to (that information is stored in the `Post.in_reply_to` column). If you want to display messages in threaded order, you simply have to sort them appropriately and indent each reply.

✔ **BBcode:** If you've visited many Web forums, you've probably encountered a feature known as *BBCode*. BBCode is an easy way for a novice user to mark up a message. For example, to italicize a phrase, you simply type in **[i]this is italicized[/i]**; to include a smiley face, just type in **:-)**. The PHP Extension and Application Repository (PEAR) provides a package, HTML_BBCodeParser, that can convert BBCode into equivalent HTML form.

✔ **Forum Management:** After your forum is up and running for a while, you'll probably find a few tasks that you'd like to automate. You might want to create a Web form that makes it easier to add (and remove) Forum and Topic records. You might want another form that truncates a thread or consolidates two similar threads. You *can* manage your forum from the MySQL command line, but Web forms can certainly simplify the task. Just be sure to secure any management tools that you create, so they can't fall in the wrong hands.

✔ **File uploads/downloads:** Most Web forums provide a way for a visitor to attach a file to a message. If you're hosting a forum devoted to household pets, your users will surely want to share photos. Check out the HTTP_Upload package at PEAR (pear.php.net) to see how to add this feature to your forum.

✔ **Search tools:** The MySQL server provides a set of full-text search functions that you might want to add to your forum. You can use a full-text search to find words and phrases within any table in your MySQL server. The most useful search (in this application) locates messages by searching the Post.body and Thread.subject columns.

Part V
The Part of Tens

The 5th Wave   By Rich Tennant

SITE MAP STRATEGY BY JERRY

"Okay, well, I think we all get the gist of where Jerry was going with the site map."

In this part . . .

Chapter 9 contains tips for application development based on my experiences. They can serve as short-cuts for you on your journey to becoming a Web developer.

Chapter 10 contains a list of Web sites where you can find code libraries and other useful information about applications.

Chapter 9

Ten Hints for Application Development

An application can be a five line script that outputs `Hello World!`. Application development for this script is pretty simple. However, an application is likely to be more complex, often requiring many scripts and many coordinated programmers. Application development for a complex application can be very tricky. This chapter includes some suggestions for coding practices that will make development proceed more smoothly, no matter how complicated the application is.

Plan First

Restrain your desire to jump in and start coding immediately. A plan, on paper, is essential. A plan should answer the following questions:

✔ What tasks does your application need to perform?

✔ What programming methods will you use to implement each task?

✔ How do the tasks interact with each other?

✔ How easy is your application to maintain?

✔ How will you add features to the application in the future?

✔ How does the application meet the needs of the user?

Nothing is more painful than realizing after half your application is coded that you forgot an important factor and must start all over again.

Be Consistent

Many decisions are made in the course of coding an application. Make each decision once and then be consistent throughout the application. For instance, decide on naming conventions at the beginning and use the same conventions throughout. If you use all lowercase letters for variables and camel caps for function names at the beginning of your application or in one class, use the same conventions throughout the application or in all classes. Consistency makes the code much easier to understand and to maintain.

Test Code Incrementally

A program consists of many code blocks. Building and testing an application proceeds best when each small code block is tested on its own. Test a simple piece of code until it performs as expected. Add functionality to the code one element at a time, testing as each new piece of code is added. For instance, if a program task requires a loop within a loop, build and test one loop. When it works, add the other loop.

Remember Those Who Follow

Keep your code as simple and easy to read as possible. At some point in the future, someone will try to understand your code so they can maintain or modify it. Code that can't be easily understood is a problem, no matter how clever it might seem or how many lines shorter it is.

Use Constants

Constants greatly simplify maintenance. If you use the same value more than once in your application, such as a tax rate or a company name, store it in a constant and use the constant in your application. This serves two purposes. First, the constant name is much more enlightening than an obscure number to someone reading the code. That is, TAX_RATE is much more informative than 6.5. Secondly, if the value changes, you have to change it only once, at the beginning of the program, rather than finding and changing it in many places in your application.

Write Reusable Code

Look for opportunities to write reusable code. Any time you find yourself writing the same code in different parts of the application, write a function. It saves a great deal of time and makes the program much easier to read. Over a period of time, you will build up a library of functions that you can use in many different applications.

Of course, if you're writing object-oriented code, you're always writing reusable code.

Separate Page Layout from Function

Maintenance is easier if you separate the Web page layout code from the program logic code. You can write the code that displays the page in a separate file, a file that outputs HTML code. The main PHP script that contains the program logic can include the file containing the display code when the page needs to be displayed. Given this separation, it's much easier to change the look of a Web page. You change only the display code in the layout file; you don't need to change any of the program logic code.

Don't Reinvent the Wheel

Before you spend hours writing a piece of code that refuses to do what you want it to do, search the Internet for the code that you need. Thousands of PHP developers are willing to share their code. PHP code repositories store code for various purposes, perhaps exactly the purpose you have in mind. Chapter 10 provides a list of places to find code.

If your application is a common one, you might be able to find a ready-made application that you can use, instead of building your own. Many PHP applications — for free or to purchase — are available on the Internet. Several applications are available for Content Management Systems, Shopping Carts, Message Boards, Templating Systems, and many other uses. Try googling for a complete solution before deciding that you must build your own.

Use the Discussion Lists Frequently, but Wisely

Users of PHP and MySQL are more than willing to help if you are stumped. Take advantage of this resource. However, be sure your question is organized and to-the-point. "I tried to access my database but it didn't work. What should I do?" is not a message that anyone can answer. And, anyone who responds is likely to point out the foolishness of this message that doesn't provide any details. Include the following information in a message asking for help:

- Supply the software and versions that you are using, such as Windows XP, PHP 5.0.2, MySQL 4.1.7, Apache 1.3.27.

- Explain what you did, in detail. If your problem is that the code produces an error message or the code doesn't give you the results you expected, include the code. If your code is a huge program, include just enough code to show the problem. Or, perhaps, construct a simplified piece of code that has the problem.

- State what you expected the outcome to be.

- State what actually happened differently than your expected outcome.

In addition, be sure to do your homework before you ask a question. Read the manual. Google for answers. Turn to the list only when other resources fail. You can find a document with a lot of good advice about asking questions on a list at www.catb.org/~esr/faqs/smart-questions.html.

The most useful lists for PHP and MySQL help are

- www.php.net/mailing-lists.php
- http://lists.mysql.com

Document Everything

While you're writing an application, the details seem indelibly burned into your mind. However, in six months, when you want to make changes to the application, you'll be amazed to discover that most of those details are gone. So don't depend on your memory. Write down all your decisions. Use comments liberally in your scripts.

Chapter 10

Ten Sources of PHP Code

In This Chapter

▶ Finding code libraries

▶ Discovering other useful resources for PHP programmers

*O*ne advantage of PHP is that its developers are willing to share code. Several online code libraries are available where you can obtain code donated by experienced PHP programmers. Whatever your need, you can often find code that you can use as is or with a little modification. There's no need to reinvent the wheel for every programming task.

SourceForge.net

www.sourceforge.net

SourceForge.net is the largest repository of open-source code and applications available on the Internet. You can find software for all purposes at this site. Many of the projects on SourceForge are large software applications that you can download and use. For instance, phpmyadmin, a popular application used to manage MySQL databases, is available on SourceForge.

You don't need to log in to SourceForge to download software. You can find software written specifically in PHP by following these steps:

1. **Click the Software Map tab at the top.**

2. **Click Programming Language in the column on the right.**

3. **Click PHP in the column of alphabetically listed programming languages on the left.**

As of today, SourceForge.net shows over 9,000 projects in PHP.

WeberDev

`http://weberdev.com`

WeberDev is one of the most comprehensive resources for PHP programmers. Started in 1998 as a page to post examples, the site has grown dramatically and includes both code snippets and complex programs. The almost 4,000 examples (as of this writing) fall into the following major categories: PHP, MySQL, JavaScript, and Databases. You can download the code without logging into the site. User comments about the code are displayed with the code. WeberDev also provides articles, manuals, discussion forums, a coding contest, templates, PHP Web logs (blogs), and other resources.

You can register on WeberDev and receive a password. Logging in allows you to add code, post to the discussion forums, add comments to code examples, enter a coding contest with prizes, receive a newsletter, receive notification when new examples are added to the site, and other advantages. You must provide your name and e-mail address to register. You can elect not to receive e-mail from the site when you register.

PHP Classes

`www.phpclasses.org`

PHP Classes is a repository for hundreds of classes written in PHP. You can search or browse through many categories or by author to find classes. User ratings are provided with the class information. You don't need to log in to download the code. This Web site also provides reviews of PHP books.

Codewalkers

`http://codewalkers.com`

The Codewalkers Web site calls itself "A resource for PHP and SQL developers." You can find code in the following categories: Content Management, Database Related, Date and Time, Discussion Boards, E-Mail, File Manipulation, Link Farm, Look and Feel, Miscellaneous, Searching, Site Navigation, Statistics and Counters, and User Management. Each code submission displays a rating provided by site visitors. The code gallery contains both procedural and object-oriented code. The site also offers tutorials, reviews of books and software, a coding contest, and forums for discussions.

The site provides a member registration and login. You don't need to register as a member of the site to download code, but you must register before you can contribute code. You can post to the forums without logging in, but you must register to use some advanced features of the forums. Registration requires a user ID and a password that you create. An e-mail address is also required. Other information is requested but not required.

PHP Builder

www.phpbuilder.com

PHP Builder is a Web site containing a variety of resources for PHP coders. It provides a library of code snippets, scripts, and functions for a broad range of uses. You can search for code in such categories as databases, calendars, shopping carts, games, graphics, and many others. In addition, you can find news and a list of useful articles as well as search for jobs or people available for hire.

HotScripts.com

www.hotscripts.com

HotScripts is an Internet directory to programming-related resources. HotScripts provides information and scripts for PHP, CGI, Perl, JavaScript, and ASP. Almost 10,000 scripts are currently listed for PHP.

The listing for each program provides information about the software, with a link to the Web page for the software. Each listing also includes reviews and ratings of the software provided by visitors.

Zend

http://zend.com

The Zend Web site includes a code gallery. Zend is the company that develops the PHP engine. You don't need to log in to the Web site to download code. PHP code is available for categories such as math, databases, algorithms, new, most requested, and top rated. Visitors can post ratings of the software.

Many other resources are available here, including some excellent articles. Zend, in partnership with WeberDev (which I describe earlier in this chapter), sponsors a PHP coding contest.

PHP Freaks

www.phpfreaks.com

PHP Freaks offers about 600 scripts in several categories. It also provides easy access to the ten most popular scripts and the newest scripts. Ratings of the code are provided. You don't need to log in to download scripts or to add a script. However, you must provide a name and valid e-mail address to add a script.

The site also provides articles and tutorials, news, and forums. The Web site states that it has, as of this writing, 25,189 active members.

PX: The PHP Code Exchange

http://px.sklar.com

PX allows users to post and download PHP code. It's a simple Web site that just provides access to code. The home page consists of a list of categories for browsing and a field for entering search terms. You don't need to be logged in to download code, but you must register and log in before you can post or rate code.

Free PHP and MySQL Hosting Directory

www.oinko.net/freephp

This site is a list of free Web hosting companies that offer PHP. Hosts are rated up to five stars.

Part VI
Appendixes

The 5th Wave   By Rich Tennant

"Why, of course. I'd be very interested in seeing this new milestone in the project."

In this part . . .

This part provides a brief introduction of object-oriented programming (Appendix A) and also a summary of concepts and syntax for object-oriented programming in PHP (Appendix B).

Appendix C provides information on PHP functions used to interact with MySQL. It provides tables for converting from mysql functions to mysqli functions and/or mysqli objects.

Appendix D discusses the useful goodies you can find on the CD: all the code from the book, a list of useful PHP- and MySQL-related links, and a bonus chapter that shows you how to build and manage a mailing list.

Appendix A

Introducing Object-Oriented Programming

* *

*I*f you're unfamiliar with the concepts and terminology of object-oriented programming, this appendix is for you. I explain the principles and terms of object-oriented programming here. In Appendix B, I describe how to write object-oriented programs. If you are familiar with the vocabulary and concepts of object-oriented programming and know object-oriented programming using another language, such as Java or C++, you can go directly to Appendix B where I explain the syntax of PHP's object-oriented programming features.

Understanding Object-Oriented Programming Concepts

OO programming (that is, object-oriented programming) is an approach to programming that uses objects and classes. As I explain in Chapter 1, changing from procedural programming to object-oriented programming is more than just using a different syntax. It's a different way of analyzing programming problems. The program is designed by modeling the programming problem. For example, a programmer designing a program to support a company's sales department might look at the programming problem in terms of the relationships among customers and sales and credit lines — in other words, in terms of the design of the sales department itself.

Object-oriented programming developed new concepts and new terminology to represent those concepts. This section introduces and explains the major object-oriented programming concepts.

Objects and classes

The basic elements of object-oriented programs are *objects*. It's easiest to understand objects as physical objects. For example, a bicycle is an object. It has properties, such as color, model, and tires, which are also called *attributes*. A bike has things it can do, too, such as move forward, turn, park, and fall over.

In general, objects are nouns. A person is an object. So are animals, houses, offices, customers, garbage cans, coats, clouds, planets, and buttons. However, objects are not just physical objects. Often objects, like nouns, are more conceptual. For example, a bank account is not something you can hold in your hand, but it can be considered an object. So can a computer account. Or a mortgage. A file is often an object. So is a database. Orders, e-mail messages, addresses, songs, TV shows, meetings, and dates can all be objects.

A *class* is the code that is used to create an object — the template or pattern for creating the object. The class defines the properties of the object and defines the things the object can do — its responsibilities. For example, you write a class that defines a bike as two wheels and a frame and lists the things it can do, such as move forward and change gears. Then when you write a statement that creates a bike object using the class, your new bike is created following the pattern in your class. When you use your bike object, you might find that it is missing a few important things, such as a seat or handlebars or brakes. Those are things you left out of the class when you wrote it.

As the person who writes a class, you know how things work inside the class. But it isn't necessary to know how an object accomplishes its responsibilities in order to use it; anyone can use a class. I have no clue how a telephone object works, but I can use it to make a phone call. The person who built the telephone knows what's happening inside it. When new technology is introduced, the phone builder can open my phone and improve it. As long as he doesn't change the interface — the keypad and buttons — it doesn't affect my use of the phone at all.

Properties

Objects have *properties,* also sometimes called *attributes.* A bike might be red, green, or striped. Properties — such as color, size, or model for a bike — are stored inside the object. Properties are set up in the class as variables. For example, the color attribute is stored in the object in a variable and given a descriptive name such as `$color`. Thus, the bike object might contain `$color = red`.

The variables that store properties can have default values, can be given values when the object is created, or can have values added or modified later. For example, a house might be created white, but when it is painted later, $color is changed to chartreuse.

Methods

The things that objects can do are sometimes referred to as responsibilities. For example, a bike object can move forward, stop, and park. Each thing an object can do — each responsibility — is programmed into the class and called a *method*.

In PHP, methods use the same syntax as functions. Although the code looks like the code for a function, the distinction is that methods are inside a class.

Classes are easier to understand and use when method names are descriptive of what they do, such as `stopBike` or `getColor`. Methods, like other PHP entities, can be named with any valid name but are often named with camel caps, by convention (as shown in the previous sentence).

The method are the interface between the object and the rest of the world. The object needs methods for all its responsibilities. Objects should interact with the outside world only through their methods. If your neighbor object wants to borrow a cup of sugar, for example, you want him to knock on your door and request the sugar. You don't want him to just climb in the kitchen window and help himself. Your `house` object should have a `front door`, and `neighbor` objects should not be able to get into your house without using the `front door`. In other words, your house object has a method for `openFront Door` that the neighbor must use. The neighbor should not be able to get into the house any other way. Opening the `front door` is something your `house` object can do, via a method called `openFrontDoor`. Don't leave any open windows in your object design.

A good object should contain all it needs to perform its responsibilities but not a lot of extraneous data. It should not perform actions that are another object's responsibility. The `car` object should travel and should have everything it needs to perform its responsibilities, such as gas, oil, tires, engine, and so on. But the `car` object should not cook and does not need to have salt or frying pans. And the `cook` object should not transport the kids to soccer practice.

Abstraction

Abstraction is an important concept in object-oriented programming. When you're designing a class, you need to abstract the important characteristics of the object to include in your class, not include every single property and responsibility you can think of. You abstract the characteristics that are important for your application and ignore the characteristics that are irrelevant for your task.

Suppose you're developing an application for a grocery store. Your application will assist with the work schedule for the grocery clerks, so you design a checkout clerk object. You can include many characteristics of the grocery clerks, such as name, age, hair color, hours worked per week, and height. However, your goal is to abstract the grocery clerk characteristics that are relevant to the scheduling task. Age, hair color, and height are not useful information. However, the grocery clerks' names and the hours they're scheduled to work per week are necessary for the schedule, so those characteristics are included in the object.

Methods are similarly abstracted for their relevance. Such methods as `startWork` and `stopWork` are needed for the application, but `brushesTeeth` and `drivesCar` are not.

Inheritance

Objects should contain only the properties and methods they need. No more. No less. One way to accomplish that is to share properties and methods between classes by using *inheritance*. For example, suppose you have two Car objects: a sedan and a convertible You could write two classes: a `Sedan` class and a `Convertible` class. However, a lot of the properties and responsibilities are the same for both objects. Both have four wheels, both have color, and both move forward in the same way. Inheritance enables you to eliminate the duplication.

You can write one class called `Car`, which stores the information, such as `$color` and `$engine_size`, and provides the methods, such as `openDoor` and `moveBackward`, used by both types of cars. You can then write two subclasses: `Sedan` and `Convertible`. The `Car` class is called the *master class* or the *parent class*. `Sedan` and `Convertible` are the *subclasses*, which are referred to as *child classes*, or the *kids*, as my favorite professor fondly referred to them.

Child classes inherit all the properties and methods from the parent class. But they can also have their own individual properties and methods, such as `$sunroof = yes` or `$sunroof = no` for the `Sedan` class and `lowerTop` and `raiseTop` methods for the `Convertible` class. A `$sunroof` property doesn't make sense for the `Convertible`, because it isn't going to have a sun roof, ever. The `lowerTop` or `raiseTop` methods make no sense for the `Sedan` because you can't lower its top.

A child class can contain a method with the same name as a method in a parent class. In that case, the method in the child class takes precedence for a child object. You can use the method in the parent class by specifying it specifically, but if you don't specify the parent method, the child class method is used. For instance, the cars both can move forward. In most cases, they move forward the same, regardless of the type of car, so you put a method called `moveForward` in the `Car` class so both child classes can use it. However, suppose that the `Convertible` moves forward differently than the `Sedan` (for instance, all convertibles are standard shift, but a sedan can be standard or automatic). You can put a method called `moveForward` in the `Convertible` class that would override the method in the parent class with the same name.

Information hiding

Information hiding is an important design principle in object-oriented programming. The user of a class doesn't need to know how an object performs its actions. The user just needs to know the interface of the object in order to use it.

For instance, take a look at a checking account. As the user of a checking account, you need to know how to pay money from your account to your landlord. You know that you can pay money from the account to your landlord by writing a check with your landlord's name on the payee line. You don't know the details involved when your landlord cashes that check; you don't know who handles the check, where the check is stored, or where or how the teller enters the information about the check into the bank's computers, or any similar details You don't need to know. You need to know only how to write the check. The bank can alter its procedures, such as using a different teller or changing the computer program that handles the transaction, without affecting you. As long as the bank doesn't change the interface between you and the bank, such as how you fill out the check, you continue to use the bank without knowing about any internal changes.

If you're writing a banking application that includes an account object, the same principles apply. The account class needs to include a method such as `cashCheck`. The person using the class needs to know how to pass the information, such as the payee and the amount of the check, to the `cashCheck` method. However, the person using the `cashCheck` method doesn't need to know how the method performs its actions, just that the check is cashed. The person writing the class can change the internal details of the `cashCheck` method, but as long as the interface doesn't change, the user of the class isn't affected.

The same principle applies to properties of an object. For instance, the checking account object needs to know the balance in the account. However, no one outside the class should be able to change the balance directly. The balance should be accessible only to bank employees, such as the teller. The balance should not be public, where anyone can change it.

To accomplish information hiding in PHP (and other languages), you use keywords to designate public versus private properties and methods. Private properties and methods can be accessed only by methods contained in the class, not by statements outside the class. Appendix B explains the details of using public and private properties and methods.

Creating and Using the Class

By their nature, object-oriented programs require a lot of planning. You need to develop a list of objects — along with their properties and responsibilities — that covers all the functionality of your application. Each object needs to contain all the information and methods needed to carry out its responsibilities without encroaching on the responsibilities of other objects. For complicated projects, you might need to do some model building and testing before you can be reasonably confident that your project plan includes all the objects it needs.

After you decide on the design of an object, you can create and then use the object. The steps for creating and using an object follow:

1. **Write the `class` statement.**

   The `class` statement is a PHP statement that is the blueprint for the object. The `class` statement has a statement block that contains PHP code for all the properties and methods that the object has.

2. **Include the class in the script where you want to use the object.**

   You can write the `class` statement in the script itself. However, it is more common to save the `class` statement in a separate file and use an `include` statement to include the class at the beginning of the script that needs to use the object.

3. **Create an object in the script.**

   You use a PHP statement to create an object based on the class. This is called *instantiation*.

4. **Use the new object.**

   After you create a new object, you can use it to perform actions. You can use any method that is inside the `class` statement block.

Appendix B provides the details needed to complete the preceding steps.

Appendix B

Object-Oriented Programming with PHP

● ●

*I*f you know object-oriented (OO) programming in another language, such as Java or C++, and just want to know how object-oriented programming is implemented in PHP, you are in the right place. In this appendix, I tell you how to write PHP programs by using object-oriented programming methods, assuming you already understand object-oriented terminology and concepts. If you don't know object-oriented programming concepts and terminology, check out Appendix A, where I introduce object-oriented programming.

Much of the syntax that I describe in this appendix is valid only for PHP 5 and doesn't work in PHP 4.

Writing a Class Statement

You write the `class` statement to define the properties and methods for the class.

The class statement

The `class` statement has the following general format:

```
class className
{

    #Add statements that define the properties
    #Add all the methods
}
```

Naming the class

You can use any valid PHP identifier for the class name, except *reserved words* — words that PHP already uses, such as echo, print, while, and so on. The name stdClass is not available because PHP uses the name stdClass internally. In addition, PHP uses Iterator and IteratorAggregate for PHP interfaces, so those names are not available. In general, if you use the name of a PHP command or function for a class name, you get a parse error that looks something like the following error for a class named echo:

```
Parse error: parse error, unexpected T_ECHO, expecting
  T_STRING in d:\Test.php on line 24
```

If you use a name that PHP already uses for a class, you get a fatal error similar to the following:

```
Fatal error: Cannot redeclare class stdClass in
  d:\Test.php on line 30
```

Adding the class code

You enclose all the property settings and method definitions in the opening and closing curly brackets.

The next few sections show you how to set properties and define methods within the class statement. For a more comprehensive example of a complete class statement, see the section "Putting it all together," later in this appendix.

Setting properties

When you're defining a class, declare all the properties in the top of the class. PHP does not require property declarations, but classes with declarations are much easier to understand. It's poor programming practice to leave them out.

Declaring public properties

Use public to declare public properties when needed, as follows:

```
class Airplane
{
    public $owner;
    public $passenger_capacity;
    public $gas;

    Method statements
}
```

You can leave out the keyword `public`. The property is then public by default. However, the code is easier to understand with the word *public* included.

You can also use constants as properties, with the following format:

```
const SIZE = 20;
```

Declaring private properties

You can declare properties either private or protected by using a keyword:

- ✔ `private`: No access from outside the class, either by the script or from another class.
- ✔ `protected`: No access from outside except from a class that is a child of the class with the protected attribute or method.

You can make an attribute private as follows:

```
private $gas = 0;
```

With the attribute specified as private, a statement that attempts to access the attribute directly gets the following error message:

```
Fatal error: Cannot access private property Airplane::$gas
in c:\testclass.php on line 17
```

The `public` and `private` declarations are new with PHP 5. In PHP 4, all properties were declared as follows:

```
var $gas = 0
```

However, the new `public` and `private` keywords replace `var` in PHP 5. If you use `var` in PHP 5, your script still runs correctly, but you receive an `E_STRICT` warning as follows:

```
Strict Standards: var: Deprecated. Please use the
public/private/protected modifiers in c:\test.php on line 5
```

Don't use the `var` keyword, because it will possibly be removed in a future version of PHP.

While testing new code during development, you want to see all the messages (error, warning, notice, strict) that PHP can display. The information is useful for debugging new code. The error setting `E_ALL` doesn't include the "strict" messages. So, use the setting `E_ALL | E_STRICT`. You, of course, should turn off these messages when the application is made available to users, because any error messages provide information that's useful for the bad guys. At this point, you can turn error messages off, or better still, write them to a log file.

Setting values for properties

To set or change a property variable's value when you create an object, use the constructor (which I describe in "Writing the constructor," later in this appendix). Or, to set or change the property variable's value after you create the object, use a method you write for this purpose.

You can set default values for the properties, but the values allowed are restricted. You can declare a simple value but not a computed one, as detailed in the following examples:

✔ The following variable declarations are allowed as default values:

```
private $owner = "DonaldDuckAirLines";
private $passenger_capacity = 150;
private $gas = 1000;
```

✔ The following variable declarations are *not* allowed as default values:

```
private $color = "DonaldDuck"." AirLines";
private $passenger_capacity = 30*5;
private $gas = 2000-1000;
```

An array is allowed in the variable declaration, as long as the values are simple, as follows:

```
private $doors = array("front","back");
```

Adding methods

Methods specify what an object can do. Methods are included inside the `class` statement and are coded in the same format as functions. For example, your checking account might need a method that deposits money into the account. You can have a variable called `balance` that contains the amount of money currently in the account. You can write a method that deposits a sum into the `$balance`. You can add such a method to your class as follows:

```
class CheckingAccount
{
  private $balance = 0;
  function depositSum($amount)
  {
    $this->balance = $this->balance + $amount;
    echo "$${amount} deposited to your account";
  }
}
```

This looks just like any other function, but it's a method because it's inside a class. Methods can use all the formatting of functions. For instance, you can specify a default value for your parameters as follows:

```
function depositSum($amount=0)
```

If no value is passed for $amount, $amount is 0 by default.

PHP provides some special methods with names that begin with __ (two underscores). These methods are handled differently by PHP internally. This appendix discusses three of these methods: construct, destruct, and clone. Don't begin the names of your own methods with two underscores unless you're taking advantage of a PHP special method.

You can make methods private or protected in the same way you can make properties private or protected: by using the appropriate keyword. If you don't use any keyword for a method, it's public by default.

It's good programming practice to hide as much of your class as possible. Only make methods public that absolutely need to be public.

A *static method* is a method that can be accessed directly, without instantiating an object first. You declare a method static by including a keyword, as follows:

```
static function functionname()
```

For details on using a static method, see the section "Using a Class," later in this appendix.

Accessing properties and methods

When you write methods for your class, you often want to access the properties of the class or other methods in the same class. A special variable — $this — is available for accessing properties and methods within the same class. You use the variable as follows:

```
$this->varname
$this->methodname
```

You can use $this in any of the following statements as shown:

```
$this->gas = 2000;
$product[$this->size] = $price;
if($this->gas < 100)
    {echo $this->gas};
```

As you can see, you use $this->varname in all the same ways you would use $varname.

Notice that a dollar sign ($) appears before this but not before gas. Don't use a dollar sign before gas — as in $this->$gas — because it changes the meaning of your statement. You might or might not get an error message, but it isn't referring to the variable $gas inside the current class.

The following class includes a method to add gas to your car: addGas. However, you want to be sure that people buy the gas that is added; you don't want any stolen gas in your car. So, you make the gas property and the addGas method private. You add a buyGas method for public use, as follows:

```
class Car
{
  private $gas = 0;
  private function addGas($amount)
  {
    $this->gas = $this->gas + $amount;
    echo "$amount gallons added to gas tank";
  }
  function buyGas($amount)
  {
    $this->addGas($amount);
  }
}
```

In this class, the only way that gas can be added to the car from outside the class is with the buyGas method. The $gas property is private, so it can't be modified from outside the class. The addGas method is also private. The only public method for adding gas is the buyGas method, which accesses the addGas method by using $this->addGas. If a statement outside the class attempts to add to $gas directly or to use addGas, a fatal error is displayed, as follows:

```
Fatal error: Call to private method Car::addGas()in
 c:\testcar.php on line 10
```

You can't use the special variable $this in a static method because $this refers to the current object and you don't necessarily create an object when accessing a static method.

You can't use $this to access class constants. Instead, you use a line like the following to access a class constant named SIZE:

```
$this->gas = self::SIZE;
```

Writing the constructor

The *constructor* is executed automatically when an object is created by using the class as a pattern. In PHP, only one constructor is allowed. A constructor is not required.

The constructor has a special name so that PHP knows to execute the method when an object is created. Constructors are named __construct (two underscores). A constructor method looks similar to the following:

```
function __construct()
{
    $this->balance = 100;    # account is opened with $100
    echo "Current balance is $$this->balance.";
}
```

This constructor defines the new bank account. When the account is created, it has $100 in it (a reward for opening the account).

Prior to PHP 5, constructors had the same name as the class. You might run across classes written in this older style. PHP 5 looks first for a method called __construct() to use as the constructor. If it doesn't find one, it looks for a method that has the same name as the class and uses that method for the constructor. Thus, older classes still run under PHP 5. If your class has both a method named __construct() and a method with the same name as the class, a message warns you that you are redefining the constructor, and then the script proceeds, using __construct() and ignoring the method with the same name as the class.

Putting it all together

Your class can have as few or as many properties and methods as it needs. These methods can be very simple or very complicated, but the goal of object-oriented programming is to make the methods as simple as is reasonable. Rather than cram everything into one method, it's better to have several smaller methods and have one method call another, as in the following example:

```
class Message
{
  private $message = "No message";
  function __construct($message)
  {
    $this->message = $message;
  }
  function displayMessage()
  {
    echo $this->message."\n";
  }
  function changeMessage($new_message)
  {
    $this->message = $new_message;
    echo "The message was changed to: ";
    $this->displayMessage();
  }
}
```

This simple Message class has a constructor, two methods, and one property. The property is the text of the message, which is passed into the object when the object is created and stored in the property variable when the constructor executes. The displayMessage method displays the message stored in the property. The changeMessage method changes the text of the message and then uses the displayMessage method to display the changed message text.

Using inheritance in your class

A class can be a subclass that inherits properties and methods from a parent class. Suppose you need two car objects: a sedan and a pickup truck. The two objects have many similarities, such as four wheels, an engine, and a steering wheel. However, the two objects also have differences, such as trunk versus bed, two doors versus four doors, passenger capacity, cargo capacity, and so on. You can write a parent class, Car, that contains the similarities and a subclass, Pickup, that contains the properties and methods that are unique to the pickup. You write the Pickup class as follows:

```
class Pickup extends Car
{
    Add the property statements
    Add the methods
}
```

The object created from this class has access to all the properties and methods of both the Car class and the Pickup class. The Car class, however, does not have access to properties or methods in the child class Pickup. You can access the properties and methods of the parent from a child class by using either of the following statements:

```
$this->gas
parent::gas
```

If you add a method to a child class with the same name as a method in the parent class, the child class method overrides the parent class method. That is, if you create a child object and call the method, then the child method rather than the parent method is used. If the signature (the number of arguments passed) for the child method doesn't match the signature of the parent method, a warning is displayed.

To prevent a method from being overridden in a child class, use the keyword final with the method in the parent class, as follows:

```
final function functionname()
```

You can prevent a class from being inherited by declaring it final, as follows:

```
final class classname
```

Using a Class

The class code needs to be in the script that uses the class. Define the class before you use it. Most commonly, the class is stored in a separate include file and is included in any script that uses the class.

To use an object, you first create the object from the class. Then that object can perform any methods that the class includes. Only static methods can be used without creating an object first.

Creating an object

To create (or *instantiate*) an object, use statements with the following format:

```
$objectname = new classname(value,value,...);
```

For example, to create a Message object, use the following statement:

```
$my_message = new Message("Slow. Aardvark crossing.");
$my_message2 = new Message("Happy 100th Birthday!");
```

The Message object is stored in $my_message. The constructor method stores "Slow. Aardvark crossing." in the $message property.

Different objects created from the same class are independent entities. If you change the message in $my_message, it doesn't affect the message in $my_message2. You can copy an object by using PHP's __clone method, which I describe later in this appendix.

Using methods

After you create the object and store it in a variable, you can use any method in the class, except private or protected methods, with statements of the following format:

```
$my_message->displayMessage();
$my_message->changeMessage("Stop. Aardvark in crosswalk.");
```

Static methods can be used directly from outside the class, without creating an object first. The following example is a class with a static method:

```
class TestStatic
{
    static function writeMessage()
    {
        echo "I am a static method";
    }
}
```

You can access this method directly in your script with the following statement:

```
TestStatic::writeMessage();
```

Accessing properties

After you create an object, you can access the public properties with the following statements:

```
$my_message->message;
$my_message2->message;
```

However, private and protected properties can't be accessed this way. They can be accessed only from inside a class. It's good programming practice to hide as much of your class as possible. Only make properties public that absolutely need to be public, which is seldom the case.

Using Exceptions

PHP provides an error-handling class called `Exception` that you can use to handle undesirable things that happen in your script. For example, in the `Car` class, you might keep track of the gas in the car and stop the car when it runs out of gas. You expect your program to detect 0 gallons and react. You don't expect the gas in the gas tank to be a negative amount; you consider that to be an exception, and you want to be sure that won't happen in your script. To deal with this, you can write a routine that uses the `Exception` class to watch for a negative gas amount. The following statements check for this situation:

```
$this->gas = $this->gas - 5;
try
{
```

```
      if ($this->gas < 0)
      {
        throw new Exception( "Negative amount of gas.");
      }
  }
  catch (Exception $e)
  {
      echo $e->getMessage();
      echo "\n<br />\n";
      exit();
  }
```

The preceding script contains a try block and a catch block:

✔ In the try block, you test a condition. If the condition is TRUE, you throw
an exception — in other words, you create an Exception object. The
Exception object has a property that stores the message you sent when
you threw the exception.

✔ In the catch block, you catch the exception and call it $e. Then you exe-
cute the statements in the catch block. One of the statements is a call to
a method called getMessage in the Exception class. The getMessage
method returns the message that you stored, and your statement
echoes the returned message. The statements then echo the end-of-line
characters so the message is displayed correctly. The script stops on
the exit statement.

If no exception is thrown, the catch block has nothing to catch, and it's
ignored. The script proceeds to the statements after the catch block.

Copying Objects

PHP provides a method you can use to copy an object: __clone (with two
underscores). If your class contains a __clone method, PHP uses the method
to copy; if the class doesn't contain a __clone method, PHP uses its default
__clone method, which copies all the properties as is. As shown by the two
underscores beginning its name, the clone method is a special method, and
thus is called differently, as shown in the following example.

For example, you can write the following class:

```
class Car
{
  private $gas = 0;
  private $color = "red";
  function addGas($amount)
  {
```

```
      $this->gas = $this->gas + $amount;
      echo "$amount gallons added to gas tank";
   }
   function __clone()
   {
      $this->gas = 0;
   }
}
```

Using this class, you can create an object and copy it as follows:

```
$firstCar = new Car;
$firstCar->addGas(10);
$secondCar = clone $firstCar;
```

After these statements, you have two cars:

- ✔ $firstCar: This car is red and contains 10 gallons of gas. The 10 gallons were added with the addGas method.

- ✔ $secondCar: This car is red but contains 0 gallons of gas. The duplicate car is created by using the __clone method in the Car class. This method sets $gas to 0 and doesn't set $color at all.

If you didn't have a __clone method in the Car class, PHP would use a default __clone method that would copy all the properties, making $secondCar both red and containing 10 gallons of gas.

Destroying Objects

You can create and destroy an object with the following statements:

```
$myCar = new Car;
unset($myCar);
```

After $myCar is unset, the object no longer exists.

PHP provides a method that is automatically run when an object is destroyed: __destruct. For example, the following class contains a __destruct method:

```
class Tower
{
   function __destruct()
   {
      echo "The tower is destroyed";
   }
}
```

When you destroy the object with an `unset` statement, the `__destruct` method runs, and the output is echoed. The `__destruct` method is not required.

Using Abstract Classes

PHP allows you to use *abstract methods* — patterns that specify the methods to be used and the information to be passed, but don't contain any code. Any class that contains an abstract method must be declared abstract. An abstract class can contain both abstract methods and methods that are not abstract. You define an abstract class with a keyword, as follows:

```
abstract class Message
{
    protected $messageContent;
    function __construct($text)
    {
        $this->messageContent = $text;
    }
    abstract public function displayMessage($color);
}
```

An object can't be created from an abstract class. The function of an abstract class is to serve as a parent for one or more child classes. The abstract class specifies the methods, including abstract methods that contain no code. The following two child classes actually implement the `displayMessage` method:

```
class BiggestMessage extends Message
{
    public function displayMessage($color)
    {
        echo "<h1 style=\"color: $color\">
            $this->messageContent</h1>";
    }
}

class BigMessage extends Message
{
public function displayMessage($color)
    {
        echo "<h2 style=\"color: $color\">
            $this->messageContent</h2>";
    }
}
```

Notice that the child classes do not contain a constructor. When an object is created from either child class, the constructor from the parent class is used. Both child classes must implement the abstract method specified in the parent class. If `displayMessage` is not included in a child class, a fatal error occurs. Notice that the implementation of `displayMessage` is different in each class, specifying different sized text. However, because the abstract method in the parent class specifies one argument ($color) for the method, the child classes must implement the abstract method with one argument.

Notice that the child classes can access the $messageContent property in the parent class. A child class can access a protected property. If the property were private, the child class would get an error message when trying to access it.

Using Interfaces

Interfaces, like abstract classes, can't be instantiated. Interfaces differ from abstract classes in that all methods in an interface must be abstract. You define an interface as follows:

```
interface Moveable
{
    abstract public function moveForward($distance);
}
```

Then suppose you have a Car class as follows:

```
Class Car
{
    protected $gas = 0;
    function __construct()
    (
        $this->gas = 10;
    }
}
```

You can create a subclass as follows:

```
Class Sedan extends Car implements Moveable
{
    public function moveForward($distance)
    {
        $this->gas = $this->gas - $distance * $mileage;
    }
}
```

When a Sedan object is created, it adds 10 gallons to $gas as coded in its parent, the Car class. It also implements the Moveable interface, which means it must implement a moveForward method that accepts one parameter.

You can implement more than one interface by using the following format:

```
Class Baby implements Feedable, Washable, Changeable
```

Testing an Object

You can test an object to determine its class by using the `instanceof` operator, as follows:

```
if( $myCar instanceof Car )
     echo "It's a car!";
```

This statement returns TRUE whether $myCar is a Car or is created by a child class of Car, such as when $myCar is a Sedan.

Object-Oriented Concepts That PHP 5 Omits

If you're familiar with object-oriented programming in other languages, you might find that some features you're accustomed to using aren't available in PHP 5:

- ✔ **Polymorphism:** PHP doesn't allow more than one method, even a constructor, to have the same name in a class. Therefore, you can't implement polymorphism as you're used to doing. You can't have two or more methods with the same name in the same class that accept different types or numbers of variables. Some people use switches and other mechanisms to implement the functionality of polymorphism.

- ✔ **Multiple inheritance:** PHP doesn't allow multiple inheritance. A class can inherit from one parent class only.

Appendix C

The MySQL and MySQL Improved Extensions

• •

*P*HP interacts with MySQL by using built-in functions. Currently, PHP provides two sets of functions for use when accessing MySQL databases: the MySQL extension (mysql) and the MySQL Improved extension (mysqli).

The MySQL extension is enabled automatically when PHP 4 is installed. The functions provided by this extension have the format

```
mysql_action(parameters);
```

where *action* is the part of the function name that indicates what the function does, and *parameters* are the parameters that the function requires. For instance, the following is a typical function:

```
$connect = mysql_connect($host,$user,$password);
```

The function connects to the MySQL server and returns a connection that is stored in $connect.

The MySQL extension isn't enabled automatically when you install PHP 5. You need to activate it yourself, as described in the installation instructions provided on the PHP Web site (www.php.net).

The MySQL extension can interact with MySQL versions 4.0 and 4.1. However, several additional features were added with MySQL 4.1. To take advantage of the new features, you must use the MySQL Improved extension. You activate mysqli, instead of mysql, when installing PHP 5. The functions provided by this extension have a similar format:

```
mysqli_action(parameters);
```

The beginning of the function name is mysqli, rather than mysql. Parameters are also passed to the mysqli functions. In some cases, the syntax is the same, such as for the following function:

```
$connect = mysqli_connect($host,$user,$password);
```

However, for some functions the syntax is slightly different, as shown in the following two functions:

```
mysql_select_db($dbname,$connect);
mysqli_select_db($connect,$dbname);
```

Notice that the parameters are in a different order.

The MySQL Improved extension also provides objects for those who prefer object-oriented programming. Basically, it provides two objects with several methods available. The two objects used in the applications in this book are:

```
$connect = new mysqli($host,$user,$password);
$result = $connect->query("SELECT * FROM Test_table");
```

$connect is an object that represents a connection to the MySQL server. $result is an object that contains the results from an SQL query. Both objects have several methods. For instance, as shown in the preceding code, query is a method in the mysqli class, used in the second line to return the $result object. You can see a complete list of all the objects and queries available in the mysqli extension at www.php.net/manual/en/ref.mysqli.php.

In this book, I use mysqli functions in the procedural programs and mysqli objects in the object-oriented programs. You can convert any script to use a different method of interacting with MySQL. For instance, if you prefer to use PHP 4, you can enable the mysql extension and convert the functions to mysql functions.

The following two tables show the differences in syntax for statements used in the applications in this book. The tables assume that the parameters are passed in variables. For instance, the connection to the MySQL server is stored in a variable named $connect, as shown previously in this section. The results of a query are stored in a variable named $result.

Table C-1 compares mysql and mysqli functions. Table C-2 compares mysqli functions with mysqli methods.

Table C-1	Syntax for mysql and mysqli Functions
mysql Function	*mysqli Function*
mysql_connect($host, $user,$passwd)	mysqli_connect($host, $user,$passwd)
mysql_errno() or mysql_errno($connect)	mysqli_errno($connect)
mysql_error() or mysql_error($connect)	mysqli_error($connect)

mysql Function	mysqli Function
`mysql_fetch_array($result)`	`mysqli_fetch_array($result)`
`mysql_fetch_assoc($result)`	`mysqli_fetch_assoc($result)`
`mysql_fetch_row($result)`	`mysqli_fetch_row($result)`
`mysql_insert_id($connect)`	`mysqli_insert_id($connect)`
`mysql_num_rows($result)`	`mysqli_num_rows($connect)`
`mysql_query($sql)` or `mysql_query($sql,$connect)`	`mysqli_query ($connect,$sql)`
`mysql_select_db($dbname)`	`mysqli_select_db ($connect,$dbname)`

Table C-2   mysqli Functions and Object-Oriented Statements

mysqli Function	mysqli Method or Property
`mysqli_connect($host, $user,$passwd)`	`new mysqli($host, $user,$passwd)`
`mysqli_errno($connect)`	`$connect->errno`
`mysqli_error($connect)`	`$connect->error`
`mysqli_fetch_array($result)`	`$result->fetch_array()`
`mysqli_fetch_assoc($result)`	`$result->fetch_assoc()`
`mysqli_fetch_row($result)`	`$result->fetch_row()`
`mysqli_insert_id($connect)`	`$connect->insert_id`
`mysqli_num_rows($result)`	`$result->num_rows`
`mysqli_query($connect,$sql)`	`$connect->query($sql)`
`mysqli_select_db ($connect,$dbname)`	`$connect->select_ db($dbname)`

Note that some items in the object-oriented column do not have parentheses () at the end of the statement. This means that those items are properties, not methods. Thus, they are used as variables, as in the following:

```
echo $connect->error;
```

Appendix D

About the CD

. . . .

I've included a CD to provide you with all the source code that I present in the book. I wanted to save you all that typing. And because I had the CD anyway, I decided to stick in a list of links to PHP and MySQL sites that I think you'll find useful. In this appendix, I describe the computer requirements for using the CD. I also tell you about the material you can find on the CD and how to access that material. I end the appendix with a brief troubleshooting section that I hope you won't need.

System Requirements

Make sure that your computer meets the minimum system requirements shown in the following list. If your computer doesn't match up to most of these requirements, you might have problems using the files on the CD. For the latest and greatest information, please refer to the ReadMe file located at the root of the CD-ROM.

- ✔ A PC with a Pentium or faster processor, or a Mac OS computer with a Power PC-based or faster processor
- ✔ Microsoft Windows 98 or later, or Mac OS system software 8.5 or later, or Linux OS
- ✔ At least 32MB of total RAM installed on your computer, but for best performance, at least 64MB of RAM
- ✔ A CD-ROM drive
- ✔ A monitor capable of displaying at least 256 colors or grayscale
- ✔ A modem with a speed of at least 14,400 bps

If you need more information on the basics, check out these books published by Wiley: *PCs For Dummies,* 9th Edition, by Dan Gookin; *Macs For Dummies,* 8th Edition, by David Pogue; *iMacs For Dummies,* 4th Edition by Mark L. Chambers;

Windows 98 For Dummies, Windows 2000 Professional For Dummies, and *Windows XP For Dummies,* 2nd Edition, all by Andy Rathbone; *Linux For Dummies,* 6th Edition, by Dee-Ann LeBlanc.

Using the CD

To install the items from the CD to your hard drive, follow these steps.

Note for Linux Users: Mount the CD and browse to the Author directory on the CD to access the source code files.

1. **Insert the CD into your computer's CD-ROM drive.**

   The license agreement appears.

   Note to Windows users: The interface won't launch if you have autorun disabled. In that case, choose Start➪Run. In the dialog box that appears, type **D:\start.exe**. (Replace D with the proper letter if your CD-ROM drive uses a different letter. If you don't know the letter, see how your CD-ROM drive is listed under My Computer.) Click OK.

   Note for Mac Users: When the CD icon appears on your desktop, double-click the icon to open the CD, and then double-click the Start icon.

2. **Read through the license agreement, and then click the Accept button if you want to use the CD.**

   After you click Accept, the License Agreement window won't appear again.

   The CD interface appears. The interface allows you to install the programs and run the demos with just a click of a button (or two).

What You Can Find on the CD

The following sections are arranged by category and provide a summary of the files you can find on the CD. If you need help with installing the items provided on the CD, refer to the installation instructions in the preceding section.

Source code files

All the application code in this book is located in the Author directory on the CD. The source code files provided will work with PHP on Macintosh, Linux,

UNIX, Windows 98/NT/2000/XP, and many other operating systems. These files contain all the application code from the book. The structure of the code directory is

```
Author/Authentication/Procedural
Author/Authentication/OO

Author/Login/Procedural
Author/Login/OO

Author/Catalog/Procedural
Author/Catalog/OO

Author/ShoppingCart/Procedural
Author/ShoppingCart/OO

Author/CMS/Procedural
Author/CMS/OO

Author/Forum/Procedural
Author/Forum/OO

Author/MailingList/Procedural
```

Links to useful PHP and MySQL information

In addition to all the source code files on the CD, you can also find a list of links that will take you to Web sites containing additional information about PHP and MySQL.

I describe each of the following sites in Chapter 10:

- http://zend.com
- www.sourceforge.net
- http://weberdev.com
- www.phpclasses.org
- http://codewalkers.com
- www.phpbuilder.com
- www.hotscripts.com
- www.phpfreaks.com
- http://px.sklar.com
- www.oinko.net/freephp

The following three sites wouldn't fit into Chapter 10, but they're useful, so I include them on the CD, too:

- ✔ www.mysql.com: The official MySQL Web site.
- ✔ http://janet.valade.com: My Web site, where you can find any errors or updates to the application code.
- ✔ www.php.net: The official PHP Web site.

A bonus chapter

The bonus chapter on the CD covers building an application that manages mailing lists. A *mailing list* is essentially a group of recipients. When you send a message to a mailing list, the message is distributed to each recipient. A polite, well-behaved mailing list application asks you to voluntarily subscribe before it sends any messages to you. (An impolite application simply gathers a collection of e-mail addresses and sends annoying advertisements to each recipient.) The mailing list application that I develop in this bonus chapter is a polite one. Users subscribe/unsubscribe themselves from the mailing lists and can send messages only to lists that they are subscribed to.

In addition, the application stores an archive of every message and a copy of every attachment. Users can look at any message and attachment in the archive. In addition to the features provided to all users, the application recognizes a special type of user — an administrator, who has special privileges. The administrator can create new mailing lists, send e-mail to a list that he or she is not subscribed to, and purge old messages.

The code for this application is provided on the CD, along with the code from the other chapters. However, although the other chapters provide both procedural and object-oriented code, this chapter presents only a procedural application. The bonus chapter contains some code that is a little more advanced than the code in the other chapters. You might view this application as intermediate, rather than introductory. However, the chapter provides plenty of detailed explanation for the code. I give you all the information you need to understand the code.

Troubleshooting

If any source code programs on the CD fail with error messages when run in your PHP/MySQL environment, check my Web site for information. The Web site provides information and corrections for problems or errors reported by readers. Corrected and updated versions of files might be available (`http://janet.valade.com`).

Customer Care: If you have trouble with the CD-ROM, please call the Wiley Product Technical Support phone number at (800) 762-2974. Outside the United States, call (317) 572-3994. You can also contact Wiley Product Technical Support at `www.wiley.com/techsupport`. John Wiley & Sons provide technical support only for installation and other general quality control items. For technical support on the applications themselves, consult the program's vendor or author.

To place additional orders or to request information about other Wiley products, please call (877) 762-2974.

Index

• _G_ •

Wiley Publishing, Inc.
End-User License Agreement

READ THIS. You should carefully read these terms and conditions before opening the software packet(s) included with this book "Book". This is a license agreement "Agreement" between you and Wiley Publishing, Inc. "WPI". By opening the accompanying software packet(s), you acknowledge that you have read and accept the following terms and conditions. If you do not agree and do not want to be bound by such terms and conditions, promptly return the Book and the unopened software packet(s) to the place you obtained them for a full refund.

1. **License Grant.** WPI grants to you (either an individual or entity) a nonexclusive license to use one copy of the enclosed software program(s) (collectively, the "Software") solely for your own personal or business purposes on a single computer (whether a standard computer or a workstation component of a multi-user network). The Software is in use on a computer when it is loaded into temporary memory (RAM) or installed into permanent memory (hard disk, CD-ROM, or other storage device). WPI reserves all rights not expressly granted herein.

2. **Ownership.** WPI is the owner of all right, title, and interest, including copyright, in and to the compilation of the Software recorded on the disk(s) or CD-ROM "Software Media". Copyright to the individual programs recorded on the Software Media is owned by the author or other authorized copyright owner of each program. Ownership of the Software and all proprietary rights relating thereto remain with WPI and its licensers.

3. **Restrictions on Use and Transfer.**

   (a) You may only (i) make one copy of the Software for backup or archival purposes, or (ii) transfer the Software to a single hard disk, provided that you keep the original for backup or archival purposes. You may not (i) rent or lease the Software, (ii) copy or reproduce the Software through a LAN or other network system or through any computer subscriber system or bulletin-board system, or (iii) modify, adapt, or create derivative works based on the Software.

   (b) You may not reverse engineer, decompile, or disassemble the Software. You may transfer the Software and user documentation on a permanent basis, provided that the transferee agrees to accept the terms and conditions of this Agreement and you retain no copies. If the Software is an update or has been updated, any transfer must include the most recent update and all prior versions.

4. **Restrictions on Use of Individual Programs.** You must follow the individual requirements and restrictions detailed for each individual program in the About the CD appendix of this Book. These limitations are also contained in the individual license agreements recorded on the Software Media. These limitations may include a requirement that after using the program for a specified period of time, the user must pay a registration fee or discontinue use. By opening the Software packet(s), you will be agreeing to abide by the licenses and restrictions for these individual programs that are detailed in the About the CD appendix and on the Software Media. None of the material on this Software Media or listed in this Book may ever be redistributed, in original or modified form, for commercial purposes.